Rural Social Work Practice

Rural Social Work Practice

Edited by
Nancy Lohmann and Roger A. Lohmann

COLUMBIA   UNIVERSITY   PRESS   NEW   YORK

COLUMBIA UNIVERSITY PRESS
Publishers Since 1893
New York   Chichester, West Sussex
Copyright © 2005 Columbia University Press
All rights reserved

Library of Congress Cataloging-in-Publication Data

Rural social work practice / edited by Nancy Lohmann and Roger A. Lohmann.
     p. cm.
     Includes bibliographical references and index.
     ISBN 0–231–12932–7 (cloth : alk. paper)
     1. Social service, Rural — United States.   I. Lohmann, Nancy.   II. Lohmann,
Roger A., 1942–
     HV91.R7727 2005
     361.9173′4 — dc22
                                                                          2005045566

Columbia University Press books
are printed on permanent and durable acid-free paper.
Printed in the United States of America

c 10 9 8 7 6 5 4 3 2 1

Dedicated to the students, alumni, faculty, and staff of the West Virginia University Division of Social Work and to our grandson, Brandon Thomas Lohmann

This book is also dedicated to the memory of John Michel in appreciation for the support and guidance he provided to us and other social work authors for Columbia University Press.

Contents

Part II. Interventions

Part III. Client Populations and Fields of Practice

Part IV. Education for Practice

Introduction

Roger A. Lohmann and Nancy Lohmann

This is a book on rural social work practice as it exists in the United States during the first decades of the twenty-first century. To some in social work and beyond, the news that *rurality* — the condition of being rural — still exists in the United States may be a surprise. That this book is published by Columbia University Press, in many ways the most obviously urban of university presses, may be even more of a surprise. But the fact of the book's publication is itself a kind of testimony to the continued existence of rurality.

Columbia University Press is headquartered in what has once again regained its status as the World's Greatest City. One can look out of any of the office windows at the Press in any direction and not see a cow, a barn, a coal mine, or a fishing trawler, no evidence whatsoever of the pastoral rurality of Peter Stuyvesant's purchase. Including a book on rural practice in the burgeoning social work series published by Columbia University Press is evidence not only of the existence and vitality of rurality but also of the view taken in this book that the rural-urban continuum is far more complex than a simple dichotomy. A look out of those same twenty-first-century office windows would probably also surprise many a diehard rural partisan with the abundance of trees, flowers, and wildlife that have sprouted up in the concrete canyons of the island of Manhattan. Just as in any rural area, the natural and built environments of Manhattan must coexist in some measure of symbiosis.

New York and most other American cities have changed a great deal from the days of Henry James, Sinclair Lewis, and Jane Addams and so, too, have rural areas. Our cities are no longer the gritty, industrial dens of depravity that a great many people in rural America still believe them to be. Likewise, our own rural communities are seldom merely the pastoral Jeffersonian havens of virtuous, hardy, self-sufficient artisans and farmers we would like them to be. If they were, there would be no need for a book on rural social work. But the fact is that the full range of social problems from AIDS to welfare afflicting urban America is also found in abundance in contemporary rural America. Social work may be an urban transplant to rural communities, but it has arisen there out of the same real needs that brought social work to the cities.

In this introduction we describe some of the influences that led to the development of this book. We also present several of the extant definitions of the term *rural* and discuss three dynamics (population, employment, and policies) that are important in understanding rurality in the twenty-first century.

A Rural School?

This book is testimony to the struggles over many decades of a "rural" school of social work to define itself in the context of the rather distinctive urbanization of the Appalachian region, West Virginia and Morgantown, the present or past home of many of the authors of this work. When we began this book project, Morgantown was officially a small city with a population of less than thirty thousand. Like many university towns, Morgantown had long been subjected to serious census undercounting simply because past census takers made no significant effort to include students. By the census magic of including the roughly twenty-four thousand students of West Virginia University and revising municipal limits, in the 2000 Census Morgantown became the newest metropolitan statistical area (MSA) (and undoubtedly one of the smallest!) in the United States. With a wave of the magic census wand, the residents of Morgantown went from rural to urban without even moving!

This official public change of status has been accompanied by Morgantown being included, not once but several times, in a list of the "Best Small Cities" in the east and nationally — a recognition with which we and the contributors to this volume heartily concur. But such prize-winning metropolitan status has not gone to our heads. Despite all these signs of urbanization, in our personal lives and with regard to the country we believe that there are still important things to say on the subject of rurality. We have not (yet) put on airs or taken on big city ways. A very large proportion of the authors in this book grew up and have spent most of their lives in rural areas, and the majority of the "big city" Morgantown contributors actually still live outside the city in surrounding rural (well, in some cases, suburban) areas of "the county" as well as in nearby small towns.

In the same vein, however, in addition to our very urban publishers, the reader will note that chapter 4 (on rural nonprofit human services) is authored by a team of researchers working at the Urban Institute in Washington, D.C. This is yet another indicator, if one were needed, of the continuing vitality of rurality as a topic and of the interdependence of urban and rural topics.

A Rural Program

Just as we have for more than half a dozen re-accreditation visits, the faculty of the West Virginia University social work program recently reaffirmed our commitment to rural social work practice as this book was in its final stages. We still do not know fully what the phrase *rural social work* means — defining it may be only a bit less complicated than defining the meaning of life. But we do know that the majority of our students continue to practice in the small towns and small cities of West Virginia and the region, and to serve clients and colleagues who think of themselves as rural people. Thus, as we have for more than a quarter of a century, the faculty and staff of the West Virginia University Social Work Program continue to affirm our status as a predominantly rural program, one of only a handful in the country.

Even in the majority of social work programs where the focus is not mainly rural, one is likely to find a small number of "rural specialists" among the faculty. This is one of several substantiations of the continued vitality of rurality in social work today. Another of the tests of the viability of rurality as a scholarly teaching and research interest is its ability to continue to attract new contributors. From that vantage point, this book represents a statement of the health of rural social work as a scholarly enterprise. In the chapters that follow we offer a healthy mix of old-timers and newcomers, for whom this book represents their first major publication. None of the current contributors to this book was present at the beginning of the quest for rural social work at West Virginia University. Leon Ginsberg, dean at the time of

that sea change, went on to inspire the rural social work movement nationally and has continued to contribute through multiple editions of his pioneering book, *Social Work in Rural Communities*. Three of us (Nancy Lohmann, Roger A. Lohmann, and Barry Locke) were participants in the first
national rural social work conference in 1976. The other contributors found
their rural interests in the 1980s, the 1990s, and the current decade. The
simple reality that people continue to discover their interests in rural practice
as we write this and as you read it is evidence of the continued vitality of
rurality in an urban nation.

As with any book project involving many people, several years were
needed to fully develop the book, and a good deal of change occurred in
the process. New authors have been added, others have dropped out, and a
number of faculty members in our program with rural interests chose not to
participate or arrived too recently to be included in the project. Taken together, these are all signs of a healthy and dynamic vitality in an academic
interest like rural social work at West Virginia University and nationally. We
hope in the chapters that follow to communicate that sense of vitality to you.

Definitions of Rurality

To discuss rural social work practice, it is important to define what is
meant by "rural." However, as Braden and Beauregard (1993, 915) have
indicated, "it must be acknowledged that no single definition captures the
spectrum of rurality in the United States." Nevertheless the quest goes on.
The two most common definitions of *rurality* found in the social work literature and elsewhere may be seen in the approaches taken by the Bureau
of Census (BoC), which focuses on places and has been in use since the
first census in 1790, and the Office of Management and Budget (OMB),
which focuses on nonmetropolitan areas. It is only in recent decades that
the latter has developed its nonmetropolitan approach, which is a measure
not of places but of areas — specifically clusters of counties. The OMB approach to rural definition is strictly residual: rural areas are those that are
not urban areas. The OMB definition indicates that counties that do not
meet the specified levels of social and economic integration with metropolitan counties are non-MSA, or nonmetropolitan areas, and thus are considered rural.

A third approach, built on the OMB model but too new to be reflected
in most rural statistics, is utilized in the chapter by Hager, Brimer and Pollak,

chapter 4. The U.S. Department of Agriculture has devised a set of "continuum codes" that distinguish metropolitan counties by size and nonmetropolitan counties by degree of urbanization and proximity to urban areas.

Working within the framework of the two major historic approaches to the definition of *rural*, one arrives at an interesting portrait of rural America. The census data shown in tables I.1 and I.3 indicate several noteworthy facts:

1. The actual number of rural residents has grown slowly but steadily since the first census in 1790 right up to the present.
2. At the same time, the proportion of rural population has declined steadily for more than a century, and at least four states (California, New York, Florida, and Massachusetts) are now over 90 percent urban.
3. Each of those 90 percent–plus urban states (like most other large urban states) also has a rural population that, in actual numbers, exceeds the *total* population of the smallest state(s).
4. For the country as a whole, and for most states, the proportion of the rural population living outside any "organized" place (small town or village) is almost four times the number of rural people living in towns and villages of 2,500 or less.

TABLE I.1 Rural Population Growth, 1900–2000

	Total	Urban	Rural	Urban (%)	Rural (%)
2000	281,421,906	222,360,539	59,061,367	79.01	20.99
1990	248,709,873	187,053,487	61,656,386	75.20	24.80
1980	226,542,199	167,050,992	59,494,813	73.70	26.30
1970	203,302,031	149,646,629	53,565,297	73.60	26.40
1960	179,323,175	125,268,750	54,054,425	69.90	30.10
1950	151,325,798	96,846,817	54,478,981	64.00	36.00
1940	132,164,569	74,705,338	57,459,231	56.50	43.50
1930	123,202,624	69,160,599	54,042,025	56.10	43.90
1920	106,021,537	54,253,282	51,768,255	51.20	48.80
1910	92,228,496	42,064,001	50,164,495	45.60	54.40
1900	76,212,168	30,214,832	45,997,336	39.60	60.40

Based on data taken from the U.S. Census of Population, 2000. Bureau of the Census, Washington, D.C., 2001.

Table I.2 is derived from the data in table I.1 and shows in greater detail the dynamic of limited rural population growth against the greater urban growth since 1900.

In table I.3 we see the patterns of rural and urban growth in 2000 by state. The reader will note that table I.3 is sorted by total rural population. This ordering shows clearly that the largest rural state populations are to be found in large and otherwise notably urban states including Texas, North Carolina, Pennsylvania, Ohio, Michigan, and New York, whereas those states with the highest percentages of rural (and lowest urban) population, like Maine, West Virginia, North and South Dakota, and New Hampshire, are also among the "smallest" states in terms of total population. Of note is that California, which has the largest total population overall and the largest total urban population, both by a wide margin, also has one of the largest rural populations among states. In fact, the *rural* population of California (and each of the other states listed above California in the table) is considerably greater than the *total* populations of the ten smallest states. In this table we also introduce a new and more useful state measure: proportion of the total U.S. rural population. Combined with the conventional state rural proportions familiar to the rural social work audience, this new measure

TABLE I.2 Rural and Urban Population Growth by Decade, 1900–2000

Decade	Rural Growth (%)	Urban Growth (%)	Cumulative Rural Growth (%)	Cumulative Urban Growth (%)
2000	0.96	1.05	1.18	5.29
1990	1.04	1.02	1.34	6.19
1980	1.11	1.00	1.29	5.53
1970	0.99	1.05	1.16	4.95
1960	0.99	1.09	1.18	4.15
1950	0.95	1.13	1.18	3.21
1940	1.06	1.01	1.25	2.47
1930	1.04	1.10	1.17	2.29
1920	1.03	1.12	1.13	1.80
1910	1.09	1.15	1.09	1.39
1900	100	100	100	100

Derived from the data in table I.1.

offers an additional dimension of understanding. Thus, for example, while the population of Maine is nearly 60 percent rural, that represents only 1.29 percent of the total rural population in the United States. At the same time, while New York is only a little over 12 percent rural, rural New Yorkers represent roughly 4 percent of the national rural population.

Table I.4 shows these same state populations for rural areas, broken down into five standard census categories. For Texas, for example, the table shows that 84.8 percent of that state's population lives in urban centers like Dallas, Houston, or San Antonio; that 1.5 percent live in towns with a population greater than 2,500; that 1.8 percent live in towns with populations from 1,000 to 2,499; that 1.4 percent live in towns with populations of less than 1,000; and that the bulk of the Texas rural population (16.4 percent) lives "in the country," that is, on farms and ranches, ranchettes, and other small plots of land outside organized towns or cities ("Not in Place" in the table).

Summary

Rural, urban, place, and *area* are not terms easily sorted out in census data or other national statistics. Yet these labels present a clear picture that people have continued to live in rural places and in rural areas even as the nation has become predominantly — even overwhelmingly — urban. Rural people are no longer mostly the self-sufficient producers of long ago but rather are employed by and engaged in the same national economy as their urban coresidents and are citizens of the same political union, even though their respective influence has diminished considerably in the past half-century. In the chapters of this book we will see many of the implications of this somewhat paradoxical rurality for the contemporary practice of social work in rural areas.

Living, Working, and Voting Rural

Three closely related dynamics that will help the reader to a clearer understanding of the current rural context are rural population dynamics; changes in rural labor force participation, particularly the rise of nonfarm employment; and political redistricting with its continuing impact on rural community politics. Together these three factors support the view that there are more rural people in the United States today than ever before, that only

TABLE I.3 Rural Population, by State

State	Urban Total	Rural Total	% of State Rural	% of U.S. Rural
United States	222,360,539	59,061,367	21.00	100
Texas	17,204,281	3,647,539	17.50	6.18
North Carolina	4,849,482	3,199,831	39.80	5.42
Pennsylvania	9,464,101	2,816,953	22.90	4.77
Ohio	8,782,329	2,570,811	22.60	4.35
Michigan	7,419,457	2,518,987	25.30	4.27
New York	16,602,582	2,373,875	12.50	4.02
Georgia	5,864,163	2,322,290	28.40	3.93
Tennessee	3,620,018	2,069,265	36.40	3.50
Alabama	2,465,673	1,981,427	44.60	3.35
Virginia	5,169,955	1,908,560	27.00	3.23
California	31,989,663	1,881,985	5.60	3.19
Kentucky	2,253,800	1,787,969	44.20	3.03
Indiana	4,304,011	1,776,474	29.20	3.01
Florida	14,270,020	1,712,358	10.70	2.90
Missouri	3,883,442	1,711,769	30.60	2.90
Wisconsin	3,663,643	1,700,032	31.70	2.88
South Carolina	2,427,124	1,584,888	39.50	2.68
Illinois	10,909,520	1,509,773	12.20	2.56
Mississippi	1,387,351	1,457,307	51.20	2.47
Minnesota	3,490,059	1,429,420	29.10	2.42
Arkansas	1,404,179	1,269,221	47.50	2.15
Louisiana	3,245,665	1,223,311	27.40	2.07
Oklahoma	2,254,563	1,196,091	34.70	2.03
Iowa	1,787,432	1,138,892	38.90	1.93
Washington	4,831,106	1,063,015	18.00	1.80
West Virginia	832,780	975,564	53.90	1.65
Kansas	1,920,669	767,749	28.60	1.30
Maine	512,878	762,045	59.80	1.29
Maryland	4,558,668	737,818	13.90	1.25
Oregon	2,694,144	727,255	21.30	1.23
Colorado	3,633,185	668,076	15.50	1.13
Arizona	4,523,535	607,097	11.80	1.03
Massachusetts	5,801,367	547,730	8.60	0.93
Nebraska	1,193,725	517,538	30.20	0.88

(continued)

TABLE I.3 Rural Population, by State (Continued)

State	Urban Total	Rural Total	% of State Rural	% of U.S. Rural
N. Hampshire	732,335	503,451	40.70	0.85
New Jersey	7,939,087	475,263	5.60	0.80
New Mexico	1,363,501	455,545	25.00	0.77
Idaho	859,497	434,456	33.60	0.74
Connecticut	2,988,059	417,506	12.30	0.71
Montana	487,878	414,317	45.90	0.70
Vermont	232,448	376,379	61.80	0.64
South Dakota	391,427	363,417	48.10	0.62
North Dakota	358,958	283,242	44.10	0.48
Utah	1,970,344	262,825	11.80	0.45
Alaska	411,257	215,675	34.40	0.37
Wyoming	321,344	172,438	34.90	0.29
Nevada	1,828,646	169,611	8.50	0.29
Delaware	627,758	155,842	19.90	0.26
Hawaii	1,108,225	103,312	8.50	0.17
Rhode Island	953, 146	95,173	9.10	0.16
Washington, D.C.	572,059	0	0	0.00

Based on data taken from the U.S. Census of Population, 2000. Bureau of the Census, Washington, D.C., 2001.

a tiny fraction of them are involved in agriculture, and that rural people are truly a minority.

Rural Population

A close look at the population data for the entire twentieth century immediately points up the profound paradox of modern rural population decline: on the one hand, the *proportion* of the American population living in rural areas, and the number and percentage of Americans living on farms and engaged in farm work, declined consistently throughout the entire twentieth century. In 1900 more than half the total population lived in communities of 2,500 people or less. By the year 2000 the proportion of people

TABLE I.4 Proportions of Rural Population in a State Living in Urban
Places of More Than 2,500, 1,000–2,499, Less than 1,000,
Not in Any Urban Place, and in Metropolitan Areas

State	2,500 +	1,000–2,499 (%)	> 1,000 (%)	Not in Place (%)	In Metro (%)
United States	1.50	1.80	1.40	16.40	80.30
Texas	1.60	2.00	1.10	12.70	84.80
North Carolina	1.60	1.80	1.30	35.10	67.50
Pennsylvania	0.70	1.10	1.20	20.00	84.60
Ohio	1.00	1.60	1.30	18.80	81.20
Michigan	0.50	1.70	0.90	22.30	82.20
New York	0.30	1.00	0.50	10.70	92.10
Georgia	1.30	1.50	1.20	24.40	69.20
Tennessee	2.90	2.20	1.00	30.20	67.90
Alabama	6.50	3.50	1.90	32.60	69.90
Virginia	1.40	1.30	0.70	23.70	78.10
California	0.80	0.50	0.20	4.10	96.70
Kentucky	1.60	2.30	1.50	38.90	48.80
Indiana	0.80	2.40	1.80	24.2	72.20
Florida	1.50	0.50	0.30	8.40	92.80
Missouri	1.50	3.00	3.00	23.10	67.80
Wisconsin	1.50	3.70	2.30	24.10	67.90
South Carolina	1.50	2.10	1.20	34.70	70.00
Illinois	0.40	1.90	1.90	7.90	84.90
Mississippi	4.00	3.30	2.30	41.60	36.00
Minnesota	3.20	3.50	3.60	18.70	70.40
Arkansas	4.20	4.50	4.40	34.40	49.40
Louisiana	1.50	2.30	1.20	22.40	75.40
Oklahoma	5.00	4.10	4.30	21.20	60.80
Iowa	2.40	7.40	8.10	21.00	45.30
Washington	1.60	1.50	1.20	13.70	83.10
West Virginia	0.70	3.80	2.40	47.00	42.30
Kansas	1.50	5.50	4.90	16.60	56.60
Maine	7.10	4.20	0.30	48.20	36.60
Maryland	0.80	0.70	0.50	12.00	92.70
Oregon	0.60	1.90	1.10	17.70	73.10
Colorado	1.40	2.10	1.30	10.70	83.90
Arizona	3.90	1.40	0.70	5.80	88.20

(continued)

TABLE I.4 Proportions of Rural Population in a State Living in Urban
Places of More Than 2,500, 1,000–2,499, Less than 1,000,
Not in Any Urban Place, and in Metropolitan Areas (Continued)

State	2,500 +	1,000–2,499 (%)	> 1,000 (%)	Not in Place (%)	In Metro (%)
Massachusetts	0.70	0.30	0.00	7.60	96.10
Nebraska	0.30	5.50	7.70	16.70	52.60
N. Hampshire	3.20	2.20	0.00	35.30	59.90
New Jersey	0.50	0.30	0.10	4.80	100.00
New Mexico	2.30	3.10	2.00	17.60	56.90
Idaho	0.70	2.50	3.90	26.50	39.30
Connecticut	0.50	0.40	0.10	11.20	95.60
Montana	2.00	7.40	7.00	29.50	33.90
Vermont	1.30	2.30	2.40	55.80	27.80
South Dakota	2.10	7.20	11.30	27.60	34.60
North Dakota	0.30	8.80	11.50	23.50	44.20
Utah	2.10	2.40	2.60	4.60	76.50
Alaska	12.10	5.80	11.9	4.60	41.50
Wyoming	1.50	6.90	7.00	19.40	30.00
Nevada	3.10	0.80	0.30	4.30	87.50
Delaware	0.30	1.00	0.80	17.80	80.00
Hawaii	2.70	2.10	0.80	3.00	72.30
Rhode Island	0.40	0.20	0.00	8.50	94.10
Washington, D.C.	0	0	0	0	100

Based on data taken from the U.S. Census of Population, 2000. Bureau of the Census, Washington, D.C., 2001.

living in rural areas in this original sense had fallen to around 20 percent, and the decline in agricultural ways of living was even more precipitous. Indeed, in 2000 the proportion of full-time farmers in the total population may actually have fallen below 1 percent for the very first time. Moreover, the changes in society outside the three hundred or so largest American urban centers over the course of the twentieth century were so fundamental that the indicator of a 2,500 population as the traditional lower threshold of urban places is barely meaningful for the twenty-first century. This is equally true of suburban ways of life that have arisen in the past fifty years, where a new suburb of less than 2,500 this decade may swell to 100,000 by the next census, even as many city centers continue to decline, both in absolute population and proportionally.

Another aspect of this great paradox, however, is that, despite such massive population shifts, rural areas have not disappeared, and, in fact, it is not altogether clear that they have even declined in several important respects. And, with the single exception of the expanding frontier in the middle of the country, parts of which are returning rapidly to a state of nature, it seems unlikely that they will. Close examination of the population numbers (not proportions) shows that the total number of Americans living in rural places, using the < 2,500 population measure, has actually increased in every decade but two since 1790 and nearly doubled since 1900 (see table I.1).

Rural areas have changed fundamentally over the course of the past century. But there is simply no possible way to say whether they have changed more, less, or the same as the rest of (urban) society. Again, rural areas were what they were, and, as they have changed, they are what they are. In the words of Charles Fluharty (2002) of the Rural Policy Research Institute, "If you've seen one rural community, you've seen . . . one rural community!"

Much of the literature on rural areas begins with a worrisome discussion of the dwindling proportions of the total population living in rural areas but fails to note these more important numerical increases. It is indeed the case that, since 1920, a continually expanding majority of Americans have been located in urban areas and that, more recently, growing concentrations live in the major metropolitan regions defined by the Census Bureau as Metropolitan Statistical Areas (MSAs), Consolidated Metropolitan Areas (CMSAs), and Primary Metropolitan Statistical Areas (PMSAs). Such urbanization has occurred gradually and also in personal terms that every rural family understands. Initially people (grandparents? great-great-grandparents?) settled the land; next some (grandparents? parents?) moved off the farm into town; and subsequently some of their children moved to larger towns and cities. Finally, grandchildren or later descendents moved away and wound up scattered across the continent in assorted major metropolitan areas where their own children or grandchildren stayed (or will stay) until the whole cycle begins again. At each step along the way the opposite also occurred as small numbers of urban residents moved to rural areas. In some families this process began before the Civil War. In others it started in the last decade. But such internal migration is only part of the story: in each generation some people left rural areas while many remained behind to produce the next generation(s) of rural America, and a few returned from the cities.

It is highly deceptive to see the matter of rural migration as simply one of permanent loss. Doing so leads to the myopic condition that rural social workers used to call "metropoliana" — the mistaken belief that sooner or later everyone will be living in large cities. In the social and behavioral terms in which rural families have experienced it, the much discussed proportion of rural population is actually a quite meaningless number, since proportions of population are seldom an active element in any significant social institution or relationship. And, in this case, they reinforce the false and unfortunate impression that rural areas are dwindling and of diminishing significance.

In fact, the opposite is true: there are *more* people living in rural places (those with fewer than 2,500 people) today than ever before, indeed nearly twice as many as in 1900 and twenty-five times more than in 1790 (see table I.1). The changes in proportion have occurred not because of any declines in rural numbers but solely because of dramatic increases in urban residence.

Simply put, that there are nearly six times as many people living in urban areas today as in 1920 is plainly *not* evidence of rural decline. That would be akin to suggesting that just because the population of France is up, Holland is less important as a country, even though its population has increased. In fact, when looked at closely (as, for example, in the metropolitan/nonmetropolitan distinction), more people are living in those "real" folkloric rural places (populations < 2,500) than ever before. A good portion of the continuing migration "to the city" about which rural folk so fret is actually what might be termed movement "up a notch" on the national urban continuum: farm folks have moved in great numbers into villages (population under 2,500) or small towns (under 5,000). Townies have moved upward into small cities (under 10,000) or medium cities (under 50,000). At the same time, as noted by Locke and Winship, and Hager, Brimer and Pollak, in their chapters of this book, one of the most important recent trends for rural America is the absorption of small places (rural communities) into urban regions.

Rural Labor Force Participation

A second dynamic important in understanding the rural context are changes in rural labor force participation. In earlier, simpler times, labor force participation in rural areas was concentrated heavily in the so-called primary industries: fishing, mining, and most especially farming. However, we easily underestimate how long ago declines in employment in these industries began occurring and the continuing impact this has had on rural life for many decades. Historians now generally agree that the market revolution in American society that transformed farming and fishing from subsistence activity to employment probably began around 1800. Prior to that time, rural living truly may have been the fully self-sufficient way of life of a cashless existence where things were grown, made at home, or done without. But at least, since that time, rural life for most has included a strong, if sometimes minor dimension of "store-bought goods," and most rural communities moved from simple villages to towns where organized buying and selling occurred regularly. Only in a relatively few backwoods areas was this not the case even by 1920.

There is almost nowhere in the United States where urban markets and consumer goods (and accompanying jobs in sales and service occupations) do not reach today. While certainly not an unmixed blessing, as illustrated by concerns with Walmarts and MacDonalds, access to national markets is a reality of rural life. It is certainly also the case that mechanization, increased productivity, and relocation of industries, particularly over the past half-century, have taken a ferocious toll on the number of traditional rural jobs.

This is perhaps clearest in the dramatic declines in employment in traditional rural categories of farming, fishing, and mining. For example, near the end of World War II an estimated 220,000 miners were employed in coal mining in West Virginia. By the turn of the millennium that number had been reduced to approximately 14,000, or less than 10 percent of the earlier figure. In fact, a recent study of nonprofit employment in West Virginia estimated that the number of jobs in nonprofit organizations (primarily in health care) now exceeds the number of those employed in mining (Dewes and Salamon, 2001).

The figures and proportions in the national decline of farm employment are even more impressive: As just one of several possible examples, operating a threshing machine in 1940 to harvest grain on a 180-acre farm required a crew of ten to twelve. Today a single farm worker with a large combine may harvest upward of 1,000 acres with little or no assistance. The *primary* form of employment in the U.S. economy prior to 1920, by the year 2000 approximately 1 percent of the nation's labor force was engaged in farm-related employment, and huge numbers of part-time farmers working "in town" was a universally recognizable feature of rural and small-town life.

And yet, through such wrenching declines in traditional rural employment, the total numbers of people living in rural areas have increased. How do rural people survive? In the case of many Native American reservations (almost all of which are located in rural areas) and other distressed communities, the answer is that many rural people barely survive and do so only on the basis of public aid and their own grit despite staggering barriers and challenges. The phenomenon of some rural communities being entirely or largely dependent upon Social Security, pensions, Temporary Assistance for Needy Families (TANF), food stamps, and other transfer payments is altogether too real. But in addition to the hard-core poor in rural areas, there is a huge number of slightly better-off workers in low-wage, non-benefit, insecure employment in rural America who have rapidly become an entirely new class of service workers to which rural social work will have no choice but to devote increased attention in the coming years. Our students sometimes refer to these rural residents as the "Walmart Class."

Political Representation

A third factor contributing to an understanding of the rural context is that of political representation. One of the background factors that contributed to the rise in contemporary interest in rurality is the rapid and dramatic decline in the political position of rural representation in Congress brought about by the 1962 *Baker v. Carr* ruling by the U.S. Supreme Court. Known at the time as the "One Man [*sic*], One Vote" ruling, the Court determined that the existing system of congressional representation vastly overrepresented rural populations and underrepresented urban ones.

The changes wrought by this ruling did much to level the political playing field, regardless of residence. However, the resulting loss of political influence by rural communities was real, immediate, and traumatic for many rural communities, and its effects have continued right up to the present day. While the revival of the congressional rural caucus in 2000 with its 140 members may be a positive sign, there is no denying that rural political influence has declined (Preston 2000). A review of the web site (http://www.rupri.org/) of the Rural Policy Research Institute provides evidence of the many issues affecting rural residents that often appear to be ignored.

The numbers of rural people may continue to rise in the future, but political representation is the one place where proportion truly matters. Thus it is unlikely that rural areas will ever again attain the primacy in the national polity that they held in the late 1950s.

The Chapters in This Book

The data in the tables above along with employment and political changes show the complexity of the rural-urban situation in the United States today. In the chapters that follow, aspects of practice in rural areas are explored.

The first five chapters of the book examine components of the context of rural social work practice today. In chapter 1, Barry Locke and James Winship look at aspects of rural social work over the twentieth century and, in particular, the interconnected phenomena of the rural caucus, the annual rural social work institutes, and the efforts to create a professional journal. They also discuss trends in rural practice. In chapter 2 Eleanor Blakely and Barry Locke examine welfare reform as it has unfolded in rural America within the context of rural poverty. Norma Wasko, in chapter 3, takes a close and detailed look at the impact of information and telecommunications technology on rural social work practice. Technology is often seen as a way to overcome service delivery problems posed by geography and low density in rural areas.

In one of the most innovative treatments in the rural social work literature, Mark Hager, Amy Brimer, and Tom Pollak, the authors of chapter 4, present an important analysis of the growing body of statistical information on nonprofit organizations. They were able to extract a random sample of rural human service nonprofits from a national data set and identify their characteristics. Following this statistical look at nonprofits, Roger Lohmann, in chapter 5, offers a discussion of how his interdisciplinary theory of the commons fits in rural areas and may help practitioners and educators better understand those areas.

Chapters 6, 7, and 8, which comprise part 2 of the book, examine aspects of rural interventions. Warren Galbreath, in chapter 6, discusses an issue that has been of fundamental importance in direct rural practice for several decades: dual relationships. In chapter 7 Dennis Poole looks at community practice in rural communities and strategies for building stronger communities. In chapter 8 Nancy and Roger Lohmann consider the multiple roles of rural social agency administrators.

Between parts 2 and 3 there appear photographs by Neal Newfield. A marriage and family therapist by training, Newfield has in recent years developed a considerable interest in documentary photography. Working in the tradition pioneered by Jacob Riis and Walker Evans, his photos have appeared often in *Social Work Today* and in state and regional exhibitions.

Part 3 of the book deals with client populations and fields of practice. Elizabeth Randall, in chapter 9, looks at services for the chronically mentally ill in rural areas, and in chapter 10, with Dennis Vance Jr., examines directions in rural mental health practice. Chapter 11, by Doris Nicholas, focuses on the health of rural minorities.

In chapters 12, 13, and 14, respectively, Chatman Neely looks at what he terms "the invisible people of Appalachia" — gays and lesbians living in rural communities; Dong Pil Yoon investigates the impact of religiosity and social support on the well-being of HIV/AIDS clients in rural West Virginia; and Craig Johnson, concluding this section, discusses the characteristics of the rural elderly.

In chapter 15, which comprises part 4 of the book, Nancy Lohmann explores the issues associated with educating social workers for rural practice.

The book concludes with a discussion by the coeditors of their conclusions regarding what is unique and universal about rural social work practice.

References

Braden, J. J., and K. Beauregard. 1993. *Moving beyond Nonmetropolitan as a Definition of Rural America*. Retrieved from www.amstat.org/sections/srms/Proceedings/ papers/1993_155.pdf on May 20, 2004.

Dewes, S., and L. Salamon. 2001. *West Virginia Nonprofit Employment*. Baltimore, Md.: Center for Civil Society Studies, The Johns Hopkins University.

Fluharty, C. W. 2002. Keynote Speech Presented at the Twenty-seventh Annual National Rural Social Work Conference, Frostburg, Md., July 17.

Ginsberg, L. H., ed. 1998 [1976]. *Social Work in Rural Communities*. 3rd ed. Alexandria, Va.: Council on Social Work Education.

Preston, M. 2000. *Inside Washington: Congress Revives Rural Caucus*. Electronic document. http://www.americancityandcounty.com/mag/government_inside_washingtoncongress_revives/ retrieved May 20, 2004.

Rural Social Work Practice

Part I

The Context of Practice

1 Social Work in Rural America

Lessons from the Past and Trends for the Future

Barry L. Locke and Jim Winship

> County workers out on social work frontiers have to make adaptations of their skills to fit pioneer situations. When grass roots are too tangled and tough for the plows of urban social work methodology, we get us a pickaxe and tackle our job realistically. We learn to improvise, to initiate, to change and adapt. Our aim is to achieve with professional conformity if possible, but achievement comes first and if we cannot have both, conformity must go.
>
> —J. Strode, *Survey Mid-Monthly*, 1939

The epigraph to this chapter captures a central idea about social work practice in rural areas, namely, that the social worker will, by the very nature of the rural context, be expected to practice out of a generalist model or orientation. This idea has been a consistent theme in the literature from the earliest days of the profession's work in rural areas. This chapter presents a brief history of social work in rural areas and explores a number of historical themes about practice in rural environments. Also briefly examined are the ways in which social work education has responded to the need for preparation of social workers for rural areas. The chapter concludes with observations about the impact rural issues may have on social work practice in the twenty-first century.

A Brief History

Concern about how one works effectively in the rural community is not new to the social work profession. One early development illustrating this concern was the creation of the Country Life Commission in 1908. Established by President Theodore Roosevelt, this body was instrumental in shaping the "Country Life Movement, which advocated for rural interests until World War II" (Davenport and Davenport 1995, 2082). Not all early efforts were driven by the public sector, however. With the entry into World War I, the American Red Cross established a regional service model as part of its Home Service Program. A number of leading figures in rural social work were involved in this program including Jesse Steiner, Henrietta Lund, and Josephine Brown (Martinez-Brawley 1981).

As Trattner (1999) has noted, the social work profession intensified its quest for recognition as a legitimate profession during the 1920s. The effort to demonstrate that it was maturing as a profession led to interest in developing a professional knowledge base and the attendant literature. Building from the work of Mary Richmond and others writing about social casework, a seminal work for rural social workers was published by Josephine Brown in 1933. This book, *The Rural Community and Social Case Work*, sets forth one of the earliest arguments for rural social work as differing from urban work and included a recommended curriculum that still has applicability today.

When the United States entered World War II social work played a less central role, and much of the momentum of Brown's work was lost. The field continued its efforts to be recognized as a legitimate profession. As these efforts intensified, a split occurred among schools that were preparing social workers. Social work programs associated with private urban colleges and universities tended to follow a two-year graduate model leading to a master's degree in social work (MSW). The public education social work programs, including those of land grant universities, tended to prepare social workers at the baccalaureate level (BSW). With the rise of professionalism, specialized accreditation was implemented at the graduate level under the direction of the Council on Social Work Organization. As the graduate curriculum became standardized it was organized around practice methods, including casework, group work, and community work, and the social work profession came to embrace the idea that professional practice required graduate-level education. As a result of this development, many social work programs in small towns and rural areas were lost. Martinez-Brawley (1981) noted that by 1949 attention to social work practice in small towns and rural areas had all but disappeared from the professional literature.

It can be argued that the modern rebirth of interest in social work practice in small towns and rural areas can be traced to an address to the 1969 Meeting of the National Conference on Social Welfare. Dr. Leon H. Ginsberg, who was dean of the School of Social Work at West Virginia University at the time, focused attention on what he saw as a lack of appropriate attention to the needs of the social worker who practiced in rural areas. He called for social work education to respond to this perceived gap. Several individuals and social work education programs successfully took up his challenge. The response has resulted in an increasing literature base and the initiation of an annual National Institute on Social Work and Human Services in Rural Areas (now in its thirtieth year). These efforts were closely aligned with the establishment of an informal advocacy group known as the National Rural Social Work Caucus. The caucus worked to create a special refereed journal, *Human Services in the Rural Environment*. Although successful for several years, the journal ceased publication in the 1990s.

Since the 1980s several studies have attempted to answer the question of what is unique about social work practice in rural areas (Eisenhart and Ruff 1984; Locke 1988; Kelley and Kelley 1985; O'Neill and Horner 1982; Whitaker 1984; and Whittington 1985). The results from these studies are inconclusive and the differences noted did not support the idea that a unique theory base was needed for rural and small-town practice. As a result there is less emphasis on the need to adapt the existing professional knowledge base for the rural practice context.

The start of this century finds a small but committed group of scholars and researchers interested in social work practice in the rural context. A wide range of issues including homelessness, mental health and health care delivery, the effects of welfare reform, as well as long-standing interest in community development remain high on the agenda for those focused on how to serve the approximately forty million people living in small towns and rural places.

Practice Themes

A consensus appears to exist among scholars in social work education about the skills, attitudes, and knowledge needed for social work practice within small towns and rural areas. A review of the literature suggests that at least five thematic areas are viewed as significant in the preparation of social workers for practice in rural areas. These themes are the social worker as generalist, an emphasis on community development, the importance of external relations, the importance of cultural influences, and desirable personal and professional traits that support social work practice in rural contexts.

Generalist Social Workers

Throughout the profession's history most scholars have agreed that social workers who practice in small towns and rural areas need to use a generalist orientation (Brown 1933; Levin 1974; Ginsberg 1998 [1976]; Hanton 1978; Irey 1980; Martinez-Brawley 1981; Neale 1982; and Davenport and Davenport 1995). This orientation to social work practice is now mandated by the profession's accreditation standards. While several variations are found in social work education, at the core of educational preparation the generalist social worker is one who is skilled in working with individuals, families, small groups, organizations, and communities as they attempt to address social needs.

The rationale for this approach is based on the structural realities of most rural areas. Rural areas are often characterized by a lack of formal resources, including private-sector social services. Social workers who serve rural areas are generally employed in the public sector and are asked to deal with a wide range of problems and issues presented by those seeking help. Within this context, especially valued are social workers possessing such traits as creativity, flexibility, knowledge about how to access both informal and formal helping services, and the ability to modify services as necessary to be more responsive to needs. Generalist social work practice is designed to prepare social workers with such knowledge and skills.

Practice realities in many rural areas are such that the social worker will be called upon to handle a wide range of tasks and carry diverse helping roles. This is not new. Josephine Brown, in her classic text on social work in the rural community, stated that it was important that the social worker be trained both in community organization and casework (1933, 29). This view has been refined over the years to incorporate not only helping roles but also to include an understanding of how systems interact and how the social worker builds relationships across systems to help people have their needs more fully addressed (Ginsberg 1998 [1976]; H. W. Johnson 1980; Wharf 1985; Brenden and Shank 1985). For a review of a recent model of generalist practice that builds on the idea of exploring the client's story, an approach ideally suited to many rural cultures, see the work of Locke, Garrison, and Winship (1998).

Community Development

While the literature has consistently supported social workers using a generalist orientation, many scholars (Brown 1933; Mermelstein and Sundet 1976; Webster and Campbell 1977; Jacobsen 1980; Martinez-Brawley 1981) have also called for social workers in rural areas to be actively engaged in some form of community practice. This emphasis reflects, in part, the realities and challenges faced by many rural communities, namely, that they continue to lack needed resources. Community development knowledge and skill can assist the social worker in addressing these concerns. The generalist orientation, valuing intervention with multiple client systems, is ideally suited to assist the social worker in understanding and seeking opportunities to address these community challenges as they are encountered in daily practice.

While community development is often needed, social workers are advised to enter into such activities in a way that is consistent with and supportive of the norms and values of the community (Morrison 1976). This is not to suggest that hurtful norms and values should be supported. The advice is associated with the nature of the rural environment where relationship and trustworthiness are important "coins of the realm." For example, some rural areas have been looked down on for so long that persons living there have internalized the negative stereotypes about them. Over time many such persons may adopt a "hangdog attitude" that can leave them unable to take needed actions. Such contexts call for models of change that recognize that patience, extra effort, and hard work to become trusted may be necessary before certain actions are possible. It is essential to work in the community in a way that is respectful of its norms and traditions, and to be sensitive to how the future is viewed if efforts at change are to be effective.

At least two models of community development, "Locality Development" and "Asset-Based Community Development," appear to be well suited to many rural communities. While these models are equally appropriate in urban practice, they are especially useful in the rural context. Jacobsen (1980) presents a rather strong argument in support of locality development as fitting well with the lifestyle and ebb and flow of the rural community, given this model's emphasis on doing work that is closely integrated in the community. The social worker using this model must be prepared to work well with local government, make appropriate use of power, assess community environments, work well with group process, and know how to relate to a diverse set of key stakeholders, a set of skills consistent with the generalist orientation.

Asset-Based Community Development (Kretzmann and McKnight 1993) has recently been viewed as a good alternative for working with communities, especially low-income communities. This model attempts to shift the prevalent paradigm for community practice from deficits and needs assessments to one focusing on existing community assets. The argument is advanced that community development, especially with low-income communities, works best when based on the assets and resources already found within the community. Such assets might include the gifts and talents of people living there, the existing informal networks of positive relationships, and the strengths that can be brought into play to deal with community issues.

Both these models would appear to hold promise for work in rural settings as they take advantage of one strength of that context, human relationships. Beyond that, these models also establish expectations for active participation and involvement by those most directly concerned. Such models are acceptable to the independent people most often found in the rural environment.

External Relations

Several scholars (Omer 1977; Webster and Campbell 1977; and Woehle 1982) have discussed the importance in rural practice of the awareness of key external actors and factors, and the ability to relate to them. One important skill is the capacity to interact within the existing power structure (Ginsberg 1998 [1976]; Johnson 1980; and Wharf 1985). The power structure may be viewed as any person or organization in a position to exert influence on the decisions and outcomes experienced by the local community. Knowledge of power and power holders, or rather the lack of sophisticated use of such knowledge, has been identified as one of the weaknesses of many social workers who operate in rural areas (Mermelstein and Sundet 1976). With the continuing devolution of programs from the federal to state and local levels, this skill takes on even greater importance for the social worker in a rural community (Woehle 1982).

Managing external relations is important in addressing a common need often identified with rural areas: community and economic development. Deaton and Bjergo (1978) suggest that social workers seek opportunities to involve themselves in this activity as one way to assist people in meeting a fundamental need for economic opportunity. As the profession has matured,

social work has increasingly understood the need for greater political involvement as a strategy for managing external relationships that impact on
the economic opportunities and quality of life available in a community.
For those social workers who live and work in small towns and rural areas,
one way to provide needed leadership is to seek local political office such
as on the city council or county commission .

Culture

One of the keys to understanding a rural environment is familiarity with
its culture. Rural areas in the United States are quite diverse. Depending on
the rural area you work in, you may need to know about Italian or other
middle European cultures, traditional English culture, different African cultures, the Hmong culture, the Latino culture, or Native American cultures;
that is, social workers need to understand the culture of origin of the residents of the community as well as how local customs and traditions have
developed (Ginsberg 1998 [1976]; Johnson 1980; Neale 1982; Locke, Garrison, and Winship 1998).
Sensitivity to the culture and lifestyle of clients has been a universal
principle of social work practice. This principle is especially important to
the social worker in small towns and rural areas because of the rural traditions of human relationships based on the person's trustworthiness rather
than on any professional role (Ginsberg 1998 [1976]; Neale 1982). Rural
areas are traditionally tied to the land and the rhythms of nature. Time often
takes on a different meaning and the pace of living is different from the
urban environment. Social workers must take the time necessary to learn
about the norms and traditions of the area where they practice.
Rural areas are often characterized by the social worker's greater visibility
(Ginsberg 1998 [1976]; Fenby 1978; and Whittington 1985). It is not unusual for one's personal and professional business to be common knowledge
in small towns and rural areas. This means that social workers must be
especially sensitive to their clients' confidentiality issues and must also be
prepared to encounter their clients in contexts other than an office. This
reality has been the source of some debate within the social work profession
as the Code of Ethics has been modified to address the issue of "dual relationships."[1] While the intent behind the standard is appropriate, dual relationships may be very difficult to avoid in rural areas. Additionally the social
worker will need to be comfortable with this visibility and may have to give

up some degree of privacy and autonomy around their personal lifestyle as they become known in the community. This trade-off may be necessary to maximize one's acceptance as a professional within the community. See chapter 6 of this book for an extended discussion of dual relationships in direct practice and chapter 8 for a discussion of dual relationships in administrative practice.

The visibility found in most rural areas may mean that maintaining confidentiality becomes more difficult. Kirkland and Irey (1978) have suggested that social workers in rural areas may need to view confidentiality differently. Social workers report the experience of having a sensitive professional discussion in the morning with a client only to run into the same person that evening at the local market while shopping for the evening meal (Fenby 1978). Social workers must also be prepared to relate to their clients as neighbors, a task that requires sensitivity to rural attitudes toward being helped. The stigma often associated with many of the program auspices for social work may make this even more challenging.

Understanding the importance that social institutions such as the school, family, and church hold for rural communities is part of the cultural awareness needed for effective practice (Ginsberg 1998 [1976]; Turner 1985; Collier 1978; and Whittington 1985). These institutions have historically shaped rural traditions. For example, the rural church has not only served to help people with their spiritual needs but has also defined what is acceptable in the daily life of the community (Ginsberg 1976). Rural social workers have reported that the success or failure of an intervention effort may be influenced by the views held by a powerful lay leader or minister about the nature of the help being given as well as the individual(s) receiving it.

In many rural areas the family remains a central social institution. Scholars note that effective work in small towns and rural areas requires that social workers have an appreciation of the value placed on the family (Collier 1978; Jacobsen 1980; Walsh 1981). This concern for rural families, especially those engaged in farming, has been a long-standing one. The Country Life Commission, established in 1908, called for action on behalf of the family farmer. While our myth continues about the rural family being a farm family, in reality only 1.78 percent of the rural population is engaged in farming as a primary occupation (Fluharty 2001) In fact, the fastest growing family group in rural areas are the nonfarm families who are often subject to the same stresses and issues as their urban counterparts.

Interest in strengthening the rural family continues, especially as the experiences of these families have changed, with social stresses such as divorce, loss of employment, drug use and abuse, and domestic violence becoming more commonplace in rural areas. Many rural areas, like West Virginia, continue to have well-defined extended families that may be a source of support and informal help in some of these situations. However, even though extended families may still exist, many rural regions have seen their influence wane as younger members leave the area because of the lack of economic opportunity.

Finally, social workers have to be sensitive to the needs of minority groups in rural areas. Many rural areas are characterized by a diverse population. This means that, as in urban areas, social workers must be prepared to respond to the requirements of persons who may differ from them culturally or racially. Icard (1978) suggests that the social worker must be aware that what may work in one situation or minority group may not be appropriate for other situations or groups. Social workers need to think carefully about these differences as they intervene and assure that interventions are consistent with the value orientation of the clients being served.

Personal and Professional Traits

Throughout the recent rebirth of interest in social work practice in rural places there has been consistent discussion of the personal and professional traits that support effective rural social work practice. One issue of some controversy has been the belief that, to be effective in many small towns and rural areas, social workers must be committed to the task at hand, seen by the community as supportive of and interested in preserving a rural life style (Fenby 1978; Hanton 1978). This idea is partly linked to the attraction that rural areas may hold for the people living there. The social worker is thought to be an important resource who can often help such places remain viable (Martinez-Brawley 2000). Irey (1980) suggested that a commitment to the rural area is important if the social worker is to be seen as part of the community. Unless this status is achieved, the social worker is likely to be less effective. Hanton (1978) also supported this view but for a slightly different reason, arguing that having such a connection would help the social worker better understand the community and its people and thereby enable the social worker to use professional interventions more effectively.

There is agreement in the literature on social work practice that social workers in small towns and rural areas practice in relative isolation from other professional social workers (Brown 1933; Ginsberg 1998 [1976]; Jankovic and Anderson 1979; and Johnson 1980). The isolating climate often means that the social worker in rural areas must be able to work effectively with limited peer support, supervision, or consultation, and also relate effectively to a range of people who are not social workers but play important roles. Rural social workers may be confronted with practice situations that call for immediate professional responses and must be able to evaluate these situations carefully and act with a sense of confidence in their own professional judgment, knowing that colleagues may not be available for consultation. Rural social workers who exhibit the capacity for patience, flexibility, and creativity are more likely to be successful (Snyder et al. 1985; Neale 1982; Whittington 1985; and Johnson 1980).

Finally, like all social workers, social workers who practice in rural communities need to plan for their professional growth and development (Ginsberg 1998 [1976]). Reading the professional literature and seeking access to continuing educational opportunities is very important for the social worker in small towns and rural areas because such workers are often physically isolated from their colleagues. Technology has facilitated new ways to access such support. Social workers who live and work in small towns and rural areas may take advantage of the Internet, for example, to keep abreast of current events and developments within their field.

Understanding the history and issues associated with social work practice in rural contexts is essential if social work is to fully meet its potential to work effectively in such places. Applicable here is the well-known saying that we are doomed to repeat our past mistakes if we fail to learn from them. However, it is equally limiting to focus only on the past and on past traditions. The nature of rural areas is ever changing and will continue to shift as we move through the twenty-first century. Social workers must "catch the winds of change" and find meaning in those changes. We argue that the historical wisdom associated with social work practice in rural contexts still holds as we contemplate those issues and challenges that face us as rural practitioners. Here we highlight five issues that we see as important as we reflect on the future of social work in rural contexts.

Trends Important to Social Work in Rural Areas

Speculating on the future of social work in the rural context, like speculating on the winners of sports events, is imprecise at best. Edward Cornish (2001), the president of the World Future Society, has written that when one speculates about the future, one needs to consider the continuity between the past, the present, and the future. Much that exists today (the four seasons, the affection of grandparents toward their grandchildren, the addictive potential of alcohol) will still be present in the 2030s. Furthermore, existing trends in certain areas can be projected. For example, although it is difficult to predict the degree to which a trend, such as the increasing concentration of ownership of radio stations and newspapers, will continue or accelerate, it is likely nonetheless that the trend will persist in some form (Cornish 2001).

Two of the five trends explored here affect a number of rural counties throughout the United States regardless of region. These are the movement of Latinos into rural America and the widespread use of illegal drugs by rural adolescents. The three other trends discussed below affect specific parts of rural America, namely, counties in the Great Plains that have been losing population and continue to do so, persistently poor counties, and counties that are increasingly commuter-based.

Movement of Latinos into Rural Communities

The late 1890s and early 1900s saw the first migration of large numbers of Mexicans to the United States. Large landholders and speculators in Mexico had been seizing small farms and uprooting rural families, sending many of them to "El Norte" to the United States (Takaki 1993). They were not universally welcomed. The Dillingham Commission in 1906 concluded that "it was evident that in the case of the Mexican, he was less desirable as a citizen than as a laborer" (Lund 1994, 19). For the most part, the early immigrants stayed in Texas or California or worked the fields as migrants, returning to Mexico or to the Southwest when the crops were harvested.

In the last two decades there has been another period of rapid growth of Hispanics in the United States, spurred by immigration by Mexicans and Central Americans as well as Puerto Ricans who opt to reside on the mainland. The 2000 Census documented the status of Latinos (or Hispanics) as the largest ethnic minority group in the country. Thirty-five million Latinos, 12.5 percent of the population, slightly outnumber African Americans, who comprise 12.1 percent of all U.S. residents.

Latinos are highly concentrated. More than half live in California and Texas, with another 20 percent living in New York, Florida, Illinois, Arizona, and New Jersey. However, although over 90 percent live in urban areas, there has been an increasing movement of Latinos to states and rural areas that have not traditionally had high Latino populations. Three examples of this are North Carolina, Minnesota, and Washington state.from 1990 to 2000 there was a 394 percent increase in Latinos residing in North Carolina. This population shift has been especially apparent in the rural eastern regions of North Carolina. As in many other parts of the country, this has been caused by chain migration. When a family settles in an area and finds that there are both economic opportunities and at least an acceptable quality of life, extended family and friends will also often migrate there (Anguiano 2002).

Minnesota's Latino population almost tripled between 1990 and 2000. The growth was not just in urban areas but also in the state's smaller towns. Much of that growth has occurred in a few west central Minnesota communities where industry has attracted large numbers of workers from Mexico. In Todd County (Minnesota), some longtime residents of Long Beach are struggling with the increasing diversity. The town of about 3000, which has been overwhelmingly white for much of its history, now is close to one-third Latino.

In the northwest corner of Washington state, Latino residents in rural Skagit County grew to 8.1 percent of the population by 1998. Skagit's Hispanic population represents the largest percentage of people of Hispanic origin in any Washington county west of the Cascades. Their contributions are appreciated by some. Without the population growth that resulted from Latino newcomers, several schools would have had to be closed. If Hispanic labor were lost, "it'd wipe out farming," says the Reverend Bob Ekblad, director of Nueva Tierra del Norte, an organization that provides support to Latinos throughout Skagit County (Stiffler 1999). While many here agree that Hispanics are becoming integrated and accepted by the predominantly white society, Ekblad still sees a gap. "There's very little interaction and little social connection with each other," he says (Stiffler 1999, C1).

Widespread Use of Illegal Drugs by Rural Adolescents

A study by the National Center on Addiction and Substance Abuse at Columbia University published in 2000 was the first comprehensive assessment of substance abuse to compare substance abuse in urban, suburban, and rural areas. The study found that drug use is at least as common in rural areas and towns the size of Manhattan, Kansas, as in the better-known Manhattan borough of New York City and other urban areas. Since 1990 drug law violations have increased at a higher rate in small communities than in large cities; drugs are as available in small communities as they are in large cities.

According to the report, adult drug use in rural communities is equal to that in large metropolitan centers. However, there are pronounced differences among the youth: eighth-graders living in rural America are 34 percent likelier than those in urban centers to smoke marijuana; 83 percent are more likely to use crack cocaine; 29 percent are more likely to drink alcohol; and 70 percent are more likely to have been drunk, more than twice as likely to smoke cigarettes, and nearly five times more likely to use smokeless tobacco (National Center on Addiction and Substance Abuse at Columbia University, 2000). At the same time mid-sized cities and rural areas are less equipped to deal with the consequences. Methamphetamine use has hit many areas of the West and Midwest especially hard, placing enormous pressure on hospitals, child-welfare systems, and treatment and law enforcement (National Center on Addiction and Substance Abuse at Columbia University, 2000).

Decreasing Population in the Great Plains

Rural areas saw their population rebound in the 1990s, more than reversing the out-migration of the 1980s. Seventy percent of rural counties gained in population during the last decade of the twentieth century. However, this population growth was largely concentrated in 40 percent of the rural counties (Fluharty 2001). While the nation's population grew by 13 percent, in 676 of the nation's 2,305 rural counties there was a decrease in population. There were 13 percent more counties that had a decrease in population than had lost residents in the previous decade

Most of the decline came in the states of the Great Plains. About half the counties on the plains had a decrease in population in the 1990s — some to levels lower than during frontier days in the 1800s. In Kansas, for example, there are now more "frontier counties," defined by the Census Bureau as having from two to six people per square mile, than there were in 1890 (Johnson 2001).

One example of this loss is Bisbee, North Dakota, population 227, which had a decrease in population by 30 percent in the last decade. There is no longer a doctor or lawyer in Bisbee, nor a plumber. The one restaurant in town remains open, although the owner says that she loses money every time she opens for business. The priest at Holy Rosary Catholic Church left town because parishioners cannot afford to support him. Even the police department closed. Perhaps most important to many residents, the combined high school/middle school closed its doors last year because of low enrollment (Johnson 2001).

Morland, Kansas, had only 164 residents in 2000, down from 234 in 1990. In Morland's case, the decline was brought on by the mechanization of agriculture and nearly two decades of low wheat prices and shrinking oil fields. Over the past two decades the town lost its rail service, in addition to its weekly newspaper, lumber yard, two-story hotel, automobile dealership, three gasoline stations, four clothing and shoe stores, one of its two banks, and two of its three grocery stores (Kilborn 2001).

The population decline in Morland and other small towns has led to precipitous declines in real estate prices to levels reminiscent of frontier days. A woman who moved back to Morland to take care of an aging mother bought a four-bedroom house on Main Street in 1999 for $13,000.

For many counties on the Great Plains and in other remote rural areas, the challenge is not community betterment but community survival. This trend is likely to be most obvious in those places of poverty we call persistently poor counties.

Persistently Poor Counties

More than five hundred rural counties are defined as persistently poor, with poverty rates that have exceeded 20 percent since 1960 (Findies and Mark 2001). Of these, thirty-seven counties also had child poverty rates above 45 percent in 1999. They were clustered in the South, Southwest, and in South Dakota. Many of these counties are persistently poor, with high poverty rates that have been characteristic for many decades (Findies and Mark 2001).

Between 1990 and 1995 Cynthia Duncan (1999) examined long-term trends in county census data and interviewed more than 350 people in three counties representative of Central Appalachia, the Mississippi Delta, and Upper New England in order to probe the causes of persistent rural poverty.

Blackwell (in Appalachia) and Dahlia (in the Delta)[2] are portrayed as similar. Both are among the poorest counties in the United States and have

500 Poorest Counties in the U.S., 2000

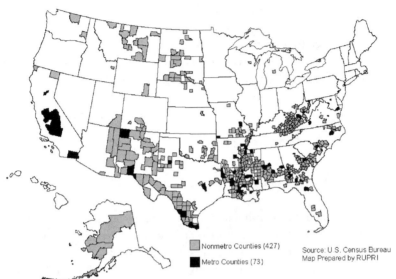

Counties with the highest poverty rates as of 1999 and reported in Census 2000. Metropolitan status as of 2003.

been for decades. It is in these counties, according to Duncan, that the poor are the most socially isolated ("worlds apart"), oppressed by systems of rigid class stratification and, in the Delta, by racial segregation of long duration. In upper New England rural poverty exists in Gray Mountain as well, but, despite contemporary challenges posed by economic restructuring and the retrenchment of government services, poverty is not as extensive, severe, or entrapping as it is in Blackwell or Delta. Duncan's book is an effort to explain why "it is that when people who are poor in Gray Mountain want to do better, they can find ladders" (Duncan 1999, 163).

In the industrial communities of Appalachia's coal fields and the farming communities of the Delta's plantation economy, local elites have ruled with oppressive power and short-sighted policies for decades, depriving local populations of economic and political justice. In both contexts communities are highly stratified; small and weak middle classes identify with elites, rarely challenge their power, and distance themselves and their children from the lives of the poor. Education for the poor has been devalued or opposed. Patronage and corruption determine access to jobs and government services. Fear predominates (Duncan 1999).

Increase of Urban Commuters in Rural Areas

Although the population in rural areas increased in the 1990s, the upsurge largely occurred in the first part of the decade, was uneven, and was concentrated in rural counties adjacent to urban areas. Although 70 percent of rural counties experienced growth, the great majority of this growth occurred in only 40 percent of counties, those close to urban areas. Since 1995 all rural counties, except those close enough to be commuter counties, have declined in population (Fluharty 2001).

Implications for Social Workers in Rural Areas

How do these trends influence the five significant thematic areas for social workers practicing in rural areas identified earlier in the chapter? The last one identified, desirable personal and professional traits, appears to be unaffected by the trends. It seems likely that social workers in rural areas in 2030 will still need to be self-directed, creative, and able to function in situations of high visibility.

Although the nature of some of the challenges that individuals, families, and organizations face will change in the coming decades, there will be an unaltered and perhaps expanded need for social workers who are generalists. The growing illegal drug use by rural adolescents in the late 1990s is an issue in itself and also an indication of the severity of the issues confronting rural communities. Without the specialized resources available to their urban counterparts, social workers in rural areas will need to know how to weave together formal and informal resources to meet needs and support people. The emphasis on external relations, on knowing the people and knowing how to work with a number of the important institutions in the community, will continue to be important as will the social workers role in community development.

As Mermelstein and Sundet (1995, 9) state,

The traditional expertise in community building that was the hallmark of this profession has been, by default, passed on to others. More and more special interest groups such as rural economic developers, health care planners, youth service advocates, ecologists, elementary and secondary education reformers and political activists are promoting broadbased citizen coalitions as a primary tool. Terms such as empowerment, leveraging, indigenous resource, assets assessment and systemic analysis are suddenly being discovered and popularized in these disciplines. While we should rejoice that community building is having such a renaissance, are social workers in the forefront? Not in many areas.

In persistently poor counties issues of social justice are joined with community building, since community development in those areas has historically been for the elite, with limited opportunities for other residents. In the context of the Great Plains, the task of community building may be replaced by the task of community survival. While other regions may not place their need for community development in such stark terms, their need is no less real. One commonality among the changes identified is that they indicate that rural communities, often seen by their residents as places of constancy, are experiencing great changes. The changes may be in the nature of the new residents, who may be Latinos (or other immigrants) or commuters whose work life is outside the counties or both. Although we noted above the importance for social workers to understand the culture of those living in the community, this may need to be expanded to include acting as a "cultural broker" between the groups in the community. New residents in a county moving to rural areas from urban areas for affordable housing or for other reasons may be predominantly Caucasian, like the longtime residents. However, their values and ideas of what community life should be like may be very different. This is equally true for communities and rural areas experiencing an influx of minorities such as Latinos. Social work should be uniquely qualified to assist communities experiencing such changes to come to a position of greater cultural understanding and valuing of all its citizens.

That the social work profession has to a large degree removed itself from the development arena is of concern at several levels. At a professional level it has tended to keep social service programs isolated from the community, as access to them is often restricted, resulting in continuing stigma about their use. Social workers in rural areas have an opportunity to position themselves in roles where they can effectively challenge such thinking. At an ethical level, noninvolvement in the community may result in missed opportunities to influence the course of local policy and program development. Earlier we mentioned a need for social workers to seek leadership roles in local politics to provide a voice in this area. At a personal level, such work is often very rewarding and even fun. Many small towns and rural places cry out for new leadership. Social workers who respond may find themselves in the position of using their knowledge and skill to the benefit of all citizens. Such efforts can only add value to the profession in the rural context.

Conclusion

Rural America is changing. Whether the change is about the dying of a midwest community or the transition of a rural area in eastern West Virginia into a suburb of Washington, D.C., change is a constant for the rural environment. Such change will be managed either by a proactive effort to shape it or by a reactive response to it. It is our view that it is better to manage such change proactively. Further, we see social work as a profession with a mission and obligation to serve, which places it in a strong position to help rural people mange such change.

The Mermelstein and Sundet quote cited above captures an important point. In our history we have the tradition of having worked to build stronger communities not only for the most vulnerable among us but for all citizens. Social work needs to reclaim that tradition in the rural context. In many respects we are an urban society and yet over 75 percent of the counties in this country are classified as rural. That being the case, social work needs to continue its mission of service to rural people. Such a mission will no doubt need those "pickaxes" mentioned in the epigraph to this chapter, if it is to be a successful one.

Notes

1. For an extended discussion of dual relationships, see chapter 6.
2. The county names used in this section — Blackwell, Dahlia, and Gray Mountain — are pseudonyms.

References

Anguiano, R.P.V. 2002. Planting seeds family enrichment program: Serving rural immigrant Hispanic families and their youth in eastern North Carolina. *Journal of Extension* 39 (6). http://www.joe.org/joe/2001december/ retrieved May 12, 2001.

Brenden, M. A., and B. Shank. 1985. Educating rural social workers: A program model. In W. H. Whitaker, ed., *Social work in rural areas: A Celebration of rural people, place, and struggle,* pp. 295–308. Orono: University of Maine Press.

Brown, J .C. 1933. *The rural community and social casework.* New York: Little and Ives.

Collier, K. 1978. Education for rural social work practice: The Saskatchewan experience. In E. B. Buxton, ed., *2nd National institute on social work in rural areas,* pp. 83-93. Madison: University of Wisconsin Press.

Cornish, E. 2001. How we can anticipate future events? *The Futurist* 35 (4): 26–33.

Davenport, J. A., and J. Davenport III. 1995. Rural social work overview. In R. Edwards, ed., *Encyclopedia of Social Work,* 19th ed., pp. 2076–2085. Washington, D.C.: NASW Press.

Deaton, R., and A. Bjergo. 1978. An appropriate role for social work: Small business development in the rural community. In E. B. Buxton, ed., *2nd National institute on social work in rural areas,* pp. 61-67. Madison: University of Wisconsin Press.

Duncan, C.M. 1999. *Worlds apart: Why poverty persists in rural America.* New Haven, Conn.: Yale University Press.

Eisenhart, M., and T. Ruff. 1984. Doing mental health work in rural versus urban places. In J. Gumpert, ed., *Toward clarifying the context of rural practice,* pp. 33–49. Lexington, Mass.: Ginn.

Fenby, B. L. 1978. Social work in a rural setting. *Social Work* 23 (2): 162–163.

Garcia, J. R. 1979. The people of Mexican descent in Michigan: A historical overview. In H. Hawkins and R. W. Thomas, eds., *Blacks and Chicanos in urban Michigan,* pp. 44–55. Lansing: Department of State, Michigan History Division.

Ginsberg, L. H., ed. 1976. *Social work in rural communities.* New York: Council on Social Work Education.

———, ed. 1998. *Social work in rural communities.* 3rd. ed. Alexandria, Va.: Council on Social Work Education.

Findies, Jill, and Henry Mark. 2001. Welfare reform in rural areas: A review of current research. Columbia, Mo.: RUPRI.

Fulton, J., G. Fuguiitt, and R. Gibson. 1997. Recent changes in metropolitan-nonmetropolitan migration streams. *Rural Sociology* 62 (3): 363–384.

Fluharty, C. W. 2001. Trends in rural America and the implications for economic development practitioners in rural Illinois. Presented to the Sixth Annual Southern Illinois Economic Development Conference, Carbondale, Illinois. November 7.

Hanton, S. 1978. A case for the generalist social worker: A model for service delivery in rural areas. In B. L. Locke and R.A. Lohmann, eds., *Effective models for the delivery of services in rural areas: Implications for practice and social work education,* pp. 192–201. Morgantown: West Virginia University School of Social Work.

Icard, L. 1978. Blacks in rural areas: Consideration for service effectiveness. In E. B. Buxton, ed., *2nd National institute on social work in rural areas,* pp, 68–75. Madison: University of Wisconsin Press.

Irey, K. V. 1980. The social work generalist in a rural context. *Journal of Education for Social Work* 16 (3): 36–42.

Jacobsen, G. M. 1980. Rural communities and rural development. In H. W. Johnson, ed., *Rural human services: A book of readings*, pp. 196–202. Itasca, Ill.: Peacock.

Jankovic, J., and R. J. Anderson. 1979. Professional education for rural practice. *Social Work in Education* 1 (2): 5–14.

Johnson, H. W., ed. 1980. *Rural human services: A book of readings*. Itasca, Ill.: Peacock.

Johnson, D. 2001. Death of a small town. *Newsweek*, September 10.

Kelley, V., and P. Kelley. 1985. Differences between rural and urban social work practice as perceived by practitioners. In W. H. Whitaker, ed., *Social work in rural areas: A celebration of rural people, place, and struggle*, pp. 239–253. Orono: University of Maine.

Kilborn, C. 2001. May 10. Bit by bit, tiny Morland, Kansas slips away. *New York Times*. Electronic document. http://www.citizenreviewonline.org/may_2001/bit_by_bit_tiny_morland_kansas_fades_away.htm/ retrieved May 15, 2003.

Kirkland, J., and K. Irey. 1978. Confidentiality: Issues and dilemmas in rural practice. In E. B. Buxton, ed., *2nd National institute on social work in rural areas*, pp. 142-150. Madison: University of Wisconsin.

Kretzmann, J. P., and J. L. McKnight. 1993. *Building communities from the inside out*. Chicago: ACTA Publications.

Levin, L. I. 1974. *Educating social workers for practice in rural settings*. Atlanta: Southern Regional Education Board.

Locke, B. L. 1988. Role expectations for social work in small towns and rural areas. Unpublished Ph.D. dissertation, West Virginia University, 1988. *Dissertation Abstracts International* 49 (11): 3507 (AAT 8905120).

Locke, B., B. Garrison, and J. Winship. 1998. *Generalist social work practice: Context, story, and partnerships*. Pacific Grove, Calif.: Brooks/Cole.

Lund, J. M. 1994. Boundaries of restriction: The Dillingham Commission. *University of Vermont History Review* 6. Electronic document. http://www.uvm.edu/~hag/histreview/vol6/lund.html/ retrieved May 16, 2003.

Martinez-Brawley, E. E. 1981. *Seven decades of rural social work: From country life commission to rural caucus*. New York: Praeger.

———. 2000. *Close to home: Human services and the small community*. Washington, D.C.: NASW Press.

Mermelstein, J., and P. Sundet. 1995. Rural social work is an anachronism: The perspective of twenty years of experience and debate. *Human Services in the Rural Environment* 18 (1): 6–12.

Morrison, J. 1976. Community organization in rural areas. In L. H. Ginsberg, ed., *Social work in rural communities: A book of readings*, pp. 57–61. New York: Council on Social Work Education.

National Center on Addiction and Substance Abuse at Columbia University.

2000. *No place to hide: Substance abuse in mid-size cities and rural America*. Electronic document. http://www.casacolumbia.org/publications1456/publications_show.htm?doc_id = 23734/ retrieved May 15, 2003.

Neale, N. K. 1982. A social worker for all seasons: Rural social work in the 1980s. In L.A.B. Jorgensen and J. A. Smith, eds., *The 80s: A decade for new roles in social work*, pp. 169–180. Salt Lake City: University of Utah Press.

Omar, S. 1977. Rural practice models: Community development. In R. K. Green and S. A. Webster, eds., *Social work in rural areas: Preparation and practice*, pp. 107–136. Knoxville: University of Tennessee School of Social Work.

O'Neill, J. F., and W. C. Horner. 1982. Two surveys of social service practice in the Northwest: Comparing rural and urban practitioners. In M. Jacobsen, ed., *Nourishing people and communities through the lean years*. Iowa City: University of Iowa.

Pipher, Mary. 2002. *The middle of everywhere: The world's refugees come to our town*. New York: Harcourt.

Post, Tim. 2001. Hispanic population changes the face of rural Minnesota. Electronic document. http://news.mpr.org/features/200103/28_newsroom_census/rural_hispanics.shtml/ retrieved November 9, 2003.

Singelmann, J. 1996. Will rural areas still matter in the 21st century? Can rural sociology remain relevant? *Rural Sociology* 61 (1): 143–158.

Snyder, G. W. et al. 1978. Block placements in rural veteran administration hospitals: A consortium approach. *Social Work in Health Care* 3 (4): 331–341.

Stiffler, L. 1999. Growing Hispanic populace helping save rural lifestyle. *Seattle Post-Intelligencer*. Electronic document. http://seattlepi.nwsource.com/neighbors/burlington/grow22.html/ retrieved May 12, 2003.

Takaki, R. 1993. *A different mirror: A history of multicultural America*. Boston: Little, Brown.

Trattner, W. I. 1999. *From poor law to welfare state: A history of social welfare in America*. New York: Free Press.

Turner, K. A. 1985. Local churches and community social work providers as collaborators in rural social service delivery. In W. H. Whitaker, ed., *Social work in rural areas: A Celebration of rural people, place, and struggle*, pp. 111–128. Orono: University of Maine Press.

Walsh, M. E. 1981. Rural social work practice: Clinical quality. *Social Casework* (October): 458–464.

Webster, S. A., and P. M. Campbell. 1977. The 1970s and changing dimensions in rural life: Is a new practice model needed? In R. K. Green and S.A. Webster, eds., *Social work in rural areas: Preparation and practice*, pp. 75–94. Knoxville: University of Tennessee School of Social Work.

Wharf, B. 1985. Toward a leadership in human services: The case for rural communities. In W. H. Whitaker, ed., *Social work in rural areas: A Celebration of rural people, place, and struggle*, pp. 9–40. Orono: University of Maine Press.

Whitaker, W. H. 1984. A survey of perceptions of social work practice in rural and urban areas. In S. C. Matison, ed., *The future of rural communities: Preservation and change*, pp. 221–235. Cheney: Eastern Washington University Press.

Whittington, B. 1985. The challenge of family work in a rural community. *Social Worker* 53 (3): 104–107.

Woehle, R. 1982. Economic uncertainty and planning social services in a nonmetropolitan county. In M. Jacobsen, ed., *Nourishing people and communities through the lean years*, pp. 1–12. Iowa City: University of Iowa Printing Service.

2 Rural Poverty and Welfare Reform
Challenges and Opportunities

Eleanor H. Blakely and Barry L. Locke

For many in the United States the image of rural America is one of quaint villages surrounded by rolling and open pastures where cattle graze, children play in sweet innocence, and most families live without a care in the world. Unfortunately this image holds little credence for many of the nearly seven million residents of rural areas and small towns whose reality may be one of little or no income, inadequate housing, limited education, and a bleak future shaped by living in what has come to be known as persistent rural poverty.[1]

This chapter reviews poverty in the rural context. It examines some of the outcomes for rural families associated with the current welfare reform effort and identifies certain challenges rural areas may face in the continuing evolution of the Temporary Assistance for Needy Families (TANF) program. Finally, it discusses some of the issues surrounding poverty that the profession of social work needs to address if it wants to be an important player in addressing this continuing social problem.

The Rural Poor

Who are the rural poor? While this appears to be a relatively simple question, part of the challenge of finding the answer lies in defining what we mean by "rural." In our home state of West Virginia residents distinguish between the state's rural areas and urban areas, and yet the state does not have a single city larger than 53,000 people. However, one of the authors was recently in a small city of approximately 54,000 in the Midwest, and residents there characterized themselves as living in a rural area. Clearly factors other than population density influence the concept of "rurality."

To illustrate, one of the authors lives in a large town of 2,500 that is basically a residential area with several small service-oriented businesses. A sister lives in another state in a community of similar size that also serves as the county seat. The resource differences between these two areas are quite striking. The different roles associated with the county seat means that the level of economic and governmental activity is much greater than in a community of like size without those functions. Thus even rural areas with the same population are likely to experience significant differences that impact upon the kinds of opportunities likely to be found there, an important variable to keep in mind as we examine the concept of rural poverty. As Chuck Fluharty, executive director of the Rural Policy Research Institute, (RUPRI) noted at a recent national meeting on social work and rural areas, in trying to define rural America it is important to remember that "when you have seen one rural community, you have in fact seen one rural community" (Fluharty 2002).

In its presentation of data on poverty, the U.S. Bureau of the Census uses the designations "metropolitan area," "central city," and "nonmetropolitan area." A metropolitan area (MA) is defined as a large population nucleus, together with adjacent communities that have a high degree of economic and social integration with that nucleus (some MAs are defined around two or more nuclei). "Metropolitan area" is a collective term, established by the federal Office of Management and Budget and used for the first time in 1990, to refer to metropolitan statistical areas (MSAs), consolidated metropolitan statistical areas (CMSAs), New England county metropolitan areas (NECMAs), and primary metropolitan statistical areas (PMSAs). In a metropolitan area "central city" indicates the largest place, and in some areas one or more additional places meet the standards for a central city. A few primary metropolitan statistical areas do not have a central city. Thus those areas not defined as "metropolitan" are designated as "nonmetropolitan," a term we will use interchangeably with "rural."

Overall Numbers

According to the 2000 Census 11.3 percent of the U.S. population is poor, which is defined as having an annual income below $17,603 for a family of four or $8,794 for an individual (figures for 2000). Most of us tend to think of poverty as being associated with metropolitan areas, particularly inner cities, and while the latter do have the highest poverty rates (16.1 percent), rural areas do not lag far behind, with an overall poverty rate of 13.4 percent. Not surprisingly the lowest rates are for metropolitan areas outside the central cities, at 7.8 percent. The overall rate for metropolitan areas, which includes both central cities and areas outside central cities, is 10.8 percent. Thus rural areas have a higher rate of poverty than metropolitan areas. While all areas have experienced a decline in the poverty rate since 1993, the highest rate of decline has been for persons living in central cities (5.3 percent), with metropolitan areas as a whole and nonmetropolitan areas experiencing declines of 3.8 percent.

Poverty Subgroups

While the numbers presented above provide an overview of the extent of poverty in rural areas, to more fully understand poverty and the rural context it is necessary to examine the differential impacts of poverty on various subgroups.

Blacks and Hispanics   While the majority of those living in poverty in rural areas are white, racial and ethnic minorities continue to be disproportionately represented, as indicated in Table 2.1. The table shows that minority groups still experience poverty rates much higher than one would expect based on their proportion in society. But particularly striking is that poverty rates for blacks and persons of Hispanic origin are higher in rural areas than in central cities, which contradicts the image of poverty most often presented in the popular media.

TABLE 2.1 Percent of Population in Poverty by Race and Place

	Whites	Blacks	Hispanics
U.S.	9.4	22.0	21.2
Metro	8.8	21.2	17.6
Central cities	13.2	25.8	23.8
Nonmetro	11.6	27.8	27.0

The Elderly   The reduction of poverty among the elderly is often touted as a public policy success story. Owing in part to the implementation of programs such as the Social Security Cost of Living Adjustment (COLA), Medicare, and Supplemental Security Income, the poverty rate among the elderly has declined dramatically since the 1960s. However, according to the 2000 census data, poverty is highest among the elderly living in rural areas, where it is 13.2 percent compared to 12.4 percent in central cities, 7.5 percent in metropolitan areas, and 10.2 percent overall. More than half the rural elderly have family incomes less than 200 percent of the federal poverty level compared to approximately 40 percent of the elderly in urban areas (Rural Policy Research Institute [RUPRI] 2002).

Children   Since 1993 the United States has experienced a gradual decline in child poverty rates, with the overall rate now standing at 16.2 percent. According to the 2000 census data, the breakdown by place of residence is as follows: metropolitan, 10.7 percent; central cities, 24.3 percent; nonmetropolitan, 19.0 percent. However, according to the Children's Defense Fund (2002), there are thirty-eight counties with child poverty rates higher than the poorest big cities, and nearly all are rural counties. Children in rural areas are 50 percent more likely to have no health insurance and to have periods when they are not insured; they attend schools that receive less funding than those in nonrural areas; and they have access to fewer child and youth development opportunities such as after-school recreational and educational programs (Save the Children 2002).

Working Families   One feature of rural poverty is that it is poverty of the working poor. According to the Rural Policy Research Institute (2002), low-income persons in rural areas are more likely to be employed and still poor than are their nonrural counterparts. In 1998 two-thirds of poor rural families had at least one family member working at some time, 16 percent had two or more members working, and 29 percent had one or more members working full-time year-round.

Single Female-headed Households   The family structure of the nonmetropolitan poor is different from that of metropolitan areas in that the rural poor are more likely to live in married couple families. However, the emphasis often placed on this difference tends to obscure the fact that, as noted by Lichter and Jensen (2000, 9), there is "unexpected similarity" in structure between today's nonmetropolitan and metropolitan families. Female-headed families with children are nearly proportionately represented in nonmetropolitan areas, and poverty rates among female-headed households in nonmetropolitan areas and central cities are almost identical, at 35.1 percent and 34.5 percent, respectively.

The Rural Context of Poverty

While the statistics presented above help inform the reader regarding the incidence of poverty in rural areas, it is necessary to place these numbers within a context to gain a fuller understanding of rural poverty. The following statistics apply to the beginning of the twenty-first century:

- nonmetropolitan poverty is 2.6 percentage points higher than poverty in metropolitan areas (U.S. Census Bureau 2001a)
- nonmetropolitan areas lag behind metropolitan areas in both per capita income and earnings per job (Whitener, Duncan, and Weber 2002)
- between 1999 and 2000 nonmetropolitan real median income declined by 3.8 percent compared to a 1.7 percent increase in metropolitan areas (U.S. Census Bureau 2001b)
- unemployment and underemployment are higher in nonmetropolitan labor markets than in metropolitan labor markets, and job growth is slower (Whitener, Weber, and Duncan 2001)
- employment in nonmetropolitan areas is more concentrated in low-wage industries (RUPRI 2002)
- rural workers are more than twice as likely to earn minimum wages as urban workers and 40 percent less likely to move out of low-wage jobs than are central city residents (RUPRI 2002)
- work support services such as formal child care and public transportation are less available in nonmetropolitan areas than in metropolitan areas (Whitener, Duncan, and Weber 2002; Whitener, Weber, and Duncan 2001)

More than five hundred nonmetropolitan counties are classified as persistently poor counties, defined as having a poverty rate of 20 percent or more for the last four decades. These counties cluster in certain regions, most notably in Appalachia, the South, and in the North Central region (specifically in North Dakota, South Dakota, and Missouri). According to Whitener, Duncan, and Weber (2002), these counties have a disproportionate number of economically at-risk residents, higher unemployment and poverty rates, lower earnings per job, lower per capita income, and generally weaker economies than do nonmetropolitan counties as a whole.

As we try to understand rural poverty, one thing becomes clear: place matters. As indicated above, rural residents are more disadvantaged than are their urban counterparts in terms of employment opportunities and earnings per job, as well as the availability of work support services such as formal child care arrangements and public transportation. Unless these differences are taken into account in the development and implementation of federal policies, unanticipated and unintended consequences may result (RUPRI 2002).

Rural Areas and Welfare Reform

Given the long history of poverty in rural areas, it is appropriate to examine one of the most sweeping public policy changes in the past sixty years, and its impact on rural communities and families. With the signing of PL 104–193, The Personal Responsibility and Work Opportunity Reconciliation Act of 1996 (PRWORA), President Bill Clinton was able to declare that the United States had "ended welfare as we know it." Welfare reform, as the act is commonly known, drastically changes the nature of the social contract between society and those less able to compete successfully in the economic marketplace. The act created the program of Temporary Assistance for Needy Families (TANF) as a replacement for Aid to Families with Dependent Children (AFDC). This new law provides a new set of criteria and expectations for receiving public assistance. These new criteria include:

- work requirements for adult recipients (with some exceptions) after two years of assistance
- a five-year lifetime cap on benefits
- a requirement that mothers under eighteen years of age must live with an adult relative or other adult supervisor to be eligible for cash benefits
- the de-linking of eligibility for Temporary Assistance for Needy Families (TANF) and eligibility for Medicaid
- barring of legal immigrants from eligibility to receive Supplemental Security Income (SSI) and food stamps until they become citizens
- tightening of SSI eligibility criteria, with some states electing to count SSI as a family resource and thereby making the family ineligible to receive TANF

- restriction of food stamp eligibility, with states given greater authority over the program, including the right to deny participants for at least a three-month period if they received the stamps in the previous thirty-six months and did not work or participate in a work or training program (Ozawa and Kirk 1997, 93–94)

Impact of Welfare Reform in Rural Areas

Since the implementation of the welfare reform policy, a number of research studies have been conducted that provide information about the impact of this policy on both the recipients of benefits and the service delivery system. Two such studies have been completed in West Virginia, which continues to rank as one of the most rural of the fifty states, with a majority of its residents living in rural areas. While the research data reported here are specific to West Virginia and its WV WORKS program, and no claim for generalizability beyond that state is made, the data help to fill a void in welfare reform research. Because most of the research has been conducted in urban areas, these studies contribute to our knowledge about the impact in rural areas.

As noted previously, West Virginia is one of the most rural states in the United States as defined by the percentage of its population that reside in small towns and rural areas. West Virginia also has a long history of persistent poverty. It presents a case study of the public policy challenges facing a rural area that has not been primarily linked to agriculture and has a history of consistently high unemployment and poverty rates. Given that many critics of welfare reform argue that the true test of the policy will come during recessionary times, the experience of West Virginia may serve as a harbinger of things to come for states that enjoyed strong economies during the early years of the policy's implementation (Dilger 2004).

The two studies that were conducted, one on "welfare leavers" (Dilger et al. 2000) and the other on those remaining on TANF (Dilger et al. 2001) consisted of statewide mailed surveys of each group, conducted using a generalizable sampling technique. The response rates were 50 percent and 57.4 percent, Respectively. Key findings for each study are summarized below.

Welfare Leavers Study (n = 962)

- most of those who left the AFDC/TANF program did so to accept employment (43 percent)

- the median wage for those employed was $5.90 per hour
- most of the respondents (82.9 percent) had a total annual household income of less than $10,000 in 1998
- while generally optimistic about their future, large numbers of the respondents reported that since leaving TANF they had experienced times when they did not have enough money to buy food (42.9 percent), medicine (40.2 percent), eyeglasses (59.3 percent), go to the dentist (48.9 percent), or see the doctor (39.6 percent)
- those remaining unemployed noted that the reasons were associated with disability (39.1 percent), labor market conditions (37.7 percent), child care (26.1 percent), a transportation problem (25.6 percent), or a lack of job skills (25.2 percent)
- enrollment in other public assistance programs (such as Medicaid and Food Stamps) decreased after the respondents left TANF
- when asked how they could improve their well-being, the two most frequently cited responses were finding a job or a better-paying job and obtaining additional education
- when asked what they would change about the TANF program, the two most frequently cited suggestions were to improve the sensitivity of the program staff and to provide additional help in finding work (Dilger et. al 2000)

Current Recipients Study (n = 1206)

- recipients over the age of thirty, lacking a graduate equivalency diploma (GED) or high school degree, residing in an economically distressed county (defined by the Appalachian Regional Commission), and having used AFDC or TANF more than three different times report having the most difficult time coping both financially and socially, placing them at greater risk of making the transition from WV WORKS to self-sufficiency
- many of the recipients did not have a GED or high school degree (39.6 percent)
- many of these respondents (43 percent) lacked access to a working telephone
- a very large number (71 percent) of respondents did not know how many months of TANF eligibility they had left
- many respondents reported that they did not have sufficient information about other benefits or services they might qualify for (e.g., only 26 percent reported having enough information about transportation bene-

fits, the federal earned income tax credit, or WV Works dental and vision benefits)

- large numbers of respondents (ranging from 53 to 72 percent) felt they did have enough information about food stamps and various rules and regulations associated with the TANF program in West Virginia
- approximately 26 percent of respondents were employed in subsidized or unsubsidized employment with a median wage of $5.32 per hour
- the most frequently cited reasons for not working or participating in a work-related program were lack of transportation (48.4 percent), disability (39.7 percent), child care (38.4 percent), and a poor job market (37.7 percent)
- most of the respondents reported a total household income of less than $5,000 in 1999 (65.1 percent), and they expected to stay in that income range in 2000 (56.2 percent)
- a large number (41.5 percent) reported that they had completed at least one job-training program, including: Jobs Training Partnership Act (JTPA) (17.2 percent), a job-readiness class (15.7 percent), or adult basic education or GED classes (13.4 percent)
- the most frequently mentioned factors that could improve the well-being of the respondents included finding a job or a better-paying job (33 percent), becoming more education (12.5 percent), and improving one's health (10.2 percent) (Dilger et al. 2001)

The results of these two studies reflect good news and bad news. The good news is that rural recipients are moving off the welfare rolls and into employment. The bad news is that this employment is unlikely to move families out of poverty, many families are experiencing hardships such as not having enough money for food and medical care, and often they are not receiving benefits for which they remain eligible (particularly food stamps). When combined with results from studies in other rural states, a picture begins to emerge highlighting some of the challenges rural areas will continue to face as welfare reform enters its next phase of reauthorization and implementation.

Caseload Increases   While, on average, rural areas have experienced declines in TANF caseloads about as large as those in urban areas, there is evidence that these declines are beginning to taper off. In fact, in West Virginia the caseloads are already increasing (West Virginia Department of Health and Human Resources 2002). As the economy begins a slowdown, we may see very different scenarios unfold in rural and nonrural areas, and may also find differences between the rural areas themselves.

Ability to Find Work   While many former recipients have entered the workforce, the data indicate that single mothers with little education living in rural areas have not experienced the employment gains of their nonrural counterparts. Unless there is an increased emphasis on education in the reauthorization of the Personal Responsibility and Work Opportunity Reconciliation Act (PROWRA), this group is unlikely to experience any gains. Evidence also indicates that employment increases are much smaller and more temporary in rural as compared to urban counties (Gennetian, Redcross, and Miller 2002). In the West Virginia research 38 percent of respondents who were unemployed (current TANF recipients as well as those who had left the program) reported poor labor market conditions as the primary reason for their unemployment. Both current TANF recipients and those who had left the program were asked the open-ended question "If there was one thing you could do to improve your own well-being, or that of your family, what would it be?" The most frequent response was "get a job or a better-paying job."

Welfare to Work Transition   Research on the welfare to work transition indicates that proximity of jobs and access to support services are key variables (Findeis et al. 2001). Those recipients living in or close to urban areas have access to more better-paying jobs than do recipients in remote rural areas. Transportation and child care have consistently been identified by recipients as barriers to employment, with rural areas offering less access to affordable and flexible child care (Findeis et al. 2001). As the West Virginia studies confirmed, rural recipients often turn to family members as preferred child care providers; however, this is not always an option, and the possibility of family care is not a substitute for the certainty of formalized child care arrangements.

The need for what are often called transitional benefits, but may more appropriately be thought of as benefits that help sustain employment, was also reinforced by the studies data, particularly given the low levels of earnings and lack of job benefits reported by respondents. Most (82.9 percent) of those who had left TANF reported a total annual household income of $10,000 or less in 1998. Many also reported an increase in the incidence of such life circumstances as not having enough money to buy food or medicine since leaving WV WORKS/TANF. Yet the percentage of these respondents receiving benefits that are not contingent upon being a TANF recipient, such as Medicaid, food stamps, free/reduced price meals, low-income energy assistance, and Women, Infants, and Children (WIC), was smaller when they went off the program, which is consistent with data from other states. In addition to indicating the need for such benefits, the data also point to a need for better outreach and consumer education about the supports and benefits that are available regardless of participation in the TANF program.

Economic Well-being   Although many former welfare recipients are now employed, data from various state studies indicate that recipients are unlikely to escape poverty through work, with smaller welfare reform impacts on employment and earnings in rural areas than in urban areas. In the West Virginia Leavers study, 82.9 percent of respondents reported a total household income of less than $10,000 for 1998. When former TANF recipients in rural areas do find jobs, they are more likely to earn the minimum wage and to be employed and still poor than their urban counterparts (Findeis et al. 2001). Fewer job opportunities and lack of work supports help to explain these rural/urban employment and earnings differences (Whitener, Weber, and Duncan 2001).

Administrative Flexibility   One of the challenges administrators face in both rural and urban areas has been the effort to implement a public policy based on the premise "one size fits all." The fallacy of this approach is particularly evident in the regulations on work requirements and the time limits for the receipt of TANF benefits. While it may be realistic to expect a recipient facing few structural or personal barriers to find employment and leave the TANF rolls within the allotted time, the West Virginia data indicate that large numbers of recipients confront a very different set of circumstances than those just described. For example, according to the survey of current TANF recipients, respondents living in rural areas and those living in one of West Virginia's twenty-six economically distressed counties (as defined by the Appalachian Regional Commission) were more likely to be unemployed for longer periods of time than those living in a town or city and those not residing in an economically distressed county.[2] While this result is not a particularly startling one, the current welfare reform approach does not take into account regional economic variations across and within states. Rural areas are particularly disadvantaged by this because an "urban bias" in the policy assumes that recipients have access to jobs, transportation, child care, and other institutional supports necessary to support a work program. In announcing new initiatives to respond to the needs of rural areas, Department of Health and Human Resources Secretary Tommy Thompson (2002, 1) acknowledged this bias, stating that, "for too long our rural health care and social service providers have been burdened with rules and regulations designed for urban and suburban communities." However, it remains to be seen if this acknowledgment will be translated into administrative flexibility that will allow variations both within and across states to be considered.

Challenges and Opportunities

Has welfare reform been a successful public policy in rural areas? The answer depends on how the term "successful" is defined. Many politicians on both sides of the aisle have pointed to the substantial decrease in the number of persons receiving cash assistance as a measure of success. They believe that the program should be extended, but with the addition of increased work requirements for both single and two-parent families. Others, however, want a change in focus from caseload reduction to one that emphasizes economic self-sufficiency and the reduction of poverty. To that end, the social work profession needs to take a leadership role in reframing the welfare reform debate so that equal attention is given to the issue of reducing poverty as has been given to the issue of reducing the number of cases on the public welfare rolls. Additionally we must help move the focus from one that views poverty as solely an individual-level problem to one that recognizes that many responsible low-income individuals are trapped in poverty by a variety of institutional barriers. The current TANF program is a symptom of society's inability to think of poverty as other than an individual problem. This is particularly problematic for the rural poor, in that they often lack access to the resources needed to permit the exercise of responsible choice.

The efforts of the social work profession must extend beyond active participation in the public debate over poverty. We must reassert our presence in the public welfare arena where services are provided to low-income individuals and families. Over the years some have criticized the social work profession for moving away from its historical roots often associated with poverty and social advocacy (e.g., see Specht and Courtney 1995). Employment data suggest that the primary roles and professional jobs held by social workers have taken the profession away from being a central player in the poverty arena. According to the website of the National Association of Social Workers, approximately 5 percent of its members are employed by public agencies (National Association of Social Workers 2002).

This becomes important in examining the response of the social work profession to poverty, since it can be argued that beginning in the New Deal era the public sector has carried programmatic responsibility for the care of the poor. With the implementation of welfare reform, the role of the case-worker has shifted from eligibility determination to intensive case management with families facing a variety of institutional and personal barriers to self-sufficiency. This is a role that professionally educated social workers are prepared to carry out. However, given the low salaries and high caseloads characteristic of practice in the public sector, particularly in rural areas, it is not surprising that graduates of accredited BSW and MSW programs seek employment opportunities elsewhere, which leaves a void in the public sector that is often filled by persons with degrees in disciplines other than social work. One of the challenges to the social work profession is to educate legislative bodies about the roles and functions of social workers in public welfare positions so that salaries and working conditions will become a positive factor in recruiting and retaining social workers who have a BSW or MSW.

An additional challenge is to educate both social workers and others about the realities of poverty in rural America. The myths and stereotypes associated with rural poverty (e.g., everyone grows his own food so hunger isn't a problem) need to be replaced with facts. One way to accomplish this is to assure that content on rural poverty is included in the social work curricula. Attention must also be paid to the contextual variables associated with "place," emphasizing not only how place impacts direct practice but also how it influences the conceptualization and implementation of public policy.

When asked what it would take to change her situation, one of the respondents to the West Virginia survey of current TANF recipients wrote, "I don't know . . . I guess I need a miracle." That same sentiment was expressed more than thirty years ago by an African American minister in Greenville, Mississippi, in response to Senator Robert Kennedy's observation that the dire circumstances he had witnessed as he visited Appalachia and the Mississippi Delta "cannot last forever":

Yes sir, maybe by the end of this century, the end of this second millennium, it'll be different here. Maybe the Lord will smile on us, and give us a better life, so you don't have a few with everything and most everybody else with nothing. There are days that I think it'll take the Second Coming for that to come about — but who knows? With the year 2000 the Lord might decide to pay us some attention here, and turn things around. (Duncan 1999, x)

The year 2000 has come and gone, and the miracle of social and economic equality hoped for by the minister in Mississippi has not occurred. The social work profession must put into action its stated commitment to disadvantaged populations so that rural citizens do not once again become the "people left behind" (U.S. President's National Advisory Commission on Rural Poverty 1967, ix.).

Notes

1. Unless otherwise indicated all data in this chapter are from the 2000 U.S. Census.
2. These descriptors are based on responses to the question, which of the following best describes the place where you live — a city or suburb, a small town, or a rural area?

References

Children's Defense Fund. 2002. Child poverty tops 50 percent in 38 U.S. counties. Electronic document. www.childrensdefense.org/release020604.php. Retrieved July 6, 2002.

Dilger, R. J., et al. 2000. West Virginia case closure study. *The West Virginia Public Affairs Reporter.* 17(1), 2–15.

———. 2001. WV WORKS: The recipients perspective. *The West Virginia Public Affairs Reporter* 18 (3): 2–19.

———. 2004. Studying welfare reform in West Virginia. In R. J. Dilger et al., eds., *Welfare reform in West Virginia*, pp. 1–22. Morgantown: West Virginia University Press.

Duncan, C. M. 1999. *Worlds apart: Why poverty persists in rural America.* New Haven, Conn.: Yale University Press.

Findeis, J., M., et al. 2002. Welfare reform in rural America: A review of current research. Columbia: University of Missouri. www.rupri.org. Retrieved July 10, 2002.

Fluharty, Charles W. 2002. Toward a community-based national rural policy: Implications for social workers and human services practitioners. Presentation to the Twenty-seventh Annual National Institute on Social Work and Human Services in Rural Areas, Frostburg State University, Frostburg, Md. www.rupri.org. Retrieved August 2, 2002.

Gennetian, L., C. Redcross, and C. Miller. 2002. Welfare reform in rural Minnesota: Experimental findings from the Minnesota Family Investment Program. In B. A. Weber, G. J. Duncan, and L. A. Whitener, eds., *Rural dimensions of welfare reform*, pp. 287–312. Kalamazoo, Mich.: W. E. Upjohn Institute for Employment Research.

Henry, M., W. Lewis, L. Reinschmiedt, and D. Hudson. 2000. Reducing food stamps and welfare caseloads in the South: Are rural areas less likely to succeed than urban centers? Paper presented at Rural Dimensions of Welfare Reform: A Research Conference on Poverty, Welfare and Food Assistance, May 4–5. Washington D.C.: Georgetown University.

Lichter, D., and L. Jensen. 2000. Rural America in transition: Poverty and welfare at the turn of the 21st century. Paper presented at Rural Dimensions of Welfare Reform: A Research Conference on Poverty, Welfare and Food Assistance, May 4–5. Washington, D.C.: Georgetown University.

National Association of Social Workers. 2002. Electronic document. www.naswdc.org. Retrieved July 20, 2002.

Ozawa, M., and S. A. Kirk. 1997. Welfare reform. In P. L. Ewalt, E. M. Freeman, S. A. Kirk, and D. L. Poole, eds., Social policy: Reform research and practice, pp. 93- 95. Washington, D.C.: NASW Press.

Rural Policy Research Institute. 2002. Electronic document. www.rupri.org. Retrieved July 6, 2002.

Rural Sociological Society Task Force on Persistent Rural Poverty. Persistent poverty in rural America. 1993. Boulder, Colo.: Westview.

Save the Children. 2002. America's forgotten children: Child poverty in rural America. Electronic document. www.savethechildren.org/americasforgotten.shtml. Retrieved July 5, 2002.

Specht, H., and M. E. Courtney. 1995. *Unfaithful angels: How social work has abandoned its mission.* New York: Free Press.

U.S. Census Bureau. 2001a. Poverty in the U.S.: 2000. Current Population Reports: Consumer Income, P60–214. Washington, D.C.: U.S. Government Printing Office. www.census.gov/prod/2001pubs/p60–214.pdf. Retrieved June 25, 2002.

———. 2001b. Money income in the United States: 2000. Current Population Reports: Consumer Income, P60–213. Washington, D.C.: U.S. Government Printing Office. www.census.gov/prod/2001pubs/p60–213 www.census.gov/prod/2001pubs/p60–214.pdf. Retrieved June 25, 2002.

U.S. Department of Health and Human Services. 2002. HHS takes new steps to promote quality health care and social services in rural America. Press release retrieved on August 5, 2002, from www.omhrc.gov/wwwroot/OMHRC/pressreleases/2002press0726a.htm.

U.S. President's National Advisory Commission on Rural Poverty. 1967. The people left behind. Washington, D.C.: U.S. Government Printing Office.

West Virginia Department of Health and Human Resources. 2002. WV WORKS Caseload Statistics 2002. Charleston: West Virginia Department of Health and Human Resources. Available online at www.dhhr/ofs/Monitoring/ WORKSCaseload2002.htm.

Whitener, L. A., B. A. Weber, and G. J. Duncan. 2001. Reforming welfare: Implications for rural America. *Rural America* 16:2–10. www.ers.usda.gov/publications/ruralamerica/ra163. Retrieved June 30, 2002.

Whitener, L.A., G. J. Duncan, and B. A. Weber. 2002. Reforming welfare: What does it mean for rural areas? U.S. Department of Agriculture Economic Research Service, Food Assistance and Nutrition Research Report No. 26–4. Electronic document. www.usda.gov/publications/fanrr26/fanrr26–4/. Retrieved July 6, 2002.

Whitener, L. A., and D. A. McGranahan. 2003. Rural America: Opportunities and challenges. *Amber waves: The economics of food, farming, natural resources, and rural America.* Electronic document. www.ers.usda.gov/Amberwaves. Retrieved May 28, 2003.

3   Wired for the Future?

The Impact of Information and
Telecommunications Technology
on Rural Social Work

Norma H. Wasko

This chapter began as a technical exploration and descrip-
tion of the way that advances in information and telecommunications technology, and particularly the Internet, are extending social work across tem-
poral and geographic boundaries. The specific intent was to describe how
technology is impacting service delivery in rural areas. The beginning assumption was that technology is simply a tool to apply existing practice
methodology and the chapter would be a guide to the new tools. Two years
and three revisions later, what is striking to this author is the range of applications and the potential of these technologies to dramatically alter the content and form of mainstream social work. The impacts of technology are
already found across the spectrum of professional endeavor; however, there
does not appear to be widespread awareness within the profession of the
magnitude of change on the horizon. Social workers and other practitioners
are using advanced information and communications technologies (ICT)[1]
to provide an array of direct practice activities online including individual
and family counseling, delivery of support group services, and advocacy and
community building (Stamm 1998; Geraty 2000a, 2000b; Bernal 2001). The
tools they use include e-mail, listservs, bulletin boards, chat rooms, interactive websites, one-way web casts, CD-ROMs, interactive television, desktop videoconferencing, and various combinations of these modalities (Freddolino 2002). ICT is also serving administrative and educational functions
(Freddolino 2002; Schoech 2002). As described below, ICT applications and
resource requirements are proliferating broadly and at a geometric rate.

The new information and telecommunication technologies appear to promise solutions to persistent problems in rural areas: lack of access to education and to efficiently delivered, high-quality health and human services. The provision of online behavioral (mental health and counseling) health services[2] suggests that high-tech communication could provide a means of service delivery not currently or conveniently available to many rural residents. Moreover, these technologies are potential vehicles for rural economic and community development, thus offering a way to improve the economic well-being of rural people. For most social workers, however, the impact of ICT is most obvious in the provision of counseling services.

Generally the reaction of the social work community to ICT has been mixed (Freddoino 2002; Schoech 2002). A growing number of entrepreneurial practitioners are providing and defending psychotherapy online (McCarty and Clancy 2002; O'Neill 2002). This has generated considerable controversy, centering mainly on the limitations of current technology to provide secure, confidential and accurate communication, as well as around issues of accountability and liability (Fenichel et al. 2001; McCarty and Clancy 2002; O'Neill 2002). As yet, the social work profession has taken no clear policy stand on online psychotherapy, perhaps, in part, because of the rapidity of change in this area and the lack of knowledge about online practice.

Efforts are under way to develop reliable knowledge (Miller-Cribbs 2001) about ICT and about the comparability of "e-social work" and its close relative, distance education, with face-to-face encounters. Because both activities make use of the same technology to provide comparable services, it is assumed that knowledge derived from one area is applicable to the other (Freddolino 2002). In the agencies, the demand for standardized reporting and outcomes measures combined with state efforts to upgrade information systems are changing the context of public social service delivery systems (National Governor's Association 2001, 2002; Schoech 2002). However, knowledge and resources to enhance technology skills are thin (Freddolino 2002; Schoech 2002). And this is true for the academic as well as the practice community (Freddolino 2002; Schoech 2002). Resistance of practitioners to the technology appears also to be a factor (Freddolino 2002). It seems that while some authors perceive the opportunities of ICT to reformulate and revivify social work by reinterpreting education and practice within a technologically altered global context, the mainstream of the practitioner/educator community does not share this vision.

In the belief that describing the territory is a necessary step toward achieving factual and conceptual clarity, this chapter provides a brief overview of the application of ICT to the major areas of direct practice (including both micro- and macro-level activities) as these apply in the rural context and often in urban areas as well. The chapter also defines some of the salient issues that result from the use of ICT in micro-level counseling practice, and discusses the implications for rural (and other) social workers who increasingly find themselves operating in a new, technologically altered context.

Definitions in Advocacy and Community Organization Practice

In most cases it is easier to describe activities than to articulate the defining characteristics of the online forms of modalities that distinguish "virtual" from "face-to-face " practice. For example, ICT strategies of "community building" appear to use traditional elements of the definition of "community" but without the concept of locality and the assumption of simultaneous communication (Bernal 2001). It is the indeterminacy of a geographic boundary that is the apparently distinguishing feature of these applications. This raises issues around rules for the various forms of community participation among the players, and suggests that knowledge about the nature of communities needs to be revisited, and community organization and development strategies and tactics reformulated, consistent with the way technology alters the definition of community and the nature of participation and communication.

One definition of "online community" indicates that it "involves convening people in virtual space and describes a range of online activities including electronic collaboration, virtual networks, web-based discussions or electronic mailing lists" (Bernal 2001). Practice functions of these virtual communities include mobilization, advocacy, service extension, collaboration around common goals and issues, and practitioner development (Leithead 1999). The operational base in most instances appears to be a nonprofit organization. Advocacy on the Internet educates about issues, broadcasts calls to action, and makes use of the characteristics of ICT to help targeted participants fulfill their advocacy objectives (Benton Foundation 2001). For example, advocacy groups use web technology to customize participation; individuals sign up to receive e-mail alerts about particular issues of interest and are provided a web address where current content devoted to the particular action issue is maintained. The website may provide updates of the results of actions taken. Advocacy websites also provide online databases that connect activists with local data about their area of interest (Benton Foundation 2001). One of the distinguishing characteristics of these forms of practice is the rapidity with which information can be transferred and action taken (McNutt 2002). Electronic communication also permits both rapid collection and dispersal of activists. Thus advocacy using ICT appears to require less (or perhaps different) formal organizational structure than face-to-face , traditional advocacy activities.

These characteristics of e-advocacy would suggest that there is a substantive difference in practice strategies and tactics between traditional and ICT-mediated community organization practice. For example, rural activists concerned about the impact of Federal Communication Commission (FCC) policy on media concentration and the development of broadband services in rural areas can download web-based data and analyses from the Rural Policy Research Institute (RUPRI; www.rupri.org). These analyses detail the potential (and complex) and differing impacts of proposed legislation on rural economic development in various rural areas. The advocates can then network via e-mail with their colleagues in their own and other rural states to lobby members of Congress on specific statutory language. To the extent that organizers network with key local and national leaders, and use e-mail or websites to generate local constituent letters about the specific legislative action that is wanted, the advocacy effort can somewhat offset the concentrated economic impact of corporate interest groups on the policy-formation process in Washington.

In this example, ICT-mediated advocacy would seem to differ from traditional, face-to-face community organization mainly in terms of the speed of knowledge transfer, and the ease and relatively low cost of state and national political coordination. The strategies are familiar ones of political advocacy enhanced by technology. But what if the target is not a governmental entity? Suppose the policy decision rests with a corporate conglomerate not accountable to the usual political process (for example, a U.S. corporation that privatizes the aquifers and restricts the rights of a rural Third World people to drinking water). What ICT-mediated strategies would the advocacy organization adopt? Would media events be staged that would draw on web-based organizational tactics to quickly assemble advocates sophisticated in image presentations for the nightly news? And where would these events be staged? In the United States only? Or would the organizational effort be global in scope? What interests would hold an international advocacy coalition together? What forces would tend to splinter it? Would the advocacy strategies/tactics be consistent with current conceptualizations of community organization theory and practice?

The example also suggests that rapid dissemination of information may promote flat organizational structures in advocacy organizations and thus tend to decentralize power within the advocacy organization itself. What strategic accommodations does this effect impose on advocacy organizations and how does such decentralization impact the capacity of the organizations to achieve their objectives?

This brief example addresses only a few of the questions about how ICT changes definitions of advocacy and community organization practice. The actual impact is far-reaching and complex. Recent work by Hick, McNutt, and Menon suggest that nothing less than a major reorientation of concep-tualization, research, teaching, and practice is required for social work to understand and adapt to the impact of ICT on advocacy and macro practice (McNutt and Menon 2001; Hick and McNutt 2002; McNutt 2002).

Definitions in Online Counseling and Psychotherapy

The literature suggests that definitions and examination of the common-alities and differences between virtual and face-to-face practice appear more developed (and the history of ICT applications longer) in the provision of counseling and therapy services.

Before turning to the use of ICT at the micro level of practice, a comment is in order about the sources used. Information about online practice with individuals, couples, and families presented here will draw heavily on the literature of the application of ICT to health and behavioral health services and very little on the use of ICT in the social services. This decision reflects the fact that, so far, reports of health and behavioral health dominate the literature in this area. The initial efforts to define behavioral health practice at the micro level thus begin with the experience of "telemedicine." Because the technical issues are similar across domains, and social workers are sig-nificantly involved in the delivery of both health and behavioral health ser-vices, it is argued here that the service issues will be similar.

Despite its relative longevity, it is difficult to develop stable definitions of practice in health and mental health in such a rapidly evolving field. The evolution of terms commonly found in the literature that begins with "tele-medicine" refers to the use of electronic communications and information technology to provide or support clinical care at a distance (U.S. Department of Commerce 1997; quoted in Stamm 1998). Telemedicine began by pro-viding medical consultations to remote areas lacking specialty providers.

Over a thirty-year period telemedicine consultations have come to include mental health as well as an array of traditional medical services provided at home and in institutional settings, for example, prisons, Veteran Administration hospitals, and armed forces personnel under the care of the Department of Defense (American Telemedicine Association [ATA] 1999).

Telemedicine subsequently evolved to "telehealth" reflecting the broadened functions of health services delivered via the technology. Nickelson defined "telehealth" as "the use of telecommunications and information technology to provide access to health assessment, diagnosis, intervention, consultation, supervision, education and information across distance," (Nickelson 1998, 527; cited in Stamm 1998). "Behavioral telehealth" refers specifically to behavioral health care[3] (Nickelson 1998) and includes provision of the full spectrum of health, behavioral health, and the related social support services. The most recent definition of telehealth used by the Office for the Advancement of Telehealth is the most inclusive: Telehealth is defined as the use of electronic information and telecommunication technologies to support long-distance clinical health care, patient and professional health-related education, and public health and health administration (Office for the Advancement of Telehealth [OAT] 2001). Telehealth targets populations in rural and Third World countries as well as underserved urban areas. It requires partnerships that link physician offices, rural clinics and hospitals, schools, home care agencies, mental health agencies, and tertiary care centers (Stamm 1998).

The term "e-health" reflects the growing commercialization of health care and the efforts of the private sector to position itself to capture a very lucrative market. E-health "refers to all forms of electronic healthcare delivered over the Internet, ranging from informational, educational and commercial 'products' to direct services offered by professionals, non-professionals, businesses or consumers, themselves" (Maheu 2000, 1). A recent variant of e-health is the emergence of "e-therapy," the provision of behavioral health counseling and "coaching" online. E-therapy appears to have emerged in response to a growing need and an awareness of a vast (untapped) market for mental health services that was identified by the Surgeon General's Report (*Mental Health: A Report of the Surgeon General* 1999). Although accompanied by disclaimers that e-therapy is not psychotherapy, websites advocating its benefits do not appear to draw substantive distinctions between the two.[4]

As online counseling services are expanding, so are the payment machinery and the development of population-level administrative data sets (Maheu 2000). These are "smart" data sets capable of generating relational

reports of all the data elements in the system (Maheu 2000). The significance of these administrative data sets for direct practice is that they permit
development of statistically valid, population-level studies of various health
conditions and the relative effectiveness of different service delivery strategies, as well as assessments of the quality of services delivered by individual
counseling professionals (Wasko 2001).

Forms of Technology Used for Telehealth and Social Service Delivery

According to Stamm (1998) two basic forms of technology undergird
telehealth programs: store-and-forward technology (such as e-mail or websites), and real-time videoconferencing. In this chapter, references to ICT
and "online practice" will refer to both text-based and videoconferencing
unless otherwise indicated. The important distinction between these technologies is whether communication between client and practitioner is simultaneous or whether it is visual (that is, makes use of videoconferencing)
or is text-based. The technical factors governing the speed with which video
data are transmitted determines the quality of the image and the extent to
which the medium is visually adequate for diagnostic and therapeutic purposes. As described below in the section on text-based practice issues, restricting communication to the exchange of written messages imposes limitations and creates risks not present when communication involves visual
and audio transmission. Many current limitations of ICT can be addressed
once broadband technology is available. However, the limited availability of
broadband service in rural areas presents ongoing issues of access and contributes to the economic disparities between urban and rural areas.[5]

Application of Information and Telecommunications Technology in Rural Education and Human Service Systems

The states are currently acting to update their human service and information systems. Initial efforts focused on education. Federal legislation (the
Snowe-Rockefeller-Exon -Kerry amendment to the Federal Telecommunications Act of 1996) paved the way for this development in state capacity.
The law requires that the FCC establish and fund models for public-private
collaboration to connect students in the classroom to the Internet. Potential
partners include federal and state government, state and local education

agencies, public utility regulators, and business. The necessary pieces of the models include "negotiated discounts and regulatory support for Internet service, hardware and software, teacher training, curriculum development, and monetary and philosophical commitment by state agencies, government and business" (AEL Policy Services 1997). The act was designed to offset economic disparities in computer literacy between metropolitan and rural schools. Funding is provided by means of discounted telecommunications access charges based on the lowest available market price and using the criteria of disadvantage and rural location (AEL Policy Services 1997).

State welfare programs are also undertaking infrastructure makeovers that will allow them to use the complex information-processing capacities of the new technologies. Among these are smart cards, electronic-benefits-transfer, and child-support collection (Newcombe 2000a). State social service departments are also using ICT for service delivery and educational purposes. Funding for updated state information systems was included in the Personal Responsibility and Work Opportunity Reconciliation Act in 1996. Other applications include decision support systems (interactive software systems that combine diagnosis and assessment or eligibility criteria with data on individual client characteristics, thus facilitating clinical or administrative decision making) and integrated, one-stop eligibility and program enrollment services (Newcombe 2000b). Nonetheless, high-tech applications in social service agencies are behind that of other rural state agencies.

The states are also working to apply digital technologies to law enforcement and court processes. Among the desired applications are provision of court opinions online, citizen access to public safety personnel by e-mail, and, where enabling legislation permits, use of digital signatures. Still to come is the installation of digital mobile technology in state police cars that would provide immediate access to the Department of Corrections offender tracking system and the state courts records information systems. These systems are developing rapidly in rural as well as urban states (Towns 2000).

Examples of Rural State Applications

Technology has been the key to delivering services to sparse populations located across large geographic areas. For example, in Helena, Montana, Video Link of St. Peter's uses ICT to provide mental health services to a twelve county area occupying 28,509 square miles and serving a population of 190,000 people. Its constituent agencies include the St. Peter's Hospital in Helena, the Community Service Center in Anaconda, the Law and Justice

Center in Bozeman, the Montana State Hospital in Warm Springs, the Montana Developmental Center in Boulder, and the Montana State Prison in Deer Lodge. Through links with other networks, VideoLink connects twenty-six Montana communities. Practice activities that make use of the videoconferencing link include psychological testing, discharge and follow-up planning, forensic evaluations, medical consultations, and family therapy. Other activities include preadmission screening and family visitation. In situations involving family therapy at great distances, the family gathers at the video teleconferencing (VTC) station in their hometown, and the therapist and the patient are at the unit in the institution (Stamm 1998).

According to Stamm (1998) telehealth programs exist in almost all the states and in the provinces of Canada. Not surprisingly rural and frontier states tend to report the highest levels of activity, particularly in the provision of behavioral health services. Grigsby (1998; cited in Stamm 1998) reported that Hawaii, Alaska, Eastern Montana, Northern Arizona, Kansas, Missouri, Nebraska, and Oregon made widespread use of telehealth programs. Stamm (1998) reported that twenty to thirty-one states have some kind of telebehavioral health program in place. Two of the best established are in Alaska and in Hawaii. These programs were all funded initially by federal and state grants.

Technology carries its own development imperative. In West Virginia, the project Non-Profit Collaboratives to Facilitate Rural Community Networking, has as its primary focus the development of infrastructure and technological information and skills in nonprofit organizations and rural communities; the goal is to promote community networking. The secondary focus includes the delivery of management training and continuing education to community-based service providers in social service agencies including welfare, health, education, community action, employment, and corrections agencies (Harper-Dorton 2000).

As these examples indicate, the initial applications of ICT have been to deliver public, agency-based services to rural populations. Recently ICT has been used to deliver private-sector counseling and psychotherapy services.

Social Work Provision of Private Practice Counseling Services Online

Although entrepreneurial private practice of social work online might seem to be an urban phenomenon, the fact that online communication technologies obliterate time and geographic boundaries suggests that this form of practice in rural areas may be limited only by the ability to connect to the Internet. Many of the current forms of private practice online are accomplished by using a modem to access standard telephone lines through an Internet Service Provider.

Both urban and rural social workers seem willing to venture out on the telecommunications highway using a variety of technologies for their practice activities (Seabury and Maple 1993; Finn and Lavitt 1994; Finn 1995; Weinberg et al. 1996; Levinson 1996, 1997; Craig 1997; Galinsky, Schopler, and Abell 1997; Giffords 1998; Schopler, Abell, and Galinsky 1998). They disagree, however, about the extent to which individual and group practice should occur online (O'Neill 2002). As the discussion below of issues of online practice indicates, individual and other forms of practice that is text-based and relies on existing software for security purposes is inherently risky. Nonetheless the field of social work, as well as other disciplines, are responding to a growing demand for online services.[6]

The Demand for Online Services

Maheu (2000) reported that fifteen thousand health care sites existed online as of February 2000. In 1998 an estimated 60 million adults used the Web to find health-related information (ibid.). Consumer spending for online health goods and services is projected to increase from $1 million in 1999 to $8 million in 2004 (Intellihealth 2000; cited in Maheu 2000). Among the most commonly sought service was behavioral health. According to Stamm (1998) 1997 data ranked behavioral health as the fifth most common telehealth consultation. By the end of that year it was first (Grigsby 1998; cited in Stamm 1998). These data are consistent with the prevalence estimates of the Surgeon General's Report (1999) that one of every five adults will experience some form of mental illness during his or her lifetime. Despite the relatively high rate of mental disorders, the Report found that approximately half the number of persons with a mental health condition do not seek treatment services. Stigma and cost were cited as deterrent factors. CBS News (2000) reported the results of a 1999 Harris Poll that 60 million people had searched the web seeking health information. Four of the top ten most-searched health topics were related to mental health. Thus it would appear that a significant number of Americans are at risk for mental health problems at some time in their lives but are reluctant, for whatever reason, to seek traditional psychotherapy services. The growth in the more anonymous involvements of online behavioral health suggests that many would-be clients are seeking help online (CBS News 2000; WebMD 2000b, 2001). The market potential here has not been lost on the managed care industry: "Managed care firms see the Internet as a means to improve their bottom line. Money once invested in managed care companies is being pumped into Internet health-care sites. Meanwhile, health-maintenance organizations are partnering with Internet companies or starting their own websites" (Rabasca 2000, 2). Maheu suggests that the Internet will offer opportunities for managed care companies to drop reimbursement rates or use unlicensed providers such as "lifestyle managers" to avoid regulation by state licensing boards (Maheu 2000; cited in Rabasca 2000).

Direct Behavioral Health Practice Online

The social work response to the demand for online service is determined by whether online work is considered adjunct to or the primary form of communication with the client.

Edward Geraty (2000a) labels online practice of social work as "cyber practice." By this he means "the utilization of Internet technology to enhance traditional practice and service lines" (Geraty 2000b, 1). Enhanced practice includes the integration of e-mail, listservs, web pages, chat room technology, search engines, and other interactive web-based technologies to facilitate a number of social work practice activities. Among these are communication with patients, clients, and colleagues; collection and dissemination of information related to practice, advocacy, consultation to individuals and organizations, research, marketing practice services, professional development of individuals, and the professional community; distance education; and networking (ibid.).

Geraty thus presents cyber practice as an activity that serves as an adjunct to face-to-face counseling with clients with whom one already has a therapeutic relationship rather than as an independent form of practice undertaken with new clients. In contrast, Laszlo, Esterman, and Zabko (1999) surveyed behavioral telehealth practice on the Internet and found considerable evidence that social workers are engaging in strictly online practice primarily using text-based modes of communication. "Behavioral telehealth, the use of telecommunications and information technology to provide access to behavioral health assessment, diagnosis, intervention, consultation, supervision, education and information across distance is more and more often cited as an alternative mode of providing mental health services to individuals, families and groups" (ibid., 1). Recently reported debate over the appropriateness of conducting therapy online suggests that activity in this arena is expanding (O'Neill 2002).

Research on Online Practice

How Online Practice Compares to Face-to-Face Practice   The evaluation of similarities and differences between online practice and traditional practice depends in large part on whether the technology is text-based or makes use of videoconferencing. Where funding has made videoconferencing available, the issues of sameness and difference seem to center on the quality of the video image, the comfort of the people in using the technology and (in the case of diminished speed of data transfer) limitations imposed by the requirement for participants to remain still (Stamm 1998). Stamm reviewed the studies available through 1998 and found that participants were generally as satisfied with video as with face-to-face consultations. Therapeutic alliance was also judged to be similar in both types of consultation (Stamm 1998). McCarty and Clancy (2002) report a Massachusetts study that obtained a .85 correlation between the telecommunication and face-to-face diagnoses of acutely ill psychiatric patients. Because funds are limited for service provision and for research, knowledge about the comparability of virtual and face-to-face therapy remains sparse (McCarty and Clancy 2002).

Knowledge About the Impact of Text-Based Practice Issues   Relatively little research exists on this form of practice, although it has a growing number of supporters (O'Neill 2000; McCarty and Clancy 2002). Fenichel and colleagues have begun the work of analyzing the similarities and differences between online and face-to-face practice in psychotherapy (Fenichel 2001, 2002; Fenichel et al. 2001).

The nature of the medium would suggest caution in using this technology in counseling practice. In contrast to videoconferencing, text-based communication differs significantly from face-to-face contact and creates conditions that may hinder understanding between practitioner and client. These include (a) the absence of nonverbal cues to provide contextual information about the intent of the message; (b) the fact that text-based communication may be experienced as more intense than face-to-face messages; (c) the possibility that the client may interpret messages more positively or negatively than the therapist intended; (d) the lack of control experienced by the clinician when the client (who may be experiencing a high degree of upset or be at risk for destructive behavior or both) is geographically removed; (e) the issue of how to achieve an adequate and realistic therapeutic alliance without a face-to-face encounter; (f) the possibility that the client may not be providing truthful information about his or her identity; (g) the fact that the therapist may not have the ability to use the technology adequately (Barak1999; Lazlo, Esterman, Zabko 1999).

Considerable discussion has occurred online around these issues. Suggestions and guidelines for text-based practice attempt to address each of them. Suffice it to say that there are widely differing opinions as to whether these limitations can be addressed effectively and with what kind of clients.[7] McCarty and Clancy (2002, 155) state that "despite enthusiastic defenses of chat therapy . . . there is no published study that gives empirical support to claims of effectiveness."

Limitations of Research   The fact remains that there is very little research on which to base conclusions about what form of online practice works best with whom (McCarty and Clancy 2002). Indeed, until funding becomes more readily available for services across age and population groups, and broadband technology more widely deployed, the amount of online practice accessible for evaluation is likely to remain relatively small. The studies that do exist are based on limited experience with small samples. In the case of private practice, researchers lack systematic means of identifying online practitioners or accessing data sets of sufficient size to draw valid inferences. A particularly difficult issue is posed by the nonrepresentative nature of Internet samples (Murray and Fisher 2002). This problem may diminish with the growth of behavioral telehealth in the delivery of Medicare and Medicaid services, and the capacity this will create to explore large data sets of service delivery information about populations with known demographics.

Issues of Online Practice

For reasons of space, much of the following discussion centers on micro practice and the risks of online counseling and psychotherapy. Macro practice issues associated with education, advocacy, and community organization and economic development (such as intellectual property rights, economic monopoly, social justice, human rights and civil liberties, and economic rights) are beyond the scope of this chapter. Nonetheless, macro-level issues define the context and shape the salient concerns of the following discussion.

Economic Barriers and Policy Issues Impacting Rural Internet Access

As the gap between income levels in the United States has increased during the decade of the 1990s, so has the gap between those who have access to the world of high-tech telecommunications and those who do not. Beginning in 1995 the National Telecommunications and Information Administration (NTIA) (1995, 1998, 1999, 2000) began to track computer usage and Internet access of people in various sections of the country. Despite overall growth in computer ownership and use, these reports document the growing disparity between persons on the higher end of the income scale and those on the bottom, the so-called "digital divide." According to an analysis of the Rural Policy Research Institute (1999), rural people are most at risk for technical and economic obsolescence. Income poverty alone does not account for this difference in urban-rural connectivity. The "telecommunications infrastructure supporting the information economy is unequally deployed in the US and in this respect too rural regions are at a disadvantage" (RUPRI 1999, 2).

Currently any level of rural access to the Internet is determined by the availability of local Internet Service Providers (ISPs). The key to economic local Internet access is the local telephone company and its relationship with the local ISP. However, national providers serve the majority of homes in rural areas. These providers have no economic incentives to extend services to thinly populated areas (RUPRIc 1999). Federal policies that support development of last-mile connectivity and maintain rate subsidies to rural areas are of critical importance for rural access to the Internet (Staihr 2000).

Limitations of the Technology

In an effort to define the realities of information and telecommunications technologies for policy formation purposes, the National Research Council (NRC) of the National Academy of Science undertook a major review of the potential for near-term technology applications in health services (NRC 2000) and found that a number of technical shortcomings will serve to slow the widespread adoption of ICT.

Current software applications are often incompatible, lack reliable connectivity, quality, and security of transmission. Further, technical incompatibility creates the potential for error, delays in transmission, and gaps in data at critical moments (NRC 2000). Technical standards are needed to assure the reliability of the technology (ibid.). How to resolve these issues and which players should be involved at what levels of government and the private sector are critical policy issues (OAT 2001; Eng and Gustafson 1999; NGA 2001; Mendelson and Salinsky 1997).

The NRC found that clinical care is the functional use area that requires the highest levels of technological capacity for bandwidth, low lag time in data transfer, reliability of Internet availability, security, and access to the system. Video teleconferencing that is suitable for group and family therapy, for example, requires wide bandwidth and digital phone lines to function adequately and reliably. Synchronous, text-based communication requires access to ISPs across the workday hours and in the early evening. During heavy traffic times, present telephone connections are slow and subject to disruption. The telephone system in those areas of the United States that would most benefit from online practice (the rural frontier and inner-city areas) may be hard-pressed to adequately serve the needs of expanded growth of the Internet. Despite the flurry of initial activity and high levels of media publicity, the NRC found that the technology is not yet sufficient to meet the levels of system demand required to make online practice reliable and cost-effective (NRC 2000).

Evaluation of Effectiveness of Applications

Currently few statistically significant studies of the effectiveness of telehealth and telemedicine exist (OAT 2001; NRC 2000). Because the rate of technological innovation has been so rapid, evaluations have been difficult to complete. Similarly, there is little data on cost effectiveness of telehealth applications vis-à-vis standard service provision. The few studies that do exist suggest that patient satisfaction and outcomes are equivalent, while telemedicine achieves cost savings primarily through avoided hospitalizations (OAT 2001).

Privacy, Security, and Confidentiality

Significant limitations to privacy, security, and confidentiality exist because of the lack of uniform technical standards and security practices. Security threats occur at the level of stand-alone computers and internal networks, with software, and on the Internet. Currently no uniform standards exist for protocols for disclosure of potential risks to healthcare consumers (NRC 2000; OAT 2001).

Specific Threats to Confidentiality in Online Clinical Practice

Clinical practice in this context requires protocols designed to assure truly informed client consent and awareness of the threats to confidentiality that may occur. A number of professional groups have formulated principles and standards for Internet practice.[8] At this writing social workers disagree on the safety and ethics of practice online, and the profession has not published standards for social work practice online.[9] Given the importance for the client, it seems useful to describe here what some of the specific threats are that affect security and confidentiality of social work communication in rural (and other) areas.

Video Teleconferencing   Threats to security and confidentiality result when (a) multiple parties are involved in the technical broadcasting and transmission of data; (b) there are no uniform protocols for security and confidentiality at either end of the transmission; and (c) there are no uniform standards for informed consent that address risk (information and technical failure, security breach) and disclosure (NRC 2000).

E-mail   The paradox of communication via e-mail is that it is only apparently private (Patterson 2000). Despite having the form of the written note, the message is not private. Potential security issues of e-mail occur because (a) technical staffs that tend the worksite or network server have access to any and all messages; (b) using computers at work and at home for therapeutic communication may result in others reading messages not intended for them; and (c) most software systems are easy targets unless stand-alone encryption software has been used to secure the e-mail on each end of the transaction (ibid.). Given the proliferation of systems and lack of standards, there is no guarantee that one-to-one client exchanges can be secured unless the clinician and the client each have an encryption system that meets the current security specification of 128 bit minimum encryption key in its security software (ibid.).

Chat Rooms   Even if participants are screened in advance and limited to groups with a defined purpose, chat room discussion cannot be secured because no encryption occurs during the exchange of messages. This leaves chat room participants at risk for invasion of privacy, eavesdropping, harassment, breaking of passwords, and fraud (Patterson 2000).

Ethical Obligation of Social Workers

Section 1.07m of the NASW Code of Ethics asserts the obligation of the practitioner to protect confidentiality of information electronically transmitted. The practitioner has specific responsibility to inform clients of the risks to confidentiality that exist in the particular form of communication. Given the current state of the art of software technology, the following would seem for the present to provide some guidance for achieving the standard for ethical practice: videoconferencing that makes use of clearly defined protocols for informed consent, the maintenance of client confidentiality on the part of all technicians as well as therapists, and a secure system for storing and accessing tapes and digital data. E-mail that uses appropriate encryption technology at both ends of the transaction and in the context of clearly defined protocols detailing risk may be within the NASW Code. Given the limitations of the current technology, chat room participation is not.

Lack of Consumer Protections

As more and more client-consumers assume an active role in managing their own health care they seek information and support on the Web. Often, however, they lack expertise in evaluating the information they find there. Furthermore, many fail to understand that visits to websites are not anonymous or that most privacy safeguards fall short of their promise; personal information may not be adequately protected. There are currently no regulatory mechanisms or uniform standards that require persons who are providing health and mental health information, or counseling via the Internet, to provide information about their credentials, accreditation, licenses, or experience. Although major professional health care organizations (not including NASW) have developed policy statements with recommended standards for disclosure of this information to consumers of health information and services, there currently is no uniform practice applied to telehealth (OAT 2001; NRC 2000).

In an effort to provide greater protection, the FCC is actively monitoring privacy protection and deceptive trade practices on commercial websites. Based on Section 5 of the Federal Trade Commission Act and the Children's Online Privacy Protection Act of 1998, the FCC has established regulatory oversight of personal data collected online. However, the Commission does not have authority to require Web-based companies to adhere to standard information practices (OAT 2001).

Licensure, Accreditation, Certification

Many state licensing statutes do not address practice on the Internet. Moreover, it is difficult for consumers or state regulatory agencies to track whether disclosures on websites comply with state licensure laws (OAT 2001). Currently the states are attempting individually to regulate Internet practice. By 2000 twenty-six states had introduced licensure laws pertaining to the practice of telemedicine across state lines (ibid.). However, there is no uniformity of approach and little or no reciprocity among the states in establishing and enforcing uniform standards of electronic practice. It remains unclear which state has jurisdiction over the practitioner (ibid.). This in turn creates issues of liability. A social worker serving a client in another state, for example, could be subject to a malpractice suit for practicing without a license in the client's state (McCarty and Clancy 2002).

In an effort to take the initial step toward uniformity in licensure, the Joint Working Group on Telemedicine, a cross-agency federal policy group, plans to work with state governments and professional organizations to assess the feasibility of developing a common licensure application form (OAT 2001). State agreement on the content of professional competence that is to be assessed is considered the first step toward achieving greater uniformity in licensure. A key issue here is whether practice online requires new and different knowledge and skills and thus whether special accreditation or certification is required for competent practice. A number of professional groups have proposed such special credentialing (ibid.). However, until the similarities and differences between face-to-face and online practice are better formulated and more widely understood there would seem to be no adequate basis for defining the terms of such special credentialing.

Liability and Accountability for Technology Failure

A number of factors create risks and liability for clients and telehealth practitioners. Perhaps the most difficult to evaluate are risks generated by the lack of technical reliability of the software. Information transmitted by software used in interactive clinical decision support,[10]clinical assessment systems, and so forth, is subject to decay, glitches, and failures that may result in the transmission of wrong or harmful information (NRC 2000). To complicate matters, software developed for use in one decision process may produce wrong logical outcomes when incorporated into a different decision support process. The Science Panel on Interactive Communication and Health is studying this situation and has issued a preliminary report defining the parameters of the problem and highlighting the risks involved. The primary issue here is one of client protection and practitioner liability. To the extent that social workers make use of interactive software in their practice (for example, using interactive electronic scales to evaluate depression, suicide, etc.) the question of liability for damages is relevant.

Lack of Sources of Payment for Online Services

A myriad of federal programs, mainly offering grants and loans, were created over the past decade to stimulate the growth of the telemedicine infrastructure; most of these programs appear to be based on the assumption that ongoing operating costs would eventually be reimbursed by traditional insurances or state and local grants. However, most private insurers do not cover telehealth services and Medicare (which, under the 1997 Balanced Budget Act, initiated payments for telehealth consultations among primary and specialty care physicians and included payments for social work services) has been slow to develop adequate funding mechanisms (Puskin 2001). Medicaid also pays for telehealth services. To date, approximately twenty states have elected to cover telehealth services (Health Care Financing Administration [HCFA] 2001). However, because it is a state option, Medicaid coverage tends to be variable and limited (Puskin 2001). Despite the fact that it is the most highly sought health service on the Internet, behavioral health has been more or less ignored, except as it is covered under Medicare payments for mental health services delivered by a psychiatrist.

Although the Benefits Improvement and Protection Act of 2000 removed obstacles and extended Medicare funding for telehealth (Puskin 2001), fed-

eral policy on reimbursement remains cautious. Until there is more experience with claims for telehealth services to reliably calculate utilization
costs, both public and private insurers will continue to be reluctant to provide more generous coverage (Berenson 2000). The National Research
Council Report (2000) recommends that public- and private-sector organizations should work with the Department of Health and Human Services
to evaluate various health applications of the Internet to better understand
their effect on access, quality, and cost of care. Given the complexity of the
technical and policy issues that are not well understood it seems likely that
there will continue to be limited funding for telehealth in the foreseeable
future.

Implications for Social Work Education and Practice

What does all this mean for social work educators and practitioners working in rural areas? It does seem clear that high-tech telecommunications
systems are changing the context of practice. ICT is creating opportunities
as well as raising barriers in various applications to education, health, and
human services. How these opportunities will play out, which professional
groups and organizational entities, and what values, will drive the development and extension of electronic delivery of health and human services
remains to be seen.

Rural social workers, like their clients, differ in their level of access to
ICT infrastructure and in their knowledge, skill, and comfort in using the
technology. As with most adult learning, most practitioners adopt a new
technology when there is a practical problem to solve and when technical
mastery is a requirement of the setting in which they work. As ICT spreads
through traditional social service delivery systems and has a genuine direct
service delivery function (beyond collecting data on number of clients
served), social work staff will be trained in its use by the agencies. As time
goes on, however, agencies (and private-sector employers as well) are likely
to become less willing to invest scarce resources in bringing new employees
up to speed. Mastery of basic ICT will become a requirement for getting
hired.

This process alone should move schools of social work toward developing
better conceptualizations about the applications of ICT and its relationship
to the existing curriculum as well as training students in its use as an integral
part of practice. Rural social workers especially have much to gain in using

ICT to expand service delivery to rural clients. Potentially they also have much to lose. If local services are to continue to be provided by rural social workers and agencies and not competitively overrun by privatized ICT services delivered from urban centers, strategies (such as the development of rural social service, education, and health consortia) need to be explored, barriers addressed, and economically viable solutions developed.

The opportunities for innovation are many. Social workers interested in macro-level health and human service delivery can build coalitions with old and new partners, both public and private (such as reported by Harper-Dorton 2000) to extend rural ICT infrastructure, develop technology competence among rural people, and create multifunctional uses of ICT delivery systems to make them economically viable. Social workers who want to buffer clinical practice from the profit-driven focus of corporate health care, could establish organizational alliances among nonprofit organizations, professional practice groups, and academic centers to secure funds to deliver, test, compare, and evaluate the relative effectiveness of traditional and online services.

The race is now under way to develop reliable knowledge about the effectiveness of ICT-mediated communication. If social work does not participate and bring its multilevel systems perspective to this process, it seems likely that evidence-based (and -funded) strategies will be conceptualized in terms of the frames of reference of the professionals conducting the research, most of whom do not make the connections between the micro and the macro system levels and how these interact to impact the lives of rural people.

The fluidity of the present situation presents an opportunity for the profession of social work to reexamine traditional knowledge and direct practice skills at both the micro and macro levels of practice. This would entail examining the impact of ICT on frameworks, models, and strategies of education and practice. Some of this work has already begun (Campbell and Queiro-Tajalli 2000; Cooper-Altman 2000; Hick and McNutt 2002; McNutt 2002; McNutt and Menon 2001; Miller-Cribbs 2001; Schopler, Abell, and Galinsky 1998).

However, the reasons for coming to terms with technology should not just be based on the need to maintain professional relevance. Social work values need to be brought to bear in the context and methods of online practice. In fulfilling this task, educators should also address the related issues of social and economic justice that emerge in a global society where technology has fostered the growth of supranational economic entities whose decisions are often made without legal or political accountability for their effect on rural peoples.[11]

Online practice, in any of its present manifestations, will not displace traditional forms of service delivery in the near future. However, despite current barriers, ICT applications to health and human services will certainly expand significantly in the coming decade. This growth will occur as a consequence of experimentation and market competition among multiple players to "wire America." In this race, regional economic disparities and the difficulty of achieving competitive economies of scale place many rural areas at a disadvantage. In the short run, the technical and policy barriers that slow technology adoption provide a window for social work to bring itself technologically up to date. How the profession responds to the challenge of ICT will determine its relevance to the plight of rural peoples in the global society of the twenty-first century. If the tasks indicated here are the measure of what must be accomplished, a sea change lies ahead for both rural and urban educators and practitioners. The history of the profession has been to confront change with enormous creativity, energy, dispute, passion, and acrimony, and, in the long run, to adapt productively. There is no reason to expect a different response to ICT. The question is whether the profession can change quickly enough to truly help rural people in the struggles that lie ahead.

Online Resources for Social Work Practice

Advocacy: http://www.benton.org/publibrary/toolkits/advocacy.html.
Community building resources: http://www.benton.org/publibrary/toolkits/
    community.html.
Cyber social work: http://members.aol.com/Egeraty/Page6.html.
Democracy at work. Nonprofit use of Internet technology for public policy pur-
    poses. OMB Watch; annotated bibliography of websites: http://www.
    ombwatch.org/npt/resource/reports/scan.pdf.
Electronic journal of social work: http://www.ejsw.net/IssueView1.asp.
Internet resources for rural America: http://www.ruralamerica.org/hotlinks.htm.
The new social worker online: http://www.socialworker.com/websites.htm.
New technology in the human services: http://www.chst.soton.ac.uk/nths/watson.
    htm.
Non-profit management and skills resources online: http://home.connection.com/
    ˜regan/.
Non Profits Internet connections: http://www.icomm.ca/.

Online community resources: http://www.fullcirc.com/commresources.htm.
Resources related to human services and information technology: http://www2.
uta.edu/cussn/cussn.html.
Rural economic and development resources: http://www.nal.usda.gov/ric/ruralres/
economic.htm.
Shirley's social work web resources: http://kml.uindy.edu/resources/socialwork/
policy.html.
Social work resources on the Web (comprehensive list broken down by subject
area): http://wwwlibrary.csustan.edu/lboyer/socwork/bysubj.htm.
Social work access network (SWAN): http://www.sc.edu/swan/topics.html.
The social worker's Internet handbook: http://www.socialworker.com/swintbk1.htm.

Notes

1. The definition of information and communication technologies used here follows Freddolino and includes computers, the Internet, software, telecommunications, information systems, and, potentially, robotics.
2. Behavioral health in this and subsequent references in this chapter generally
   refers to the full array of mental health and alcohol and drug abuse treatment
   services. It is not restricted to those interventions that draw on behavioral theory.
3. "Behavioral health" is a generic term as defined above.
4. See, for example, Metanoia 2002. "Talk to a Therapist Online." "Online counseling — 'e-therapy' is when a professional counselor or psychotherapist talks
   with you over the Internet to give you some kind of mental health assistance
   or emotional help. . . . E-therapy is not psychotherapy. It should not be compared to psychotherapy. . . . E-therapy is a form of counseling which, though
   it falls short of full-fledged psychotherapy, is still a very effective source of help."
   Available online at http://www.metanoia.org/imhs/index.html.
5. The essential technical characteristics of ICT include:

   a. *Store-and-forward technologies.* In these technologies various kinds of data
   (text, photos, psychological tests, images, etc.) can be stored in a computer,
   forwarded, and then stored in the receiving computer. Because information is
   stored at both ends of this transaction the parties to the communication do not
   have to be present at the same time. Thus communication may be simultaneous
   or asynchronous (the parties may respond to each other at different times).
   Data can be sent on secured, closed intranets (such as that maintained by a
   university system or the Veterans Administration). Date may also be sent over
   the open, unsecured Internet by using software with or without built-in security
   safeguards (Stamm 1998).

   b. *Video teleconferencing equipment.* The other telehealth technology is
   video teleconferencing (VTC). Here audio and video data are sent simultaneously from both ends simulating face-to-face contact. (Thus the term "synchronous technology" is applied to these applications.) VTC requires cameras,

monitors, and computer processors. At this writing, four types of VTC were on the market: dedicated VTC units; desktop computer units that pass data via telephone lines; desktop computer units that pass data via the Internet; and retrofit videophone units that use existing television and telephones. The videophone is a camera unit that is smaller than a VCR. It has television and telephone attachments that permit the use of a TV and a touch-tone telephone for videoconferencing without a computer (Stamm 1998).

c. *Technical specifications affecting the quality of the VTC image.* The quality of the video cast is determined by the transfer speed measured in the frames per second (fps) as data pass through the system (Stamm 1998). The higher the fps, the clearer the image and also the greater the cost. The optimal speed is 30 fps but because of the relatively high cost of the equipment to achieve this speed, most units have a maximum capacity of 15–20 fps. This speed permits clear resolution provided the sending image remains still. Unless lack of movement is a clinical deterrent (such as, for example, family therapy or counseling with a hearing-impaired client who requires sign language), slower frames may be adequate for many service needs (Stamm 1998).

d. *Broadband service.* As broadband capability is achieved, these limitations are expected to diminish. Current broadband connections provide data transfer at speeds at least four times faster than 56 kilobits per second, the maximum speed of transfer offered by ordinary telephone lines. Top broadband transfer speeds may exceed 10 million bits per second, over a hundred times faster than standard telephone transfer (Staihr 2000). Broadband is thus well suited for the massive data transfer required for audio-visual teleconferencing and other health, education, and business uses.

Three broadband technologies are currently available in some local markets (Staihr 2000). Digital subscriber lines (DSL) offered by local telephone companies achieve data transfer speeds of up to 8 megabytes per second. Cable modems offered by cable television companies use upgraded cable lines and transfer data at speeds up to 10 megabytes per second. Wireless technology makes use of satellite or microwave transmission. Wireless data transfer speeds can range from 2 megabytes to 10 megabytes per second (Staihr 2000). Because the cost of cable and DSL lines depends on the number of subscribers and have distance limitations (to achieve high-speed data transfer, the customer must be less than 16,000 to 18,000 feet from the cable node or DSL telephone office), wireless systems would appear to offer the greatest promise for bringing high-tech transmission to more remote rural areas (Staihr 2000).

6. For a thoughtful discussion of the issues of telehealth practice, see McCarty and Clancy 2002.

7. See International Society for Mental Health Online 2000. "Suggested Principles for the Online Provision of Mental Health Services, version 3.11." Available online at http://www.ismho.org/suggestions.html.

8. See The American Psychiatric Association (APA) 1998. "APA Resource Document on Telepsychiatry via Videoconferencing." Available online at http://www.psych.org/pract_of_psych/tp_paper.cfm. This document, approved by the APA Board of Trustees in July 1998, assumes that the technological medium is videoconferencing. It does not address text-based communication. See also International Society for Mental Health Online 2000. "Suggested Principles," as given in note 7 above.

9. The Clinical Social Work Federation has published a position paper opposing text-based practice. Available online at http://www.cswf.org/therapy.html. NASW has published a Social Work Practice Update, "Online Therapy and the Clinical Social Worker" (Coleman 2000), exploring the pros and cons of therapy on the Internet. The May 2000 Update appears to assume that text-based communication is the medium of transmission and warns practitioners, "Should online therapy become one of your choices of practice, proceed with caution . . . and be aware that you are placing yourself at a higher risk for malpractice litigation" (4). So far, the organization has not established standards and protocols for social workers engaging in the delivery of telehealth services.

10. It is the social, political and economic justice impacts of ICT that best reflect the magnitude of contextual change ahead. For a glimpse of the issues see Blumer and Coleman 2001, available online at http://www.citizensonline.org.uk/pdf/realising.pdf; Amt 2002, available online at http://www.nado.org/pubs/apr023.html (3) Holley 2002, available online at http://www.mwg.org/epublishing/cyberplaces/archives/000011.html; Center for Digital Democracy 2002, available online at http://www.democraticmedia.org/news/FCCcabledecision.html; American Civil Liberties Union 2002, available online at http://www.aclu.org/Cyber-Liberties/Cyber-Liberties.cfm?ID = 10579c = 16; "You Have to Have a Telephone!" available online at http://www.edu-cyberpg.com/Teachers/telephone.html; Benner 2002, available online at http://www.alternet.org/print.html?StoryID = 12168; Sen 2002, available online at http://www.prospect.org/print/V13/1/sen-a.html; Vaidhyanathan 2002, available online at http://chronicle.com/free/v48/i47/47b00701.htm.

11. Clinical decision support systems are interactive software systems that combine diagnosis and assessment data with information on individual client characteristics, thereby facilitating clinical decision making. See the following online resources: Social Work Practice Advocacy, at http://www.benton.org/publibrary/toolkits/advocacy.html; Community Building Resources, at http://www.benton.org/publibrary/toolkits/community.html; Cyber Social Work, at http://members.aol.com/Egeraty/Page6.html; Democracy at Work: Nonprofit Use of Internet Technology for Public Policy Purposes. OMB Watch (annotated bibliography of websites), at http://www.ombwatch.org/npt/resource/reports/scan.pdf; Electronic Journal of Social Work, at http://www.ejsw.net/IssueView1.asp; Internet Resources for Rural America, at http://www.

ruralamerica.org/hotlinks.htm; The New Social Worker Online, at http://www.socialworker.com/websites.htm; New Technology in the Human Services, at http://www.chst.soton.ac.uk/nths/watson.htm; Nonprofit Management and Skills Resources Online, at http://home.connection.com/˜regan/; Nonprofits Internet Connections, at http://www.icomm.ca/; Online Community Resources, at http://www.fullcirc.com/commresources.htm; Resources Related to Human Services and Information Technology, at http://www2.uta.edu/cussn/cussn.html; Rural Economic and Development Resources, at http://www.nal.usda.gov/ric/ruralres/economic.htm; Shirley's Social Work Web Resources, at http://kml.uindy.edu/resources/socialwork/policy.html; Social Work Resources on the Web (comprehensive list broken down by subject area), at http://wwwlibrary.csustan.edu/lboyer/socwork/bysubj.htm; Social Work Access Network (SWAN), at http://www.sc.edu/swan/topics.html; The Social Worker's Internet Handbook, at http://www.socialworker.com/swintbk1.htm.

References

American Civil Liberties Union. 2002. No competition: How monopoly control of the broadband Internet threatens free speech. An ACLU White Paper. Online at http://www.aclu.org/Cyber-Liberties/Cyber-Liberties.cfm?ID = 10579&:c = 16. Accessed August 27, 2003.

AEL Policy Services. 1997. The Telecommunications Act of 1996: A guide for educators. Online at http://www.ael.org/rel/policy/fcc97.htm. Accessed August 27, 2003.

American Psychiatric Association resource document on telepsychiatry via videoconferencing. 1998. *APA Online practice of psychiatry.* Online at http://www.psych.org/pract_of_psych/tp_paper.cfm. Accessed August 23, 2003.

American Public Human Services Association. 2002. HIPAA: What states should know. Online at http://www.aphsa.org/wmemohipaa.pdf. Accessed August 27, 2003.

American Telemedicine Association. 1999. Telemedicine: A brief overview developed for the congressional telehealth briefing. Online at http://www.atmeda.org/news/overview.htm. Accessed August 27, 2003.

Amt, W. 2002. Rural America pays heavy price with Free Trade. *Economic Development Digest.* Washington, D.C.: NADO Research Foundation. Online at http://www.nado.org/pubs/apr023.html. Accessed August 27, 2003.

Baker, P., and J. Swett. 2000. Bringing the information world to life. Paper presented at the Fourth Annual Technology Conference on Social Work Education and Practice, August 27 – 30, Charleston, S.C.

Barak, A. 1999. Psychological applications on the Internet: A discipline on the threshold of a new millennium. *Applied and Preventive Psychology* 8:231–246. Online at http://construct.haifa.ac.il/%7eazy/app-r.htm. Accessed August 27, 2003.

Benner, J. 2002. Public money, private code. Alternet.org. Online at http://www.alternet.org/print.html?StoryID = 12168. Accessed August 27, 2003.

Benton Foundation. 2001. Advocacy. Washington, D.C.: Benton Foundation. Online at http://www.benton.org/publibrary/toolkits/advocacy-html. Accessed August 27, 2003.

Bernal, V. 2001. Building Online communities: Transforming assumptions into success. Washington, D.C.: Benton Foundation. Online at http://www.benton.org/publibrary/practice/community/assumptions.html. Accessed August 27, 2003.

Berenson, R. 2000. Testimony of Robert A. Berenson, M.D., Director of the Center for Health Plans and Providers Health Care Financing Administration before the House Commerce Subcommittee on Health and Environment, on telemedicine, September 7. Online at http://www.hhs.gov/asl/testify/t000907a.html. Accessed August 27, 2003.

Blumer, J., and S. Coleman, S. 2001. Realising democracy Online: A civic commons in cyberspace. IPPR/Citizens Online Research Publication No. 2. London: Institute for Public Policy Research. Online at http://www.citizenson-line.org.uk/pdf/realising.pdf. Accessed August 27, 2003.

Campbell, C., and I. Queiro-Tajalli. 2000. Utilization of information technology by field instructors: Implications for curriculum development. Paper delivered at the Fourth Annual Technology Conference on Social Work Education and Practice, August 27 – 30, 2002, Charleston, S.C.

CBS News.com. 2000. Surfing for peace of mind. March 31. Online at http://www.cbsnews.com/stories/2000/03/20/tech/main174167.shtml. Accessed August 27, 2003.

Center for Digital Democracy. 2002. FCC's decision on cable broadband services broadens cable industry's media monopoly. March 14. Washington, D.C.: Center for Digital Democracy. Online at http://www.democraticmedia.org/news/FCCcabledecision.html. Accessed August 27, 2003.

Coleman, M. 2000. Online therapy and the clinical social worker. *NASW Social Work Practice Update*. Washington, D.C.: National Association of Social Workers.

Cooper-Altman, J. 2000. The creative use of technology in a foundation social work practice course. Paper delivered at the Fourth Annual Technology Conference on Social Work Education and Practice, August 27 – 30, 2002, Charleston, S.C.

Consumers Union. 1999. Lessons from 1996 Telecommunications Act: Deregulation before meaningful competition spells consumer disaster. Online at http://www.consumersunion.org/teleco/lessondc201.htm. Accessed August 27, 2003.

Craig, J. 1997. Convening groups on "voice-mail" systems. *Social Work with Groups Newsletter* 12:13.

Eng, T., and D. Gustafson. 1999. Wired for health and well-being: The emergence of interactive health communication. Science Panel on Interactive Communication and Health. Washington, D.C.: U.S. Department of Health and Human Services. Online at http://www.health.gov/scipich/pubs/report/execsummary.htm. Retrieved August 27, 2003

Fenichel, M. 2001. Online psychotherapy: Technical difficulties, formulations and processes. *Current Topics in Psychology*. International Society for Mental Health Online. Available at http://www.fenichel.com/technical.shtml. Accessed August 27, 2003.

———. 2002. The here and now of cyberspace. *Current Topics in Psychology*, International Society for Mental Health Online. Available at http://www.fenichel.com/herenow.shtml. Accessed August 23, 2003.

Fenichel, M., et al. 2001. Myths and realities of Online clinical work. *Current Topics in Psychology*. International Society for Mental Health Online. Available at http://www.fenichel.com/myths/. Accessed August 27, 2003.

Finn, J., and M. Lavitt. 1994. Computer-based self-help for survivors of sexual abuse. *Social Work with Groups* 17:21–47.

Finn, J. 1995. Computer-based self-help groups: A new resource to supplement support groups. In M.Galinsky and J. Schopler, eds., *Support groups: Current perspectives on theory and practice*, pp.109–117. Binghamton, N.Y.: Haworth.

Freddolino, P. 2002. Thinking "outside the box" in social work distance education: Not just distance anymore. *Electronic Journal of Social Work* 1, 1 (February 15). Online at http://www.ejsw.net/IssueView1.asp. Accessed August 27, 2003.

Galinksy, M., J. Schopler, and M. Abell. 1997. Connecting group members through telephone and computer groups. *Health and Social Work* 22:181–188.

Geraty, E. 2002a. Welcome to cyber social work. Online at http://members.aol.com/Egeraty/Page6.html. Accessed August 27, 2003.

———. Welcome to cyberpractice. Online at http://members.aol.com/BehavioralsciCon/cyber.html. Accessed August 27, 2003.

Giffords, E. 1998. Social work on the Internet: An introduction. *Social Work* 43:243–251.

Grigsby, B. 1998. ATSP report on U.S. telemedicine activity. Portland, Oreg.: Association of Telemedicine Service Providers. Online at http://www.atsp.org/survey/reports/1998.asp. Accessed August 27, 2003.

Grigsby, B., and N. Brown. 2000. 1999 report on U.S. telemedicine activity. Portland, Oreg.: Association of Telemedicine Service Providers. Online at http://www.atsp.org/survey/reports/1999.asp. Accessed August 27,2003.

Harper-Dorton, K. 2000. Technology access: Bridging the digital divide with rural nonprofits. Paper delivered at the Fourth Annual Technology Conference Social Work Education and Practice, August 27 – 30, Charleston, S.C.

Health Care Financing Administration. 2001. States where Medicaid reimbursement of services utilizing telemedicine is available. Online at http://cms.hhs.gov/states/telelist.asp. Accessed August 27, 2003.

Healy, L. 2002. Internationalizing social work curriculum in the twenty-first century.

Electronic Journal of Social Work 1, 1 (February 15). Online at http://www.ejsw.net/IssueView1.asp. Accessed August 27, 2003.

Hick, S., and J. McNutt, eds. 2002. Advocacy and activism on the Internet: Perspectives from community organization and social policy. Chicago: Lyceum.

Holley, J. 2002. Creating cyber places telecommunications policy in the public interest: Putting communities first. Online at http://www.mwg.org/epublishing/cyberplaces/archives/000011.html. Retrieved August 27, 2003.

International Society for Mental Health Online. 2000. Suggested principles for On-line provision of mental health services (version 3.11). Online at http://www.ismho.org/suggestions.html. Retrieved August 27, 2003.

Kikuchi, S., and S. Sorensen. 2000. The P.A.C.E. Model: interactive television (ITV) teaching strategies for social work educators. Paper presented at the Fourth Annual Technology Conference on Social Work Education and Practice, August 27–30, Charleston, S.C.

Laszlo, J., G. Esterman, and S. Zabko. 1999. Therapy over the Internet? Theory, research and finances. *CyberPsychology and Behavior* 2:293–307. Online at http://www.ismho.org/issues/therapy_internet.htm. Accessed August 27, 2003.

Leithead, M. 1999. Community connections: Using technology to further your mission. Paper presented at the Strategy Institute Conference: Leveraging the Power of Technology and the Internet for Non-Profits, September 21. Online at http://www.charityvillage.com/cv/research/rofr13.html, Accessed August 27, 2003.

Levinson, D. 1996. The Internet: A new social work tool. *NASW News* 41, 3 (October).

———. 1997. Online counseling: Opportunity and risk. *NASW News* 42, 3 (September).

Maheu, M. 2000. Delivering behavioral telehealth via the Internet: e-health. Online at http://telehealth.net/articles/deliver.html. Accessed August 27, 2003.

McCarty, D., and C. Clancy. 2002. Telehealth: Implications for social work practice. *Social Work* 47 (April): 153–161.

McNutt, J. 2002. New horizons in social work advocacy. *Electronic Journal of Social Work* 1, 1 (February 15). Online at http://www.ejsw.net/Issue/Vol1/Num1/Article3.pdf. Accessed August 27, 2003.

McNutt, J., and G. Menon. 2001. Teaching Internet-based social work advocacy practice in cyberspace: A course example and conceptual framework. Online at http://www.cosw.sc.edu/Conf/Tech/2001/abstracts/PDFs/McNutt.pdf. Accessed August 31, 2003.

Mendelson, D., and E. Salinsky. 1997. Health information systems and the role of state government. *Health Affairs* 16 (May/June): 106–119.

Menon, G. M. 2002. Using the Internet as a research tool for social work and human services. New York: Haworth.

Mental Health: A Report of the Surgeon General — Executive Summary. 1999.

Rockville, Md.: U.S. Department of Health and Human Services. Online at http://www.mentalhealth.org/features/surgeongeneralreport/summary.asp. Accessed August 27, 2003.

Metanoia. 2002. Talk to a therapist Online. Available at http://www.metanoia.org/imhs/index.html. Accessed August 27, 2003.

Miller-Cribbs, J., ed. 2001. New advances in technology for social work education and practice. New York: Haworth.

Murray, D., and J. Fisher. 2002. The Internet: A virtually untapped tool research. In G. Menon, ed., *Using the Internet as a tool for research.* Binghamton, N.Y.: Haworth.

National Academy of Science, Committee on Broadband Last Mile Technology. 2002. Broadband bringing home the bits. Online at http://books.nap.edu/html/broadband/. Accessed August 27, 2003.

National Research Council, Committee on Enhancing the Internet for Health Applications: Technical Requirements and Implementation Strategies. 2000. Networking health prescriptions for the Internet: Conclusions and recommendations. Online at http://www.nap.edu/html/networking_health/ch6.html. Accessed August 27, 2003.

National Telecommunication and Information Administration. 1995. Falling through the net: A survey of the have-nots in rural and urban America. Online at http://www.ntia.doc.gov/ntiahome/fallingthru.html. Retrieved August 27, 2003.

———. 1998. Falling through the net II: New data on the digital divide. Online at http://www.ntia.doc.gov/ntiahome/net2/falling.html. Retrieved August 27, 2003.

———. 1999. Falling through the net: Defining the digital divide. Revised. Online at http://www.ntia.doc.gov/ntiahome/fttn99/contents.html. Accessed August 27, 2003.

———. 2000. Falling through the net: Toward digital inclusion. Online at http://www.ntia.doc.gov/ntiahome/fttn00/contents00.html. Accessed August 27, 2003.

———. 1997. Telemedicine report to Congress. Online at http://www.ntia.doc.gov/reports/telemed/evaluate.htm. Accessed August 27, 2003.

Neuberger, N., M. Payne, and M. Wakefield. 2001. Rural health care and the Internet: Issues and opportunities for using interactive communications to improve rural health care services. Health Tech Strategies, LLC. Online at www.gmu.edu/departments/chpre/ruralhealth. Accessed August 27,2003.

Newcombe, T. 2000a. Reinventing welfare for the digital age. Online at http://www . govtech . net / publications / gt / 2000 / apr / digitalstates2 / digitalstates2. phtml. Accessed August 27, 2003.

———. 2000b. Technology helps states transform welfare. Online at http://www.govtech.net/publications/gt/2000/apr/feature/feature.phtml. Accessed August 27, 2003.

NGA Center for Best Practices. 2001. Building better e-government: Focus of e–

government task force. Online at http://www.nga.org/center/divisions/ 1,1188,C_ISSUE_BRIEF D_2851,00.html. Accessed August 27, 2003.

―――. 2002. e-Governance. Online at http://www.nga.org/cener/topics/ 1,1188,D_410,00.html. Accessed August 27, 2003.

Nickelson, D. 1998. Telehealth and the evolving health care system: Strategic opportunities for professional psychology. *Professional Psychology: Research and Practice* 29 (6): 527–535. Available at http://www.apa.org/journals/pro/ pro296527.html. Accessed August 27, 20003.

Office for the Advancement of Telehealth. 2001. Report to Congress on telemedicine. Washington, D.C. Online at http://telehealth.hrsa.gov/pubs/report2001/ telcom.htm. Accessed August 27, 2003.

Office of Rural Health Policy. 1997. Exploratory evaluation of rural applications of telemedicine. Washington, D.C. Online at http://tie.telemed.org/telemed101/ plan/eval_links.asp. Accessed August 27, 2003.

O'Neill, J. 2000. Internet-based therapy draws criticism. *NASW News* 45:12.

Patterson, D. 2000. *Personal computer application in the social services.* Boston: Allyn and Bacon.

Puskin, D. 2001. Telemedicine: Follow the money. *Online Journal of Issues in Nursing* 6 (3): manuscript 1. Online at http://nursingworld.org/ojin/topic16/ tpc16_htm. Accessed August 27, 2003.

Rabasca, L. 2000. Self-Help sites: A blessing or a bane? *Monitor on Psychology* 31, 4. Online at http://www.apa.org/monitor/apr00/selfhelp.html. Accessed August 27, 2003.

Rural Policy Research Institute. 1999. Telecommunications infrastructure development: The state and local role. Online at http://www.rupri.org/publications/ archive/reports/1999/p99–12/. Accessed August 27, 2003.

Seabury, B., and F. Maple. 1993. Using computers to teach practice skills. *Social Work* 38:430–439.

Sen, A. 2002. How to judge globalism. *American Prospect* 13:1–7. Online at http:// www.prospect.org/print/V13/1/sen-a.html. Accessed August 27, 2003.

Schoech, D. 2002. Technology challenges facing social work. *Electronic Journal of Social Work* 1 (1). Online at http://www.ejsw.net/IssueView1.asp. Accessed August 27, 2003.

Schopler, J., M. Abell, and J. Galinsky, J. 1998. Technology-based groups: A review and conceptual framework for practice. *Social Work* 43:254–267.

Shultz, P., and R. Sukow. 2000. Building the last mile: Broadband deployment in rural America. Online at http://www.ntca.org/leg_reg/white/dp5_pdf. Accessed August 27, 2003.

Staihr, B. 2000. The broadband quandary for rural America. Center for the Study of Rural America, Federal Reserve Bank of Kansas City. Online at http:// www.kc.frb.org/RuralCenter/mainstreet/MSE_0800.pdf. Accessed August 27, 2003.

Stamm, H. 1998. Clinical applications of telehealth in mental health care. *APA*

Journals 29:536–542. Online at http://www.apa.org/journals/pro/pro296536.html. Accessed August 27, 2003

Towns, S. 2000. Digital justice Georgia leads the pack as states integrate technology and law enforcement. Online at http://www.govtech.net/publications/gt/2000/apr/digitalstates1/digitalstates1.phtml. Accessed August 27, 2003.

U.S. Department of Commerce. 2002. A nation Online. Online at http://www.techpolicybank.org/2002/commercereport.html. Accessed August 27, 2003.

Vaidhyanathan, S. 2002. Copyright as cudgel. The chronicle of higher education. Online at http://chronicle.com/free/v48/i47/47b00701.htm. Accessed August 27, 2003.

Wachter, G. 2000. Two years of Medicare reimbursement of telemedicine: A postmortem. Telemedicine Information Exchange (TIE) Legal Issues in Telemedicine. Online at http://tie.telemed.org/legal/medic/reimburse_summary.asp. Accessed August 27, 2003.

Wasko, N. 2001. Internet technology makes clinical data systems technically and economically practical: Are they politically feasible? In J. Miller-Cribbs, ed., *New advances in technology for social work education and practice*, pp. 41–62. New York: Haworth.

Weinberg, N., J. Schmale, J. Uken, and K. Wessel. 1996. On-line help: Cancer patients participate in a computer-mediated support group. *Health and Social Work* 21:24–29.

WebMD. 2000a. Is Online help safe? Online at http://my.webmd.com/printing/article/1674.50618. Accessed August 27, 2003.

———. 2000b. Therapy from a distance. Online at http://my.webmd.com/printing/article/1674.50865. Accessed August 27, 2003.

———. 2000c. When cybertherapy goes bad. Online at http://my.webmd.com/printing/article/1674.50863. Accessed August 27, 2003.

———. 2001d. From couch to keyboard: Cyber therapy booms. Online at http://my.webmd.com/printing/article/1728.73112. Accessed August 27, 2003.

4 The Distribution of Nonprofit Social Service Organizations along the Rural-Urban Continuum

Mark A. Hager, Amy Brimer,
and Thomas H. Pollak

Cook County, Illinois, is the central county of the Chicago metropolitan area and home to more than five million people. Not surprisingly it is also the home to a large number of nonprofit social service organizations. In fact, more than one thousand such organizations are located in Cook County, including nearly three hundred programs aimed at preschool children or youth and teens, and more than one hundred programs for physical and mental health.

However, Cook County is not a typical U.S. county. Out of the more than three thousand counties in the United States, about thirty claim 1 million inhabitants. In contrast, nearly seven hundred counties have fewer than ten thousand people living in them. One of the consequences of the growth of America's cities in the past century is that rural areas have remained sparse despite the overall growth in the country's population. While Cook County is a prime example of an urban county with a broad array of social services, a more typical county is Valley County in central Nebraska. Valley County is home to fewer than five thousand people, half in the county seat and half spread around in farms and very small towns throughout the county. Valley County has one nonprofit social service charity — Senior Classics — which provides hot meals to elderly residents of the county. County government provides other services, but the small population supports only a small array of charitable services.

In 2000 more than fifty-seven thousand nonprofit social service organizations across the United States filed Form 990, the annual reporting form required of most charities by the Internal Revenue Service. Nearly twenty-six thousand of these organizations operate in the minority of counties that make up the central cities of metropolitan areas with at least 1 million people. In contrast, fewer than one thousand tax exempt organizations operate in the 520 counties with fewer than twenty-five hundred people. Nearly 400 counties in the United States (roughly 13 percent of the total) have no nonprofit social service providers. Nonprofit social service organizations operate where people are, which means that sparsely populated rural areas generally have fewer social service charities.

This chapter examines the distribution of nonprofit social service organizations in the United States. It is a statistical profile of the nonprofit social service sector, with special attention to differences between urban and rural counties.

Why is it important to know about these things? Sometimes we hear anecdotes about the differences in support services and resources between cities and rural communities, and many of us have observed some of these differences firsthand. However, unless we look at the big picture, we might be misled by anecdotes or atypical situations that do not accurately reflect the similarities or differences between rural and urban communities across the country. Are rural counties experiencing a shortage in social service providers compared to urban counties? Are there substantial differences between urban counties and rural counties in the number of social service organizations per capita? Is there a substantial difference in the amount of money spent on social services between urban and rural counties? These are some of the questions we take up in this chapter. Understanding the statistical profile of nonprofit services can help you better understand the realities of social service opportunities, services, and resources in rural areas.

We proceed in three steps. First, we describe the kinds of social service organizations included in the profile. Second, we discuss how we define our continuum of counties from the biggest major cities to rural areas not adjacent to a metropolitan area. Third, we use these two categorizations to investigate differences in average number of social service nonprofits, the influence of population density on the number of nonprofits, and per capita spending on services.

Nonprofit Social Service Organizations

While many everyday social problems are addressed informally by the kindness of neighbors, most social services are delivered through formal organizations. Scholars and policy makers differentiate between four different kinds of entities: government, for-profit businesses, religious congregations, and public charities. Each approaches social service delivery in a different way, and each is an important part of the community ecology of social service delivery.

This chapter focuses exclusively on public charities. "Public charity" is the official name for nonprofit organizations that gain favorable tax treatment under section 501(c)3 of the Internal Revenue Code by promising to carry out missions that serve the public good. Favorable tax treatment means that public charities do not pay income tax on their own revenues and that a donation to them may be a charitable deduction for the donor. Public charity does not connote an association with government. While it is certainly possible that social services in rural areas may be delivered by public governmental organizations or for-profit corporations, comparable data on the existence of such entities in counties throughout the country are not currently available. Moreover, the tendency in recent decades for state and local governments to divest their service operations to nonprofit organizations is well known and widely commented upon. Many of the nonprofit organizations that appear in this study may, in fact, have come into operation in this way.

While religious congregations also fall under the broad definition of "nonprofit organizations," they are not required to register with or file annual reports with the Internal Revenue Service. Thus, without a large-scale research effort, we cannot know which congregations are engaged in the delivery of social services and which are not. For these reasons, we exclude congregations from our presentation and use the term "nonprofit organization" interchangeably with "public charity." Our statistical profile includes only those nonprofit social service organizations that are large enough to file with the Internal Revenue Service, and these are the ones we counted in our opening statements about social service nonprofits in Cook County and Valley County. Organizations that do not have $25,000 worth of receipts in a given year are not required to file either the annual Form 990 or the short Form 990EZ. Consequently very small independently incorporated food pantries, thrift shops, and other like organizations are also not included here.

We do include the 57,426 nonprofit social service organizations that filed a Form 990 with the IRS in 1999 or 2000. Because this number excludes small charities, it is a conservative estimate of the number of social service nonprofits in the United States and may be biased against rural areas. Another factor that contributes to the conservatism of the estimate is that the 57,426 organizations in our study are those that are coded by the IRS or the National Center for Charitable Statistics as being *primarily* a social service organization. This excludes the large number of *primarily* health, educational, environmental, arts, or international charities that provide social services. Table 4.1 provides an overview of the categories and numbers of each kind of organization included in our profile.

Rural-Urban Continuum Codes

Since the primary purpose of this chapter is to examine differences between nonprofit social services in different kinds of counties, we need a system to differentiate rural from urban localities. The Economic Research Service of the U.S. Department of Agriculture has made great strides in sorting counties into major groupings. *County Typology Codes* identify counties according to their primary economic activity, including such designations as "farming-dependent" and "mining-dependent." *Urban Influence Codes* sort counties according to their proximity to urban areas of different sizes. However, the most popular scheme is the *Rural-Urban Continuum Code*. Based on the 2000 decennial census and the subsequent designations of counties by the Office of Management and Budget as either metropolitan or nonmetropolitan, these codes distinguish metropolitan counties by population size and nonmetropolitan counties by population size and adjacency to metropolitan areas. Although the Rural-Urban Continuum system has nine separate codes, we combine several codes to create a seven point system. The definitions and numbers of counties in each category are represented in table 4.2.

The codes used in this chapter depart from the true Rural-Urban codes by ignoring whether counties with small cities or towns are adjacent to metropolitan areas or not. However, we preserve this distinction for the rural counties. A county is designated as "adjacent" if it physically adjoins a metropolitan county *and* has at least 2 percent of its employed labor force commuting to metropolitan counties. Adjacency to metropolitan counties is potentially important because of ease of access to social services in these neighboring counties.

Across the Continuum

Table 4.3 shows how the average number of social service charities is distributed across different kinds of counties. For example, the 414 counties with the biggest cities have an average of 68.5 social service charities. On the other hand, the 435 rural counties not adjacent to metropolitan areas

TABLE 4.1 Social Service Nonprofits in the United States, ca. 2000

Number of Organizations	Category of Social Service Organization	Types of Organizations Included
12,684	Multipurpose Programs	Urban League Salvation Army Young men's or women's associations Neighborhood centers Volunteers of America Centers for the developmentally disabled Ethnic and immigrant centers Human services not classified elsewhere
9,438	Community organizations and housing	Urban and community economic development Housing development, construction, and management Public housing Temporary housing Community and neighborhood development Community coalitions Neighborhood and block associations
7,043	Programs for preschool children	Preschools Child day care
5,543	Physical and mental health	Reproductive health care Family planning Substance abuse dependency, prevention, and treatment Community mental health centers Community clinics Hospices
4,980	Programs for the Elderly	Senior centers Senior continuing care communities Meals on Wheels

(continued)

TABLE 4.1 Social Service Nonprofits in the United States, ca. 2000 (Continued)

Number of Organizations	Category of Social Service Organization	Types of Organizations Included
4,487	Emergency services	Food programs Food banks and pantries Homeless shelters Congregate meals Soup kitchens Homeless centers Travelers' Aid Family violence shelters Emergency assistance Victims' services Spouse abuse prevention Child abuse prevention Sexual abuse prevention
4,018	Programs for youth and teens	Family services for adolescent parents Children and youth Services Youth centers and clubs Boys' and girls' clubs Adult and child matching programs Big Brothers and Big Sisters
3,802	Adult programs for work readiness	Adult education Goodwill Industries Sheltered employment Vocational rehabilitation Employment not elsewhere classified Employment preparation and procurement Vocational counseling Job training
2,867	Group homes	Residential care
2,564	Family services	Family services Single-parent agencies Family counseling Adoption Foster care

TABLE 4.2 Rural Urban Designations of U.S. Counties

Number of Counties	Category	Definition
414	Counties with biggest cities	Counties in metropolitan areas with 1 million people or more
325	Counties with bigger cities	Counties in metropolitan areas of 250,000 to 1 million people
351	Counties with big cities	Counties in metropolitan areas of fewer than 250,000 people
323	Counties with small cities	Nonmetropolitan counties with an urban population of 20,000 or more
1,059	Counties with towns	Nonmetropolitan counties with an urban population of 2,500 to 20,000
235	Rural, near metropolitan area	Urban population of less than 2,500, adjacent to metropolitan area
435	Rural, not near metropolitan area	Urban population of less than 2,500, not adjacent to metropolitan area

average only 1.5 charities. As one might expect, the number of social service organizations declines steadily as one moves along the continuum from urban to rural.

This trend generally holds for different kinds of social service organizations as well. Numbers less than 1.0 indicate that a town or rural county is more likely to *not* have a particular kind of social service charity.[1] Even counties with big cities are not likely to have group homes or charities that focus specifically on family services. Still, they are more likely than rural areas to have these kinds of charities. Elderly programs are more prominent in counties dominated by towns or rural areas. Although there are fewer such programs in rural areas than in urban areas, they are the most abundant type of social service charity in rural areas. In fact, in rural counties not adjacent to metropolitan areas, elderly programs are twice as abundant as any other kinds of charity, including multipurpose social service charities.

The numbers of social service organizations in a county of a particular type is not always the best indication of the scale of services available to local residents. A better indication might be the number of charities available to a certain number of people. In our opening paragraph, we said that Cook

TABLE 4.3 Average Number of Social Service Nonprofits along the Rural-Urban Continuum

			Counties with					
	Biggest Cities	Bigger Cities	Big Cities	Small Cities	Towns	Rural, near metro	Rural, not near metro	All
Multipurpose programs	15.0	8.0	4.1	3.4	1.1	0.4	0.2	4.0
Community organizations and housing development	12.4	5.6	2.4	2.3	0.7	0.3	0.2	3.0
Programs for preschool children	8.8	4.2	2.0	1.6	0.6	0.3	0.2	2.2
Physical and mental health programs	6.4	3.6	1.7	1.7	0.5	0.1	0.1	1.8
Elderly programs	5.0	2.9	1.6	1.5	0.7	0.3	0.4	1.6
Emergency services	4.9	2.8	1.6	1.5	0.4	0.1	0.1	1.4
Programs for youth and teens	4.8	2.6	1.4	1.2	0.3	0.1	0.1	1.3
Work-readiness programs	4.7	2.4	1.2	1.0	0.3	0.1	0.0	1.2
Group homes	3.2	1.9	0.9	0.8	0.3	0.1	0.1	0.9
Family services	3.3	1.8	0.7	0.6	0.1	0.0	0.1	0.8
Any Social Service nonprofit	68.5	35.8	17.6	15.6	4.8	2.0	1.5	18.3

County's five-million-plus people were serviced by more than one thousand social service charities. This works out to about nineteen such charities for every one hundred thousand people. On the other hand, Valley County has only one social service nonprofit to go with its nearly five thousand residents. If Valley County grew to one hundred thousand people and the number of social service nonprofits grew accordingly, it would have twenty-one such charities. So, on a per capita basis, Valley County has more social service charities than Cook County does. Put another way, rural Valley County has more social service delivery organizations per person than the densely populated central county of Chicago.

Table 4.4 presents the per capita counts of social service nonprofits in counties along the rural-urban continuum. This table reveals that nonmetropolitan areas, specifically counties dominated by small cities, have the greatest wealth of social service organizations per person. These counties average twenty-five social service organizations for every one hundred thousand residents, and they have the greatest per capita number of social service organizations of all types.

When looking at social service organizations per capita, rural counties do not look so different from the counties dominated by major cities. Rural counties not adjacent to metropolitan areas have more community organizations, preschool programs, physical and mental health, and elderly programs per capita than counties dominated by our biggest cities. These counties also have more of these nonprofits (per capita) than rural counties adjacent to metropolitan counties. This suggests that rural counties near metropolitan areas are more likely to rely on their neighboring counties for these kinds of services, while rural counties that are further removed from metropolitan areas must develop their own programs.

Especially notable are the number of elderly programs per capita in rural areas. The 4.6 organizations per one hundred thousand residents in rural counties near metropolitan areas and 7.1 in counties further removed from metropolitan areas are the highest per capita totals in table 4.4. This finding reflects the greater concentration of elderly residents in rural counties. It also reflects the ability of communities to create and sustain programs best suited to the needs of the people who live there.

Number of organizations per capita is helpful in describing the commitments of different counties to different kinds of nonprofit services. However, such an accounting ignores the fact that social service nonprofits come in a variety of shapes and sizes. One way to think about the size of social service organizations is the amount of money they spend each year, including the

TABLE 4.4 Average Number of Social Service Nonprofits per 100,000 Residents

					Counties with			
	Biggest Cities	Bigger Cities	Big Cities	Small Cities	Towns	Rural, near metro	Rural, not near metro	All
Multipurpose programs	3.9	4.0	4.2	5.5	4.7	3.7	3.3	4.3
Community organizations and housing	2.6	2.6	2.7	3.7	3.1	2.6	3.4	3.0
Programs for preschool children	1.9	2.3	2.3	2.6	2.8	2.7	3.6	2.6
Physical and mental health	1.5	1.7	1.7	2.6	2.1	1.4	2.0	1.9
Elderly programs	1.5	1.7	2.3	2.6	3.3	4.6	7.1	3.3
Emergency services	1.5	1.3	1.7	2.5	1.8	0.8	1.2	1.6
Youth and teens	1.1	1.2	1.4	1.9	1.0	0.4	0.7	1.1
Work ready programs	1.1	1.1	1.3	1.6	1.1	1.1	0.8	1.1
Group homes	0.9	0.9	0.8	1.4	1.0	0.9	0.8	1.0
Family services	0.7	0.7	0.7	0.9	0.5	0.3	0.5	0.6
Any Social Service nonprofit	16.7	17.6	19.3	25.3	21.5	18.5	23.4	20.6

costs of programs, administration, and fund-raising. The more than one thousand social service nonprofit organizations in Cook County, Illinois, reported a total of $2.4 billion in annual expenditures on their Form 990. That means that each social service nonprofit in the county spent an average of $2.3 million, although some spent a lot more and some much less. In contrast, the one social service organization in Valley County, Nebraska, spent $63,000. Of course, a large part of this discrepancy can be explained by the difference in the number of people in each county. However, when we consider per capita spending, the disparity remains quite large. Cook County's social service nonprofit spending works out to $44.5 million dollars for every one hundred thousand people. In Valley County, if the population grew to one hundred thousand and the amount of spending by social service nonprofits grew accordingly, the amount spent would only reach $1.4 million dollars. If these counties are typical urban and rural counties, these numbers point to a much greater wealth of spending and economic activity in urban counties.

Table 4.5 shows how average per capita spending by different kinds of social service nonprofits differs across the rural-urban continuum. The table shows that Cook County's $44.5 million dollars in expenditures per one hundred thousand people is higher than the average for other counties of this type, which average only $23.5 million in spending per one hundred thousand residents. Similarly Valley County's $1.4 million per one hundred thousand people is low relative to its peer counties. Other rural counties not adjacent to metropolitan areas average $11.8 million per one hundred thousand residents.

Nonetheless, the disparity between rural and urban counties is clear in table 4.5. Social service nonprofits in the three varieties of metropolitan counties (those with biggest, bigger, and big cities) spend about the same per capita, around $23 million per one hundred thousand residents. Just as table 4.4 indicated that counties with small cities are richest in terms of numbers of social service nonprofits, table 4.5 demonstrates that they are also richest in terms of per capita spending. However, counties with towns spend less per capita than metropolitan counties, and rural counties spend notably less per capita than do nonrural counties. In fact, nonprofit social service organizations in rural counties spend less than half per capita than counties with higher populations.

This disparity holds across different kinds of social services. It is less pronounced for per capita spending on group homes, but the disparity is particularly large in emergency services and programs for youth and teens. Most

TABLE 4.5 Average Total Nonprofit Expenditures per 100,000 Residents (in millions of dollars)

				Counties with				
	Biggest Cities	Bigger Cities	Big Cities	Small Cities	Towns	Rural, near metro	Rural, not near metro	All
Multipurpose programs	$6.2	$6.3	$5.8	$7.4	$6.4	$2.1	$3.3	$5.7
Community organizations and housing	$1.8	$1.3	$1.5	$2.0	$1.6	$0.5	$1.1	$1.5
Programs for preschool children	$1.2	$1.1	$1.0	$0.9	$0.9	$0.7	$0.3	$0.9
physical/mental health	$3.9	$3.6	$4.6	$6.6	$3.2	$1.6	$2.3	$3.6
Elderly programs	$3.5	$3.9	$4.9	$3.4	$2.4	$2.0	$2.0	$3.0
Emergency services	$1.2	$1.0	$0.8	$1.2	$0.5	$0.1	$0.2	$0.7
Youth and teens	$0.9	$1.6	$0.8	$0.9	$0.4	$0.1	$0.3	$0.7
Work ready programs	$2.0	$1.9	$2.0	$2.5	$1.3	$0.6	$0.4	$1.5
Group homes	$1.6	$1.5	$1.3	$2.5	$1.3	$1.1	$1.1	$1.5
Family services	$1.3	$0.6	$0.7	$1.0	$0.3	$0.1	$0.7	$0.6
Any Social Service nonprofit	$23.5	$22.8	$23.4	$28.3	$18.3	$9.0	$11.8	$19.5

notably the difference in per capita spending between urban and rural counties holds for elderly services. Even though rural counties, and especially rural counties not adjacent to metropolitan counties, have a higher number of elderly service nonprofit organizations per capita, the elderly service nonprofits in rural counties spend notably less per capita than the same services in urban counties.

Summary

Are urban counties better off than rural counties in terms of social services? This chapter provides three different kinds of answers to this question. First, we illustrated that urban counties have more social service nonprofit organizations than rural counties. This should not be surprising, since we expect that more charities will be founded in counties that are more densely populated. Therefore, we looked secondly at the number of social service organizations per one hundred thousand people, and we found that rural areas hold their own on per capita numbers of social service organizations. Rural counties even have some kinds of services in greater numbers (per capita) than urban counties, especially elderly service organizations.

However, when we looked thirdly at the amount of money spent by social service organizations per capita, rural counties lagged far behind urban counties. On average, social service charities in metropolitan counties spend roughly twice per person what social service charities spend in rural counties. Even compared to more heavily populated nonmetropolitan areas, rural counties come up short. Charities in rural counties not adjacent to metropolitan areas spend one-third per person the amount spent by charities in nonmetropolitan counties with urban populations of twenty thousand or more. This finding highlights a large disparity between the resources available to residents of rural counties. While these charities frequently have nonprofit social services available, the amount of money accessible to them lags far behind their counterparts in more urbanized areas.

Note

1. It bears repeating that the organizations in the study are those that file their required form with the Internal Revenue Service. Our profile does not include charities that do not file or do not need to file. Our profile covers most of the charities whose primary mission is the delivery of social services, but not all of them. We also do not include county or city services, or services provided by local congregations.

5 The Third Sector in Rural America

Roger A. Lohmann

The third, or nonprofit, sector has long played an important role in rural social work practice and will continue to do so in the future. Three waves of activity characterize the nonprofit sector. The first was the rise in importance of voluntary associations and nonprofit organizations in rural life in general. Hayrides, square dances, 4-H clubs, church socials, ladies aid societies, barn raisings, volunteer fire departments, church camps, local cemeteries, and many more organizations and groups are all part of the traditional rural third sector. They structure the associational galaxy of rural community life that Alexis de Tocqueville chronicled in his famous tour of America in the 1830s, with strong emphasis on voluntary action, participation, citizenship, and civic duty.

In the latter part of the nineteenth century and early part of the twentieth a second wave of third-sector activity occurred as agricultural cooperatives and associations from the Grange and the Farm Bureau to the National Farmers' Organization (NFO) took root in rural America. The emphasis of this second wave of activity was primarily concern for economic issues such as control of production, distribution of profits, and stabilization of incomes. It is noteworthy that, although there is a close tie between agricultural and rural, part of the focus of this second wave of activity was on organizing among rural industrial workers. For much of its history the United Mine Workers, for example, was a predominantly rural union in the same sense that the steel workers' union and autoworkers' union were predominantly urban.

More recently Head Start programs, community mental health centers, community action agencies, hospices, senior centers, after-school programs, the Red Cross, the United Way, Boys' and Girls' Clubs, and a host of other nonprofit social services and the nonprofit organizations that deliver them have become part of the fabric of rural America. Together they constitute the third wave of rural third-sector activity with a strong accent on community development. In the case of evolving rural nonprofit social services, the emphasis has been less on civic involvement or economic production than on establishing community services delivered by paid professionals.

Two aspects of this third wave of activity are particularly evident: The first occurred largely as rural communities availed themselves of federal grant funds originally intended for urban areas. The dynamics of this "grantsmanship" differed significantly from the types of indigenous community dynamics that gave rise to the first two waves of activity. The second aspect resulted as fewer rural community people were involved in these efforts, with greater emphasis placed on creative action by rural community leaders and professionals. Further, most of the social services that have sprung up in rural communities since the 1960s can be seen as "transplants" of already established urban services and institutions rather than as unique rural institutions or innovations (Lohmann and Lohmann 1977).

In many ways the United Way movement is emblematic of what has occurred in rural social services. For at least the first half of the twentieth century, all the pioneering federated financing or workplace giving plans in the United States were located in major urban centers. This has given rise to the mistaken impression that the contemporary movement itself is primarily an urban one. The reality is that while most of the money is raised in large urban communities by highly professionalized staff, a great many United Way organizations are small, rural operations and depend heavily on volunteers. There are an estimated fourteen hundred United Way organizations in American communities today. According to the 2000 Census, there are just under three hundred major metropolitan areas in the United States. Thus it should be relatively clear that a sizable number of the United Way organizations in the country are located in smaller, nonmetropolitan communities like Buckhannon, West Virginia; Roswell, New Mexico; Warren, Pennsylvania; and Lihue, Hawaii.

Something very similar to the proliferation of rural United Way organizations also occurred with community action agencies, senior citizens' centers, and hospice care, to name just three examples. And in the late 1990s and the first decade of the twenty-first century another similar pattern developed with an increase in the number of community foundations. Most large urban centers and a few pioneering smaller cities like Parkersburg, West Virginia, have had community foundations since the 1940s; however, only after the economic boom of the 1980s and 1990s did they begin to emerge in smaller communities. Thus a state like West Virginia that had five community foundations as recently as 1990 currently has twenty-two. All the newest foundations arose in smaller cities with the intent of serving the cities and the surrounding rural areas. Overall, nationally, the number of community foundations grew from around three hundred — roughly the number of metropolitan areas — to more than twice that number in the past fifteen years.

In fact, the pattern of new service development in the United States tends to follow a well-known standard diffusion curve, beginning with an *innovation* somewhere, with most of the *early adopters* concentrated in the largest metropolitan centers. Sometimes, as with community foundations before the 1980s, matters rest there for many years and the innovation spreads no further. In other cases some innovations truly "go national" diffusing first from the largest urban centers to ever smaller communities that eventually include most or all of rural America. This is as true of hospice programs as it is of the independently owned coffee bars that began in Seattle and have currently spread to small towns such as Zumbrota, Minnesota, among many other examples. Thus it is the case that, in our time, much of what occurs in urban areas also takes place in rural areas; things just happen later as diffusion takes its course.

Definitions

To better understand the role of the third sector in rural America, we need to understand a few terms. The term *third sector* describes a variety of national clusters of organizations and activities outside the private domain of families or households and distinguishable from the public domains of market economies (business) or political states (government). The third sector is generally understood as a domain of organizations and corporations, rather than persons. In the United States it is largely the domain of "nonprofit," tax-exempt entities governed by nondistribution constraints.[1] Some would prefer the term *independent sector*, coined by the corporate CEO and independent scholar Richard Cornuelle in 1965 (Cornuelle 1965).

For much of the first half of the twentieth century the nonprofit social services of the third sector in the United States were designated by social workers and others as *voluntary* social services; a usage still current in Great Britain, where the full set of such activities are referred to as the *voluntary sector* (Harris 1998; Billis and Glennster 1998; and others). In much of the rest of the world similar organizations are known as *nongovernmental*. In the United States the term *nonprofit sector* has become a term of choice since the federal government began allowing grants to such entities in the 1960s, mandating incorporation and tax-exempt status as a condition for funding. The Filer Commission anointed the term in the 1970s, and academic disciplines began recognizing *nonprofit studies* as specialties in the 1980s. Even so, the term *nonprofit* still lacks exact or rigorous meaning.

Charity is one important component of the American third sector and nonprofit law, where it has a broad meaning encompassing not only health and human services but also education and the arts. Another element of modern third sectors is *philanthropy*, a word that has roots in ancient Greek, referring to action for the general good, with its root, *philia*, usually translated as brotherhood [*sic*], fellowship, mutuality, or civic friendship. In its most expansive modern meaning, philanthropy refers to what Robert Payton (1988) called *private action for the public good*. In its somewhat narrower everyday usage philanthropy refers to the activities of foundations and fundraising.

Nationally the third sector is composed of a rather indefinite mélange of perhaps a million and a half nonprofit corporations, at least forty-five thousand foundations, and untold numbers of additional informal groups, voluntary associations, self-help and mutual aid groups, and other similar organizations, significant portions of them in rural America. Chapter 4 of this book is the very first published account of rural nonprofits, using a method Mark Hager and Tom Pollak devised to identify such organizations from the IRS files that are the principal source for contemporary research on nonprofit organizations.

Needs and Services

According to the management guru Peter Drucker (1990), orientation to mission and purpose (as opposed to profit) is one of the most distinctive characteristics of nonprofit organizations. The "needs and services" paradigm of social work would suggest that the mission of public and nonprofit social work is to meet needs by providing services. One of the principal ways to do that is through nonprofit organizations.

The needs and services paradigm dates from the scientific philanthropy of early social work in the late nineteenth century, and incorporates the intertwined notions that individual human needs can be readily identified, tabulated, and aggregated into ad hoc sets of social problem categories known as *community needs* through a generic process of *needs assessment*. On the basis of such tabulations, *community priorities* can be established, usually by noting the needs with the highest incidence. Community needs and priorities in turn provide the rationale for attracting the financial and human resources required to create and sustain networks of social services to address those community needs. Asking social workers and other firsthand observers their opinions on community needs is a second variation of this approach. Most federal and state social service planning efforts in rural areas as well as the standard United Way Resource Allocation model closely follow the needs and resources paradigm (Lohmann 1991; Lohmann, Locke, and Meehan 1984).

The needs and resources paradigm assumes the existence of several kinds of voluntary or nonprofit organizations and groups: *client groups* and groups that speak for the community; *social agencies* that strive to recognize and address community needs; and community *planners* and *decision makers*. By following the model, the usual assumption is that the legitimacy of social service interventions is an expression of the general will of the community.

Sector Theory

Real world events of the last two decades, particularly the collapse of a large portion of the "Second World" of communist totalitarianism and the rise of neo-conservatism in the "First World" have produced something like a worldwide hegemony for the market economy and political democracy. This has resulted in renewed emphasis in the international political world and social science community on market economics, political democracy, and civil society. One interesting multidisciplinary by-product of this new emphasis is something that can be called "sector theory." Derived originally from economics, it was percolated into, and helped to define, the interdisciplinary matrix of the newly emerging field of nonprofit or third-sector studies.

On a more or less ad hoc basis, researchers and theorists interested in nonprofit, voluntary, and nongovernmental organizations have suggested various three- and four-category models of "sectors" of organizations. The

German social philosopher Jürgen Habermas (1984) projects two institutional "systems," economy and state, characterized by instrumental rationality and a sphere characterized by communication which he calls the "lifeworld." Jean Cohen and Anthony Arato (1992) see economy and state as well as a third sector of "civil society," which they argue consists of communication media, voluntary associations, and social movements. Burton Weisbrod (1998), Lester Salamon (1992), and others posit the third sector arising out of the economic market and political state through processes they dub, respectively, "market failure" and "government failure." Roger Lohmann (1992), David Billis (1993), and others also include a fourth — household — sector.

Mediating with Urban America

The single most important contribution of third-sector organizations in rural America is what has been termed "mediation with outside forces in urban America." "Grassroots associations" perform a somewhat similar role in urban, ethnic, inner-city neighborhoods. The idea of mediation is an important one in current understandings of the third sector. It is implicit in Alexis de Tocqueville's perspective, but much more recently sociologist Peter Berger, theologian John Neuhaus, and political commentator Michael Novak focused explicitly on the role of such mediation by the third sector. As they identify it, mediation is the buffering provided by associations and other organizations between the "lifeworld" of ordinary citizens as individuals and the large institutions of modern society — particularly the market economy and the democratic state. Although their argument makes no distinctions between urban and rural communities, it does differentiate between the more and less powerful, and suggests that mediation from third-sector organizations plays a role in protecting and empowering those with fewer resources.

Mediation of this sort is an essential feature of the precarious position of rural communities in an increasingly urban society. In the following I concentrate on two key aspects of third-sector social mediation in rural areas, and then examine an approach to the third sector known as commons theory in an effort to isolate the precise dynamics of nonprofit charity and philanthropy that allow such buffering to take place. The two aspects of mediation central to rural social work practice are the creative management of tradition and "rurban" change, that is, the introduction of urban institutions and practices in rural areas, and vice versa.

Reinforcing Tradition

An important mediating role played by the third sector in rural areas is to reinforce and stabilize tradition and traditional ways of being and doing in rural areas. It is a role that sometimes includes not only the protection of existing traditions and the revitalization of weak or dying traditions but also the invention of entirely new traditions. Foremost in this regard are the many thousands of small Christian churches dotting the rural landscape.[2] One cannot understand the role of the third sector in rural America without paying some attention to the role of the rural church. Nationally approximately 45 percent of all charitable donations are made to religious groups and organizations. In comparison, the percentage of charitable donations to all social services has now fallen below 10 percent (Hodgkinson et al. 1996).

In marked contrast to such urban-based religious developments as the social gospel movement, liberation theology, and faith-based social services, rural religion is typically foursquare in its support of tradition.[3] Rural religious traditionalism sometimes pits rural social workers, particularly those on the cutting edges of "rurban" social change, against the most intransigent of the rural clergy. This sometimes results in drawing the false dichotomy of social work versus religion that is currently belied by the rising interest in faith-based social services in rural areas.

There are other, similarly benign and comforting aspects of rural religious enforcement of tradition in rural life. One of the most powerful and hopeful aspects of rural religion from a social work standpoint is the invocation of charitable and humanitarian responses that, particularly in times of disaster, flow easily and powerfully from rural churches and rural church people. It usually requires only a series of very small steps from ad hoc disaster relief to support for ongoing mental health and for children's or geriatric services.

In a very real sense, contemporary rural traditions of lending assistance largely flow from religious sources. Indeed, the Great Awakenings, eighteenth- and nineteenth-century religious revivals that brought, among other things, Sunday Schools, revival meetings, and religiously inspired fundraising and contributed significantly to the strength of evangelistic Christianity in America, were largely rural movements if only because the country was predominantly rural at the time. And the kind of evangelical, fundamentalist religion they fostered still resonates strongly throughout much of contemporary rural America. Thus the origins of support in rural communities for social services, nonprofit charity, philanthropy, and "that old time religion" are deeply intertwined.

A second set of sources of active enforcement of rural traditions is less overtly religious and was, at one time, seen as the very antithesis of the traditional, namely, a great many contemporary rural institutions stemming from an ongoing series of secular rural revivals, most notably the Country Life Movement of the first decades of the twentieth century. In particular, 4-H Clubs, the Future Farmers of America (FFA), county extension agents and programs, county fair boards, community festival associations, celebration and holiday committees, and, most recently, senior citizens centers have arisen from change-oriented, modernizing, progressive sources to become over time significant rural traditions, and the organizations associated with them function as important defenders of rural traditions.

The various religious and progressive groups aligned in a rural community to defend what they perceive as its most important traditions, from a Memorial Day program at the local cemetery to the beard growing contest at the county fair, usually represent a broad cross-section of rural community leadership. They are often both staunch defenders of rural tradition and important generators of social capital of trust and networking. Thus it is often an effective if somewhat paradoxical and challenging strategy for rural social workers to build alliances with traditionalist leaders, and to seek to creatively redefine needed changes in terms of community traditions. In the case of children's services, senior programs, and faith-based initiatives of all sorts, such alliances may depend primarily on the knowledge and skills of the rural social worker.

This may not be as complex or counterintuitive as it first appears. There is a tendency in social work, and in the social sciences in general, to counterpoise tradition with social change in roughly the same way that we contrast urban and rural or modern and old-fashioned. From this perspective, rural traditions are easily — and mistakenly — aligned with opposition to needed change in areas such as child-rearing practices, gender relations, and handling diversity. The paradox is that this may be true right up to the moment when it ceases to be true and real change occurs. If this were consistently the case, one could hope to bring about change in rural communities only by cultural revolutions overthrowing traditions that, in the process, rejected dominant aspects of rural culture and community life. As the acceptance over time of everything from Sunday Schools to 4-H Clubs and senior citizens centers confirms, rural traditions are much more dynamic, flexible, and changing than they may appear to be at any given moment. The challenge is how to understand and cope with this seeming paradox. In marked contrast to the model of cultural revolution or transformation is the perspective of "invented tradition" identified by the historians Eric Hobsbawm and Terance Ranger, who define the phenomenon as

> a set of practices, normally governed by overtly or tacitly accepted rules and of a ritual or symbolic nature, which seek to inculcate certain values and norms of behavior by repetition, which automatically implies continuity with the past. In fact, where possible, they normally attempt to establish continuity with a suitable historic past. . . . However, insofar as there is such reference to a historic past, the peculiarity of 'invented' traditions is that the continuity with it is largely fictitious. In short, they are responses to novel situations which take the form of reference to old situations, or which establish their own past by quasi-obligatory repetition. (Hobsbawm and Ranger 1983, 7)

Hobsbawm and Ranger argue that far from being stable, unchanging, and deeply rooted in the past, many traditions are, in fact, dynamic and of surprisingly recent origin. That this is true of such rural traditions as senior centers should require little defense. The historical record will support the claim that it is also true of Sunday Schools, county fairs, 4-H Clubs, and agricultural co-ops.

Hobsbawm and Ranger distinguish between three types of invented traditions, each with a distinctive function: (a) tradition establishing or symbolizing social cohesion and collective identity; (b) tradition establishing or legitimatizing institutions and social hierarchies; and (c) traditions socializing people in particular social contexts (Hobsbawm and Ranger 1983, 9). As examples from rural communities, one might cite the constantly updated social cohesion and collective identity arising from local lore and legend; the community legitimacy associated with "our school"; and the role of churches, service clubs, and other associations and nonprofits in socializing youth to the expectations of citizenship in "our" communities.

A bit of reflection and local historical investigation in most rural communities will lend further support for the assertion that, in the context of rural social work practice, one of the most effective and far-reaching strategies available to the rural practitioner is the invention of tradition. Each of the three functions noted by Hawbsbowm and Ranger offers its own important possibilities for invention of such traditions. For example, a surprising number of what are seen as "traditional" rural arts and crafts from quilting to toll painting and "country music" are relatively recent inventions.[4] They

play important roles in shaping the collective identify of rural people, determining and sustaining positive rural identities even under adverse social
conditions like the virtual disappearance of agricultural and mining
employment.

Opportunities for invention of rural traditions may be more available in
some venues than in others. In particular, those programs and services most
actively committed to social justice for the poor, for minority groups, for gay,
lesbian, bisexual, and transgendered persons, and for women's issues are, in
the most fundamental and thorough-going ways, threats to the traditional
order, which may include large measures of secrecy, public hypocrisy, and
even threats and intimidation. One should not expect that those seeking to
overturn rural traditions of discrimination and bias will be particularly well
received. Rural social workers need to be aware that, to various degrees, rural
social work practice may be an unavoidable threat to rural traditions and an
active agent of social change. Or, with suitable attention, social programs
and services may be part of the creative invention of traditions in the renewal
of rural life.

Rurban Social Change

The second major role for the third sector in rural life involves mediating
"rurban" change. People who write and talk about rural social work often
treat rural and urban as polar opposites. Doing so neglects the very important
"rurban" dimension — the introduction of urban institutions and practices
in rural areas, and vice versa. The rurban process is definitely a two-way one.
Those familiar with rural areas recognize — however reluctantly — that market economies, paid employment, automobiles, and television are all urban
institutions imported to rural communities. Similarly many of the best improvements to cities and suburbs — grass, trees, quiet spaces, and so on —
represent the introduction of rural amenities to city life. This process of what
I term "rurbanization" is a long-term one.

Throughout the twentieth century rural ways of isolated and independent
living inherited from eighteenth- and nineteenth-century American life and
from earlier centuries of peasant[5] life in Europe gradually gave way to more
modern ways of rural living that can still be described as characteristically
rural, in part because of the invention of tradition and rurbanization. As
previously noted, the difference between urban and rural is often a matter
of degree or a matter of time. For example, modern rural people with vehicles and access to the Internet generally have access to the same products

and services as urban people do, although they may have to drive further or delivery may take longer. The senior citizens center was a thoroughly urban institution, created on the streets of New York City in the 1940s (Lohmann and Lohmann 1977). But rural communities everywhere have embraced the idea and made it completely their own.

The advent of state and interstate highways, rural electrification, large consolidated high schools, and, most notably, the automobile and television were primary catalysts in this process. Through these media and highway travel throughout the North American continent, rural residents gradually became aware that rural living is one among many ways of life in a highly diverse nation. This awareness of diversity is one of the conventional hallmarks of urban living, but it is a "rurban" feature that for many decades has characterized much of rural America. For previous centuries, although it seems foreign today, one of the stable features of life for the vast majority of rural people was the famed "six-mile limit." It was estimated that, until the twentieth century, the majority of people everywhere seldom traveled more than six miles from their birthplace in their entire lives.

Although radio, television, and highways were the principal media for advancing this great change, which can be characterized as the advent of a newer, more cosmopolitan rurban society in rural America, the third sector also played an important role. In the case of social services, social work professionals and their programs often constitute major rurban influences in rural communities. Incorporation of associations and membership groups, the formation of new types of nonprofit organizations, and the formation of groups committed to preserving and celebrating rural ways of living were all part of this trend.

Commons Theory

How is it that the third sector plays a central role in the invention of tradition and the transmission and legitimization of urban practices and ways to rural areas? And what does this tell us about social work practice in the third sector in rural areas? The key to a deeper understanding of the third sector in rural America both in terms of the invention of tradition and rurban change is to be found in the concept of the commons. In particular, commons theory offers explanations of the origins of "social capital" that give third-sector organizations their unique power, and also elucidates approaches to intervention in rural communities that transcend the static, limited nature of the needs and resources model in the present era. As such, it offers a general theory of mezzo- and macro-level intervention compatible with the assumptions of the "strengths perspective."

Commons theory is an interdisciplinary body of theory that makes use of an actual, historical rural institution, the agricultural commons or shared pasture land, as a model, metaphor, and exemplar of the best or most desired features of voluntary and membership associations. Different variants of commons theory have evolved in environmental studies and in economics (Hardin 1968; Ostrom 1992). The approach developed here is based on my version of commons theory (Lohmann 1992; Lohmann and Lohmann 2002).

From the vantage point of commons theory, the key to understanding the rural third sector is to consider Aristotle's term for it, namely, *koinonia politike*, which has been variously translated to mean society, community, civil society, political community, and commons, as well as several other possible translations. Following on this, *koinonia*, or the commons, has five essential characteristics (Finlay 1974; Lohmann 1992). Three of these are constitutive of the commons and bring it into being: (1) participation is voluntary, that is, optional, not forced or coerced; (2) purposes, or missions, are shared — jointly agreed upon; and (3) resources are shared in common resource pools, not owned or controlled by any individual participant.

The remaining two characteristics are emergent, arising out of the circumstance of people interacting in a social situation thus constituted. No one can dictate or enforce them upon others. Rather, they emerge from interpersonal interaction that meets the three formative characteristics. Thus the final two of the five essential characteristics include (4) *philia* (the Greek root from which the word *philanthropy* is derived) and can be translated approximately as civic friendship, or mutuality. It is a special instance of what every introductory sociology course discusses as the we-group sense; that special feeling of "us" that develops among co-participants. The second emergent characteristic of social action is (5) voluntary, the pursuit of a shared mission using pooled resources, and is the advent of a shared sense of justice indigenous to the group. In the case of formal nonprofit organizations, this begins with a formalized set of by-laws, but it may also extend to a strong sense among the group of "what is right," as in the case of social action or advocacy groups.

It is essential to note that the concept of the commons is an ideal type. Actual organizations demonstrate these characteristics only approximately and to varying degrees, particularly the ability to generate social capital. Historic voluntary social services like charity organization societies and settlement houses closely model these characteristics of a commons. A highly entrepreneurial nonprofit service organization purposely created to receive grant or contract funds may model the commons ideal to a much lesser extent. Typically rural nonprofit organizations represent blends of commons characteristics (A) with those of government bureaus (GA), businesses (AB), or one of the other, more complex hybrid theoretical possibilities GAB, AHB, or GABH. A number of contemporary economic development non-profits, for example, blend state or local tax money with private investment of the GAB type.

Philia and Social Capital

The emergence of *philia* in commons explains the otherwise strange connection that social theorists have drawn between trust and networking in definitions of social capital, and also accounts for the unique ability of third-sector entities, especially voluntary associations, to generate social cap-ital (Bourdieu 1993; Coleman 1988; Putnam 2000) In brief, community members who might otherwise not do so learn to trust one another — and also learn how far that trust legitimately extends — through working together on church councils, as scout leaders, and on social service agency boards, and by volunteering as a group in flood relief efforts and visitation of the elderly. And, on the basis of that trust, networks of interaction and com-munication serving all manner of additional useful purposes — functioning as social capital — come into being.

The abundance of this type of social capital is, in fact, precisely what many rural people find so appealing about their communities. This dynamic is also a distinctly rurban phenomenon, even though that conclusion is not consistent with standard rural images of the city. It is as true in any rural community today as it was in the northern Italian city-states of the Renais-sance where Robert Putnam first identified this process of social capital formation (Putnam 1995). The *philia* or mutuality that arises through such efforts is not only the "active ingredient" in philanthropy; it is the powerful engine of social capital formation.

Generating Social Justice

Numerous examples of invented traditions, as discussed above, have given renewed strength and vigor to rural life and problem-solving capacities. At the same time, applying the theory of the commons to the rural third sector, voluntary associations and nonprofit organizations that approximate the ideal commons type have it within their power to create or reinvigorate social norms. A rather mundane instance of this is the ability of every nonprofit organization to set its own operating rules. Thus, by establishing a new rule that board members are expected to donate annually to the organization, the nonprofit may be inventing a new tradition by adopting a practice that may have applied in the distant past only to organizations in the urban, voluntary sector. But it is important to note that however much this expectation of board member donations may have applied in the past to urban voluntary-sector organizations, this particular norm has been conspicuously absent in the many rural nonprofits created as vehicles for receiving public grants and contracts since the 1960s. Thus bringing it to the rural third sector represents a clear case of rurbanization.

The world of social action nonprofits offers countless additional examples of the application of these aspects of commons theory. Mothers Against Drunk Driving (MADD) has not only called for greater adherence to a universal public law (against driving a vehicle while intoxicated). The organization has also spawned a wealth of "copycat" groups with similar messages (the act of networking), thus enhancing the capacity of law enforcement officials to enforce laws against drunk driving, and to do so even against the wealthy and powerful (thereby building public trust in law enforcement). While MADD is not a predominantly rural organization — it is, in fact, a rurban one with deep roots already embedded in some rural communities — the point applies equally well to other national and local rural social action organizations.

A powerful social capital argument of this type can be made for the engagement of rural social workers with affirmative action with all types of oppressed groups. Such an argument covers much of the same territory but takes us well beyond the "positive role model" arguments frequently made in this area. Simply put, social services and other organizations will be markedly stronger with the involvement of diverse populations and cultures. This is so not only because of the additional "cultural capital" that derives from diverse perspectives and cultures, but also because the involvement of members of what, from the perspective of affirmative action, is termed the "protected class" fosters greater trust of the organization among those members of that class, thus creating networks that reach out to and diffuse within their communities. For this reason it is a key strategy in efforts to empower oppressed communities. This, of course, is another facet of the mediation function of organizations that is not exclusive to either rural or third-sector organizations but certainly includes them both.

Conclusion

The rural third sector is a distinctive component of rural life as well as a powerful engine for the protection and revitalization of what is important in rural life for those who live there. While nonprofit social services came to most rural communities relatively late, and with very limited bases of support, thanks to the availability of grant and contract funding many like the senior center have become as important to their communities as earlier third-sector entities such as county fair boards and agricultural associations.

In the contemporary rural community one of the most important functions of the third sector is mediating with the mainstream economy and political system of urban America. Two aspects of this mediation that are especially important include accommodating changes in the rural community to local tradition through, first, a process known as inventing tradition, and, second through the transfer of urban practices to the rural setting (and vice versa) in the process of rurbanization.

A fuller understanding of the mediating operations of inventing tradition and rurbanization can be gained by recognizing that many nonprofit organizations are, to varying degrees, commons, constituted by voluntary participation, shared missions, and shared resources. Over time their operations provoke social capital development through the growth of *philia*, or mutuality, and by the deliberate generation of norms of social justice. Third-sector organizations that function as commons are not only capable of generating entirely new traditions and norms of justice. Through their mediating roles they are also able to generate trust and entirely new and expanded networks of interaction that make their wider acceptance possible.

Notes

1. In this usage the term *peasant* refers to the social class of rural residents that emerged in middle and late medieval Europe. Some contemporary connotations of the word are as unpleasant as names such as *hick, rube,* or *hayseed.* Yet the fact remains that the term *peasant* is as descriptive of a rural social class as the terms *burger* and *bourgeoisie* are of urban classes.
2. Nondistribution constraints, that is, legal and ethical limits on the distribution of profits to shareholders or owners, are currently held to be one of the defining

characteristics of nonprofit organizations in the United States. Most state laws and IRS regulations for tax-exempt entities require nonreversible language of this sort in the basic legal documents of a nonprofit organization, usually the Articles of Incorporation. It is this, rather than the far more ambiguous "lack of a profit motive" and "not making a profit," which is said to truly define nonprofit organizations. However, this is a characteristic of American law and tradition. Equally "nonprofit," voluntary, or nongovernmental entities throughout Europe and elsewhere in the world manage to function effectively without such nondistribution constraints.

3. There is no intent here to suggest that rural America is exclusively Christian. Jews, Moslems, Buddhists, and other religionists as well as atheists and agnostics are found among the diverse populations of rural America, albeit certainly in smaller numbers than the predominantly Christian population. It is an untested hypothesis that wherever such populations have lived in rural America for extensive periods (such as Jews in the rural South) their traditionalism may be equally as strong — and as creative — as that attributed to rural Christianity there.

4. Some of these issues are being approached very indirectly in current discussions over the role of "spirituality" in the practice of social work. The discussion here avoids most concerns of spirituality and concentrates entirely on the institutional and organizational dimensions of the issue.

5 A contemporary example of a tradition in process of being invented is that of Appalachian weaving. See, for example, Philis Alvic 2003.

References

Alvic, Philis. 2003. *Weavers of the southern highlands.* Lexington: University of Kentucky Press.

Berger, P. L., R. J. Neuhaus, and M. Novak. 1996. *To empower people: From state to civil society.* 2nd ed. Washington, D.C.: American Enterprise Institute.

Billis, D. 1993. *Organising public and voluntary agencies.* London: New York: Routledge.

Billis, D., and H. Glennerster. 1998. Human services and the voluntary sector: Towards a theory of comparative advantage. *Journal of Social Policy* 27:79–98.

Bourdieu, P. 1993. *The field of cultural production: Essays on art and literature.* New York: Columbia University Press.

Coleman, J. 1988. Social capital in the creation of human capital. *American Journal of Sociology* 94:95–120.

Drucker, P. 1990. *Managing the non-profit organization: Principles and practices.* New York: HarperCollins.

Cohen, J. L., and A. Arato. 1992. *Civil society and political theory.* Cambridge, Mass.: MIT Press.

Cornuelle, R. C. 1965. *Reclaiming the American dream.* New York,: Random House.

Finlay, M. I. 1974. *Ancient economy*. Berkeley: University of California Press.

Habermas, J. *The theory of communicative action*. Vol. 1, *Reason and the rationalization of society*. Boston: Beacon.

Hanifan, L. J. 1920. *The community center*. Boston: Silver Burdett.

Hardin, G. 1968. The tragedy of the commons. *Science* 162:1243–1248.

Harris, M. 1998. Doing it their way: Organizational challenges for voluntary associations. *Nonprofit and Voluntary Sector Quarterly* 27 (2): 144–158.

Hodgkinson, V., et al. 1996. *Nonprofit Almanac 1996–97: Dimensions of the independent sector*. San Francisco: Jossey-Bass.

Horton, M. 1990. *The long haul: An autobiography*. New York: Anchor Books.

Lohmann, R. A. 1991. Social planning and the problems of old age. In P. Kim, ed., *Serving the elderly: Skills for practice*, pp. 209–232. New York: Aldine-DeGruyter.

———. 1992. *The commons: Perspectives on nonprofit organization and voluntary action*. San Francisco: Jossey-Bass.

Lohmann, R. A., B. Locke, and K. Meehan. 1984. A model for human service planning. In *Proceedings of the Tenth National Institute for Social Work in Rural Areas*. Columbia: University of Missouri School of Social Work.

Lohmann, R. A., and N. Lohmann. 1977. Urban services for the rural aged: Are they exportable? In R. Green and S. Webster, eds., *Social Work in Rural Areas: Preparation and Practice*, pp. 284–297. Knoxville: University of Tennessee School of Social Work.

———. 2002. *Social administration*. New York: Columbia University Press.

Ostrom, E. 1990. *Governing the commons: The evolution of institutions for collective action*. Cambridge: Cambridge University Press.

Payton, R. L. 1988. *Philanthropy: Voluntary action for the public good*. New York: American Council on Education.

Putnam, R. D. 1995. *Making democracy work: Civic traditions in modern Italy*. Princeton, N.J.: Princeton University Press.

———. 2000. *Bowling alone: The collapse and revival of American community*. New York: Simon and Schuster.

Salamon, L. M. 1992. *America's nonprofit Sector: A primer*. New York: The Foundation Center.

Weisbrod, B. A. 1998. *To profit or not to profit: The commercial transformation of the nonprofit sector*. Cambridge: Cambridge University Press.

Part II

Interventions

6 Dual Relationships in Rural Communities

Warren B. Galbreath

A friend of mine, Louie, is thinking about changing jobs. He is a social worker in a hospital in New York City and is exploring opportunities in child welfare in West Virginia. To help him decide whether to make this move, Louie asked me what would be different about practicing in rural West Virginia compared to his urban practice in New York.

I told Louie that one of the major differences would be that in rural communities he would need to clearly define boundaries with his clients. He could not understand why this would be more important in rural communities than in his urban practice. I explained that the rural practitioner had a greater chance of becoming involved in a dual relationship with clients and that professional boundaries could become cloudy when the professional is involved in more than one type of relationship with clients. I also indicated that it was the responsibility of the practitioner to determine if either of the relationships was harmful to the client, and, if so, the practitioner needed to end one of the relationships.

Only recently has much been written about the ethical issues social workers encounter when facing dual relationships (Congress 2001; Reamer 2003; Kagle and Giebelhausen 1994). Reamer (2001) discusses the "tangled relationships" that social workers face when attempting to manage boundaries in their profession. Lazarus and Zur (2002) explore dual relationships as they relate to psychotherapy. These authors have taken the lead in their respective professions to define the issues that relate to managing dual relationships in the human services field. This chapter applies the issues discussed in these two books to social work practice in rural communities. It also provides a framework that social workers may use to assess dual relationships.

This chapter focuses on the ethical dilemmas posed by direct practice relationships in rural areas. In doing so, it both explains the nature of dual relationships often encountered and provides some insight into the nature of direct practice in rural areas. The chapter also addresses dual relationships that may occur in administrative settings. Dual relationships, and the conflicts of interest that may result from them, are of concern to all social workers practicing in rural areas, regardless of their practice approach.

Defining "Dual Relationship"

Kagle and Giebelhausen (1994, 213) state that a dual relationship occurs when the social worker "assumes a second role with the client, becoming social worker and friend, employer, teacher, business associate, family member or sex partner. A practitioner can engage in a dual relationship whenever the second relationship (the one that is not professional) begins before, during or after the social work relationship."

Social workers in rural communities are likely to become involved in dual relationships because of the nature of small communities. Smaller numbers of people in rural communities mean that social workers are more likely to encounter people in multiple relationships. It is possible that a social worker's barber, neighbor, business associate, buyer for a used car, or past, present, or future lover could become a client. How does a social worker practicing in a rural community ensure that the second relationship she or he becomes involved in is not detrimental to the client? Are all dual relationships with clients unethical? In a single word, no! In fact, some may be therapeutic and encouraged by the profession (Reamer 2003).

The Uniqueness of Rural Practice

The 2001 National Association of Social Workers (NASW) Delegate Assembly adopted a position statement focused on the unique aspects of rural social work practice. The following is a portion of the statement that focuses on dual relationships.

Ethical practice in rural areas requires special attention in dual relationship issues. Few other settings expose social workers more to the risk of violating the code of ethics that states social workers are to "take steps to protect clients and are responsible for setting clear, appropriate and culturally sensitive boundaries. (NASW *Code of Ethics* 1.06) (NASW 2003, 1)

The statement goes on to state that,

Social workers practicing in rural areas must have advanced understanding of ethical responsibilities. Not only because dual relationships or multiple relationships are unavoidable but also because the setting may require that dual or multiple relationships be used and managed as an appropriate method of social work practice. (ibid., 2)

With the adoption of this position statement, the national association acknowledged that rural practitioners must have the knowledge and tools needed to effectively manage the inevitable dual relationships, and that social workers must do so because some of the relationships will be therapeutic and beneficial to the client.

The challenge for the rural social worker is to effectively manage the multiple relationships they will encounter . The purpose of this chapter is to provide the rural practitioner with a framework for understanding the nature of dual relationships and to help the practitioner manage these multiple relationships.

Managing Boundaries

Managing dual relationships requires understanding the boundaries social workers must maintain between themselves as professionals and their clients. Social workers must be able to distinguish between actions that are boundary violations and those that are boundary crossings.

Managing dual relationships also involves the client. This means that the client must also be aware that the social worker plays more than one role in the client's life. Explaining early on in the professional relationship the different roles you may play in the client's life may help the client understand why you behave differently in your professional role than in the role of a nonprofessional. As a result, clients may be able to understand why you may not acknowledge them on the street if they are with friends, or why you cannot attend their children's birthday parties. Involving clients and making sure they are aware of dual relationships may help them understand your behavior.

Boundary violations occur when the relationship has the potential to be harmful to the client. Boundary violations are unethical. Boundary crossings are not explicitly unethical. In boundary crossings, the professional may be involved in two relationships as long as the client is not exploited. When a relationship has the potential to be exploitative, it is clearly in violation of the NASW *Code of Ethics*. The *Code* states:

> Social Workers should inform clients when a real or potential conflict of interest arises and the reasonable steps to resolve the issue in a manner that makes the clients' interests primary and protects client's interests to the greatest extent possible. (Standard 1.06a)

Section 106c continues:

> Social workers should not engage in dual relationships with clients or former clients in which there is a risk of exploitation or potential harm to the client.

These sections of the Code place the responsibility of establishing boundaries on the social worker, not the client. Therefore it is critical that one keep in mind the potential of exploitation or harm through a dual relationship. The client may be vulnerable and is not in a position to take responsibility for establishing appropriate boundaries.

In a rural community there may not be many options other than multiple relationships. Thus it may be more difficult for the rural practitioner than the urban one to separate him- or herself from one or the other relationship. The rural social worker may need to be skillful and creative to ensure that the client is not exploited or harmed by an unavoidable dual relationship.

Boundary Violations

As indicated above, a boundary violation occurs when a dual relationship has the potential to be harmful to a client. Clear examples of boundary violations include having a sexual encounter with a client, borrowing money from a client, getting a client to include the social worker in her or his will, or working with the client to fraudulently bill insurance companies.

Other boundary violations may not be as clear. One example is that of dating a former client. Some professions define the length of time that should elapse before a professional should date a former client. The social work profession has no such stipulation in its *Code*. Thus it may be inferred that once a client, always a client, and that dating a former client, no matter how long ago the professional relationship ended, would be a boundary violation.

At the 1999 NASW Delegate Assembly, a small rural faction of the assembly attempted to modify the NASW *Code of Ethics* to include a specific time period that should elapse before a social worker dates a former client. The rationale was that in rural areas options for relationships are limited and that, by prohibiting the dating of a former client, the profession was curtailing the options social workers had to find a good relationship. It should be noted that the faction of delegates favoring the amendment did not represent the whole rural caucus of the Delegate Assembly. Indeed, the rural caucus did not support it. In the end the assembly soundly defeated the amendment.

Boundary violations clearly must be avoided, as they cause harm to the client. Also, because such violations represent unethical behavior, state licensure boards could decide to revoke or suspend the license of a social worker found guilty of a boundary violation. It is critical for professional social workers to understand that the client must be the primary concern and that, in an intimate relationship, the power that exists in the professional relationship is likely to be exploited, which undoubtedly would do harm to the client.

Boundary Crossing

You may question whether all dual relationships are inappropriate, to be avoided regardless of their nature. The simple response is no; social workers do not need to avoid all possible outside relationships with clients. This is good news for rural social workers because, in most rural communities, all possible dual relationships cannot be avoided, even if that were desirable. It is inevitable that when social workers practice in rural areas they will have relationships with clients outside the office. Many of these relationships can be defined as "boundary crossing."

"Boundary crossing" describes a dual relationship that is not intentionally exploitative or harmful. Yet boundary crossings may be harmful when the relationship between social worker and client has negative consequences for the client. Gutheil and Gabbard (1993, 190) state that professionals should "determine the impact of a boundary crossing on a case-by-case basis that takes into account the context and situation-specific facts, such as the possible harmfulness of this crossing to his patient."

Boundary crossings are common in rural communities. Given the limited numbers of places to live, shop, partake in recreational activities, worship, and so on, clients often encounter their social workers outside the professional relationship. Again, responsibility remains with the social worker to ensure that clients are not taken advantage of or harmed.

For example, if a client works as a cashier at the local convenience store, it would be inappropriate for the social worker, stopping by for a gallon of milk, to ask the cashier about her progress on the goals of the previous week's session. Such a question puts the clerk in a difficult position. The social worker may not be aware that someone else is listening to the conversation. The discussion could distract the cashier from her job responsibilities. Also, she may not have informed her employer that she had sought the help of a social worker; should the employer overhear the conversation, this may put the cashier in an awkward or vulnerable position. Convenience stores routinely videotape all activity in the store, which could result in others hearing the conversation on the videotape. This does not mean, however, that the social worker should approach the encounter in a cold or distant manner, which could be taken by the cashier as demeaning and possibly damage the professional relationship between the two. Instead, the social worker might approach the cashier in a friendly way, allowing the latter to determine how she wishes to handle the chance meeting. The social worker may even be able to make therapeutic use of the encounter in their next session.

Consider another situation that is less straightforward. A social worker was counseling a recently divorced young parent in a rural community. After a few sessions the young mother started to feel better about her life and felt that the therapist had helped her take better control of her life. The young mother wanted to express her appreciation to the therapist. At one of their sessions the social worker had mentioned that she was looking for a used bicycle to get some exercise. The young woman was willing to give her own bicycle to the social worker, but the latter felt awkward accepting it. How would it affect their relationship? Was the client's gesture only in appreciation of the social worker's assistance, or did it reflect the client's feelings for the therapist and her desire to develop a friendship? Moreover, what would happen to the client/social worker relationship if, after a short time, the bicycle no longer met the social worker's needs and she wanted to discard it? Would the client feel that she had failed her therapist? Because there were limited opportunities to buy used bicycles in a rural community, should the social worker buy the bicycle from the mother rather than accept it as a gift? But what would be a fair price? The social worker did not want to take advantage of her client; nor did she want to pay too much. In the end the social worker decided to be candid with her client regarding the question of ethics. She then suggested that if the client was indeed wishing to sell the bicycle that she place an ad in the community "Swap and Shop." The social worker would then have the chance to purchase it if it was within her price range.

Although this may seem like a minor conflict of interest, the social worker must still explore the potential harm or disadvantage to the client, and use her judgment to protect the client. While accepting the bicycle is not clearly unethical, the potential harm or disadvantage it might bring to the client is real. The social worker must also explore her own motivation for her action. If her sole aim is to gain the use of the bicycle to meet her own needs, then the action could be identified as unethical.

A rural practitioner must be able to identify when a relationship is a boundary violation (which should always be avoided) and when it is a boundary crossing (which is sometimes acceptable). If the relationship is one of crossing boundaries, then the social worker must ask, is there potential harm to the client? If the answer is yes, then the relationship should clearly be avoided. If there is no risk of potential harm, then the social worker should consider how the relationship may be beneficial to the client.

Models for Guiding the Social Worker's Involvement in a Dual Relationship

In her book, *Social Work Values and Ethics*, Congress (1997) describes a model for evaluating ethical issues. This model is also useful in evaluating dual relationships. Indeed, it can be used as a guide for rural practitioners. It is not prescriptive, of course, because ethical issues are rarely black and white. Rather, the model guides practitioners through areas they will need to explore and gather information on so as to make an informed decision. The practitioner still needs to evaluate all aspects of the situation before making a final decision.

Congress makes use of the word "ethics" to describe her model. The first letter, "e," stands for "examine": when confronted with a dilemma one must *examine* relevant personal, societal, agency, client, and professional values related to the decision. Rural practitioners cannot rely solely on their own professional values related to the decision. They must take into account the values of the client and the community as well as those of the profession.

When an ethical dilemma appears, the social worker should first examine the values of all involved. By identifying these values the social worker may also get a better idea about how to intervene in the situation and a clearer perspective as to how the client will interpret the intervention. To illustrate this point, we can look back to the late 1960s, when Volunteers in Services to America (VISTA) came to southern West Virginia. Many of the VISTA volunteers had middle-class values and came to southern West Virginia attempting to instill these values in the poor of the community. Many good VISTA projects failed because local politicians and citizens did not trust the volunteers. They were outsiders and their values differed from those in the community. Moreover, outsiders had previously exploited the Appalachian culture. Many of the VISTA volunteers failed to recognize the cultural and political values of the rural communities in which they were working and were often asked to leave before their projects became successful.

The second step in Congress's model, taking its name from the second letter in "ethics," involves the social worker *thinking* about "what ethical standard(s) from the NASW *Code of Ethics* might apply to the situation as well as relevant laws" (32). When considering the *Code of Ethics*, social workers must keep in mind that they have responsibilities to the client, colleagues, practice settings, other professionals, the social work profession, and society as a whole. But when evaluating the dilemma from these different perspectives, the client's needs must take top priority.

The following situation illustrates how the social worker must consider the impact the decision will have on the client. A Child Protective Service (CPS) caseworker's car fails to start after a home visit. The father of the child who is the caseworker's client is a mechanic and he suggests having the car towed to his shop where he can have it looked at. The social worker feels awkward about this but has heard from others that this man is the best mechanic in the county. What does the caseworker do? The *Code* states that the social worker should barter only under extreme situations. But this is not bartering because the caseworker will pay for the towing and repair. The social worker is in a bind, and the father may be able to help. Does the father hope to influence the caseworker's decision about his child through his offer?

Reamer (2001) states that the social worker must be cautious of accepting advice or services from a client, as this has the potential of confusing the boundary between worker and client. "Over time the professional may feel indebted to the client" (135), and this may cloud the judgment of the professional. The NASW *Code of Ethics* does not prohibit the social worker from taking advice from the client nor does it state that the social worker cannot obtain services from a client. However, the social worker must take care to ensure that the client, or other clients in the social worker's caseload, are not harmed by a second relationship that may may develop.

Congress's third step *hypothesizes* the different courses of action a social worker might take to resolve the dilemma. At this stage the social worker projects different responses, and identifies advantages and disadvantages of each course of action. For example, the social worker would consider the two options available in the situation mentioned above, when his car breaks down and he is stranded at the client's house: the social worker can either accept the client's offer and have the car towed to the client's shop for repair, or he can decline the offer, call his own mechanic, and have the car towed to another garage.

The fourth step in Congress's model *identifies* the person who will benefit or potentially be harmed by the behavior of the social worker. Social workers must consider their commitment to clients who are most vulnerable. In the case of the stranded social worker, the rural practitioner must keep in mind that the client is his primary responsibility. What are the practitioner's motives? How will the action be viewed by the client? If the social worker accepts the client's offer to tow the car, will the client then feel that the practitioner is obligated to him? What happens if the car is made worse by the repairs in the client's garage? Will the client then feel obligated to extend his usual agreements with customers because the practitioner is also the family's CPS worker?

And what if the social worker declines the offer? Will it be necessary to wait at the client's home, perhaps for many hours, before another mechanic arrives? This would not be unusual in a rural area where services may be at a distance and the wait lengthy. Would this not be awkward for all concerned? And what if this waiting time occurs when lunch is imminent? Will the client feel you mistrust him if you decline his invitation for lunch? Will this refusal affect the professional relationship you share? Although the immediate situation may benefit from accepting the client's offer to help, the social worker must look beyond the present circumstance and consider both short- and long-term consequences of accepting the offer.

In the fifth and last step of Congress's model, playing on the final letter "c" in "ethic," social workers need to *consult* their supervisors and colleagues about the ethical choice. Often the first person a social worker looks to for advice is the supervisor. However, the rural social worker should be cautious about discussing a dilemma with his or her supervisor, for, as is true for many rural agencies, supervisors are not trained social workers who adhere to the NASW *Code of Ethics*. Therefore, in some rural communities, the rural social worker may not find even one trained social worker to consult and may need to seek social workers outside the immediate community for consultation.

A point not included in Congress's model, and yet one critical to the process, is that, after the social worker consults with colleagues, it is he or she who must make the final decision. Too often social workers discuss ethical issues but fail to reach their own conclusions. The result is that the decision is made be someone else and is not always in the client's best interest.

Finally, social workers need to document the ways they reach their decisions and monitor the consequences in order to be accountable to clients, employers, and funding sources, and, if necessary, to provide documentation in the event of an ethics complaint, malpractice claim, or lawsuit.

A Typology for Classifying the Dual Relationship in Rural Practice

Reamer (2003) describes a typology for classifying dual relationships. The typology identifies five categories of dual relationships in terms of their nature: intimate relationships, pursuit of personal benefits, how professionals respond to their own emotional needs, altruistic gestures, and responses to unanticipated circumstances.

Intimate Relationships

An intimate relationship with a client is identified by all as unethical and could result in the loss of one's social work license. The NASW *Code of Ethics* (1999, 1.09b) states: "Social Workers should not engage in sexual activities or sexual contact with client's relatives or other individuals with whom clients maintain a close personal relationship." Here the boundaries are clear that intimate relations with a client's family members are unacceptable. But is it unethical to have intimate relationships with a colleague with whom you share a case? Here the boundaries are not so clear.

Two questions need to be asked about such a relationship: Are you treating this client differently because you have an intimate relationship with the other worker? Has this intimate relationship clouded your judgment? If you answer yes to either question, there may be a conflict of interest requiring that either you remove yourself from the case or end the intimate relationship. This problem is more likely to occur in rural communities. Because dating options are limited, social workers may be more likely to develop intimate relationships in the workplace.

Consider the following scenario regarding the complications involved in engaging in intimate relationships with a colleague. Two social workers in a residential child care facility were dating. Sue worked in a cottage as Jane's therapist. Bill, who was dating Sue, ran an independent living program for the facility. Jane, seventeen years old, was living in the girl's dormatory but was ready to begin independent living, for which there were limited slots available. It was Bill's responsibility to decide which clients would enter the program; it was Sue's obligation to advocate for her client, Jane, to get into the program. This was the only independent living program within a radius of one hundred miles.

In this situation Bill must determine whether his relationship with Sue clouds his decision about whether Jane gets into the program. If Bill accepts Jane because of his relationship with Sue, is this the best decision for Jane and for other clients? If Jane is accepted by the program, then Sue and Bill must make sure that the time they spend with Jane as a means of being together does not deter them from the work that needs to be done with other clients.

As this scenario makes clear, rural practitioners must be cautious when choosing the person with whom they will have intimate relationships. The *Code* does not prohibit intimate relationships with colleagues, but it does state that when social workers choose to do so, they must assure that a conflict of interest does not exist and does not develop during the course of the relationship. Since it is difficult to anticipate future potential problems, it may be better to avoid such relationships.

Pursuit of Personal Benefits

Reamer (2001, 12) states that "human services professionals can become involved in dual relationships that produce forms of personal benefit, including monetary gain, goods and services or useful information." This cautionary statement leads to the exploration of two issues as they relate to rural practice: (1) bartering; and (2) advice and other useful information. Barnett and Yutrzenka (2002) state that the general characteristics of the rural community create a milieu from which dual relationships emerge.

On occasion professionals receive goods or services or both in exchange for their services. This is termed "bartering." Historically bartering has been common in rural communities. On the surface bartering may not appear to be unethical. Both parties receive goods or services that they need. However, the NASW *Code of Ethics* (1999, 1.13b, 9) states the following: "Social workers should avoid accepting goods or services from clients as payment for professional services. Bartering arrangements, particularly involving services, create the potential for conflicts of interest, exploitation, and inappropriate boundaries in social workers' relationship with clients." The *Code* goes on to state that social workers should avoid bartering and that they should accept goods and services from clients as payment for professional services only in limited circumstances (Reamer 1998).

This is an important issue when working with clients in rural communities because the bartering system is grounded in the roots of the rural economy. Historically those in rural communities have traded one service for another. Whether trading vegetables from the garden for a tune-up of a tractor or trading a handmade quilt for roof repairs, bartering continues to be an important part of many rural communities in America.

The question of bartering in rural communities easily becomes entangled with questions of service provision. Presently health insurance companies are the primary source of payment for services for most health and mental health professionals. Many clients living in rural communities do not have health insurance, however, and they also may not have the money to pay for services. Does this mean that these individuals will not get the services they need? Ethically can we deny services to those who cannot pay for them? Or do we allow some clients to barter for service? The simple response is, "yes, but . . ."

Bartering is ethical if a fair exchange is made for the services rendered. In many instances this is fairly easily established using concepts such as fair market value. But bartering raises other concerns. For example: What is the guarantee for the quality of services rendered in exchange for the professional services? What if the rug laid in an office in lieu of payment for services does not fit correctly? When bartering, the roles change from that of a professional relationship between a client and a worker to a business relationship that is complicated if and when the service received is unacceptable. There is another factor the social worker must take into account when a client offers to barter for services: Who has the potential to benefit from the barter? Who has the potential to be harmed? The short- and long-term effects of the barter also must be considered. Who is responsible for the quality of the services offered through the barter?

Rural practitioners must be cautious as well when it comes to accepting advice from clients. In rural communities there may be a limited number of individuals from whom one can get personal advice. The advice might relate to anything from personal preferences to the best pizza place to car maintenance problems to help with taxes. That there are limited numbers of people in the community and the surrounding areas restricts the options the professional would have to obtain personal services. The longer professionals remain in the area, the greater the chance that they will encounter the need for services that a client or former client may offer. Such dual relationships are likely unavoidable. But the professional needs to be concerned about the impact that the service delivery will have upon the client. Will the client feel obligated to the professional for having relied on her for services? Will this new relationship, which has developed because of the need of the professional, jeopardize the therapeutic relationship the professional has with the client? If it will, or if there is even the possibility that the client will be harmed by the relationship, the professional must not engage with the client in that relationship.

We can also look at this issue from another perspective. What happens when you have had a nontherapeutic relationship with an individual who then comes to you for professional services? Do you tell that person that you cannot provide professional services because it would be unethical to do so? Unlike their urban peers, rural practitioners, because of limited options in rural communities, are often unable to refer such potential clients to other appropriate service providers. Therefore the overlapping of professional-personal boundaries is often unavoidable, and so rural practitioners must take caution about dismissing the possibility of providing services to those with whom they have had nonprofessional relationships. If the rural practitioner does get involved with the individual professionally, then he or she must be aware that the nonprofessional relationship may change. The professional, therefore, needs to consider how such a change will impact the client. As in any decision that is made in the professional or nonprofessional relationship, the client's welfare must take first priority.

Professionals Seeking to Meet Their Own Needs through Clients

The third category in Reamer's typology is that of professionals becoming involved with clients so as to meet their own personal needs. Social Workers need to explore their motivation to fully understand dual relationships in this category. They may not always be able to separate their personal motivation from their decision about the possible dual relationship. Therefore, the professional may need to consult a supervisor or colleague to ensure that the best interests of the client are considered when making a decision.

Consider the following situation. A social worker in a rural community is going through a divorce. There are only a limited number of individuals she can talk to about her frustrations. While providing services to a single mom in the community, the social worker begins to feel comfortable disclosing personal information to the client. She realizes that after every session with this mother she feels better about herself. The mother makes progress in her sessions with the social worker as well, and it is time for closure. Ethically what should be done?

The professional would like to continue the relationship in either a professional or personal manner. How should this be handled? The *Code* does not prohibit the professional from engaging in a personal relationship with the client. Therefore developing a personal relationship would not be unethical. But she must take into consideration how the new relationship will affect the client. If this new relationship would negatively impact the client, the relationship should be avoided. This is a perfect example of when one should consult with others before making a decision. Colleagues may be able to help the social worker explore the nature of the new relationship and the potential support or harm that the client may reap from such a relationship.

Altruistic Gestures

The fourth category in Reamer's typology is altruistic gestures. Social workers often have a genuine interest in being helpful. This is a positive characteristic common to social workers. But, how does the client view these altruistic behaviors? Will the client misinterpret the gesture as an offer to develop a nonprofessional relationship? Will the gesture add to the professional relationship? Will the gesture be therapeutic for the client?

Reamer (2003) shares a scenario concerning a social worker who practiced in a rural elementary school and was working with a boy, whom I shall call Jim, who was struggling with low self-esteem. The social worker was also the coach of the only youth basketball team in the community. The social worker thought that Jim would benefit from participating on the basketball team. However, when Jim does so, he is not very good and his playing is detrimental to the team. If he continues to play with the team, the team will not perform as well than if he does not play. Being removed from the team, however, could be a further blow to Jim's self-esteem.

This social worker/coach is playing two roles with his client. How can the dilemma be resolved without doing harm to Jim? Can Jim understand the different roles that the social worker is playing? If not, should the social worker find another way for the boy to work on his self-esteem rather than suggesting that he join the basketball team? There are usually no clear-cut answers when dealing with dual relationships. Social workers must make certain that they explore all possible solutions and use their own best judgment to select the one that is least harmful to the client.

Unanticipated Circumstances

The final category in Reamer's typology is unanticipated circumstances. It is inevitable that a social worker practicing in a rural community will encounter the client when neither expects it. This could be a chance meeting at the grocery store, attending a wedding of someone you both know, belonging to the same church, eating dinner at the same local restaurant, and so on. The encounter may be awkward for the client, especially if the client is with someone who is unaware that the individual is involved with a human services organization. In all cases it is the social worker's responsibility to ensure that this awkward situation is handled so as to minimize the possible harm to the client.

Standards for Practice in Rural Communities

Barnett and Yutrzenka (2002) believe that dual relationships are to be expected in rural communities, and, moreover, they contend that not all dual relationships should be prohibited as some can be therapeutic. These authors suggest eleven standards of practice that should be followed when rural human services professionals are attempting to make ethical decisions concerning dual relationships.

1. *Acknowledge the facts.* Understand that dual relationships are inevitable in rural communities and be prepared to deal with these relationships rather than ignore or overlook them.

2. *Be sensitive to community expectations.* Be aware that in rural communities you may find that you "live in a fish bowl." Others outside the office are going to know what you are doing in the community. In an urban community you may be able to have an unconventional lifestyle and blend into the community. That will not happen in a rural setting. Community members will have certain expectations of you from the start. You should understand this and attempt to live up to those expectations.

3. *Compartmentalize your roles, not your relationships.* Human Services professionals cannot afford to be accepting and nurturing in the office and unapproachable in the community when encountering a client. There needs to be consistency in your relationships. This may mean that you may need to educate your client on the different roles that you play in the client's life and teach the client how to operate within the established boundaries of those roles.

4. *Know thyself.* You should be the first to know when you are treading on thin ice with professional relationships. Understand your motivations for the decisions you have made and ensure that you document the rationale for the decisions. If you think that your motivation may be personal, stop and reevaluate your decision. You do not want your client (or his attorney) to be the one to let you know you have a problem.

5. *Know others.* Rural social workers are often professionally isolated. They may be the only professionally trained social workers at their agency and may find that even their supervisor is not professionally trained. Therefore it is important that rural social workers identify social workers in the community or the state whom they can consult when ethical dilemmas arise.

6. *Nurture networks and resources.* Rural practitioners must develop positive relationships with other agencies in their community. Even if the agency does not have any professionally trained social workers, staff within the agency may be able to help provide necessary services to the client if you are unable to do so because of a dual relationship.

7. *Make referrals.* When a dual relationship does exist, the rural practitioner should explore the possibility of referring the client to another practitioner. In fact, if the social worker is aware of the dual relationship at intake and believes that it may interfere with professional judgment, the social worker should refer the client to another practitioner. Not doing so would be unethical.

8. *Remain cognizant of confidentiality.* Within a rural community you will inevitably encounter clients outside the office. It is critical that when this occurs the social worker allow the client to decide whether to recognize you. Others who know your client may come to you with information. At no point is it your responsibility to acknowledge that the individual they are discussing is a client of yours. If the information others provide is necessary for your treatment of the client, you should include it in treatment. However, it is not appropriate to share information about a client with others without your client's consent.

9. *Keep documentation.* In our litigious environment, it is important that you document your rationale for making a decision concerning a dual relationship. This documentation could demonstrate your effort to provide reasonable treatment for the client.

10. *Remain current on professional issues.* Rural practitioners should be active in keeping up to date on social work literature. Participating in continuing education workshops and reading the professional literature on the issue of dual relationships will help prepare the rural practitioner for making ethical decisions.

11. *Enter the professional dialogue and be part of needed changes.* Dual relationships are commonplace in rural communities. Rural practitioners are not always aware of how to handle these experiences. By sharing your experiences in presentations at workshops or in agency in-service programs you can help others better understand these dilemmas. Rural practitioners must keep in mind that many of the human services personnel in rural communities may not be trained as professional social workers and therefore may not understand how to behave professionally with regard to dual relationships. Sharing your experiences increases the awareness of nonprofessionals about dual relationships and may help guide their decision making.

Conclusion

Social workers practicing in rural communities should expect to encounter dual relationships routinely. For my colleague, Louie, whom I introduced at the start of the chapter, as well as others practicing in urban areas, the pervasiveness of such relationships in rural social work practice will be surprising. Managing such relationships in an ethical way is one of the continuing challenges facing rural practitioners and requires great skill and sensitivity.

Any dual relationship may represent a boundary crossing or a boundary violation. Boundary violations must be avoided, since they represent unethical practice and could result in damage to the client. In addition, they could cause the loss of the social worker's license to practice. Boundary crossings are more ambiguous and may even be appropriate depending upon the situation and the potential for harm to the client. Resources exist for the worker to sort out the complexities: Reamer (2003) provides a typology of possible dual relationships, and Congress (1997) and Barnett and Yutrezenka (2002) provide ways that such relationships may be analyzed. This chapter offers a set of standards to evaluate situations. In general, dual relationships must be dealt with cautiously so that the client is not harmed.

While dual relationships represent a particular challenge to the rural practitioner, by exercising appropriate caution and attending to the standards of ethical practice it is possible for the practitioner to enjoy the benefits of a rural practice while assuring that clients are not harmed.

References

Barnett, J., and B. Yutrzenka. 2002. Nonsexual dual relationships in professional practice, with special attention to rural and military communities. In A. A. Lazarus and O. Zur, eds., *Dual relationships and psychotherapy*, pp. 273–286. New York: Springer.

Congress, E. 1997. *Social work values and ethics: Identifying and resolving professional dilemmas*. Chicago: Nelson Hall.

———. 1997. Do the right thing; Social work ethics: Sex and the new code of ethics. New York: National Association of Social Workers. Available online at www.naswnyc.org/e14.html. Retrieved July 22, 2002.

———. 2001. Dual relationships in social work education: Report on a national survey." *Journal of Social Work Education* 37 (2): 255–266.

Gutheil, T. G., and G. O. Gabbard. 1993. The concept of boundaries in clinical practice: Theoretical and risk-management decisions. *American Journal of Psychiatry* 150 (2): 188–196.

Kagle, J. D., and P. N. Giebelhausen. 1994. Dual relationships and professional boundaries. *Social Work* 39 (2): 213–220.

Lazarus, A. A., and O. Zur, eds. 2002. *Dual relationships and psychotherapy*. New York: Springer.

Mack, K., and S. Boehm. 2001. Rural Child Welfare 101. *Children's Voice*. Available online at www.cwla.prg/articles/cv0111rcw.htm. Retrieved July 25, 2002.

Mamalakis, P. M., and M. R. Hill. 2001. Evaluating potential dual relationships: A response to Butler and Gardner. *Family Relations* 50 (3): 214–219.

National Association of Social Workers. 1999. *Code of Ethics. National Association of Social Workers*. Available online at https://www.socialworkers.org/pubs/code/code.asp. Retrieved July 22, 2003.

——. 2003. *Social work speaks: Rural social work*. Available online at http://www.socialworkers.org/resources/abstracts/abstracts/rural.asp. Retrieved August 20, 2003.

Poole, D. L., and J. M. Daley. 1985. Problems of innovation in rural social services. *Social Work* 30 (4): 338–349.

Reamer, F. G. 1998. *Ethical standards in social work: A critical review of the NASW Code of Ethics*. Washington, D.C.: NASW Press.

——. 2001. *Tangled relationships: Managing boundary issues in the human services*. New York: Columbia University Press.

——. 2003. Boundary issues in social work: Managing dual relationships. *Social Work* 48 (1): 121–133.

Reilly, D. R. 2003. Not just a patient: The danger of dual relationships. *Canadian Journal of Rural Medicine* 8 (1): 51–53.

Zur, O., and A. A. Lazarus. 2002. Six arguments against dual relationships and their rebuttals. In A. A. Lazarus and O. Zur, eds., *Dual relationships and psychotherapy*, pp. 3–24. New York: Springer.

7   Rural Community-Building Strategies

Dennis L. Poole

Rural communities are dynamic, ever-changing environments. Boom and bust cycles in the energy industry, fluctuations in the farm economy, corporate mergers, restructuring in mills and factories, influx of packinghouse and waste disposal operations, improved access to information technologies, depopulation and rural turnaround, shifts in human and cultural diversity — these dramatic environmental changes disrupt rural community systems and processes, and alter the context of social work practice (Beyers and Nelson 2000; Fong 1998; Fruedenburg and Gramling 1992; Kirkey and Forsyth 2001). Environmental jolts to human service industries have ripple effects as well. Managed care, block grants, devolution, privatization, welfare reform, and cutbacks in federal and state funding also require adaptations, especially in rural human services systems and programs (Egan and Kadushin 1997; Ferguson et al. 2002; Gringeri 2001; Taylor 2001).

From an ecological perspective, community adaptations to the environment may be either beneficial or harmful (Germain 1999). Relevant questions posed to social workers have less to do with the possibility of adaptation than with the consequences of choice and response. Rural communities can respond proactively to changes in the environment, or they can react passively to situations thrust upon them. As with rural families, the challenge for social workers is to strengthen their capacity to mobilize collective resources for positive collective ends — a daunting challenge, as environmental transformations over the past thirty years have significantly diminished or weakened community resources available for this purpose (Lacy 2000).

To meet the challenge rural practitioners must have knowledge and skills in rural community building; they must know what rural community building is and how to help rural communities adapt to change. At the same time they must be ever vigilant of the social worker's professional mission to promote social and economic justice in behalf of vulnerable populations in rural communities (Council on Social Work Education 2002).

Rural Community Building Defined

Rural community building is the process of developing and sustaining partnerships between groups of citizens and practitioners to bring about planned change for the public good in rural communities.[1]

Community stems from the Latin word *communis*, which implies something shared and public. When applied to a group of people, *communis* refers to something done for the common public good. *Building* reflects the reality that community is an ideal concept — always evolving, never fully attained. While community is not limited to spatial boundaries, most public goods are delivered at the local level, where the identity of a person is built around other people and their government (Boulding 1967). Since spatial boundaries are usually determined by the number of residents in a geographic area, *rural* community building is concerned with the distribution of public goods to people living in isolated rural residences, rural neighborhoods, villages, towns, small cities, and nonmetropolitan areas with fewer than fifty thousand residents (DuBord 1979).

Another key term is *partnership*. Partnership draws meaning from its derivative *partner*. In shipbuilding, the term *partner* once referred to a board or piece of timber used to buttress the deck or mast of a wooden sailing vessel — a fitting analogy here. Partners in community building join together for the common public good. Each partner is vital, but partners working together can accomplish more than any one individual alone. As with the deck or mast of a sailing ship, partners working together in community building support something above and beyond the reach of any one person, namely, common public goods such as health care, housing, education, safety, transportation, employment, and a viable economy.

The two central partners in rural community building are citizens and practitioners. A *citizen* is a person who qualifies for the status of membership in a community, with rights and obligations codified by constitutions, charters, and laws. "Ethical citizenship" refers to the citizen's right and obligation to participate as volunteers in all aspects of community life, where duty to others and communal ties overrule preoccupation with self-interest (Cooper 1991, 6). A *practitioner*, on the other hand, is a person who qualifies for membership in a socially sanctioned profession, such as social work or medicine. Citizens pay professionals to render a relevant public service, with the understanding that pecuniary gain will be secondary to the public interest (Lubove 1965). Professionals are citizens, too, of course; but, unlike volunteer citizens, they have a built-in conflict of interest — pay. Thus they tend to resist change when it threatens the way they earn a living, even when change is in the public interest (Lucas 1976). The best defense against professional tyranny in rural community building is volunteer citizen participation.

Other key terms in rural community building are *planned change* and *process*. *Planned change* refers to systematic efforts to alter conditions in a community that harm its members. Unplanned change is an unintended consequence of the forces of society or nature. Many "tactics of actions," Alinsky (1965, 52) observed, "aren't planned or engineered. Often they're irrational. They just happen." Planned change is deliberate and purposive. Practitioners are trained to use models or strategies to guide them through the *process*. Some call this process "problem solving," others "capacity building," and still others "community enhancement" (Delgado 2000). Among social workers it is called *community building*.

The process of community building usually occurs in *groups* — in this case, groups of citizens and practitioners. As Dahl (1956) observed many years ago, decision making in democratic society is a steady appeasement of relatively small groups. Although relatively deprived groups do not have as many resources to influence decision makers as well-organized groups do (Lipsky 1968), conflicts in community building are not always resolved in favor of organized groups with the most money or with political connections. Sometimes groups with few resources or political clout win the conflict (Schattschneider 1960). Leadership is needed to ensure that the interests of vulnerable population groups are well represented in the process.

The final key term in rural community building — *the public good* — is often used interchangeably with other terms such as *the common good, the public interest,* and *the common public good*. Regrettably many professional disciplines, under the professed aim of value neutrality, shy away from references to the public good. Daley and Cobb (1989, 131) note the "large element of self-deception" in this, as well as the tendency to "favor the status quo." Fortunately value neutrality does not plague our profession. Social work throughout its history has endorsed "an enlightened view of the public good," characterized by advocacy, focused primarily on the "interests of the general citizenry and of individual clients, especially the most vulnerable" (Reamer 1994, 26). Our professional mission in rural community building is to help communities adapt to environmental changes in ways that promote fairness in social arrangements and distribute resources for the realization of human and social potential, especially among vulnerable population groups (Council on Social Work Education 2002; National Association of Social Workers 2000).

Strategies

There are many different strategies of rural community building. Weil and Gamble (1995) list eight under the rubric of community practice. Here I consolidate them into three strategies that closely parallel Rothman's (1968) classic, tri-dimensional conceptualization of community interventions as locality development, social planning, and social action. I call them community planning, community development, and community organizing. The use of the adjective "community" in the three strategies discussed here is intentional, a reminder that the chief beneficiaries of the social worker's efforts should be communities and their members.

In reviewing each strategy a historical struggle may be observed between partnership-affirming and partnership-denying approaches to rural community building. Social workers endorse partnership-affirming approaches that,

- routinely engage citizens in planning, developing, and organizing community goods and services;
- apply principles of democracy and empowerment in community decision making;
- build on the strengths and assets of local people and community organizations;
- advance the common public good over narrow private, organizational, or professional interests; and
- promote social and economic justice.

Community Planning   Community planning typically involves multiple community interventions, including needs assessment, program planning, policy analysis, and evaluation. Its appeal as a strategy derives from its potential in helping rural communities adapt to change by identifying local needs, developing interagency collaborations on policy and programming, sharing local resources to avoid waste and duplication, and ensuring efficient and effective utilization of scarce local resources.

Traditionally community planning is defined as a systematic, deliberative process for determining a course of action to achieve goals based on a rational examination of all available data for implementation at some future time (Banfield 1955; Rothenberg 1961). The "rational decision-making approach" to community planning rests on this definition. This approach places community planners in key positions to use their "technical, 'value free' expertise to identify problems, assess needs, set goals, develop programs, and evaluate outcomes in terms of the degree to which they promote the public interest" (Gummer 1995, 2180). It assumes that the ability of a community to adapt to change in complex modern society depends on the quantity and quality of services rendered by professional planners (Rothman 1995).

In contrast, the "partnership approach" to community planning is political and value-based. Rational, logical decision making, based on the collection of relevant facts, is a core feature of the approach, but emphasis is placed on citizen participation in all stages of planning and decision making. Community planners using this approach empower local citizens to identify community needs, set community goals and objectives, marshal community resources, and monitor progress toward valued outcomes in public goods and services (Baum 1983; Chambers 1994; Gummer 1991).

In rural community planning, distinctions between the two approaches surface in debates over Rapid Rural Appraisal (RRA) versus Participatory Rural Appraisal (PRA). Internationally PPA has displaced RRA as the dominant approach to rural community planning, not only in health and social welfare but also in natural resources, agriculture, and economic development (Bar-On and Prinsen 1999; Chambers 1994;). Planners (typically outsiders) using the RRA approach elicit and extract information from the community. In the PPA model, rural community planners tap into the analytical capabilities and values of local people, empowering them to share and analyze their knowledge of life and local conditions, as well as to plan and act. PPA thus represents a paradigm shift from planning being carried out by professionals to planning being carried out by rural people themselves.

Few rural social workers in the United States earn their living as community planners. The ones that do usually work for the United Way, a community council, a local planning commission, a coordinating council, a consultant firm, or a local or state agency with community-planning functions (e.g., a public health department). However, many rural social workers perform these functions as part of their regular job duties in program coordination or administration, typically as agency representatives on local planning commissions, community councils, or interagency coordinating bodies. Social work faculty members from colleges and universities frequently participate in rural community planning as well, typically through needs assessment, program evaluation, and other community-based research.

The need for social work participation in rural community planning is well documented. Molnar and colleagues (2000) report considerable variability in the operating procedures, eligibility rules, and amount of food provided by private rural food pantries, resulting in uneven distribution and irregular food supplies to rural populations. They recommend that rural social workers initiate planning efforts to link rural food pantries with large, formalized food distribution systems in urban areas. Other social workers (Badger and Ackerson 1998; Van Hook and Ford 1997) report disconnects between primary care physicians and mental health practitioners in the provision of holistic care to rural populations. They call on rural social workers to resolve political and logistic barriers that block client access to integrated systems of care. Poole and Salgado de Snyder (2002) cite similar problems in pathways to care for rural Mexican families with a high migratory tradition to the United States. They cite the need for social workers and practitioners to integrate formal systems of health and mental health care with the population's local ethno-medical systems of care. Still others document the need for rural community planning in such diverse areas as school-based social services (Astor et al. 1997), long-term and community-based care (Burholt, Wenger, and Scott 1997; Carlton-LaNey 1992), violence (Singer and Singer 2002), higher education (Poole and More 2004), welfare reform (Taylor 2001), substance abuse (Hodge, Cardenas, and Montoya 2001), public social services (Martinez-Brawley and Brawley 1992), homelessness (First and Rife 1994); and HIV-AIDS prevention (Goicoechea-Balboni 1997).

The partnership approach is also well documented in social work literature. Poole (1997b) demonstrates use of this approach in planning rural school-based services. A citizen-led community planning commission, staffed by a social worker, appointed a community needs assessment committee to examine the problem of early school failure in local public schools. Following a series of focus group meetings with parents, students, teachers, school administrators, and local professionals, the committee presented a report to the commission, detailing the scope and causes of early school failure, and a plan of action to resolve the problem through a school-based prevention project. The commission adopted the report, mobilized local resources for the project, and formed a citizen-led local advisory council to monitor its implementation and outcomes. An independent evaluator later reported significant improvements in school behavior, attendance, and academic performance among student participants in the project.

Two similar examples are found in rural community health planning. Pistella, Bonati, and Michalic (2000) describe social work strategies to empower rural women as partners in the assessment of community prenatal systems. Social workers, in collaboration with community and professional leadership, used a participatory action model to obtain participant perceptions of community barriers to prenatal care. Goicoechea-Balbona (1997) demonstrates the partnership approach, too, as a health educator in a rural migrant health center. Principles of empowerment were incorporated into every aspect of the social work process in planning collaborative relationships with indigenous health care providers. The approach proved critical in understanding sociocultural health behaviors of indigenous populations, identifying barriers to health care utilization, and creating local ownership of the HIV/AIDS prevention plan.

Social workers seeking training and employment opportunities in rural community planning can search the websites of the National Association of Planning Councils, the Planners Network, the U.S. Information Agency, and the U.S. Department of Health and Human Services. Websites of international organizations that employ social workers in rural community planning can be searched as well, including International Planned Parenthood, the United Nation's High Commissioner for Refugees, and the World Health Organization. The website of CIET (Community Information, Empowerment, and Transparency) should also prove helpful. This international organization involves community people throughout the world as partners in evidence gathering, analysis, and planning, frequently to address local issues such as sexual violence, corruption, malnutrition, inadequate health care, and gender discrimination.

Community Development   A variety of nomenclatures are applied to community development as a strategy for helping rural communities adapt to change. The most common ones include asset-based development, neighborhood development, social development, community-based development, and sustainable development.

For many years the most widely accepted definition of community development was the one adopted by the United Nations in 1956:

The process by which the efforts of the people themselves are united with those of governmental authorities to improve economic, social and cultural conditions of communities, to integrate communities into the life of the nation, and to enable them to contribute fully to national progress. cited in Sanders 1970, 20)

Not surprisingly critics charged that central authorities and outside experts often used community development to impose their own goals on communities (Warren 1978). It was a ploy to get local people to do what they wanted them to do, by manipulating them into thinking a development program was their idea. Other critics claimed that many problems associated with community development were unintentional. Government officials and professional experts often hurt more than helped local communities, because they failed to engage citizens fully in the planning, execution, and evaluation of their projects (Earle and Simonelli 2000).

A third criticism of community development stems from its historical emphasis on *needs-based* rather than *assets-based* development. Kretzman and McKnight (1993) call the traditional path of community development a needs-driven dead end. *Needs-based community development* begins with community development professionals focusing on local deficiencies and problems, thereby painting images of communities as places of crime and violence, homelessness, unemployment, poverty, and dependency, and people living there as needy, problematic, and deficient. This approach to community development proceeds from the *top down* or *outside in*, with professionals assuming responsibility for virtually every phase of the process. In contrast, assets-based development proceeds from the *inside out*. Community development practitioners and external institutions assist rural communities with the process but recognize that significant development only occurs when local citizens invest themselves as partners in the effort.

Accordingly, revised definitions of community development emphasize empowerment, assets, strengths, and local ownership. "Community development," Rubin and Rubin (1986, 20) write, "involves local *empowerment* through organized groups of people *acting collectively* to control decisions, projects, programs, and policies that affect them as a *community*." In *assets-based development*, community development practitioners and local citizens work together as partners in identifying available assets, connecting them in ways that multiply their power and effectiveness (Kretzmann and McKnight 1983). Similarly the Community Services Unit (2000) of the United Nations High Commissioner for Refugees, which employs social workers, defines community development as "a process by which the efforts of the people themselves are united with those of others (i.e., the agencies), to improve the economic, social and cultural conditions of communities . . . [I]t also involves facilitating the adjustment to the changes in the new environment and the development of new structures and practices." These definitions of community development fit well with ecological, strengths, and empowerment perspectives of social work, as well as with the partnership approach to rural community building.

Chaskin et al. (2001) report some of the most impressive efforts in this direction in their book, *Building Community Capacity*. The Rural Futures Program, administered by the Glades Community-based Development Corporation (GCDC), is one such project. This project services four physically, socially, and economically isolated rural communities that have not benefited from the growth and prosperity of Palm Beach County, Florida. The mission of GCDC is "to enable people in the Glades communities to design and implement sustainable solutions to their problems and to mobilize financial, human, and political resources both within and outside the Glades, to support these efforts" (ibid., 196). Core principles include taking a holistic approach to health, economic welfare, education, and social welfare; engaging local people in designing, implementing, and evaluating projects; and building the capacity of local institutions and community leaders to sustain development.

Relatively few rural social workers in the United States are employed in community development. Those who earn their living in community development typically work in local housing and community development agencies, community centers, agricultural extension, and public health. Yet, as with community planning, many rural social workers perform community development functions as an extension of their regular job duties, when they involve citizens, local organizations, and other practitioners in the development or revitalization of human services programs and services.

Nevertheless, community development has long been recognized as a core social work strategy to help rural communities adapt to change (Ginsberg 1998; Johnson 1981; Martinez-Brawley 1980, 1981, 1982; Poole 1981; Vice-Irey 1980). Rural social workers have a rich history of developing partnerships with local citizens to strengthen political, economic, social, and human services infrastructures of rural communities (Davenport and Davenport 1979; Farley et al. 1982; Jacobssen and Sanderson-Alberson 1987; Mermelstein and Sundet 1986). Although their job duties have become more specialized in recent years (Ginsberg 1998), rural social workers frequently use community development techniques to strengthen the capacity of communities to address unmet needs of vulnerable populations. Scales and Streeter's (2004) edited volume, *Rural Social Work: Building Assets to Sustain Rural Communities*, provides examples of community development efforts initiated by rural social workers who see the proverbial glass of opportunity as half-full rather than half-empty, and local people as citizens with assets, not merely clients with problems.

Throughout the world a wide range of rural community development projects have been launched — many by social workers — to improve public goods in rural communities. Most projects engage local people as empowered partners in these efforts. Pandey (1998), a social worker, describes a reforestation project in Nepal using the partnership approach. There rural women "make major decisions concerning the design, implementation, benefit sharing, and evaluation of development projects, and project staff are catalysts and intermediaries" (342). Li and colleagues (2001) describe a similar approach by practitioners in the Women's Reproductive Health and Development Program. Community participation, local resource mobilization, and empowerment of village women are common themes in their community development efforts to improve women's health in rural China.

Another current international theme is sustainable development. The World Commission on Environment and Development (1987, 43) defines sustainable development as "development that meets the needs of the present without compromising the ability of future generations to meet their needs." Two social work contributions to the literature are noteworthy. One is Hall's (1996) article on grassroots sustainable development in Amazonia, where social workers and other outside professionals collaborate with local leaders on a variety of projects. The other is Shobert and Barron's (2004) chapter on sustainable development in a Haitian subsistence farming community. They demonstrate how social workers in the United States can pursue sustainable development in developing countries through participatory mechanisms that preserve the right of indigenous people to control the destiny of their communities.

Social workers interested in employment and training opportunities in rural community development within the United States can explore the websites of the Community Development Foundation, the Association of Community Organization and Social Administration, the Rural Social Work Caucus, the Office of Community Development in the U.S. Department of Agriculture, the Asset-Based Community Development Institute, the Enterprise Foundation, the Kellogg Foundation, the Ford Foundation, and the U.S. Department of Housing and Urban Development. International opportunities can be explored on the websites of the International Community Development Society, the U.S. Agency for International Development, the World Resources Institute, Save the Children, the International Institute for Environment and Development, the U.S. Peace Corps, InterAction, World Vision, American Friends Service Committee, World Neighbors, and the United Nation's Children's Fund.

Community Organizing   Community organizing is another strategy that social workers utilize to help rural communities adapt to change. Multiple community interventions fall under the umbrella of community organizing, including grassroots organizing, social action, union organizing, community activism, and policy action.

Power is the central concept in community organizing. As the Center for Community Change (2003) explains, community organizing is the process of

- *building power* through a constituency in identifying problems they share and the solutions to those problems that they desire;
- *identifying* the people and structures that can make those solutions possible;
- *enlisting* those targets in the effort through negotiation and using confrontation and pressure when needed; and
- *building an institution* democratically controlled by that constituency that can develop the capacity to take on further problems and that embodies the will and power of that constituency.

Community organizers divide into three camps, however. One camp, Bilken (1983) observes, tends to be doctrinaire, with a well-defined ideological view of power. Frequently identified as "New Left" organizers, for their adherence to neo-Marxist politics, these community organizers view communities as hierarchies of privilege and power, with clusters of deprived groups suffering from disadvantage or social injustice (cf. Galper 1980; Piven and Cloward 1979, 1981). They assume that interests between human service clients and community power structures are irreconcilable, and that conflict tactics are needed to realign power relationships in the community.

Conflict-oriented, this camp draws inspiration from noted community organizer Saul Alinsky. Alinksy (1969, 132) identified conflict as the principal means of getting leaders of people of deprived groups to the community bargaining table:

A People's Organization is a conflict group. This must be openly and fully recognized. Its sole reason for coming into being is to wage war against all evils which cause suffering and unhappiness. A People's Organization is the binding together of large numbers of men and women to fight for the rights which ensure a decent way of life. Most of this constant conflict will take place in orderly and conventionally approved legal procedures — but in all fights there come times when "the law spoke too softly to be heard in such a noise as war."

Community organizers in this camp are often found on the front lines of tenant strikes, civil rights marches, legal defense, labor reform, human rights campaigns, sweatshop activism, and peace and justice movements. They take a partnership-affirming stance with poor and oppressed people, but a partnership-denying stance with traditional power structures (including professional groups) that do not share their ideological views of power, human rights, and social justice. One example reported in the literature is the "kill-floor rebellion" in rural Nebraska, led by an alliance of faith-based groups and unions against a meatpacking industry that exploits Mexican, Guatemalan, and Salvadoran workers (Bacon 2002). Another is the regional, citizens-action project in the Merrimack Valley of Massachusetts, which campaigns against sweatshop manufacturers, plant closings, and pay below acceptable levels for non-unionized immigrant workers (McArthur 2001). Edelman (2000) presents several international examples in the NACLA Report of the Americas. Most involve organizing small farmers to press demands for price supports, gain access to markets, and secure legal protection against large landowners who hire gunmen to assassinate peasant leaders.

The second camp of community organizers downplays or eschews conflict in favor of consensus building through education and persuasion. These organizers agree that power is concentrated, but they believe that powerful elites and organizations can be challenged without needing to radically restructure political and economic systems. They also cite historical research which shows that conflict tactics often do not deliver what organizers promise, and that oppressed people who gain power often become oppressors themselves (cf. Warren, Rose, and Bergunder 1974). Michael Eichler, founder of the Consensus Organizing Institute, explains: "Instead of taking power from those who have it, consensus organizers build relationships in which power is shared for mutual benefit" (cited in Chaskin et al. 2001, 96). The Institute has devised a technique called "parallel organizing," in which community organizers form partnerships with both disenfranchised residents and powerful "movers and shakers" outside their community.

The third camp of community organizers displays flexibility in the use of conflict and consensus tactics. One activist, originally trained in the Alinksy school of community organizing, offers this perspective:

> The assumptions that communities organized around twenty, thirty, and forty years ago are no longer valid. When the [Industrial Areas Foundation] began organizing during the fifties and sixties, its goal was to balance asymmetric power relationships within existing inter-mediary institutions. . . . Today's organizers and leaders face dual challenges of restoring the civic culture that traditionally gave strength to intermediary institutions. . . . The work of IAF is best characterized as strengthening democratic culture through the development of civil society and citizenship — through conversation and negotiation. (Cited in Chaskin et al. 2001, 99)

For example, Oregon Rural Action (ORA) (2002) supports and encourages community organizing between diverse groups around locally identified issues. This organization strives to "create a shared vision of a healthy, democratic, and just society" but also takes action with community groups to "promote social and economic justice, agricultural and economic sustainability, and stewardship of the region's land, water, and air" (1).

Social workers have long recognized community organizing as a core strategy for helping rural communities adapt and respond to human needs. The tradition grows out of the settlement house movement and labor movements, which organized ethnic, racial, immigrant, and other disempowered community groups to pursue — often through conflict, protest, and civil action — an equitable distribution of public goods and services. Rural social workers contributed to these movements by organizing farm workers, coal miners, racial and ethnic minorities, and the rural poor (Betten and Austin 1990; Kahn 1991; Wellstone 1978). Recently their efforts have expanded to other marginalized groups that experience discrimination, including women, gays, and lesbians (cf. Lindhorst 1997; Silvestre et al. 2002).

Few rural social workers earn their living as community organizers. Those that do are usually employed by grassroots organizations, cooperatives, community action agencies, labor unions, or human rights organizations. Bilken (1983) asserts that social workers and other professionals have discarded community organizing in favor of jobs in human services agencies, thereby aligning themselves with power structures that control their salaries rather than with the interests of oppressed people. While there is truth in this argument, it is not the whole truth. Many rural social workers in traditional human services settings have learned to incorporate elements of community organizing into their regular job duties. They do this by developing leadership among stigmatized groups, linking disempowered clients to political organizations, creating powerful community action structures, and reorganizing oppressive community services delivery systems.

Silvestre et al. (2002) provide an example in their article on HIV-prevention capacity building among gay, racial, and ethnic minority groups in small cities and towns. "Stigma and marginality," they argue, "not only explain many of the barriers facing HIV-prevention programs, but also help explain the inability of some providers to reach members of racial, ethnic, and sexual minority groups" (61). They used a feminist model of community organizing to identify indigenous leaders and develop leadership among stigmatized groups. And they followed Alinsky's (1969) first action guideline for a newly organized group — that is, begin its initial foray into activism with a project free from danger and likely to result in success. Empowering stigmatized groups to have a voice in HIV policy formulation, program planning, and implementation was chosen as their first human services objective.

Another example is found in Poole's (1997a) analysis of a community-organizing project that utilized community action structures to reform preventive health services for needy children in a rural county of Oklahoma. Prior to the project, powerful elites in the county controlled local health planning and service delivery structures that systematically excluded needy children from high-quality early screening, diagnosis, and treatment services. Community action structures, initiated by social workers in a human services agency, fostered local ownership of the problem, prompted behavioral change among health providers and practitioners, and reorganized local health systems to meet the health needs of this vulnerable population. Although community organizers emphasized consensus building, they used persuasion and conflict, at critical moments of the project, to win the cooperation and support of health agency officials and local physicians.

Social workers seeking employment, training, or service opportunities in rural community organizing within the United States can search the websites of the Consensus Organizers Institute, the Policy Action Network, the Association of Community Organization and Social Administration, the National Association of Community Action Agencies, Influencing State Policy, the Center for Law and Policy, the Rural Social Work Caucus, Sweatshop Watch, the Fair Labor Association, United Students Against Sweatshops, Oregon Rural Action, the National Labor Committee, Co-op America, and the National Interfaith Committee for Worker Justice. The websites of international organizations involved in rural community organizing can be searched as well, including Human Rights Watch, the Center for International Solidarity, Feminists Against Sweatshops, the Maquila Solidarity Network, Amnesty International, the Center for Peace and Justice, and Global Exchange.

Summary

Dramatic environmental transformations over the past thirty years have significantly diminished or weakened the capacity of rural communities to provide adequate public goods for their members. To help them respond proactively to change, social workers must have knowledge and skills in community building. Although social work has a long and rich history in community building, few practitioners earn a living today in community planning, community development, or community organizing. Thus elements of these strategies must be incorporated into the regular job duties of social workers in traditional human services settings. How this is done is important. Rural communities have a long history of being harmed by professional efforts to help them adapt to change. To avoid this mistake, social workers must engage local citizens as partners in community building, consistent with empowerment and strength perspectives in social work. At the same time practitioners must remember that their professional mission is to help rural communities respond to change in ways that promote fairness in social arrangements and distribute public goods for the realization of human and social potential, especially among vulnerable population groups.

Note

1. This definition derives from my earlier writings on community building (cf. Poole 1995; Poole 2002).

References

Alinsky, S. 1965. The professional radical moves in on Rochester. *Harper's Magazine* 232, 52–59.
———. 1969. *Rules for radicals*. New York: Vintage Books.
Astor, R. A., W. J. Behre, K. A. Franvil, and J. M. Wallace. 1997. Perceptions of school violence as a problem and reports of violence: A national survey of school social workers. *Social Work* 42:55–68.

Bacon, D. 2002. The kill-floor rebellion. *American Prospect* 13:20–23.

Badger, L. W., and B. Ackerson. 1997. The case for integration of social work psychological services into rural primary care practice. *Health and Social Work* 22:55–68.

Banfield, E. C. 1955. Note on conceptual scheme. In M. Meyerson and E. C. Banfield, eds., *Politics, planning, and the public interest*, pp. 303–329. New York: Free Press.

Bar-On, A. A., and G. Prinsen. 1999. Planning, communities, and empowerment: An introduction to participatory rural appraisal. *International Social Work* 42:277–294.

Baum, H. S. 1983. Politics in planners' practice. *Journal of Planning Education* 3:13–22.

Betten, N., and M. J. Austin. 1990. *The roots of community organizing, 1917–1939.* Philadelphia: Temple University Press.

Beyers, W. B., and P. B. Nelson. 2000. Contemporary development forces in the nonmetropolitan West: New insights from rapidly growing communities. *Journal of Rural Studies* 16:459–474.

Bilken, D. 1983. *Community organizing.* Englewood Cliffs, N.J.: Prentice-Hall.

Boulding, K. 1967. Boundaries of social policy. *Social Work* 12:3–11.

Burholt, V., G. C. Wenger, and A. Scott. 1997. Dementia, disability and contact with formal services: A comparison of dementia sufferers and non-sufferers in rural and urban settings. *Health and Social Care in the Community* 5:384–397.

Carlton-LaNey, I. 1992. Elderly black farm women: A population at risk. *Social Work* 37:517–523.

Chambers, R. 1994. The origins and practice of participatory rural appraisal. *World Development* 22:953–969.

Chaskin, R. J., P. Brown, S. Venkatesh, and A. Vidal. 2001. *Building community capacity.* Hawthorne, N.Y.: Aldine de Gruyter.

Center for Community Change. 2003. *What is organizing?* Available online at http://www.communitychange.org/CO.

Community Services Unit. 2000. *Strategy for re-orientation of community services: Toward a community development approach.* Working Paper. Geneva: United Nations High Commissioner for Refugees.

Cooper, T. 1991. *An ethic of citizenship in public administration.* Englewood Cliffs, N.J.: Prentice-Hall.

Council on Social Work Education. 2002. *Educational policy and accreditation standards.* Alexandria, Va.: published by the author.

Dahl, R. 1961. *A preface to democratic theory.* Chicago: University of Chicago Press.

Daley, H., and J. Cobb. 1989. *For the common good.* Boston: Beacon.

Davenport, J., and J. A. Davenport, eds. 1979. *Boom towns and human services.* Laramie: University of Wyoming.

Davenport, J. A., and J. Davenport. 1995. Rural social work overview. In R. L. Edwards, ed., *Encyclopedia of Social Work*, 19ᵗʰ ed., Vol. 3, pp. 2076–2085. Washington, D.C.: NASW Press.

Delgado, M. 2000. *Community social work practice in an urban context: The potential of a capacity-enhancement perspective.* New York: Oxford University Press.

DuBord, A. 1979. The rural minority in an urban society: Content for social work education. Unpublished paper.

Earle, D., and J. Simonelli. 2000. Help without hurt: Community goals, NGO Interventions and lasting aid lessons in Chiapas, Mexico. *Urban Geography* 29:97–141.

Edelman, M. 2000. The persistence of the peasantry. *NACLA Report on the Americas* 33:14–47.

Egan, M., and G. Kadushin. 1997. Rural hospital social work: Views of physicians and social workers. *Social Work in Health Care* 26:1–23.

Farley, O. W., K. A. Griffiths, R. A. Skidmore, and M. G. Thackeray. 1982. *Rural social work practice.* New York: Free Press.

Ferguson, M., D. L. Poole, D. DiNitto, and J. Schwab. 2002. Raising a flag of caution in the race for community-based approaches to welfare reform: Early findings from Texas. *Southern Rural Sociology* 18:204–221.

First, R. J., and J. C. Rife. 1994. Homelessness in rural areas: Causes, patterns, and trends. *Social Work* 39:97–112.

Fong, L. 1998. Borderland poverty: The case of the Rio Grande Valley at the United States–Mexican Border. *Social Development Issues* 20:107–115.

Freudenburg, W., and R. Gramling. 1992. Community impacts of technological change: Toward a longitudinal perspective. *Social Forces* 70:937–955.

Galper, J. 1980. *Social work practice: A radical perspective.* Englewood Cliffs, N.J.: Prentice-Hall.

Germain, C. 1999. *Human behavior in the social environment: An ecological view.* New York: Columbia University Press.

Ginsberg, L. H., ed. 1998. *Social work in rural communities.* 3rd ed. Alexandria, Va.: Council on Social Work Education.

Goicoechea-Balbona, A. 1997. Children with HIV/AIDS and their families: A successful social work intervention based on the cultural specific health care model. *Health and Social Work* 23:61–69.

Gringeri, C. E. 2001. The poverty of hard work: Multiple jobs and low wages in family economies of rural Utah households. *Journal of Sociology and Social Welfare* 28:3–22.

Gummer, B. 1991. *The politics of social administration.* Englewood Cliffs, N.J.: Prentice Hall.

———. 1995. Social planning. In R. L. Edwards, ed., *Encyclopedia of Social Work*, 19th ed., Vol. 3, pp. 2180–2185. Washington, D.C.: NASW Press.

Hall, A. 1996. Social work or working for change? Action for grassroots sustainable-development in Amazonia. *International Social Work* 39:27–39.

Hodge, D. R., P. Cardenas, and H. Montoya. 2001. Substance abuse: Spirituality and religious participation as protective factors among rural youth. *Social Work Research* 25:53–61.

Jacobsen, G. M., and B. Sanderson-Alberson. 1987. Social and economic change in rural Iowa: The development of rural ghettos. *Human Services in the Rural Environment* 11:58–65.

Johnson, H. W., ed. 1981. *Rural Human Services.* Itasca, Ill.: Peacock.

Kahn, S. 1991. *Organizing.* Washington, D.C.: NASW Press.

Kirkey, K., and A. Forsyth. 2001. Men in the valley: Gay male life on the suburban-rural fringe. *Journal of Rural Studies* 17:421–441.

Kretzman, J. P., and J. L. McKnight. 1993. *Building communities from the inside out: A path toward finding and mobilizing a community's assets.* Chicago: ACTA.

Lacy, W. B. 2000. Empowering communities through public work, science, and local food systems: Revisiting democracy and globalization. *Rural Sociology* 65:3–26.

Li, V., et al. 2001. Capacity building to improve women's health in rural China. *Social Science and Medicine* 52:279–292.

Lindhorst, T. 1997. Lesbians and gay men in the country: Practice implications for rural social workers. *Journal of Gay and Lesbian Social Services* 7:1–11.

Lipsky, M. 1968. Protest as a political resource. *American Political Science Review* 62:1144–1158.

Lubove, R. 1965. *The professional altruist: The emergence of social work as a career, 1880–1930.* Cambridge, Mass.: Harvard University Press.

Lucas, J. R. 1976. *Democracy and participation.* Baltimore, Md.: Penguin.

Lusk, M. W., and D. Stoesz. 1994. International social work in a global economy. *Journal of Multicultural Social Work* 3:101–113.

Martinez-Brawley, E. 1981. *Seven decades of rural social work.* New York: Praeger.

———. 1982. *Rural social and community work in the U.S. and Britain: A cross-cultural perspective.* New York: Praeger.

———, ed. 1980. *Pioneer efforts in rural social welfare: Firsthand views since 1909.* University Park: Pennsylvania State University Press.

Martinez-Brawley, E., and A. B. Brawley. 1992. Community care in a rural patch in Cumbira, England. *Social Service Review* 66:32–49.

McArthur, L. 2001. Organizing just-in-time in the Merrimack Valley. *Social Policy* 32:43–48.

Mermelstein, J., and P. A. Sundet. 1986. Rural community mental health centers' responses to the farm crisis. *Human Services in the Rural Environment* 10:21–26.

Molnar, J., P. Duffy, L. Claxton, and C. Bailey. 2000. Private food assistance in a small metropolitan area: Urban resources and rural needs. *Journal of Sociology and Social Welfare* 28:187–209.

National Association of Social Workers. 2000. *Social work speaks: National Association of Social Workers policy statements, 2000–2003*. Washington, D.C.: NASW Press.

Oregon Rural Action. 2002. *Sowing seeds of change*. Available online at http://www.oraction.org.

Pandey, S. 1998. Women, environment, and sustainable development. *International Social Work* 41:339–355.

Pistella, C. L., F. A. Bonati, and S. L. Michalic. 2000. Rural women's perceptions of community prenatal systems: An empowerment strategy. *Journal of Health and Social Policy* 11:75–87.

Piven, F. F., and R. A. Cloward. 1979. *Poor people's movements*. New York: Vintage.

———. 1981. *The new class war*. New York: Pantheon.

Poole, D. L. 1981. *Rural social welfare: An annotated bibliography for educators and practitioners*. New York: Praeger.

———. 1995. Partnerships buffer and strengthen. *Health and Social Work* 20:2–4.

———. 1997a. Achieving national health goals in prevention through community organization: The "bottom up" approach. *Journal of Community Practice* 4:77–92.

———. 1997b. The SAFE Project: Community-driven partnerships in health, mental health, and education to prevent early school failure. *Health and Social Work* 22:282–289.

———. 2002. Community partnerships for school-based services: Action principles. In A. Roberts and G. Greene, eds., *Social Workers' Desk Reference*, pp. 539–544. New York: Oxford University Press.

Poole, D. L., and N. V. Salgado de Snyder. 2002. Pathways to health and mental health care: Guidelines for culturally-competent practice. In A. Roberts and G. Greene, eds., *Social Workers' Desk Reference*, pp. 51–56. New York: Oxford University Press.

Poole, D. L., and S. More. 2004. Asset-based community development to increase rural youth participation in higher education. In T. L. Scale and C. L. Streeter, eds., *Rural social work: Building assets to sustain rural communities*. Pacific Grove, Calif.: Brooks/Cole.

Reamer, F. 1994. Social work and the public good: Calling or career? In P. N. Reid and P. R. Popple, eds., *The moral purposes of social work*, pp. 11–33. Chicago: Nelson-Hall.

Rothman, J. 1968. Three models of community organization practice. *Social Work Practice 1968*. New York: Columbia University Press.

Rothenberg, J. 1961. *Measurement of social welfare*. Englewood Cliffs, N.Y.: Prentice-Hall.

Rubin, H., and I. Rubin. 1986. *Community organizing and development*. Columbus, Ohio: Merrill.

Sanders, I. 1970. The concept of community development. In L. J. Cary, ed., *Com-*

munity development as a process, pp. 9–31. Columbia: University of Missouri Press.

Scales, T. L., and C. Streeter. 2004. Introduction to *Rural Social Work: Building assets to sustain rural communities,* ed. T. L. Scale and C. L. Streeter. Pacific Grove, Calif.: Brooks/Cole.

Schattschneider, E. 1960. *The semi-sovereign people.* New York: Holt.

Shobert, M., and D. A. Barron. 2004. Community development in an international setting: The role of sustainable agriculture in social work practice. In T. L. Scale and C. L. Streeter, eds., *Building assets to sustain rural communities: A resource for the social work classroom.* Pacific Grove, Calif.: Brooks/Cole.

Silvestre, A., S. H. Arrowood, S. Ivery, and S. Barksdale. 2002. HIV-prevention capacity building in gay, racial, and ethnic minority communities in small cities and towns. *Health and Social Work* 27:61–66.

Singer, K., and M. I. Singer. 2002. Children and violence: Findings and implications from a rural community. *Child and Adolescent Social Work Journal* 19:35–56.

Taylor, L. C. 2001. Work attitudes, employment barriers, and mental health symptoms in a sample of rural welfare recipients. *American Journal of Community Psychology* 29:443–463.

Van Hook, M. P., and M. E. Ford. 1998. The linkage model for delivering mental health services in rural communities: Benefits and challenges. *Health and Social Work* 23:53–60.

Vice-Irey, K. 1980. The social work generalist in a rural context: An ecological perspective. *Journal of Education for Social Work* 16:36–42.

Warren, R. L. 1978. *The community in America.* 3rd ed. Chicago: Rand McNally.

Warren, R. L., S. M. Rose, and A. F. Bergunder. 1974. *The structure of urban reform: Community decision organizations in stability and change.* Lexington, Mass.: Lexington Books.

Weil, M. O., and D. N. Gamble. 1995. Community practice models. In R. L. Edwards, ed., *Encyclopedia of Social Work,* 19th ed., Vol. 1, pp. 577–593. Washington, D.C.: NASW Press.

Wellstone, P. 1978. *How the rural poor got power.* Amherst: University of Massachusetts Press.

World Commission on Environment and Development. 1987. *Our community future.* Oxford: Oxford University Press.

8 The Multiple Roles of a Rural Administrator

Nancy Lohmann and Roger A. Lohmann

The reader may wonder why a chapter on administration is included in a book dealing with rural social work practice. While there may be some differences between administration in a profit setting and administration in a nonprofit or governmental one, administration is administration, is it not?

Basic administrative procedures are the same regardless of geographic location. The same accounting standards apply to agencies in rural settings as apply to those in urban locales. The same expectations exist for accountability, sound personnel management, and other administrative tasks regardless of setting. A discussion of these basic procedures is available in a number of sources including Lohmann and Lohmann (2002). In spite of such similarities, the setting does impact the way administrative tasks are fulfilled. This chapter focuses on the ways in which the location of a social service agency in a rural area or small town influence the performance of administrative duties.

The chapter discusses primarily nonprofit social service agency administration, although some references are made to administration in federal, state, or local government agencies. The chapter also focuses on the chief executive of the agency; much of the content, however, is relevant for other employees who have administrative assignments. As the title suggests, the primary focus is on the many roles a rural administrator must perform.

A large number of rural and small town agencies are nonprofit, and most of those are small. In many agencies the administrator may be the only professional staff member and, in some instances, she or he is the *only* staff member. Both Young and Martin (1989) and Horejsi (1979) refer to the one-person social welfare agency or department often found in rural areas. Similarly data on nonprofit organizations suggest that the majority have only a few employees and budgets under $100,000.

Rural social service administrators are often not prepared for the many roles they must perform in such settings. This is because professional social work education tends to prepare students more thoroughly for direct practice roles than for administrative ones. While one chapter cannot remedy that deficit, it can alert potential rural administrators and currently struggling ones to situations they may face.

Unlike many other chapters in this book, this one does not contain extensive citations of the literature simply because very little in the literature deals with social service administration in rural areas. For example, a search of *Social Work Abstracts Plus* for articles containing "rural" and "administration" identified fifty-six articles. Most of the those identified, however, were selected because administration was in the name of an agency mentioned, such as the Administration on Aging or the address of an author or a reference to a presidential administration, such as the Clinton administration. While the relevant literature identified is cited, the chapter also draws on the authors' experiences as administrators in rural areas and on the anecdotal experiences of others.

The Multiple Roles

One of the more significant differences between the administrator in a rural or small town setting and the administrator in an urban setting is the many roles the rural administrator must typically play. The rural chief administrator, especially in a small agency, must be ready to carry out almost any of the roles associated with agency administration, often engaging in several responsibilities simultaneously. The roles may include not only all facets of direct service but also those of personnel director, budget officer and accountant, building and maintenance supervisor, volunteer coordinator, fund-raiser, client services supervisor, group developer, community organizer, public educator, policy specialist, and director of public relations and marketing. An urban agency is likely to have employees or volunteers focusing on several if not each of these roles, which allows the chief administrator to focus exclusively on administrative roles such as agency direction and vision.

The many functions that must be performed by the rural chief administrator create challenges. Few administrators, no matter how talented, are
equally effective at this wide range of roles. Thus it is likely that not all
functions are completed with an equal level of skill or expertise. Further,
there is a natural tendency to focus on those areas in which an administrator
does well because they are often more enjoyable and rewarding. That may
leave other functions of equal importance undone or neglected.

Conscientious administrators, worried about their lack of expertise in
some areas, may find themselves identifying ways to develop such expertise.
One of the authors, for example, when administering a rural multiple-county
poverty agency, completed a full year of accounting classes to overcome his
concern about his level of expertise in that area. Had he been in a more
urbanized setting, he could have simply contracted with a qualified accountant some of the functions that were of concern to him and avoided a lot of
night classes. In the rural community, however, there was no one with whom
to contract.

The administrator in a small rural agency may also feel professionally
isolated. Not only may there be few professional colleagues in the agency,
there may not even be many in the community or county. Social worker
Emily Williams, for example, reports that there are only eight social workers
within two hundred miles of her home in South Dakota (Stoesen 2002).
Both authors recall that less than two decades ago there were few MSWs
employed in the city of (then) twenty-three thousand where we teach. If the
agency is the branch of a larger program or affiliated with a regional or
national agency, colleagues in other offices may be willing to reduce the
sense of professional isolation by discussing shared concerns or problems.
Participation in professional continuing education activities may also provide
a temporary solution to feelings of professional isolation. However, the isolation the administrator feels can be difficult to remedy.

Technology may be used to reduce isolation. Membership in electronic
discussion lists can be a way to communicate with and seek advice from
professional colleagues who may be geographically distant. The National
Association of Social Workers (NASW) Rural Social Work Caucus maintains
a discussion list focused on the interests of rural practitioners. It may be
accessed at http://www.uncp.edu/sw/rural/index.html. Through that website,
other listservs focusing on rural interests may be identified.

Sundet and Cowger (1990) found isolation to be an important factor in
their study of the sources of stress for rural child welfare workers in two
midwestern states. Other factors identified in the rural literature (worker

visibility, role contamination, a paucity of resources, job status, and client affecting work) were not found to be significant contributors to stress. They indicated the following implications of their findings for rural administrators planning staff training.

> Administrators of agencies with a heavy concentration of rural person-
> nel need to realize that staff development is as much a means of al-
> leviating professional isolation and the stress associated with it as it is
> of developing or enhancing professional skills. And those who conduct
> agency-based training for rural staff need to be aware in their peda-
> gogical methodology of the need of the staff to share and interact with
> one another. (Sundet and Cowger 1990, 108–109).

This quotation by Sundet and Cowger points up another aspect of pro-fessional isolation uniquely affecting social administrators: The admonitory tone of their language ("administrators . . . need to realize") suggests that administrators are somehow grounded, secure, and fully integrated social beings not subject to the same stresses of isolation which they are being admonished to understand. Yet the reality is that not only are rural admin-istrators subject to the same isolation as other rural professionals, in many cases they carry an additional level of isolation and distance from their co-workers that simply goes with being "the boss."

But we must be careful not to overstate the matter. While such isolation can produce stress, it does not necessarily result in burnout. Rohland (2000) surveyed the executive directors of all Iowa community mental health cen-ters to assess the relationship between burnout and the work environment. The findings indicated that rurality was not associated with burnout. Rurality was defined by location in a rural county, having fewer employees, having a smaller budget, and spending more time on direct clinical care.

In the absence of professional colleagues who can reinforce the com-mitment to professional norms, it may be difficult to resist the pressures toward conformity often found in rural areas. While there would not appear to be anything inherent in rural areas that would require conformity, the experience of many is that conformity to community norms and standards is a common expectation in rural areas. The norms and standards may deal with matters of dress or sexual orientation. They may also deal with profes-sional values like confidentiality and self-determination. The administrator may find that there is pressure from local residents to reveal more about agency clients than is consistent with professional norms, or that local residents do not understand why clients are allowed to determine for themselves the actions they wish to take. It can be helpful when resisting those pressures to have professional colleagues with whom one can consult or commiserate, but such colleagues may not be available to the rural administrator.

The homogeneity of local norms and standards in a rural community may also be less accepting of diversity, at least if we are to believe the testimony of many urbanites. There may still be chauvinistic expectations about the status of women in the community that can cause difficulties when the agency administrator is a woman. Many rural communities are not racially diverse, which may cause problems in accepting someone in a position of authority who is from a racial or ethnic background different from that predominant in the community. A sexual orientation other than heterosexual may also be difficult for the local community to accept.

Another challenge for the administrator is to identify ways in which agency clients can receive supportive services that in more urbanized areas might be available from other agencies. For example, a study in Arizona found that rural older people entered institutional care at younger ages and with lower levels of functional impairment than did urban elders (Greene 1984). One explanation for this is the absence of supportive community services that would allow the rural elders to remain in their own homes. As the rural administrator and staff attempt to deal with such issues, they may find themselves feeling frustrated by the lack of realistic alternatives.

The administrator and staff may be tempted to expand the agency beyond its original mission to create the needed services. In some instances such expansion may be possible, but in other cases expansion may dilute the agency's effectiveness in meeting its mission. The agency may work with others in the community to create needed services. However, often the funding or critical mass of clients needed to support additional services may be absent. Natural helpers may be used to provide alternatives to formal organized services in rural areas (Germain and Patterson 1988). Often, however, it is not possible to create the full range of supporting services available in more urbanized areas and thus, as in the example above, clients end up in services that provide more than is needed or end up with no services at all.

Other Employees in the Rural Agency

While many rural agencies have only one or two staff members, some have multiple employees permitting a greater division of labor. Even when there is funding for staff, recruiting staff with the needed skills can be a challenge for the rural administrator.

Although the rural labor market may offer many potential employees who are not without their strengths, the potential employees may not have the level of expertise, skill, or experience sought. The budget, for example, may provide enough funding for an accountant to be hired. But the rural labor market may not yield the necessary qualified applicants. If the local labor pool only includes potential employees who have taken a few accounting courses but none with a degree in accounting and experience, the available funding alone may not be of much help.

While staff with the needed skills can in some instances be recruited from other areas, such recruitment efforts are not always successful, and can at times be locally controversial. Some research has found that salaries for comparable employees tend to be lower in rural than urban areas, reducing the appeal of an available job (Kim and Johnson 1984). Attractive as the quality of life in a rural area is to many, others uninterested in living in an area where they may feel professionally isolated or as if they are living in a fishbowl (Stoesen 2002). In many communities urban norms of specialty and training are not well understood, and importing "outsiders" to fill local jobs, when local people are unemployed, can run counter to very powerful sentiments. If recruitment efforts are successful, those recruited may find themselves, as outsiders, distrusted and ignored (Murty 1984).

Even contracting for services may not solve the expertise and experience issue. If there is no one with whom to contract, contracting is not a realistic solution to staffing problems. A study of contracting for mental health services in California found that 62 percent of the rural programs perceived no or little competition for contracts and that rural programs contracted significantly less than programs in urban areas (Libby 1997). Where contracting is a possibility, the limited number of potential contractors and resultant lack of competition may mean that the costs of contracting are greater (Ward 1992). Thus, even if potential contractors are available, the cost may make such contracting infeasible.

The available employee pool may not include the range of diversity desired in many social service agencies. Thus the administrator committed to hiring a diverse staff may find it difficult to do so.

Nonprofessional employees, like others in the community, may have difficulty understanding professional norms like confidentiality expectations and client self-determination. While such employees may have limited contact with clients, they may have routine access to files or overhear conversations about clients and not realize that divulging such information to those outside the agency is inappropriate. While orienting employees to confidentiality expectations is important in all agencies, it may be especially important in the rural agency because the size of the community is such that inappropriately revealed information may quickly circulate.

Hiring volunteers may be a way to expand the staff of a rural agency. Many urban agencies make use of formal and informal programs of volunteers that help the agency perform needed functions. If such volunteers are available in rural areas, and if they can accept the need for confidentiality and other professional expectations, they can serve as a useful enhancement to agency services.

Volunteering is certainly not a new concept in rural areas. Co-ops are found in many rural areas and the cooperative grain elevator in the rural Midwest is, after all, a group of local residents volunteering to work together to meet one another's needs. The casserole delivered to the home when there has been a death in the family also represents a form of volunteer service. The idea, however, of volunteering for a local social service agency is a less familiar one in many rural areas, and the rural administrator may need to be proactive in order to develop such a program.

The availability of potential volunteers who can assist the agency may also limit the use of volunteer programs. The limited population in rural areas reduces the pool of potential volunteers. Transportation issues may also limit the number of volunteers. The volunteers available may not have the skills needed by the agency. However, rural administrators in areas that have become attractive to professional retirees who are moving into the area may find an ample supply of skilled volunteers available and feel like they have hit gold.

Volunteers (and employees) from the area may be helpful in educating the larger community about the services the agency provides and may help legitimate the agency. The agency, even if the director is from outside the geographic area, will be seen as less foreign and more acceptable if local residents are associated with it as volunteers and employees.

Dual Relationships in the Rural Agency

One of the most troubling ethical issues for administrators and employees in rural social service agencies is that of dual relationships. This issue as it relates to direct practice is discussed in chapter 6 of this volume.

The NASW *Code of Ethics* (1999) specifies the following with regard to dual relationships:

> Social workers should not engage in dual or multiple relationships with clients or former clients in which there is a risk of exploitation or potential harm to the client. In instances when dual or multiple relationships are unavoidable, social workers should take steps to protect clients and are responsible for setting clear, appropriate, and culturally sensitive boundaries. (Dual or multiple relationships occur when social workers relate to clients in more than one relationship, whether professional, social, or business. Dual or multiple relationships can occur simultaneously or consecutively.)

It is difficult to avoid such relationships when working in a rural community. Clients may include your child's teacher, the person who repairs your car, or the uncle of the agency secretary. Even if administrators are not directly providing services to such clients, since their agency is, the chances are there will be relationships that could be classified as dual or multiple because the agency provides services..

As the *Code of Ethics* indicates, the administrator needs to establish boundaries when dual relationships occur. Those boundaries may include advising the client of the times and places that it may be appropriate to discuss the services being provided by the agency or to register a complaint about the agency. A discussion with your child's teacher, who is also an agency client, at the PTA meeting with other parents in the room is likely not appropriate, even if the teacher is comfortable with such a discussion.

The administrator also needs to help other agency employees, not all of whom may be social workers, to understand how to manage dual relationships and what they mean for client privacy and confidentiality. While the actions required may sometimes be perceived as un-neighborly in the rural area, helping employees and clients understand why such actions are needed may help mitigate the situation. Employees may also need to be coached in how to establish appropriate boundaries without appearing abrupt in interactions with clients and other community residents. Murty (1984, 19) indicates that "firmness in protecting confidentiality, once it is understood, will be respected by the community and will help to establish trust."

The administrator and employees may find themselves disclosing more personal information than would be the practice in a more urbanized setting. It may sometimes be difficult to establish when such disclosure represents acceptance of and conformity to local norms and when it crosses a professional boundary. Murty (1984, 18), in writing about rural mental health workers, indicates that such disclosures are often expected and, even if not expected, given the "fishbowl" nature of rural life, may be difficult to avoid. She suggests responding to one or two personal questions and then returning to the purpose of the meeting.

While the *Code of Ethics* deals with relationships with clients and former clients, the rural administrator needs to recognize the personal relationships between other service providers that may influence service delivery. Dunlop and Angell (2001, 44), when reporting on rural coalition building, describe the family and friendship ties that affected the involvement and cooperation of participating coalition agencies in rural Ontario. In the instance that they describe, those relationships facilitated service delivery. They indicate that the existence of previous ties was reported by participants to have contributed to the development of coalitions. In other instances, past or current relationships may help explain resistance to cooperation.

Fund-raising

With declining federal support for social services and state budget cuts in state-supported programs, obtaining the funding needed to support social service agencies has become much more difficult. Social service agencies, even small ones, are increasingly turning to fund-raising in an effort to supplement declining public funds.

Fund-raising in rural areas and small towns can include applying to a United Way for funding. Of the fourteen hundred United Way organizations, approximately three hundred are in what are defined as metropolitan areas, leaving perhaps as many as eleven hundred in nonmetropolitan areas. In some cases these are what are usually thought of as small, rural communities. In other cases they may be regions where rural areas are part of a larger United Way service area. As a result, many rural areas are covered by a United Way. Often the United Way covers one or more counties including both rural and more urbanized areas.

Participation in a United Way can enhance the agency's budget. In a county or multicounty United Way area, there may be a redistribution effect with resources raised in the more urbanized areas supporting both urbanized and rural services. Such redistribution can be helpful to the rural area because local resources may be more limited.

Several surveys have found that most Americans report charitable giving; churches are included among those organizations to whom gifts might be made. Keirouz (1998) summarizes the findings from polls of Indiana residents, Michigan residents, and a Gallup poll of the United States conducted for the independent sector. In Indiana approximately 90 percent of those polled reported a charitable donation, with most (64 percent) reporting a donation of less than $500 in the previous year (2). Almost half the Indiana sample of 505 residents lived in small towns or rural areas (6), but differences in donation rates or levels are not reported by residence. In Michigan 85 percent reported making a donation, and the Gallup poll found that 69 percent reported donating (3).

Other than the fund-raising that occurs through the local churches and the special fund-raising drives that may be undertaken to send the high school band to a major parade, fund-raising in rural areas is generally limited. This is partly because resources are usually inadequate. Chapter 2 in this book deals with rural poverty, and the data provided illustrates the reduced financial resources generally found in rural areas. It is often assumed that the resources are too limited even to make fund-raising efforts worthwhile.

Assuming that donation rates in rural areas roughly parallel the findings in rural Indiana, Michigan, and the national poll, it may be that possibilities for fund-raising (or philanthropic sufficiency) are greater in rural areas than is generally thought (Lohmann 2004). It will likely be even more difficult for rural agencies to obtain private funds to substitute for the public funds that may have supported social service programs in the past than it will be for urban agencies to do so. However, rural administrators should assess the possibilities for fund-raising in their area rather than assuming that such efforts will be unsuccessful.

Seeking grants is be another form of fund-raising that can help assure the survival or expansion of rural social services. Friedman (2003) reports Kraybill and Labao's (2001) finding that the grant-seeking capacity in rural areas is lower than in urban areas. In particular, they found that only 28 percent of the rural counties employed grant writers. While specialized grant writers are not essential for obtaining grant funding, having personnel dedicated to seeking and applying to possible funding sources may enhance the chances of success.

Several sources that focus on rural services identify possible funding sources. The website of the Rural Social Work Caucus includes information about organizations to which one might apply for grant funding at

http://www.uncp.edu/sw/rural/grant.html. The Rural Assistance Center website (http://www.raconline.org) includes a searchable funding database. That
site also provides links to other sites with funding information. The rural
administrator may find it helpful to consult sites such as these when writing
grants.

Do the Regulations Fit?

One of the challenges rural administrators routinely face is that of fitting
programs to rural settings that were designed primarily with urban populations in mind to rural settings. The regulations and requirements associated
with those programs sometimes require actions or support that may not be
available in rural areas. Rowley (2003b, 1) indicates the following with regard
to this problem:

> As for help, many federal programs offer little at all. In communities
> where population density is sometimes measured in square miles per
> person, not the other way around, meeting eligibility requirements can
> border on the impossible. Serve at least 100 people to get funding?
> Not where there are only 200 people, period. Cough up $50,000 in
> matching contributions to get a grant? How, in a community of 500
> dependent on low-wage jobs and surrounded by federal land that pays
> no property tax?

Temporary Assistance for Needy Families (TANF), the program that replaced the welfare program Aid to Families with Dependent Children
(AFDC), illustrates some of the problems associated with making programs
work in rural areas. Because TANF allows states to exercise more choice in
the services offered to recipients than AFDC did, it could provide some of
the flexibility needed to adapt to the circumstances of rural areas. Many
states have also provided increased flexibility to localities, further increasing
the likelihood of programs designed to meet local needs. In addressing this,
Kaplan (1998) indicates, "There can be positive effects of devolution for
rural areas, such as having the ability to create programs sensitive to rural
needs and the involvement of community residents in planning to meet their
needs" (2).

However, the possible positive effects will not be fully realized so long as
certain federal requirements remain. A Rural Policy Research Institute

(RUPRI) editorial (Rowley 2003a) indicates that Bruce Weber, chair of the RUPRI Welfare Reform panel, suggests that three changes are needed to ease the application of TANF requirements in rural areas.

1. Recognize that jobs are less plentiful in rural areas and allow greater flexibility in work requirements that takes into account the reduced supply;
2. Modify time limits so that rural recipients have enough time to find jobs, given their access to fewer jobs and support systems;
3. Address the lack of licensed child-care in rural areas. (1)

The basic nature of these changes illustrates the problem rural administrators may face. Even a program intended to be more flexible than the usual social service program sometimes has requirements that are difficult to meet in rural areas. The chances that programs not intended to provide flexibility would not fit well are significant.

The regulations associated with other social service programs may also be difficult to meet in rural areas. State and other publicly funded programs sometimes specify the number of units of service to be provided per staff member or the qualifications of staff or some other factor thought to be associated with effective and efficient service delivery. Some of those requirements may be difficult to meet in the rural office.

The cost per capita of the services provided illustrates the problem that a rural or small town agency may have in meeting external requirements. The cost per capita for services tends to be higher in rural areas than in urban areas because of the lower population density (Friedman 2003). Transportation costs may also add to the cost per capita. Waltman et al. (1991) suggest that there are several factors that result in higher unit costs. These include (1) the need to be involved in community activities in the rural environment, thus reducing the time for delivering billable services; (2) the costs of a one-clinician office with much of the overhead expenses for one person that could be distributed among several people in a larger office, and (3) lower client fees because of the local market. When competing for funding, rural agencies may find themselves disadvantaged by the higher unit cost of services and may find that available funding is awarded to more cost-efficient agencies. They may also find that existing funding is threatened because the agency is perceived as less efficient.

Pugh (2003, 74) reports that in some areas of the United Kingdom the added cost of service delivery in rural areas is recognized by providing additional funds. He indicates that the Wiltshire social services department has introduced a "premium" for rural services and provides 3 percent more funding for such services. However, he adds that this is not common. We are unaware of a comparable practice in the United States. The greater costs of service delivery in rural areas usually works to the disadvantage of rural agencies rather than resulting in increased funding.

Conclusion

What, then, makes rural administration special? It is not the nature of the basic administrative tasks, which tend to be the same regardless of the geographical location of a social service agency. It is the context that makes rural administration special and worth commenting on.

A part of the context is the typical size of the agency found in rural areas and small towns. Most agencies are small, which means a limited division of labor, often requiring the chief administration to carry out a range of administrative roles which may well include providing clinical services at the same time. This variety in the work life of the administrator can be very challenging. Although it may be energizing, stimulating, and rewarding, it can also be overwhelming as the administrator tries to complete duties for which she or he has little preparation and perhaps even less interest.

Another part of the rural context is the challenge of recruiting other employees for the agency. The skills and experience sought may be less available in rural areas than in more urbanized ones. Both administrator and staff need to cope with a sense of professional isolation once employed in the rural agency.

For both administrator and staff, dual relationships may prove problematic. Such relationships are difficult to avoid. Local community members may view some of the professional actions required by the NASW *Code of Ethics* as un-neighborly and unfriendly.

Fundraising and the application of federal, state or other guidelines in the local environment may also be challenging. With declining governmental funding of social services, fund-raising has become increasingly important in assuring the survival of agencies. The limited population in a rural area and lower income levels may make fund-raising even more difficult than it is in an urban area. Guidelines for program administration are often written with urban settings in mind. Applying them while remaining sensitive to local needs and expectations may be difficult.

Given some of the challenges that are found in rural agencies, one may wonder why social workers and other human services professionals would want to work in such an agency. The reasons are varied. For some, it may be a way to return home or to a place very much like home. For others, the quality of life in a rural area may be the primary appeal. Another part of the attraction may be the chance to live in a place where the terrain is beautiful, where one can get to know one's neighbors, where the crime rate is low, and where one can eat vegetables grown by a neighbor or perhaps homegrown.

For others, the needs of local residents and limited services to meet those needs represent a professional challenge. The chance to help build services in places where they are needed makes social workers feel they are making a difference. While the song indicates that if you can make it in New York, you can make it anywhere, the rural administrator knows that one's ability to identify resources in a rural area that will meet a client's needs is probably a stronger indication that you can make it anywhere. If a social worker can pull together needed resources in rural America, doing so in a more urbanized area may seem like child's play.

Another motivation may be the chance to be a renaissance person, given the many roles the rural administrator must play. Wonderful as it may be to specialize in one relatively narrow area of practice, many find great satisfaction in being able to carry out a range of duties that sometimes appear unrelated and that require different skills.

For still others, working in a rural setting affords the opportunity to build on the strong mutual support networks that exist in many communities. It is a chance to become part of that network and to become accepted and trusted by others in the community. The coordination of services may prove easier to accomplish because it can be achieved through personal relationships.

The growth experienced in many rural areas over the last two decades means that rural administrative practice will continue to be an area of opportunity for the social worker interested in administration. As the NASW policy statement on rural practice indicates, such practice "remains a vibrant and challenging area of practice" (Stoesen 2002, 3).

References

Dunlop, J. M., and G. B. Angell. 2001. Inside-outside: Boundary-spanning challenges in building rural health coalitions. *Professional Development: The International Journal of Continuing Social Work Education* 4 (1): 40–48.

Friedman, P. 2003. Meeting the challenge of social service delivery in rural areas. *Welfare Information Network Issue Notes* 7 (2). Online at http://www.finance-projectinfo.org/Publications/meetingthechallengeIN.htm. Retrieved June 30, 2003.

Germain, C.B., and S. L. Patterson. 1988. Teaching about natural helpers as environmental resources. *Journal of Teaching in Social Work* 2 (1): 73–90.

Greene, V. L. 1984. Premature institutionalization among the rural elderly in Arizona. *Public Health Reports* 99 (1): 58–63.

Horejsi, G. A. 1979. Social work in a small hospital. *Health and Social Work* 4 (3): 9–25.

Kaplan, A. 1998. Rural challenges: Barriers to self-sufficiency. *Welfare Information Network: Issue notes* 1 (14): 1–12.

Keirouz, K. S. 1998. *Public perceptions and confidence in Indiana nonprofit organizations.* Indianapolis: Indiana University Center on Philanthropy. Online at http://www.philanthropy.iupui.edu/INPoll98report.pdf. Retrieved June 25, 2003.

Kim, P.K.H., and D. P. Johnson. 1984. Sexism and ruralism: A reality for clinical social workers in community mental health centers. *Journal of Social Service Research* 8 (1): 61–70.

Kraybill, D., and L. Labao. 2001. Changes and challenges in the new millennium. *Rural County Governance Center Research Report* 1.

Libby, A. M. 1997. Contracting between public and private providers: A survey of mental health services in California. *Administration and Policy in Mental Health* 24 (4): 323–338.

Lohmann, R. A. 2004. Lindblom County: How diversity influenced philanthropic sufficiency. In D. Fauri, E. Netting, and S. Wernet, eds., *Cases in macro social work practice*, pp. 105–123. Boston: Pearson/Allyn and Bacon.

Lohmann, R. A., and N. Lohmann. 2002. *Social administration.* New York: Columbia University Press.

Murty, S. A. 1984. Developing the trust of a rural community. *Human Services in the Rural Environment* 9 (2): 15 – 20.

National Association of Social Workers. 1999. *Code of Ethics.* Online at https://www.socialworkers.org/pubs/code/code.asp. Retrieved June 24, 2003.

Pugh, R. 2003. Considering the countryside: Is there a case for rural social work? *British Journal of Social Work* 33 (1): 67–85.

Rohland, B. M. 2000. A survey of burnout among mental health center directors in a rural state. *Administration and Policy in Mental Health* 27 (4): 221–237.

Rowley, T. 2003a. Forward, not backward, with welfare reform.. *Rural Policy Institute Weekly Editorial.* Online at http://www.rupri.org. Retrieved June 30, 2003.

———. 2003b. Life on the frontier is tough: Policies make it tougher. *Rural Policy Institute Weekly Editorial.* Online at http://www.rupri.org. Retrieved June 30, 2003.

Stoesen, L. 2002. Rural social workers embrace challenge. *NASW News* 47 (9): 3.

Sundet, P. A., and C. D. Cowger. 1990. The rural community environment as a stress factor for rural child welfare workers. *Administration in Social Work* 14 (3): 97–110.

Waltman, G. H., J. C. Czarnecki, and E. J. Miller. 1991. The rural branch office: Planning, marketing, commitment. *Families in Society: The Journal of Contemporary Human Services* 72 (1): 45 – 50.

Ward, J. D. 1992. Privatization and political culture: Perspectives from small cities and towns. *Public Administration Quarterly* 15:496–522.

Young, C. L., and L. D. Martin. 1989. Social services in rural and urban primary care projects. *Human Services in the Rural Environment* 13 (2): 30–35.

Scott's Run Settlement House, Osage, West Virginia.

"I do not like to move into town." Vesta Clark on the Kingwood Pike, approximately thirty minutes from the Morgantown Mall, Morgantown, West Virginia.

"The quality of my life here is fantastic. We have a sweet, wonderful spring that has made us incredibly healthy over the time we've lived here. No electric or running water has been the hardest part of surviving. Having no refrigerator and only $2 to $3 per person a day for food makes one a very creative cook. No lights in my camping trailer kitchen means I cook in semidarkness." Dianna Clark on the Kingwood Pike, approximately thirty minutes from the Morgantown Mall, Morgantown, West Virginia.

"When I was working, I kept the car going. Now I can't even get it fixed. The car was like part of my family. If I get a job it would have to be one that I could walk to." Donna Snider, Fairmont, West Virginia.

"I know that computers are a big part of Andy's life with his panic disorder. He doesn't make friends very easily. I wait at home during the day; if he gets upset at school, I have to go get him. Sometimes I can hear him yelling in the background. I had to quit work — I was only getting minimum wage — in order to get a medical card for my son. I have no medical insurance for myself. He's seeing the psychiatrist, and it is $150 a session and the testing was $1,200." Donna Snider, Fairmont, West Virginia.

"When we got Patience he weighed thirty-five pounds and we brought him home in a burlap sack in the back of the Subaru. He is our dinner this winter." Larry Rexroad, Reevesville, West Virginia.

"This is a quiet day at Morgantown Health Right, usually the whole waiting room is filled. Patients are sometimes standing and even sitting on the stairs. These people are waiting to get medication refills or may have provider appointments. I'm pulling charts for patients getting medications. Working here can give you great satisfaction from helping people in need. Other days are stressful when patient are more demanding." Diana Berry, Office Assistant, Morgantown, West Virginia.

"There are no guarantees in this life. Circumstances change, jobs go away, marriages end, mental or physical illness invade. There are so many causes of poverty. Anyone can find themselves in a position of not having. No one of us has reason for arrogance.

"The people who visit Health Right come with lives, families, histories, and reasons for being. They are not some subclass of citizen, and in a more reasonable society there would not be such division between the haves and have-nots, the bodies which deserve and receive health care and the bodies which do not.

"I am happy to be able to work in the environment of Health Right, which supports our humanity, equality, and right to be alive in our bodies and keep on dancing." Kathy Furbee, RN, CRC, Clinical Director, Morgantown Health Right.

Morgantown,
West Virginia.

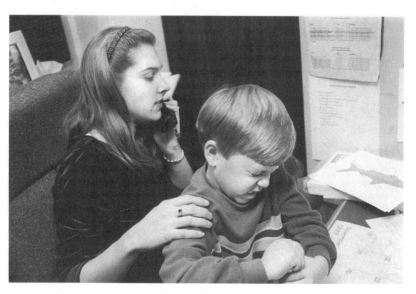

"Being a single mom, working and going to college is certainly a juggling act, but it leads me to a better life and that's how I keep going." Wendy, Morgantown, West Virginia.

"It is very important to me that people know, despite my psychiatric diagnoses, that I am a loving parent. Many people have misconceptions and stereotypes concerning people with psychiatric diagnoses. They believe that we can't take care of ourselves, let alone other people. . . . We are lucky to pull in $750 a month. From the money, we pay $360 for rent, $85 for a phone, $45 for cable television, and $165 for a used car and auto insurance, which we need if we are going to try to find work. We have to have one person in the family working so we can buy diapers, extra formula, clothes, and gas, as well as money for cleaning supplies and other necessities." Stephanie, Morgantown, West Virginia.

"My wife left, she came in one day and took everything. My daughter has decided it's her job to take care of me." Dan, Reevesville, West Virginia.

"I look at the pictures and ask the Lord to keep them. I thank the Lord for keeping us well. I thank the Lord for my aunt who is seventy-nine years of age and able to see her fifth generation." Mama Jean, Fairmont, West Virginia.

"I was an organizer of the Socialist Party in Pakistan and a lawyer. My view was that our destiny is possible only to the maximum extent, when we have an international, global society. A society with no religion, no nationality, one global human family being the salvation of humanity. Such a society is only possible when we surround ourselves with reason and logic. For these beliefs, I feared persecution from certain Islamic groups and the government. I sought political asylum in USA. I was unable to survive on my art work. Presently I am working at the stadium as a laborer. American society is scientifically advanced and highly conscious. It is my dream to enter American politics and positively affect our global destiny." Irfan Saeed, Morgantown, West Virginia.

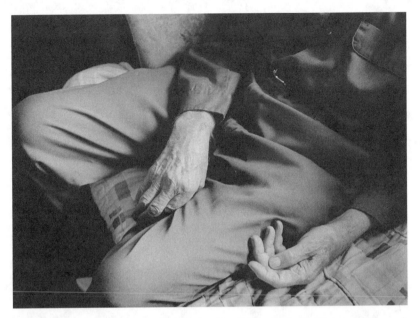

"My husband has worked the woods, the railroad, made chestnut rails and posts. Built a road until his leg got broke. He has worked all his life, eighty-four years." Mrs. Edgar Freeman, Philippi, West Virginia.

"My husband and I get social security and black lung. We both have breast cancer. The medicine Tamorifen cost $20 a month. In the winter the market doesn't make much." Mrs. Edgar Freeman, Philippi, West Virginia.

Part III

Client Populations and Fields of Practice

9   Services for the Chronically Mentally Ill in Rural Areas

Elizabeth Randall

This chapter presents a review of mental health service delivery in rural areas for the chronically mentally ill (sometimes called the severely and persistently mentally ill). At present, county and state community mental health systems remain the most important providers of these services, although the influence of managed care has significantly altered the design of most service systems and funding streams (Bazelon Center for Mental Health Law 2001a). Incremental reductions in public funding over a span of ten or fifteen years, staff downsizing, and insufficient attention to available research providing relatively clear guidelines concerning best practices have seriously undercut progress in achieving meaningful psychosocial rehabilitation for large numbers of chronically mentally ill persons (Kane and Ennis 1996; U.S. Department of Health and Human Services [USDHHS] 1999). Services that are contracted out and other cost containment efforts may also limit efforts at rehabilitation (Manning, Lieu, and Stoner 1999). Also problematic in many areas recently has been fragmentation of service systems, as contracts for particular services are carved out under capitated arrangements to subgroups of disparate, specialized providers, resulting in uncoordinated treatment plans and seemingly arbitrary inconsistencies in client eligibility. According to client advocacy groups, a number of these and other related factors have recently come together to trigger an alarming reduction in the overall quality of care (Bazelon Center for Mental Health Law 2001b; Mowbray, Grazier, and Holter 2002). In Washington State, for example, "this static funding picture has created a general sense that the mental health system in Washington State is underfunded, and some Regional Support Networks have expressed concerns about whether or not they can continue to operate the mental health system in their catchment area" (State of Washington Department of Social and Health Services [DSHS] 2002, 18). Underserved populations are estimated to be on the rise, and some commentators and policy analysts have presented data which suggest that increases in homelessness and criminal justice caseloads may correlate directly with reduced access to public mental health care over a decade or more (Mowbray and Holter 2002). In rural areas these problems are compounded by the relative disenfranchisement and political invisibility of populations at risk, as well as by the chronic dearth of trained providers and service system infrastructure in many rural areas (Beeson et al. 1998). These difficulties are particularly acute in some of the most remote regions, where local services may be strictly limited to natural or familial helping, or no services at all may exist.

Funding

Shifts in patterns of funding, going back decades but reaching a crisis level within the last ten years, have provided the impetus for the most dramatic changes in the delivery of services for the persistently mentally ill in rural areas. The push for deinstitutionalization and for the return of the chronically mentally ill to community life, resulting in the establishment of community mental health centers (CMHCs) in 1963, was originally funded entirely at the federal level. Many of these centers were staffed with a preponderance of social workers, and social workers are still the largest professional group of mental health care providers in the United States (Mowbray and Holter 2002). As these centers began to evolve, however, and as it became clear that many chronically ill clients intermittently required both inpatient and outpatient treatment, this administrative system created significant problems with coordination of care between the CMHCs and the state hospitals, which were funded and structurally organized separately. To improve coordination of care, state mental health agencies in the 1970s began to assume responsibility for the administration of both levels and systems of care under a geographical system of catchment areas, and to shoulder a larger share of fiscal responsibility for services. In 1981 federal support was further reduced with a switch from categorical program grants to a block grant system (Arons 2000). States tended to respond with increased reliance on Medicaid, a health insurance program for low-income citizens funded in part with federal dollars, as a source for reimbursement for a variety of services for the persistently mentally ill. This trend began to reach crisis proportions in the early to mid-1990s, and by 1995 Medicaid spending rose to exceed the rate of inflation by a factor of 5 (Mark et al. 1998). Currently Medicaid remains the primary funding source for treatment of chronic mental illness in rural areas, many of which are home to a preponderance of low-income or indigent residents (Fox et al. 1999).

The sharp increase in the use of managed care oversight for Medicaid reimbursed services has arisen directly from these circumstances, out of an urgent necessity to control runaway costs. For the most part, managed care plans have helped states and regions needing to balance budgets, but at a high cost in terms of service restriction, to the point where only a fraction of the need may be met in many areas. Psychiatric rehabilitation services are categorized as "optional" under federal policy guidelines to the states that are accustomed to determining how Medicaid funds are to be used (National Alliance for the Mentally Ill [NAMI] 2002a). The great majority of states have no legislative mandate against denial of services for mentally disabled citizens in need of care (Milbank Memorial Fund 2000). In most states, while some categories of service are mandated, there is no law which dictates that these services must be funded to meet the entire extent of the need (Bazelon Center for Mental Health Law 2001b). Some crucial rehabilitative services, for instance, may exist only in the form of a model or pilot program, and rural areas are often the last to draw, or be selected, for implementation of such innovative models (Arons 2000).

Other unintended consequences of Medicaid managed care plans that have been reported are fragmentation and decentralization of services, as services are delivered on the basis of what is reimbursable, instead of what is needed, and too much focus is placed on acute care while rehabilitation services, including housing and job training, are neglected. According to the Surgeon General's Report on Mental Health, "housing ranks as a priority concern of individuals with serious mental illness" (USDHHS 1999, 292), while the unemployment rate among persons with serious and persistent mental illness has been estimated to be as high as 90 percent (National Institute on Disability and Rehabilitation Research 1992). An additional barrier is created when there is such a heavy emphasis on Medicaid reimbursable services that clients who are ineligible for a Medicaid card, yet have serious disorders, are shut out of the public system entirely (Milbank Memorial Fund 2000). Others have pointed out that, in order to prevent undesirable restrictions on consumer eligibility, Medicaid managed care contracts must be written with careful attention to language, so that customary definitions of the "medical necessity" of treatments are rewritten to allow for the "social necessity" or "psychosocial necessity" of services beyond the most basic (Milbank Memorial Fund 2000). Where particular care of this kind is not taken to translate the biomedical parameters of the managed care industry into terms that make sense within mental health systems, additional barriers to access may result.

Services

A series of biomedical advances in the effectiveness of the psychoactive medications used to treat severe mental illnesses have meant that the great majority of persons affected by these disorders will receive significant benefit from psychopharmacologic case management, including an initial diagnostic interview; a trial on medication; and regular checkups to monitor their ongoing response to treatment. The majority of these steps are usually completed by mental health professionals, most often social workers (Peterson et al. 1998). These workers report their findings to physicians, who in turn write the needed prescriptions. The face-to-face contact the client may have with the physician is usually relatively brief, insuring fiscally efficient use of the physician's time. These procedures are fundamental to the effective community maintenance of most chronically mentally ill persons but are generally insufficient toward goals of significantly improved functionality or more complete psychosocial rehabilitation for those affected (Harrow et al. 1997).

According to the PORT (Patient Outcomes and Research Team) study on the treatment of schizophrenia, sponsored by NIMH, best practices with the chronically mentally ill should also include pyschopharmacology; supportive therapy; life skills training; vocational rehabilitation; family education; and family therapy, as needed (Lehmann and Steinwachs 1998a). Other authors note that optimal outcomes depend not only on the availability of these preferred services, but also on the quality and integration of the overall system of service delivery (Goldman 1998). Service systems that have been shown to be especially beneficial and effective are often grounded in particular values, including consumer empowerment and attentiveness to differing regional and cultural variables (Mowbray et al. 1997). One of the most promising integrated models is Assertive Community Treatment, or ACT, which is a multidisciplinary team approach offering around-the-clock intensive case management/therapy; manageable caseloads (approximately 1:10 staff/client ratio); coordinated treatment planning; substance abuse services for the dually diagnosed; and, sometimes, consumer representation on teams (Stein and Test 1980; Lehman and Steinwachs 1998b). Studies indicate that this model can significantly reduce the need for "revolving door" admissions to psychiatric hospitals, while improving residential stability and community involvement for otherwise hard-to-treat consumers, such as the homeless mentally ill (Mueser et al. 1998).

Unfortunately the majority of persons with chronic mental illness receive services that do not conform to PORT guidelines (Lehman and Steinwachs 1998b). Additionally seventeen states have no ACT programs, and those states that do generally offer only a few (Bazelon Center for Mental Health Law 2001b). Best practices for the persistently mentally ill are especially scarce in rural areas:

> Mental health services in rural areas cannot achieve certain economies of scale, and some state-of-the-art services (e.g., assertive community treatment) are inefficient to deliver unless there is a critical mass of patients. Informal supports and indigenous healers assume more importance in rural mental health care (USDHHS 1999, 92).

Telemedicine, or telepsychiatry, has been touted as a promising means of increasing access to psychiatric care for rural residents, whose cases may be followed by physicians in far-off urban centers, using digital technologies such as web-based streaming video. Some active programs in a number of areas in the country routinely incorporate these methods into practice (Kostreski 1997). For the most part, however, the potentialities of these innovative methods have gone unrealized, as a lack of technological support services and inadequate technology infrastructure have proven just as challenging as the lack of trained mental health providers in many areas. Werner and Anderson (1998, 1290) conclude that "telepsychiatric services are technologically feasible, pragmatically difficult, and not economically supportable at this time." The influences of technology on rural social work practice is the subject of chapter 3 in this volume.

Increased integration of mental health services and primary care, as a means of improving availability of basic treatment for the severely mentally ill, is a growing trend (Lambert and Hartley 1998; Kiesler 2000). Medicaid managed care plans in some rural areas specify that mental health care be provided by primary care physicians (Milbank Memorial Fund 2000). In

these settings mental health workers on staff can fulfill roles that are analo-
gous to their traditional roles in public mental health centers, assisting with
case management and various psychosocial services. For instance, the addition of master's level mental health professionals to the staff in a rural
primary care practice under a Medicaid managed care plan yielded several
important advantages, such as increased consumer access, coordination of
care, and reduction in stigma (Van Hook and Ford 1998; Resnick and Tighe
1997). Among mental health professionals, social workers grounded in an
ecological approach to practice are especially well positioned to work with
primary care physicians in rural areas and to promote further growth in this
trend. Lukens (2002, 84) recently described an ecologically informed social
work framework for mental health care with particular applicability to rural
practice:

> By promoting alliance and collaboration among providers, care recip-
> ients, and their supports, a kind of safety net or circle of influence and
> care is created. The greater the number of people in the informal
> support network and community who recognize signs of trouble and
> understand risk and protective factors and needs for people confronted
> by differing forms and degrees of mental illness or challenges in living,
> the more opportunity for early identification and help-seeking. This
> in turn reinforces the paradigm shift from "us versus them" to a shared
> model of care emphasizing mutual learning, respect and exchange
> among professionals, clients, and their social supports.

In 1997 an Ad Hoc Rural Mental Health Provider Work Group was convened by the Center for Mental Health Services, a unit of the U.S. Department of Health and Human Services. Among the recommendations included in the Work Group's Final Report were that federally funded rural
health programs should be required to cover mental health and substance
abuse services, and that incentives should be developed "that stimulate rural
health networks to incorporate mental health and substance abuse services
as part of their responsibility" (USDHHS 1997, 16). Mental health care
supervised by a physician with specialization in psychiatry would be pref-
erable for all who need it. In rural areas, however, mental health services
within a primary care model may provide invaluable help in filling gaps that
have been widening for decades as the publicly funded "safety net" for the
psychiatrically disabled continues to unravel (NAMI 2002b).

Stigma

Stigma, or a prejudicial attitude toward a group of persons that is "deeply discrediting" (Goffman 1963), remains a huge obstacle working against psychologically safe access to mental health services in rural areas. In regions of low population density, where "everybody knows everybody," it is often difficult or impossible for consumers to maintain privacy, if they are seen in a treatment center lobby or waiting area, or if their vehicles are spotted in the parking lot. If staff who may be "talking shop" in public areas are overheard, listeners are far more likely to be able to glean identifying information about clients, even if no names are used. According to Johnsen et al. (1997, 68):

Also interesting is the extent to which perceptions of the importance of crime as an issue may be related to perceptions of the importance of mental illness. To some extent, news coverage featuring the mental status of persons accused of crime exaggerates the link between mental illness and crime. However, in many rural areas, the linkage between mental health and the criminal justice systems is apparent even to casual observers. Because many rural areas lack effective continua of services, first-line service response to persons undergoing psychiatric crises often involves response by local sheriffs or police. In addition, in the rural areas studied, the county sheriff was heavily involved transporting persons with mental illness to state psychiatric facilities, further reinforcing the link between mental illness and crime. Finally, involvement of the courts in making involuntary commitment decisions provides additional evidence to the public of such linkage. These visible juxtapositions link mental illness and crime (and thereby reinforce stigma) in the eyes of the general public.

In addition to this perceived association between criminality and mental illness, stigmatization of the psychiatrically disabled may be reinforced by intermittent outbreaks of visible, socially disfiguring symptoms and behavioral abnormalities, giving rise on the part of neighbors or onlookers to intense fears of the unknown, and to shunning behavior. This community response can contribute to a vicious cycle that may leave consumers with no support resources, other than fellow consumers. However, in rural areas, where numbers are few, distances great, and programs nonexistent, consumers may have no realistic way to gather for peer support. This confluence of untoward environmental factors has the potential to impact the prognosis negatively for these rural consumers.

On the other hand, it has been pointed out that conditions vary dramatically from one rural or frontier area to another, and that attempts to describe disparate rural populations in similar terms may be erroneous (Wagenfeld and Geller 1998). It is also possible that, in some rural areas,

> there is an inclusiveness in rural communities and a tolerance for individual differences that provides for a strong integration between persons with mental disorder and the social fabric of the community. There is a connectedness available to persons with mental disorder living in rural communities that stands in sharp contrast to the isolation and abandonment that many of their counterparts experience in urban settings. (Beeson et al. 1998, 88)

Thus it may be seen that while privacy, confidentiality, and anonymity are often nearly impossible to maintain for rural consumers of mental health services, the degree to which these challenges contribute either to stigma and isolation — or, paradoxically, to a community response of protective envelopment — may vary widely from one rural area to another.

Considering Rurality, Race, and Ethnicity

Nearly half the populations of Alaska Natives and American Indians (42 percent) live in rural areas. African Americans also include significant numbers of rural residents (about 15 percent), especially in the South. Additionally 9 percent of Hispanic Americans are rural residents (Rural Policy Research Institute 2000). Separate and apart from issues that pertain to rural residency, planning effective mental health service systems for these populations should take into account biopsychosocial factors that are unique to each group from a racial, ethnic, or cultural perspective. While data are not available to pinpoint the numbers of persons who are both members of a cultural minority group and also rural residents, it seems clear that the interaction of having both characteristics puts persons with mental illness among these groups doubly at risk of being underserved (USDHHS 2001).

These populations are seriously underrepresented in most seminal outcome studies on treatment effectiveness and epidemiology. As a result, it is not possible to pinpoint the extent to which findings that are widely considered state of the art in mental health research may safely be generalized to these populations. However, some tentative inferences may be drawn.

Alaska Natives and American Indians, for instance, may express symptoms of mental and emotional disequilibrium in ways that do not correspond to categories in the *Diagnostic and Statistical Manual-IV* (*DSM-IV*) (Nelson and Manson 2000). Significant cultural and linguistic barriers to accurate diagnostic understanding may result if typical assessment techniques are used with these populations. Recommended modifications to standard interviewing procedures include (1) inquiring about the patient's cultural identity; (2) exploring cultural explanations for symptoms; (3) including an environmentally relevant understanding of stressors; (4) examining cultural elements in the clinician-patient relationship; and (5) forming a culturally congruent plan (American Psychiatric Association [APA] 2000).

Schizophrenia, the most epidemiologically significant category of severe and persistent mental illness, occurs in about 1 percent of the population worldwide, and there is no reason to suppose that this rate is significantly different for Native Americans. However, based on patterns of service utilization, it would appear that the chronically mentally ill among Native Americans are severely underserved, even taking into account the strict limits on access to mental health care available to most. Cultural barriers may include the extreme scarcity of Native American mental health professionals, mistrust, lack of insurance, cultural norms against seeking help from the outside, and insufficient attention among mental health professionals to spirituality as a healing force (USDHHS 2001).

African Americans are diagnosed with schizophrenia at higher than expected rates; receive higher average dosages of neuroleptic (antipsychotic) medication than whites, yet are more sensitive to side effects; and metabolize medications differently (Neighbors et al. 1989; Trierweiler et al. 2000; Segel et al. 1996; Walkup et al. 2000). Unfortunately these findings are not widely incorporated into common standards of practice. Compared to other populations, mental health care for African Americans is provided disproportionately in general hospital emergency rooms. Cultural factors blocking access to specialized care are significant for this population. According to the Office of the Surgeon General (USDHHS 2001, 63–64):

African American attitudes toward mental health care are another barrier to seeking mental health treatment. Mental illness retains considerable stigma, and seeking treatment is not always encouraged. One study found that the proportion of African Americans who feared mental health treatment was 2.5 times greater than the proportion of whites

(Sussman et al. 1987). . . . Practitioners and administrators have sometimes failed to take into account African American preferences in formats and styles of receiving assistance. African Americans are affected especially by the amount of time spent with their providers, by a sense of trust, and by whether the provider is an African American (Keith 2000). Among focus group participants, African Americans were more likely than whites to describe stigma and spirituality as affecting their willingness to seek help (Cooper-Patrick et al. 1997).

Of the three largest minority groups in the United States, Hispanic Americans represent the fastest-growing minority population but have the smallest percentage of rural residents, around 9 percent (Rural Policy Research Institute 2000). Here, again, specific data are unavailable to pinpoint numbers of persons who are Hispanic, rural, and in need of mental health services. However, it is estimated that this population is also significantly underserved by the nation's mental health care system. This problem is particularly acute for immigrants and refugees of Hispanic origin (USDHHS 2001). Hispanic Americans make up about 12 percent of the nation's population as a whole but comprise nearly 25 percent of the uninsured (Kaiser Commission 2000; Brown et al. 2000). Language difficulties represent another significant barrier to care, as 40 percent of Latinos in the 1990 Census reported limited English-speaking competency. While the exact number of Spanish-speaking mental health professionals is unknown, it is estimated to be highly inadequate to the need. A recent survey identified a ratio of only 29 Latino mental health professionals for every 100,000 Latino residents, whereas, for whites, the ratio was 173 mental health professionals for every 100,000 persons (Center for Mental Health Services 2000).

Thus it may be seen that, in addition to traditional impediments to adequate treatment in rural areas, rural minorities with persistent mental illness may also face additional, often insurmountable obstacles to effective care. Many receive care only when in crisis, and then according to standards of practice that are not culturally congruent. For most, continuity of care is completely out of reach.

Conclusions and Recommendations

Program designs insuring safety and greatly improved quality of life for the majority of the chronically mentally ill are possible, based on present knowledge. Public policy, however, is moving away from assumption of responsibility for the care and humane maintenance of these consumers. Although less visible to those in seats of power, the effects of these trends are even more deleterious in rural areas than in population centers, yielding catastrophic consequences for the majority of rural residents with severe and persistent mental illness. In a recent study by Hendryx (2000, 70), it was found that "80% of rural persons with the poorest mental health received no services from a mental health specialist." For many of these affected persons, the only remaining "safety net" has become the criminal justice system, and populations of mentally ill persons in custody because of aberrant behaviors, or crimes of desperation motivated by unmet basic needs, are on the rise (Mowbray and Holter 2002).

For social work practice, continued progress toward the integration of mental health services with primary care in rural areas may be the most promising short term solution. Social workers with training in mental health often develop great skill in recognizing patterns of dosage and response among clients being followed on a course of psychopharmacologic treatment. General medical practitioners with limited experiential knowledge of psychiatric symptoms, when faced with decisions involving clinical management of cases, often appreciate opportunities for consultation and collaboration with social workers who possess this expertise, (H. Chou, personal communication, 2002). In addition, social workers with mental health training are in a unique position to offer needed assistance with case management, client and family psychoeducation, and supportive counseling (Dixon, Adams, and Lucksted 2000).

The most widely endorsed long-term solution combines advocacy with consumerism (Frese 1998; Bjorklund and Pippard 1999; Arons 2000; Mowbray et al. 2002). The history of mental health reform over the last fifty years demonstrates that there has been considerable public sympathy, in the abstract, for the plight of the psychiatrically disabled, "coming to the fore when the plight of affected individuals periodically penetrates societal consciousness" (Mowbray et al. 2002, 168). Times have changed, and in the current economic climate mustering the political will for a return to public funding for mental health services regardless of diagnostic category or severity is unlikely. However, a recognition of responsibility for those most in need, the severely and persistently mentally ill, remains strong in public awareness. In a study on public opinion about proposed mental health parity legislation, Hanson found that "respondents . . . are more protective of inpatient care — presumably reflecting concern about persons who have catastrophic mental health care needs" (1998, 1066). At present, evidence of decline in service availability and quality could be used to bring awareness once again "to the fore," yielding the possibility of further reforms but this time based on a better understanding of effective community care for consumers.

Consumerism and family advocacy have been described as perhaps the most potent untapped forces to be used as leverage for change, "essential for the success of rural mental health" (Beeson et al. 1998, 93). For these efforts to succeed, however, numerous rural community resources must be unified and mobilized in unique and creative ways. Families and consumers cannot do this alone:

> Helping patients, consumers, and survivors to become better able to respectfully re-enter society can be a frustrating task, but increasingly this task is being seen as more central to the mission of those in the caring professions. Hopefully, mental health professionals will increasingly see themselves as much as advocates as they are scientists and practitioners in the work of serving persons with serious mental illness. (Frese 1999, 247)

To help prepare students for the political and economic realities impinging on contemporary practice, social work educators might do well to create greater opportunities for experiential learning of integrated skill sets, incorporating practice, policy analysis, and community organization. A generalist approach to field placement might be a possibility, as an alternative to models of field education based on a distinction between direct and indirect practice.

For students interested in working with the severely mentally ill in rural areas, a partial or complete dismantling of conceptual barriers separating the health and mental health fields of practice might be useful. Training in principles of business and economics would be of great benefit to many students at the master's level. In the present climate, training in grant writing might enhance the efficacy of students entering practice more than an advanced course in policy or practice would.

For most social workers interested in social justice for disadvantaged persons, increased mental health literacy may be indicated: "Our review indicates that coverage of mental health and mental illness in major social work journals seems relatively insignificant, suggesting that social work researchers are not sufficiently oriented to this topic" (Mowbray and Holter 2002). As the professional group with the largest representation among all mental health workers, and the most broadly based, value-based, and inclusive approach to practice, social work bears the largest share of responsibility for ameliorating the suffering of the chronically mentally ill in rural areas.

References

American Psychiatric Association. 2000. *Diagnostic and statistical manual of mental disorders.* 4th ed. Washington, D.C.: American Psychiatric Association.

Arons, B. 2000. Mental health services in rural America. *Vital Speeches of the Day* 66:369–371.

Bazelon Center for Mental Health Law. 2001a. *Recovery in the community: Funding mental health rehabilitative approaches under Medicaid.* Washington, D.C.: Bazelon Center for Mental Health Law.

———. 2001b. *Disintegrating systems: The state of states' public mental health systems.* Washington, D.C.: Bazelon Center for Mental Health Law.

Beeson, P. G., et al. 1998. Rural mental health at the millenium. In R.W. Manderscheid and M. J. Henderson, eds., *Mental health, United States 1998* (DHHS Publication No. SMA) 99–3285, pp. 82–98. Washington, D.C.: U.S. Government Printing Office.

Bjorklund, R. W., and J. L. Pippard. 1999. The mental health consumer movement: Implications for rural practice. *Community Mental Health Journal* 35:347–359.

Brown, E. R., V. D. Ojeda, R. Wyn, and R. Levan. 2000. *Racial and ethnic disparities in access to health insurance and health care.* Los Angeles: Center for Health Policy Research and the Henry J. Kaiser Family Foundation.

Center for Mental Health Services. 2000. *Cultural competence standards in managed care mental health services: Four underserved/underrepresented racial/ethnic groups.* Available online at http://www.mentalhealth.org/publications/allpubs/SMA00–3457/.

Cooper-Patrick, L., et al. 1997. Identification of patient attitudes and preferences regarding treatment of depression. *Journal of General Internal Medicine* 12:431–438.

Dixon, L. B., C. Adams, and A. Lucksted. 2000. Update on family psychoeducation for schizophrenia. *Schizophrenia Bulletin* 26:5–20.

Fox, J. C., et al. 1999. Mental disorders and help seeking in a rural impoverished population. *International Journal of Psychiatry in Medicine* 29:181–195.

Frese, F. 1998. Advocacy, recovery, and the challenges of consumerism for schizophrenia. *Psychiatric Clinics of North America* 21:233–249.

Goffman, E. 1963. *Stigma: Notes on the management of spoiled identity.* Englewood Cliffs, N.J.: Prentice-Hall.

Goldman, H. H. 1998. *Organizing mental health services: An evidence-based approach.* Stockholm: Swedish Council on Technology Assessment in Health Care.

Hanson, K. 1998. Public opinion and the mental health parity debate: Lessons from the survey literature. *Psychiatric Services* 49:1059–1066.

Harrow, M., J. R. Sands, M. L. Silverstein, and J. G. Goldberg. 1997. Course and outcome for schizophrenia vs. other psychotic patients: A longitudinal study. *Schizophrenia Bulletin* 23:223–231.

Hendryx, M. S. 2000. Rural adults with poor mental health: Findings from a national study. *Texas Journal of Rural Health* 19:67–73.

Johnsen, M. C., et al. 1997. Rural mental health leaders' perceptions of stigma and community issues. *Journal of Rural Health* 13:59–70.

Kane, C. F., and J. M. Ennis. 1996. Health care reform and rural mental health: Severe mental illness. *Community Mental Health Journal* 32:445–462.

Kiesler, C. A. 2000. The next wave of change for psychology and mental health services in the health care revolution. *American Psychologist* 55:481–487.

Kaiser Commission on Medicaid and the Uninsured. 2000. *Health centers' role as safety net providers for Medicaid patients and the uninsured.* Washington, D.C.: Published by the author.

Kostreski, F. 1997. Telepsychiatry gains in popularity. *Clinical Psychiatry News* 25:1–2.

Lambert, D., and D. Hartley. 1998. Linking primary care and rural psychiatry: Where have we been, and where are we going? *Psychiatric Services* 49:965–967.

Lehman, A., and D. M. Steinwachs. 1998a. Translating research into practice: The Schizophrenia Patient Outcomes Research Team (PORT) treatment recommendations. *Schizophrenia Bulletin* 24:1–10.

Lehman, A., and D. M. Steinwachs. 1998b. Patterns of usual care for schizophrenia: Initial results from the Schizophrenia Patient Outcomes Research Team (PORT) Client Survey. *Schizophrenia Bulletin* 24:11–20.

Lukens, E. P. 2002. Promoting community awareness to enhance mental health. *Health and Social Work* 27 (2) :83–86.

Manning, W. G., C. Lieu, and T. J. Stoner. 1999. Outcomes for Medicaid beneficiaries with schizophrenia under a prepaid mental health carve-out. *Journal of Behavioral Health Services and Research* 26:442–450.

Mark, T., et al. 1998. *National expenditures for mental health, alcohol, and other drug abuse treatment, 1996.* Rockville, Md.: Substance Abuse and Mental Health Services Administration.

Milbank Memorial Fund. 2000. *Effective public management of mental health care: Views from states on Medicaid reforms that enhance service integration and accountability.* New York: Milbank Memorial Fund.

Mowbray, C. T., K. L. Grazier, and M. Holter. 2002. Managed behavioral health care in the public sector: Will it become the third shame of the states? *Psychiatric Services* 53:157–170.

Mowbray, C. T., and M. C. Holter. 2002. Mental health and mental illness: Out of the closet? *Social Service Review* 76:135–179.

Mowbray, C. T., et al. 1997. Enhancing vocational outcomes for persons with psychiatric disabilities: A new paradigm. In S. W. Henggelar and B. A. Santos, eds., *Innovative approaches for difficult-to-treat populations*, pp. 311–350. Washington, D.C.: American Psychiatric Press.

Mueser, K. T., G. R. Bond, R. E. Drake, and S. G. Resnick. 1998. Models of community care for severe mental illness: A review of research on case management. *Schizophrenia Bulletin* 24:37–74.

National Alliance for the Mentally Ill. 2002a. *States in crisis: The grassroots response: Medicaid overview*. Available online at www.nami.org/cgi-bin/printfyl.cgi?/states/medicaidoverview.html.

———. 2002. *Accountability in the federal mental health block grant program*. Available online at www.nami.org/update/unitedaccount.html.

National Institute on Disability and Rehabilitation Research. 1992. *Strategies to secure and maintain employment for people with long-term mental illness*. Washington, D.C.: Published by the author.

Neighbors, H. W., J. S. Jackson, L. Campbell, and D. R. Williams. 1989. The influence of racial factors on psychiatric diagnosis: A review and suggestions for research. *Community Mental Health Journal* 24:301–311.

Peterson, B. D., J. West, M. A. Tanielian, and H. A. Pincus. 1998. Mental health practitioners and trainees. In R. W. Manderscheid and M. J. Henderson, eds., *Mental health, United States 1998*, DHHS Publication No. SMA 99–3285, pp. 8214–8246. Washington, D.C.: U.S. Government Printing Office.

Rural Policy Research Institute. 2000. Rural by the numbers: Information about rural America. Available online at www.rupri.org/policyres/rnumbers/demopop/demo.html.

Resnick, C., E. G. and Tighe. 1997. The role of multidisciplinary community clinics in managed care systems. *Social Work* 42:91–98.

Segel, S.P., J. R. Bola, and M. A. Watson. 1996. Race, quality of care, and antipsychotic prescribing practices in psychiatric emergency services. *Psychiatric Services* 47:282–286.

State of Washington Department of Social and Health Services. 2002. *Strategic plan 2004–2009*. Mental Health Division, Health and Rehabilitative Services Administration. Available online at www.wa.gov/dshs/mentalhealth/index.html.

Stein, L. I., and M. A. Test. 1980. Alternative to mental hospital treatment. Part 1, Conceptual model, treatment program, and clinical evaluation. *Archives of General Psychiatry* 37:392–397.

Sussman, L. K., L. N. Robbins, and F. Earls. 1987. Treatment-seeking by black and white Americans. *Social Science and Medicine* 24:187–196.

Trierweiler, S. J., et al. 2000. Clinical attributions associated with diagnosis of schizophrenia in African American and non–African American patients. *Journal of Consulting and Clinical Psychiatry* 68:171–175.

U.S. Department of Health and Human Services. 1997. *Mental health providers in rural and isolated areas: Final report of the ad hoc Rural Mental Health Provider Work Group.* Rockville, Md.: U.S. Department of Health and Human Services, Substance Abuse and Mental Health Services Administration, Center for Mental Health Services.

————. 1999. *Mental health: A report of the Surgeon General.* Rockville, Md.: U.S. Department of Health and Human Services, Public Health Office, Office of the Surgeon General.

————. 2001. *Mental health: Culture, race, and ethnicity–a supplement* to *mental health: A report of the Surgeon General.* Rockville, Md.: U.S. Department of Health and Human Services, Public Health Service, Office of the Surgeon General.

Van Hook, M. P., and M. Ford. 1998. The linkage model for delivering mental health services in rural communities: Benefits and challenges. *Health and Social Work* 23:53–60.

Wagenfeld, M. O., and J. Geller. 1998. Mental health services in frontier areas: Models of services delivery and special populations. *Rural Community Mental Health* 24:19–20.

Walkup, J. T., et al. 2000. Patients with schizophrenia at risk for excessive antipsychotic dosing. *Journal of Clinical Psychiatry* 61:344–348.

Werner, A., and L. E. Anderson. 1998. Rural telepsychiatry is economically unsupportable: The Concorde crashes in a cornfield. *Psychiatric Services* 49:1287–

10 Directions in Rural Mental Health Practice

Elizabeth Randall and Dennis Vance Jr.

This chapter offers a review of contemporary social work practice in rural mental health. including recent sweeping revisions in service planning driven by cost containment imperatives and managed care, the characteristics of rural cultures, profiles of rural consumers, characteristics of rural mental health workers, and the influence of computers and interactive technology on rural mental health practice. Several issues are discussed pertaining to service planning, such as the need for generalist practice in rural areas, the problem of dual relationships, and the need for collaboration with primary care clinics and other community resources. Policy and practice considerations for urgently needed improvements to the current highly threatened state of mental health practice in rural areas are described, as well as recommendations for social work education.

Funding: The Dominant Concern in Contemporary Mental Health Practice

Social work practice in the field of mental health has been shaken to its foundations all over the country within the last decade by a number of profound changes in the philosophy and implementation of service delivery systems. Most of these changes have been driven by legislative interests in health care finance reform, designed to curtail seemingly out-of-control escalation in health care costs, which are estimated to have risen from about 6 percent of domestic spending in 1965 to about 15 percent, and growing, in 2000 (Davis 1998). Costs associated with mental or behavioral health have been seen by economists and policy makers as particularly culpable. According to Cummings (1996), mental health costs rose out of all bounds in the late 1980s, becoming one of the single most important sources of health care cost inflation.

In retrospective analysis of these trends, however, others have found support for the view that over-utilization of inpatient care, which has always been far more costly than less restrictive outpatient alternatives, contributed to these inflationary pressures to a markedly disproportionate degree. The draconian solutions of restricting access to care, and other initiatives favored by the managed care industry, have since been applied as broadly as possible. Yet it has frequently been noted (Arons 2000; Fortney et al. 2001) that managed care is primarily effective as an urban model, ill suited for implementation in rural areas, where the inpatient services that managed care companies have been especially bent on restricting are, in any case, largely unavailable. Thus many rural mental health practitioners feel that they, and their clients, have been unjustly penalized for excesses committed elsewhere. The following section contains a brief review of the changes in rural mental health service delivery systems resulting from pressures for cost containment and the influences of managed care.

The Influence of Managed Care on Rural Mental Health Services

The federal Community Mental Health Centers Act of 1963 provided significant financial support for deinstitutionalization, which was designed to return persons with mental illness (many of whom had spent most of their lives in mental health facilities) to community living, with the help of outpatient case management and supportive services. However, the community mental health centers established in response to this legislation also offered an array of comprehensive services, including individual counseling and family treatment, for persons with issues or symptoms in the mild to moderately severe range. In rural areas these centers were often the only providers of mental health and substance abuse treatment for vast regions. More recently, as increasing concerns arose about the rate of inflation of health care costs in general, and mental health care in particular, a trend away from public funding for these services began to emerge, first seen in the Omnibus Budget Reconciliation Act (OBRA) in 1981, and culminating in a shift to the Alcohol, Drug Abuse, and Mental Health Services Block Grant program, with the OBRA, in 1998. These legislative changes shifted financial responsibility for services inexorably from federal sources to states, which responded increasingly with restrictions on services offered, until only those persons deemed most in need were eligible (Wagenfeld et al. 1997; Christian-Michaels et al. 1999). These clients were generally the chronically mentally ill; or, those with "serious and persistent mental illness"(SPMI) (McDonel et al. 1997). Arons (2000, 370) notes that "the trend today is away from subsidizing social services with public funding."

At present, other populations with diagnoses of somewhat less severity or chronicity (sometimes called "the worried well") are being forced more and more often to choose providers funded through private insurance or else to offer direct payment based on a sliding fee scale. In rural areas, often disproportionately impacted by poverty and unemployment, this has increasingly come to mean that large populations of citizens with non-psychotic diagnoses have no access to mental health services at all because of a lack of private insurance and an inability to pay out-of-pocket for services at a rate that is acceptable to providers in private practice.

Managed care oversight, cropping up first in health care coverage offered through Health Maintenance Organizations (HMOs) and employer-subsidized health insurance plans in the 1980s, is currently widespread in publicly funded mental health facilities and programs as well. In West Virginia a managed care contract was awarded in 2000 to provide utilization review and best-practices recommendations for all behavioral health services receiving Medicaid funding. Similarly Iowa implemented a statewide Medicaid managed care system in 1995 (Rohland 2000), and Hall et al. (2002) have described structural changes in service delivery systems because of the influences of a managed care environment in rural Iowa. In 2000 thirty-one states had Medicaid managed care plans for public mental health system clients (Milbank Memorial Fund 2000), and it is estimated that changes in service delivery systems will continue in this direction until managed care oversight is in place for all services except those provided by clinicians in private practice that may be paid for out-of-pocket by clients with the means to negotiate an acceptable fee schedule (Corwin 2002). The only remaining exceptions to this trend are services supported by grant funding, research funding, the military or the Veteran's Administration, and faith-based or other charitable organizations (Voss 1996). Yet such services as these, scarce even in more populated regions, can only meet a tiny fraction of the existing need in rural areas. In a recent study of 646 rural households by Fox et al.

(1999), it was found that nearly one-third included residents who screened positive for treatable mental health disorders. In all, it is estimated that at least 15 million rural residents struggle with treatable mental health disorders, and suicide rates in rural areas have surpassed those of more urban parts of the country (Roberts, Battaglia, and Epstein 1999).

A Gloomy Picture; Some Rays of Hope

It seems impossible to escape the conclusion that mental health practice in social work has been decimated by these fundamental changes in the way services are planned and funded. At present, anecdotal evidence reverberating throughout the field suggests that workers are often discouraged and frustrated, and that morale is low in comparison with the pre–managed care era, when workers had more autonomy and ability to exercise clinical judgment without giving up expectations of reasonable compensation. Some experience a sense of outrage or "compassion fatigue" from repeatedly having to bear tidings to clients of the severe limits on the "help" they can hope to receive. As programs are cut, and workers are transferred or let go, administrators are also subject to stress and burnout in their work. In a recent study in Iowa, a largely rural state, Rohland (2000) found that "anticipation of staff downsizing was related to increased burnout and decreased job satisfaction among mental health center directors" (234). Rohland also pointed out that "job satisfaction and burnout among rural mental health providers can influence the access, availability, and adequacy of mental health services that are provided through rural mental health delivery systems" (235–236).

Some of the changes are so new that it is impossible to know, as of this writing, what the ultimate fallout will be. For instance, Shawnee Hills, the largest mental health center in West Virginia until 1999, was reduced to the third largest in 2000, when indebtedness, owing in part to mandated paybacks imposed by Medicaid for disallowed services under newly implemented rules of managed care, forced it to sell off properties and programs. These measures, however, were not sufficient, and the agency filed for bankruptcy and ceased operations in the spring of 2002, its clients and services turned over, under the oversight of the West Virginia Department of Health and Human Resources, to a mixed bag of largely privatized providers (Davia 2002).

If one takes a long enough view, the influences of managed care on mental health practice are not altogether negative; some may have been very necessary, and others may come to prove their worth retrospectively. Reports of satisfaction with certain influences of the managed care environment on service integration may be found. For instance, Wayman (2000) points to the development within a managed care environment of collaborative arrangements with almost all regional providers as well as natural helpers in a rural area. This is seen as an aid to service planning efficiency and effectiveness that is of benefit to consumers. Corwin (2002, 6) points out the advantageous positioning of social workers within the more competitive managed care environment: "Knowledge of community resources and skills in utilizing formal and informal support networks will also be valuable in the new managed care environment, as coordination of services and a greater emphasis on client and community strengths and resources will be utilized as cost containment measures." Others point to possibilities for new and potentially satisfying roles for mental health workers in rural areas under managed care. One such role might be that of combined liaison, psycho-educational consultant, trainer, and facilitator to area health professionals, community leaders, peace officers, and clergy, toward goals of improving responsiveness to the mental health needs of citizens at the community or regional level (Chalifoux et al. 1996; Weigel and Baker 2002; Wayman 2000).

In 2000 a group of state and local health care administrators were convened in a collaborative effort sponsored by the nonprofit Milbank Memorial Fund and the Bazelon Center for Mental Health Law to garner their impressions of the effects of managed care on service delivery. Among benefits identified were (1) decreased use of inappropriate care; (2) an expanded array of services in some areas; (3) more flexibility in service delivery; and (4) more goal-directed treatment.

Unfortunately some of these benefits lack relevance in rural areas, where specialized services cannot be supported and increased directiveness may be less culturally appropriate. Additionally potential problems with managed care were also identified by this task group, including (1) unintended incentives created within risk-based contracts to underserve people with serious disorders; (2) an undue focus on acute rather than long-term care; (3) billing and paperwork difficulties; (4) inconsistencies across regions; and (5) difficulties serving non-Medicaid clients (Milbank Memorial Fund 2000).

With all this taken into account, the majority opinion among social workers in rural mental health seems to be that managed care has been more of a liability than a blessing, and most appear to hope rather fervently that "the pendulum will swing" back in the direction of fewer restrictions on access to services, as well as expanded lengths and intensities of allowable services for many diagnostic categories. How likely is this?

In an address to the National Advisory Council on Rural Health, Arons (2000) pointed out that Congress had approved a 23 percent increase in the Mental Health Block Grant for fiscal 2000, the first major increase in a decade, saying, "We in mental health care are riding an unprecedented wave of support right now, generated largely by a strong economy and a world at peace" (371). Tragically this climate was overshadowed within a year by a potentially protracted (if undeclared) war on the nation's elusive terrorist enemies, as well as economic recession. At present, these reversals appear to have yielded a domestic climate of markedly increased conservatism, which does not argue auspiciously for further increases in federal allocations for mental health in rural areas. According to the *Surgeon General's Report on Mental Health*, "Rural America is shrinking in size and political influence. . . . As a consequence, rural mental health services do not figure prominently in mental health policy" (U.S. Department of Health and Human Services [DHHS] 1999, 92).

Some hope may be seen arising from increased interest in mental health parity legislation. In April 2002 West Virginia became the thirty-fourth state to pass a law designed to abolish differing and generally more restrictive financial limits on lifetime insurance coverage for mental illness, as compared to medical and surgical diagnoses. These states have seen fit to pass legislation of their own, stemming from dissatisfaction with the federal Mental Health Parity Act of 1996, seen as a compromise measure that was weak and easy to evade by such means as capping numbers of visits, raising copayments, contesting the "medical necessity" of services, and so on, instead of imposing dollar limits on eligibility as such. How effective these new laws will prove to be at the state level is not fully known at present (Morrison 2000). Meanwhile, efforts continue on the part of some members of Congress to introduce and urge passage of stronger and more effective parity legislation at the federal level but, as of this writing, without success (Cox 2002).

Arons (2000, 370–371) points to the need for consumer advocacy in order to achieve further breakthroughs:

> It is clear by now that the government is not going to hand consumers all the services they need, and their decision to take the initiative has been — literally — a healthy one. But it is also clear that the government can do far more for them than it was inclined to do without

prompting. The needs of mental health consumers are legitimate needs, their motives are admirable, and the ultimate beneficiary of their progress is all of us.

Social work skills such as advocacy and community organization are badly needed to help end the suffering and loss of quality of life resulting from unmet need for mental health services in rural America. However, social workers interested in rural practice also need significantly increased skills in identification and development of alternatives to public funding (see also, below, "Conclusions and Recommendations").

Characteristics of Rural Consumers

While every person is an individual, several characteristics commonly seen among rural mental health consumers are described in the literature. Rural mental health patients are more likely to be poor and uninsured, and to suffer from other medical problems in addition to compromised mental health (Hendryx 2001; Abraham et al. 1993; Voss 1996). Robertson and Donnermeyer (1997) noted that rural mental health patients are 15.7 percent more likely to be uninsured than the national average. Rural mental health patients may also be older, consonant with 2000 U.S. Census figures indicating that 21 percent of elderly Americans live in rural areas (U.S. Census Bureau 2004). In addition, they may also be more depressed (Chalifoux et al. 1996). Rural residents show more disinclination to seek treatment for mental health or substance abuse (Robertson and Donnermeyer 1997; Greeno et al. 1999), even when they are contacted and provided with referrals, suggesting the need for new ways to remove barriers to treatment (Fox et al. 1999). This disinclination to seek help, combined with transportation problems, stigma, cost, and so forth, often results in rural patients not receiving mental health services. One study reported that as many as 80 percent of rural people with poor mental health did not obtain services from mental health specialists (Hendryx 2001). When rural people with mental illness do seek help, they often turn first to clergy (also see, below, "The Need for Collaboration with Primary Care Providers and Other Groups") (Wayman 2000; Voss 1996). Rural mental health patients may also have other problems that contribute to their mental illness, particularly substance abuse (Robertson and Donnermeyer 1997). In short, for rural residents with emotional or behavioral health challenges, many obstacles hinder access to care.

Rural Cultural Values

While it cannot be said that rural culture is monolithic, there are values of rural cultures in general that distinguish them from those of more densely populated parts of the country, such as self-reliance, caution in relationships with "outsiders," and increased emphasis on family and friendship ties ("He's a good guy — I've knowed him all my life"; "She's married to my second cousin"; "I'll vouch for him — he's a member of my church"). Fatalism, attunement with nature, conservative beliefs, respect for hard work, and strong religious values have also been identified as rural values, particularly in Appalachia and in the southeast (Chalifoux et al. 1996; Weigel and Baker 2002; Voss 1996). Self-reliance, in particular, is such a strong value in some rural cultures that seeking help for emotional concerns is commonly seen as an act of weakness or desperation (Voss 1996), and several authors have noted that the problem of stigma remains greater in rural areas (Beeson et al. 1998; Johnson et al. 1997) than in metropolitan areas, where group-supported self-discovery and principles of recovery are more likely to be viewed as courageous.

It is particularly important, then, for rural mental health workers to understand their communities, especially if their training reflects immersion in cultural assumptions from the greater urban society (Chalifoux et al. 1996; Arons 2000). For instance, among Native American peoples, being a good kinsman may be more important than academic achievement or "success" as it is commonly understood by the dominant culture. According to Cross et al. (2000), culturally competent interventions with Native Americans may need to be compatible with a relational worldview:

> The relational worldview, sometimes called the cyclical worldview, finds its roots in tribal cultures. It is intuitive, non-time oriented, and fluid. Balance and harmony in relationships is the driving principle of this thought system, along with the interplay of spiritual forces. The relational worldview sees life in terms of harmonious relationships; health or wellness is achieved by maintaining balance between the many interrelating factors in one's circle of life. Every event relates to all other events regardless of time, space, or physical existence. Health exists only when all elements are in balance or harmony. (20)

Cultural competence requires openness, respectful curiosity, and a willingness to learn more than one teaches, since rural values may differ widely from one region of the country to another.

The Need for Generalist Practice

The trend in health care, including the field of mental health, is toward greater specialization in training and practice. However, because of limited staff, expansive catchment areas, and resource scarcity, the rural mental health worker needs to be a generalist (Beeson et al. 1998). A rural mental health worker may find herself consulting with primary care physicians on the relative efficacy of medications (Roberts, Battaglia, and Epstein 1999); working at the individual, family, and community levels; and attempting types of treatment she has only read about. However, in many instances, she may be forced to "make do" or to improvise the closest approximation she can devise to a state-of-the-art intervention, as an alternative to allowing a client simply to do without (Weigel and Baker 2002).

As a result, recommendation reports such as *Mental Health Providers in Rural and Isolated Areas: Final Report of the Ad Hoc Rural Mental Health Provider Work Group* (Pion, Keller, and McCombs 1997) generally advise that training for rural practice should emphasize the generalist role, and also include specific content on the needs of rural residents in order to combat the urban bias of many theoretical models and assumptions about service delivery.

The Need for Collaboration with Primary Care Providers and Other Groups

Along with the need to be generalists, there is the need for rural mental health providers to work collaboratively with other local institutions, especially primary care physicians and local religious organizations. Chalifoux et al. (1996) state that nearly 60 percent of care for rural mental illness is given by primary care providers, and others (Wayman 2000; Lambert and Hartley 1998) have noted the vital importance of the "country doctor" in the rural community. Too often, however, mental health workers and primary care providers have failed to recognize the benefits of professional interdependence, despite the reality that each may often overlook issues within the expertise of the other, since clients frequently describe physical ailments that mask mental health needs, and vice versa (Lambert and Hartley 1998; Robertson et al. 1999).

To remedy this situation, Yuen et al. (1996) recommend that linkages between rural mental health workers and rural primary care providers be pursued and courted, so that mental health needs can be treated earlier, and to facilitate increased utilization of mental health care in the community at large. Wayman (2000) goes even further, placing the responsibility for collaborative initiatives on the shoulders of mental health workers. Lambert and Hartley (1998) note some successes along these lines in Maine, Pennsylvania, and Texas. Pat Murdock, director of the Mark Twain Area Counseling Center in Kirksville, Missouri, noted in an interview with the second author of this essay that her organization was working with several area primary care clinics to provide mental health care by sending therapists to those clinics during their business hours. She feels that this collaboration improves citizen access to mental health resources by reducing stigma, and by taking help closer to where people are (P. Murdock, personal communication, April 2002).

The literature also points out the importance of collaboration with other organizations such as faith groups. In many cases, rural clergy are the first line of defense against mental health emergencies (Voss 1996; Wayman 2000), but clergy may lack particular expertise in responding to pleas for help by congregants. Roberts, Battaglia, and Epstein (1999) note that this tendency is not limited to rural Christians but is also found in other rural cultures such as among Alaskan Native Americans. Wayman (2000) notes a particularly successful initiative in Iowa to use peer helpers as caregivers for mental health needs, and social workers have much to contribute, and also to gain, in collaboration with programs such as these. Speaking with Don Noble, a counselor and project specialist with Northeastern Missouri Caring Communities, the second author learned that, since 1995, Noble has been conducting training seminars in basic mental health with ministers in two counties in Missouri (D. Noble, personal communication, April 2002). Pat Murdock, mentioned above, is doing similar work with the religious community in Kirksville, Missouri (P. Murdock, personal communication, April 2002).

The Issue of Dual Relationships

The National Association of Social Workers (NASW) *Code of Ethics* states that the social worker "should not engage in dual or multiple relationships with clients or former clients in which there is a risk of exploitation or potential harm to the client" (NASW, 9). When dual or multiple relationships are unavoidable, workers are to take appropriate measures to ensure that clients are protected. Other groups of mental health professionals have similar injunctions (Arons 2000; Brownlee 1996). In rural communities this prohibition against dual relationships is often impractical or impossible to follow (Roberts et al. 1999), since "everybody knows everybody" and all parties wear more than one hat. For instance, a mental health worker may treat an appliance salesman, only to learn that the salesman, who doubles as the technician, is the only one around who can fix her washer or stove. Similar situations of varying magnitude or significance crop up all of the time in the rural setting. Moreover, "maintaining a professional distance" from the community will work against building trust, rapport, and the collaborative relationships needed to function effectively.

These dual relationships can cause problems, such as loss of confidentiality (Roberts et al. 1999, or relational hindrances in the enforcement of legal mandates. The temptations are great for the mental health professional to be self-serving rather than to be ethical, especially if acting ethically could mean loss of her position or could result in serious disadvantage.

If dual relationships are unavoidable, what can be done to preserve the best interests of both the client and the worker? Certainly the rural worker must learn to refrain completely from referring in social situations to her work, since word spreads faster in the rural community because of the high degree of personalism and the improbability of anonymity (Roberts et al. 1999). In urban areas it may be possible to make a conversational reference to an experience arising from practice and yet preserve confidentiality by the simple expedient of omitting names and details. However, the smaller the community, the more obvious the identifying information may be to the listener by process of elimination, and thus all such conversations must be scrupulously avoided.

In the end, rural workers must rely on thorough internalization of the spirit of the *Code of Ethics*, and on habits of mind that are attuned to the ethical implications of circumstances bearing on their work and citizenship in general. Additionally, when ethical dilemmas do arise, rural workers should allow time for thoughtful consideration and the weighing of possible outcomes, and also nurture and maintain relationships at a distance with colleagues who can provide neutral consultation. Rural workers facing ethical dilemmas arising from dual relationships that cannot be avoided should also discuss these issues and any possible alternatives openly with clients and, wherever possible, engage in mutual decision making. For a detailed examination of dual relationships in rural communities, see chapter 6 in this volume.

Mental Health Social Workers in Rural Areas

Do you have to be "Sweet Betsy from Pike" or "her husband Ike" to be a mental health worker in a rural area? No, but it helps. Numerous authors have described characteristics associated with goodness-of-fit with this arena of practice, and most of them have more to do with values, tastes, and temperament than with such matters as training or theoretical orientation. In essence, the ability to live and thrive socially and emotionally in a rural area is an important predictor of success, and rural treatment centers or programs that recruit staff without taking this relationship into account are often plagued with high rates of staff turnover (Pion, Keller, and McCombs 1997).

Although traditional patterns are changing in many parts of contemporary rural America, moving to "the county" often means that the large majority of one's neighbors and associates are people deeply rooted in the local area, many of whom feel a spirit of place that one whose family ties and traditions are elsewhere may only be able to understand intellectually. Anticipating this gulf in understanding, rural residents may tend to "close ranks" against recent arrivals, which may create particular difficulty in forming relationships of trust and openness (Gumpert and Saltman 1998). It can be discouraging to new workers to encounter this reserve, especially because they are eager to start reaping the internal sense of satisfaction with helping and "making a difference" that initially motivated them to pursue social work education. Patience, and the ability to refrain from "taking it personally" if local citizens appear slow to accept a newcomer, no matter how well intentioned, may be crucial. In many regions there may also be a large gap in educational attainment between the worker and the average citizen. The worker in a rural area may need to develop appreciation for ways of knowing or attaining wisdom that do not derive from science or scholarship, and refrain from conveying an impression of inflated self-importance derived from education. Respect for and sincere curiosity about local customs and folkways are also imperative.

Compounding the problems of transition may be a dearth of coworkers, dramatically reducing opportunities for peer interaction and support (Pearson and Sutton 1999). Lack of opportunities for supervision, peer consultation, and in-service training for skill development and maintenance of licensure may also be serious drawbacks.

Added to these challenges are a lack of cultural amenities, such as well stocked libraries, theaters, and concert halls; a lack of specialty stores; and possibly a scarcity of potential partners. Caseloads are heavy; there may be a need to assist with on-call or crisis services after hours; and pay scales are low. Other negatively valued features of rural practice may include discouragement over lack of resources, frustration with distance and transportation problems, and distaste for certain features of some rural cultures, such as stereotypical beliefs or perceptions of excessive conservatism (Sullivan, Hasler, and Otis 1993).

Yet despite all these factors, those who are "cut out" for rural practice may experience strong feelings of calling and personal commitment to the rural lifestyle itself, and this may offer unique rewards. Having a deep love of nature and outdoor activities such as hiking, gardening, or rock climbing, or simply appreciating a slower and more elemental pace of living, can bring deep meaning that transcends regret over absent urban luxuries. Additionally the nature of rural mental health practice offers possibilities and challenges that some workers may accept with considerable satisfaction. Among these are opportunities for educational and consultative activities (Weigel and Baker 2002); forming networks of collaborative community relationships (Beeson 1998a); and a sense of accomplishment deriving from broadly based skill development as a generalist, one who is called upon professionally to be all things to clients (Beeson 1998b). Other possible rewards and satisfactions available from rural mental health practice include opportunities for leadership, program development, and administrative responsibility, which may come more quickly and may offer career flexibility and autonomy that might be unusual in a more populous area. Several studies of job satisfaction among mental health professionals have found no significant differences between rural workers versus those based in metropolitan areas (except in situations where funding becomes threatened and cutbacks loom) (Weigel and Baker 2002; Rohland 2000; Sullivan, Hasler, and Otis 1993). In short, social work in rural mental health is not for everyone; but (given an expectation of a modest living) those who love it have felt historically that despite challenges that seemed overwhelming at times, their sense of mission and ability to derive meaning and reward from their work were unshakable.

The Influence of Information Age Technology on Rural Mental Health

Recently there have been reports in the literature of direct mental health services being delivered via distance technologies. According to McCarty and Clancy (2002), most of these reports (by a factor of 10 to 1) describe the use of interactive video systems for diagnostic interviews and medication checks, rather than ongoing psychosocial therapies or counseling. There is also an essentially unregulated private industry delivering therapy over the Internet, either by means of serial e-mail messages or via synchronous online communication ("chat"). The simultaneous use of inexpensive web cameras by both therapist and client to conduct therapy sessions at a distance has also been described (Kaplan 1997). However, such services are not presently covered by most third-party payers that require face-to-face contact for reimbursement. This huge stumbling block, together with the uncharted legal territory of liability and malpractice coverage for teletherapy, make the use of these technologies a gray area which most providers and program administrators are avoiding at present, despite their enormous potential for bringing services to remote and sparsely populated areas.

Some other uses of digital technology appear to face fewer obstacles and thus hold more immediate promise as aids to rural mental health systems. One of these is distance education, commonly used in schools of social work to increase student access to professional degree programs, and also to facilitate participation in continuing education classes for rural workers (Parker and Parker 1998). Reports are also beginning to emerge of promising uses for interactive technologies to bring case consultation and supervision to mental health professionals in rural areas (McLaren and Ball 1995; Gammon et al. 1998).

Anecdotal evidence suggests that Internet access can and does make a difference in the lives of some rural Americans. For instance, while providing supervision toward independent licensure for a mental health worker, the first author of this essay encountered the case of a rural woman with a physical disability, who achieved remission of chronic depressive symptoms for the first time in years, largely owing to reduced feelings of emotional isolation brought about by relationships formed online. Similarly a colleague in Tennessee tells of a "virtual support group" for patients with restrictions on mobility as a result of agoraphobia (M. Colson, personal communication, 2001), and a West Virginia veteran readjustment counselor describes the use of Web-based searches for long-lost comrades-in-arms as beneficial in some cases of combat-related posttraumatic stress disorder and depression (R. Whisman, personal communication, 2000). However, the particular therapeutic efficacy of these resources remains untested.

The most widespread and significant application of computer-assisted technology in mental health practice is presently telemedicine, or telepsychiatry, generally used to link rural workers and their clients to medical centers for diagnostic and psychopharmacological consultations.

For a more in-depth review of contemporary influences of technology on social work practice in rural areas, see chapter 3 in this volume.

Child and Youth Mental Health Services in Rural Areas

Much like mental health practice in rural areas generally, specialized services for children and youth have changed rather dramatically in the last decade. However, the climate of restricted funding is not quite as dire for child and youth services as it is within adult services because of widespread availability of the federally funded State Child Health Insurance Program (SCHIP). Through this program many children and adolescents from households living near the poverty line are eligible to receive health insurance, even if their parents have just enough income to be disqualified for Medicaid. Under SCHIP, all eligible children "are entitled to any medically necessary service . . . to correct or ameliorate defects, and physical and mental illnesses and conditions, even if the state in which the child resides has not otherwise elected to include that service in its Medicaid plan" (U.S. Public Health Service 2000, 51). Still, interpretations of this rule may vary widely by state or region, and rural parents and guardians are often reluctant to advocate for services to be provided beyond the local area because of family disruption and stress that such utilization would inevitably bring. In some states parents may be forced to relinquish custody of their children in order to gain eligibility for out-of-state services for their children (Bazelon Center 2000).

The lack of trained providers and available services that has historically hampered service delivery in rural areas (Pion, Keller, and McCombs 1997) may often become a more serious problem for child and youth services than funding. In West Virginia, for instance, there are no residential services for children and youth with more serious behavioral and conduct disorders, who are routinely sent to out-of-state facilities for treatment. These services, unfortunately, cannot successfully incorporate adjunctive family treatment because of the distances involved, and after-care plans are severely compromised by the same lack of appropriate in-state services that necessitated the out-of-state referral in the first place. Inevitably long-term outcomes are affected negatively by these factors, and research indicates that residential treatment for children and youth is generally the most expensive, yet least effective, of the available options (Barker 1998; Loeber and Farrington 1998; Greenbaum et al. 1998).

Under urban models of managed care, services for children and youth are often designed using a continuum of care approach, or an array of "wrap-around services" (Burns and Goldman 1999) in which referrals may be made to services that vary according to intensity or setting, depending on the urgency of the need and the presenting difficulties, at different points in time. In rural areas, however, such service plans may be impossible to structure owing to the unavailability of key components of the network of services needed. It is crucial for program planners and providers in rural areas to take into account differences in feasibility between models described in the literature that may reflect urban bias versus those that may realistically reflect regional constraints.

Some Promising Community Programs for Children and Youth

There are some reports in the recent literature of service systems that have been influenced positively by the emphasis on efficiency and flexibility originating in the managed care environment. The clinician-case manager model, in which a single worker may provide an array of services to a child as well as to family members or caregivers, represents a good fit with recommendations that rural mental health providers are best able to meet regional needs when practicing as generalists (Weigel and Baker 2002). In addition, the clinician–case manager model has potential for reducing professional time spent in coordinating and attending multidisciplinary team meetings (Sawyer and Moreines 1998). For rural areas where distances can be great and travel time disproportionately burdensome, it is estimated that this advantage of the clinician–case manager model could be of significant benefit.

Promising children's initiatives have been described in a number of rural areas under a project partially funded by the program Comprehensive Community Mental Health Services for Children and Their Families, administered by the Children's Mental Health Services branch of the U.S. Department of Health and Human Services. These demonstration projects, described as systems of care models, are designed to assist families and communities in the development of local services, toward goals of reducing out-of-home and out-of-community placements and episodes of hospitalization for emotionally disturbed youth. Grantees must develop incrementally rising levels of nonfederal matching funds over the term of the grants, and must pay particular attention to outcome evaluation. This model has been shown to be helpful at twenty-two sites, including five Native American communities (Goldman and Faw 1998; Cross 2000).

The Larger Picture in Child and Youth Services

From a short distance off, the current picture of mental health practice with children and adolescents would not seem to be quite as grim as that of adult services. Funding sources are currently somewhat more available in this area of practice, and several promising models of community care, applicable to the rural environment, and with appropriate provisions for family inclusion, continue to be refined (Burns et al. 1999). In addition, research has shown that several other practice models have been demonstrated to have significant benefit for the holistic behavioral health of children and youth. Among these are family preservation programs such as Homebuilders (Fraser et al. 1996) and multisystemic therapy (MST), an intensive, home-based intervention for delinquent youth (Henggelar et al. 1998). Also of potential benefit are therapeutic foster homes, which have been shown to reduce the need for placement in more restrictive settings for youth in child protective custody (Kutash and Rivera 1996).

However, the larger picture is still far from ideal. One of the most persistent problems in this field of practice is client and family failure to return for services following an initial appointment, a problem that unfortunately grows in proportion to the seriousness of the need (Kazdin, Holland, and Crowley 1999). It has also been found that the longer the elapsed time between a request for service and a scheduled intake, the less likely consumers are to keep appointments (Greeno et al. 1999). Lengthy waiting lists, in turn, are related to the general dearth of competent providers in rural areas (Wayman 2000). At a time when 21 percent of children and youth have diagnoses of mental health or addictive disorders (U.S. DHHS 1999), this is a serious problem for rural communities and is likely to be related to rising adolescent suicide rates (Centers for Disease Control and Prevention 1999).

Conclusions and Recommendations

In general, rural mental health care has been hard hit by major structural changes in service systems and financing within the last decade. Rural re-

gions, historically more dependent on public funding than wealthier metropolitan areas, have faced a steady abnegation of federal responsibility for
programs and services, while states, straining to take up the slack, have generally responded with increasing restrictiveness on access to services.

Many policy analysts and task groups have called for greatly stepped up
efforts in the political arena and in consumer advocacy (Pion, Keller, and
McCombs 1997; Arons 2000) toward the goal of loosening federal purse
strings on behalf of underserved rural people with mental health needs.
However, it is estimated that strict limits exist on the usefulness of this approach. According to Beeson and Sawyer, "Today, state and federal agencies
are more functionally oriented and are not swayed by emotional arguments
regarding service need" (1998, 2). The present authors believe that all such
efforts are probably best directed against any *further* erosion of service quality,
or *additional* budget cuts, rather than toward restoration of funding levels
last seen when lines separating social problems from private troubles (Longres 2000) were drawn in a different place. Meanwhile, equal emphasis
should be placed on the identification or development of alternative sources
of funding. Workers need greatly enhanced entrepreneurial, managerial, and
grant writing skills. Those who may lack the necessary qualities of temperament and inclination themselves could accomplish great things by working
in collaboration across fields of practice and disciplines with others who do
possess the requisite talents. The cause of easing mental suffering is just;
methods of proven efficacy are at hand; and workers are available who would
welcome the opportunity to do the work, if provided a modest living. If the
government will not foot the bill, it must be assumed that there are concerned others in the society who would, if the need were made known in
an effective manner. For those social workers who may have seen the partnership of social work values and public funding as a "bad marriage" anyway,
the idea of filing for separation, and eventually perhaps divorce, could be
highly liberating.

Another pressing priority for rural mental health workers is skill development with digital technologies. The use of real time interactive videoconferencing to bring direct services such as talking therapies to remote regions
is not presently feasible, but it should be assumed that it is on the way.
Meanwhile, web-based communications to bring peer consultation, supervision, and continuing education to rural workers using e-mail, chat, and
web camera conferencing, are ready to work wonders. The World Wide Web
itself is a vast and explosively growing resource that contemporary workers
can ill afford to be without, especially in rural areas.

For social work educators, there may be an immediate need to rethink courses and program designs to better reflect contingencies faced by workers in the field in the era of privatization and managed care. It may not serve students well to teach methods and models that are not allowable within present funding constraints, unless accompanied by greatly increased curricular emphases on the skills needed to secure alternative sources of funding.

Concerning the current crisis in rural mental health services, Beeson and Sawyer (1998, 4) argue:

> Many of the decisions that will affect rural mental health care delivery in the future will likely be made outside of government, and outside of rural settings. All of this requires a more business-like stance on the part of rural mental health and substance abuse providers and professionals. Rural mental health providers must become tough and well-connected. They need to understand what it costs to deliver services and to achieve desired outcomes and how to be focused on being efficient as well as effective. Within the field there is an increasing need to build and maintain the relationships necessary for success.

To prepare future social workers for these new circumstances, increased integration of micro and macro practice skills in schools of social work might be of significant benefit. One possibility would be to offer a third-year certificate program to MSW candidates in direct practice in grant writing and funding development, perhaps in partnership with business and public administration programs. This third year could be bypassed by students headed for career niches where more traditional sources of funding are expectable, but for those with interests and skills in areas of practice that are becoming nonreimbursable, this certificate program could be invaluable. Within traditional MSW programs, elective courses in collaborative development of funding partnerships, with lab experience, may be needed. Such courses might be useful in a number of fields of practice but are vital in mental health practice where, increasingly, students are discovering that just knowing how to help may no longer be enough.

References

Abraham, I. L., et al. 1993. Psychogeriatric outreach to rural families: The Iowa and Virginia models. *International Psychogeriatrics*, 5 (2): 203–211.

Arons, B. 2000. Mental health services in rural America. *Vital Speeches of the Day* 66 (12): 369–71.

Barker, P. 1998. The future of residential treatment for children. In C. Schaefer and A. Swanson, eds., *Children in residential care: Critical issues in treatment*, pp. 1–16. New York: Van Nostrand Reinhold.

Bazelon Center for Mental Health Law. 2000. Relinquishing custody: The tragic result of failure to meet children's mental health needs. Washington, D.C.: Published by the author.

Beeson, P. G. 1998a. Apples and oranges: The successful rural mental health practitioner at the turn of the century. *Rural Community Mental Health* 24 (4): 38–40.

———. 1998b. The successful rural mental health practitioner: Dimensions of success. *Rural Community Mental Health* 24 (4): 35–38.

Beeson, P. G.., et al. 1998. Rural mental health at the millenium. In R. W. Manderscheid and M. J. Henderson, eds., *Mental health United States 1998*, DHHS Publication No. SMA 99–3285, pp. 82–98. Washington, D.C.: U.S. Government Printing Office.

Beeson, P. G., and D. A. Sawyer. 1998. Rural mental health: Vision 2000 and beyond. Available online at http://www.narhm.org/pages/future.html.

Brownlee, K. 1996. Ethics in mental health community care: The ethics of nonsexual dual relationships: A dilemma for the rural mental health community. *Community Mental Health Journal* 32 (5): 497–503.

Burns, B. J., et al. 1996. A randomized trial of case management for youths with serious emotional disturbance. *Journal of Clinical Child Psychology* 25:476–486.

Burns, B. J., and S. K. Goldman, eds. 1999. Promising practices in wraparound for children with severe emotional disturbance and their families. *Systems of care: Promising practices in children's mental health.* 1998 Series, Vol. 4. Rockville, Md.: Center for Mental Health Services.

Centers for Disease Control and Prevention. 1999. *Suicide deaths and rates per 100,000.* Available online at http://www.cdc.gov/ncipc/data/us9794/suic.htm.

Chalifoux, Z., et al. 1996. Mental health services for rural elderly: Innovative service strategies. *Community Mental Health Journal* 32 (5): 463–480.

Christian-Michaels, S., G. Noll, and S. P. Wernet. 1999. Organizational reform in a community mental health center. In S. P. Wernet, ed., *Managed care in human services*, pp. 181–199. Chicago: Lyceum.

Corwin, M. 2002. *Brief treatment in clinical social work practice.* Pacific Grove, Calif.: Brooks/Cole.

Cox, T. M. 2002. Many happy about mental health parity changes. *Charleston [WV] Daily Mail*, March 13.

Cross, T., et al. 2000. Cultural strengths and challenges in implementing a system of care model in American Indian communities. *Systems of Care: Promising Practices in Children's Mental Health.* 2000 Series, Vol. 1. Washington, D.C.: Center for Effective Collaboration and Practice, American Institutes for Research.

Cummings, N. A. 1996. Does managed care offset costs related to medical treatment? In A. Lazarus, ed., *Controversies in managed mental health care*, pp. 213–227. Washington, D.C.: American Psychiatric Association Press.

Davia, J. 2002. Shawnee Hills apparently down for the count, "provisions made for all the clients." *Charleston [WV] Gazette*, May 1.

Davis, K. 1998. Managed health care: Forcing social work to make choices and changes. In G. Schamess and A. Lightburn, eds., *Humane managed care?* pp. 425–429. Washington, D.C.: National Association of Social Workers (NASW) Press.

Davis, S. R., and S. Meier. 2001. *The elements of managed care*. Belmont, Calif.: Brooks-Cole.

Fortney, J., et al. 2001. Provider choice and utility loss due to selective contracting in rural and urban areas. *Medical Care Research and Review* 58 (1): 60–75.

Fox, J. C., et al. 1999. Mental disorders and help seeking in a rural impoverished population. *International Journal of Psychiatry in Medicine* 29 (2): 181–195.

Fraser, M. W., E. Walton, and R. E. Lewis. 1997. Effectiveness of family preservation services. *Social Work Research* 21:138–153.

Gammon, D., et al. 1998. Psychotherapy supervision conducted by videoconferencing: A qualitative study of users' experiences. *Journal of Telemedicine and Telecare* 4 (Suppl. 1): 33–35.

Gilbert, P. 1992. *Depression: The evolution of powerlessness*. New York: Guilford.

Goldman, S. K., and L. Faw. 1998. Three wraparound models as promising approaches. In B. J. Burns and S. K. Goldman, eds., *Promising practices in wraparound for children with severe emotional disturbance and their families. Systems of care: Promising practices in children's mental health*. 1998 Series, Vol. 4, pp. 17–59. Washington, D.C.: Center for Effective Collaboration and Practice, American Institutes for Research.

Goldman, L. S., et al. 1998. Diagnosis and treatment of attention deficit/hyperactivity disorder in children and adolescents. *Journal of the American Medical Association* 279:1100–1107.

Gottlieb, M. C. 1993. Avoiding exploitative dual relationships: A decision-making model. *Psychotherapy* 30:41–48.

Greenbaum, P. E., et al. 1998. National Adolescent and Child Treatment Study (NACTS): Outcomes for children with serious emotional and behavioral disturbance. In M. H. Epstein, K. Kutash, and A. Duchnowski, eds., *Outcomes for children and youth with behavioral and emotional disorders and their families*, pp. 21–54. Austin, Tex.: Pro-Ed.

Greeno, C. G., et al. 1999. Initial treatment engagement in a rural community mental health center. *Psychiatric Services* 50 (12): 1634–1636.

Gumpert, J., and J. E. Saltman. 1998. Social group work practice in rural areas: The practitioners speak. *Social Work with Groups* 21 (3): 19–34.

Hall, J. A., et al. 2002. Iowa case management: Innovative social casework. *Social Work* 47 (2): 132–141.

Hendryx, M. S. 2001. Rural adults with poor mental health findings. *Texas Journal of Rural Health* 19 (1): 67–73.

Henggelar, S. W., et al. 1998. *Multisystemic treatment of antisocial behavior in children and adolescents.* New York: Guilford.

Jensen, P. S., et al. 1999. Psychoactive medication prescribing practices for U.S. children: Gaps between research and clinical practice. *Journal of the American Academy of Child and Adolescent Psychopathology* 38:537–565.

Johnson, M. C., et al. 1997. Rural mental health leaders' perceptions of stigma and community issues. *Journal of Rural Health* 13 (1): 59–70.

Kaplan, E. H. 1997. Telepsychotherapy: Psychotherapy by telephone, videotelephone, and computer videoconferencing. *Journal of Psychotherapy Practice and Research* 6:227–237.

Kazdin, A. E., L. Holland, and M. Crowley. 1997. Family experience of barriers to treatment and premature termination from child therapy. *Journal of Consulting and Clinical Psychology* 65:453–463.

Kutash, K., and V. R. Rivera. 1996. *What works in children's mental health services: Uncovering answers to critical questions.* Baltimore, Md.: Paul H. Brookes.

Loeber, R., and D. P. Farrington. *Serious and violent juvenile offenders: Risk factors and successful interventions.* Thousand Oaks, Calif.: Sage.

Lambert, D., and D. Hartley. 1998. Linking primary care and rural services: Where have we been and where are we going? *Psychiatric Services* 49 (7): 965–967.

Longres, J. 2000. *Human behavior in the social environment.* Itasca, Ill.: Peacock.

McCarton, C. M., et al. 1997. Results at age 8 years of early intervention for low-birth-weight premature infants. The Infant Health and Development Program. *Journal of the American Medical Association* 277:126–132.

McCarty, D., and C. Clancy. 2002. Telehealth: Its implications for social work practice. *Social Work* 47 (2): 153–161.

McDonel, E. C., et al. 1997. Implementing assertive community treatment programs in rural settings. *Administration and Policy in Mental Health* 25 (2): 153–173.

McLaren, P., and C. J. Ball. 1995. Telemedicine: Lessons remain unheeded. *British Medical Journal* 310 (6991): 1390–1392.

Milbank Memorial Fund. 2000. *Effective public management of mental health care: Views from states on Medicaid reforms that enhance service integration and accountability.* Available online at http://milbank.org/bazelon/.

Miller, I. W., et al. 1986. Family functioning in the families of psychiatric patients. *Comprehensive Psychiatry* 27:302–312.

Morrison, M. A. 2000. Changing perceptions of mental illness and the emergence of expansive mental health parity legislation. *South Dakota Law Review* 45 (1): 8–32.

Olds, D., et al. 1998. Long-term effects of nurse home visitation on children's criminal and antisocial behavior: 15 year follow-up of a randomized controlled trial. *Journal of the American Medical Association* 280:1238–1244.

Parker, A., and L. E. Parker. 1998. Distance education vs. in-class instruction. In

S. F. Viegas and K. Dunn, eds., *Telemedicine: Practicing in the information age,* pp. 135–152. Philadelphia: Lippencott-Raven.

Pearson, R. E., and J. M. Sutton Jr. 1999. Rural and small town school counselors. *Journal of Research in Rural Education* 15 (2): 90–100.

Pion, G. M., P. Keller, and H. McCombs. 1997. *Mental health providers in rural and isolated areas: Final report of the Ad Hoc Rural Mental Health Provider Work Group.* Rockville, Md.: The Center for Mental Health Services.

Roberts, L. W., Battaglia, J., and Epstein, R. S. 1999. Frontier ethics: Mental health needs and ethical dilemmas in rural communities. *Psychiatric Services, 50(4), 497–504.*

Roberts, L. W., et al. 1999. An office on main street: Health care dilemmas in small communities. *Hastings Center Report* 29 (4): 28–37.

Robertson, E. B., and J. F. Donnermeyer. 1997. Illegal drug use among rural adults: Mental health consequences and treatment utilization. *American Journal of Drug and Alcohol Abuse* 23 (3): 467–484.

Rohland, B. M. 2000. A survey of burnout among mental health center directors in a rural state. *Administration and Policy in Mental Health* 27 (4): 221–237.

Rohland, B. M., and J. E. Rohrer. 1998. Capacity of rural community mental health centers to treat serious mental illness. *Community Mental Health Journal* 34 (3): 261–273.

Sawyer, D. A., and S. F. Moreines. 1998. A model for rural children's mental health services. *Administration and Policy in Mental Health* 22 (6): 597–605.

Sullivan, W. P., M. D. Hasler, and A. G. Otis. 1993. Rural mental health practice: Voices from the field. *Families in Society: The Journal of Contemporary Human Services* 74 (8): 493–502.

U.S. Census Bureau. 2004. Census 2000 Summary File 1, Table P 30, Relationship by Household Type (including living alone) for the Population 65 Years and Over, United States Rural. Available at http://factfinder.census.gov. Retrieved January 19, 2005.

U.S. Department of Health and Human Services. 1999. *Mental health: A report of the Surgeon General.* Rockville, Md.: U.S. Department of Health and Human Services, Substance Abuse and Mental Health Services Administration, Center for Mental Health Services, National Institutes of Health, National Institute of Mental Health.

U.S. Public Health Service. 2000. *Report of the Surgeon General's Conference on Children's Mental Health: A national action agenda.* Washington, D.C.: Department of Health and Human Services.

Volkow, N. D., et al. 1995. Is methylphenidate like cocaine? Studies on their pharmacokinetics and distribution in the human brain. *Archives of General Psychiatry* 52:456–463.

Voss, S. L. 1996. The church as an agent in rural mental health. *Journal of Psychology and Theology* 24 (2): 114–123.

Wagenfeld, M. O., et al. 1997. Mental health service delivery in rural areas: Organizational and clinical issues. In E. Robertson, ed., *Rural substance abuse: State of knowledge and issues*, pp. 418–437. Rockville, Md.: U.S. Department of Health and Human Services.

Wayman, D. V. 2000. Rural management concerns: Management concerns in rural community mental health. *Journal of Rural Community Psychology* E3 (1): 1–5.

Weigel, D. J., and B. G. Baker. 2002. Unique issues in rural couple and family counseling. *The Family Journal: Counseling and Therapy for Couples and Families* 10 (1): 61–69.

Yuen, E. J., J. L. Gerdes, and J. J. Gonzales. 1996. Patterns of rural mental health care: An exploratory study. *General Hospital Psychiatry* 18:14–21.

11 The Health of Rural Minorities

Doris Nicholas

This chapter focuses on the health issues confronting rural minority populations. It reviews the health care challenges faced by rural minority residents and the importance of developing cultural competence among health care practitioners so they are prepared to deal with rural minority populations.

Rural communities typically have greater health care challenges than urban and suburban communities owing to their isolation, small population base, limited economic potential, and higher proportions of aging residents. All these factors drive health care costs up and limit the potential profitability of health care services. When racial and ethnic differences are added to the rural equation, the problems of access to adequate health care for rural minority residents are intensified.

The addition of race and ethnicity to the rural landscape is a stretch for many, for as Snipp (1996) suggests, the typical but misinformed view of rural America is one of homogeneity devoid of racial discord. Snipp indicates that while sociologists can be credited for their work describing rural communities and the racial and ethnic issues in these communities, the majority of literature dedicated to race and ethnicity ignores the uniqueness of rural areas in favor of more populous urban areas.

In examining the health issues of rural minorities one is immediately struck by the paucity of literature on the subject. There is substantial literature regarding rural health issues as well as minority health issues. However, when one superimposes these two criteria, rural and minority, the literature is wanting. The limited nature of the literature was confirmed in a working paper produced by the North Carolina Rural Health Research Program (Slifkin, Goldsmith, and Ricketts 2000) which states that geographic place of residence is typically missing in studies that address racial and ethnic group differences in health status or access to care. While there are other definitions of rural, place is one of the most important from the standpoint of health services access.

One minority population after another has been found to have higher-than-anticipated representation in the leading chronic illnesses of the nation. Moreover, the status of minority populations as outliers in national gains in life expectancy makes it increasingly important to identify additional factors that are co-contributors to the alarmingly high morbidity of these populations. Rural residence may be one of the factors.

Urban centers have historically received close scrutiny on health measures owing in part to their accessibility as well as the size of their populations. Such centers historically had significant health problems because of the crowding of the population and limited sanitary facilities. In the past and today rural areas present quite different challenges of access together with sparse populations that make them less attractive to researchers as well as to health care providers. Yet what evidence there is makes it clear that rural minorities have different characteristics than their urban counterparts, including geographic and social isolation and sometimes devastating poverty (Snipps 1996).

According to the U.S Census, minority persons are an estimated one in four Americans (U.S. Census 2001b). Each year the United States becomes more diverse, and projections indicate that, with the current trend, Hispanics, non-Hispanic blacks, Asians, and American Indians will account for almost half the population by 2050, in comparison with the 27 percent represented by these groups in 1998 (National Center for Health Statistics 2001). As demographics change and America continues browning, the issues facing people of color in rural areas will demand even greater attention. The Office of Minority Health (OMH) (2001) expresses continued concern for disparities in health status and access to health care that affect the lives of racial and ethnic minorities in the United States. The U.S. Department of Health and Human Services (DHHS) (2002) cites rural communities as uniquely challenged by less health and social service infrastructure, higher rates of poverty than urban areas, lower rates of employer health insurance coverage, and a systematic lack of health care providers.

According to the Office of Rural Health Policy, rural communities are experiencing a change in racial and ethnic makeup. They are becoming increasingly more diverse; this is especially true for the Hispanic population whose numbers increased by 70 percent in the 1990s (U.S. Census Bureau 2001a). Declining employment in primary industries like agriculture, mining, and fishing, the African-American diaspora from the South and the large-scale immigration of Latinos are additional factors contributing to these changes. Indeed, much of the growing minority presence in rural communities has come about because of immigration patterns resulting from employment opportunities in rural areas. This is especially true for Hispanic and Asian immigrants, particularly in Western and Southern rural areas (Rural Policy Research Institute 1999).

Rural Minority Demographics and Disadvantage

Because the focus has traditionally been on the economic and social plight of urban minority populations, particularly African Americans and Hispanics in the nation's largest urban centers, little has been written regarding related issues faced by rural poor minorities. Discussions about rural America have centered on issues of poverty, partially the result of the over-representation of the rural among the nations poor. Since poor health and poverty often go hand in hand, it is probable that the level of poverty is contributing significantly to health problems among rural minority persons.

Approximately 55 million Americans (20 percent of the U.S. population) live in rural areas. African Americans, Hispanics, and American Indians are the largest minority populations living in rural areas. African Americans currently account for about 13 percent (approximately 36.4 million) of the total U.S. population. Of this African American population, 15 percent are rural residents. An additional 12.5 percent of the U.S. population (35.3 million people) is Hispanic (Iceland, Weinberg, and Steinmetz 2002). According to the 2000 Census, 39.1 percent of the Hispanic population in the United States is foreign-born and almost half of this immigrant population arrived during the 1990s. Of the Hispanic population, 2.35 million, or 8.5 percent, live in rural areas (Therrien and Ramirez 2001). By comparison, among Asian Americans, who make up 4.2 percent of the overall population (11.9 million people), only 5 percent are rural (Iceland, Weinberg, and Steinmetz 2002). However, among American Indians and Alaska Natives, who make up 1.5 percent of the total population, 34 percent live outside metropolitan areas (ibid.). Approximately half this population lives on or near reservations (Schneider and Martinez 1997). Minority Americans, on average, tend to be poorer than whites, and elderly minority Americans are even more likely to live in poverty than their white counterparts.

Poverty in the United States increasingly has a minority face. The 2000 data reports of the Bureau of Census stated that while the poverty rate for blacks and Hispanics decreased between 1999 and 2000, the 2000 rate for blacks was still 14.6 percent higher than for whites. Similarly the Hispanic poverty rate was 13.7 percent higher than that of whites. The 2000 poverty rate for white non-Hispanics equaled an all-time low of 7.5 percent (Dalaker 2001).

A number of studies have examined the association between mortality rates and income, and have found that mortality decreases as income increases. Minority Americans on average are poorer than whites. Approximately 50 percent of African Americans, Hispanics, and Native Americans are poor in comparison with consistently less than 20 percent rates of whites (Kaiser Family Foundation 1999). Given this and the relationship between mortality and income, higher mortality rates are to be expected among minority group members, including those who live in rural areas. Life expectancy is another indicator of the health status of a society. Of the four major racial or ethnic population groups (African American, Hispanic, Native American, and Asian American) only Asian American elderly (age sixty-five or over) have a lower mortality rate than whites (Gornick 2000).

More than a decade ago, in "Minorities in Rural Society," Gene F. Summers (1991) quoted Deavers: "The Third World exists in rural America, especially among families and communities of racial and ethnic minorities" (177). Deavers's observation is as valid today as it was then. Putting aside the general misconception that rural America is ethnically homogeneous, rural minorities continue to face barriers of poverty and lack of access at disproportionate rates. In 1999 almost 23 percent of all Hispanics and 26 percent of all African Americans were living in poverty, in comparison with 13 percent of the population at large (Therrien and Ramirez 2000). Income differences often translate into limited access to health care and other services, which in turn are associated with higher morbidity.

This national picture is repeated in the enormous disparities found in public health data pertaining to minority populations. According to a report from the U.S. Department of Health and Human Services (DHHS), "although all racial and ethnic groups have experienced gains in life expectancy, differences between groups in longevity and in many other measures of health status have been apparent for as long as these measures have been collected separately by race" (National Center for Health Statistics 2001,

40). The report goes on to explain that blacks, American Indians, and Hispanics — the three minority groups with the largest percentages of rural residents — experience health status disadvantages compared to whites, and that
blacks exhibit greater disparities than any other group.

Swift (2002) reports a literature review published by Mayberry and associates on racial disparities in health care, which showed that "disparities were
documented in health services for heart disease, stroke, cancer, diabetes,
HIV/AIDS, prenatal care, immunization, asthma, and mental health services" (79). Swift goes on to cite many other studies that corroborate this
finding.

Unequal treatment is reflected in many studies that range from the differential use of pain management for African Americans and Hispanics
(Todd et al. and Bernabei, as cited in Kington, Tisnado, and Carlisle 2001)
to the denial of invasive cardiac procedures such as coronary artery bypass
surgery when it is judged to be medically appropriate (Hannan, as cited in
Kington, Tisnado, and Carlisle 2001).

Unemployment as an indicator of the most severe forms of poverty statistically mirrors other criteria characterizing marginalized America. Both
Hispanics and blacks consistently have unemployment rates twice that of
non-Hispanic whites. But the distinction also follows these minorities into
employment. For black and Hispanic men who are employed, the likelihood
is twice as high that they will work in service jobs and as laborers, jobs with
extremely limited potential for increases in socioeconomic status and improved benefits (Therrien and Ramirez 2000; McKinnon and Humes 2000).
But the relation between unemployment and ethnicity does not hold for all
ethnic populations. Asians and Pacific Islanders do not differ statistically
from non-Hispanic white men in the proportion of unemployed (4 percent
each) (Humes and McKinnon 2000).

National data consistently report substantially lower average incomes at
all levels in rural areas than in urban areas. In 1997 real per capita income
in rural areas was $18,527 compared to $25,944 in urban areas.

Yet the distribution of poverty is not geographically uniform. Rural poverty is especially concentrated in certain areas of the country, including those
with the highest concentrations of rural minorities (Rural Policy Research
Institute 1999). Social ills such as segregation, discrimination, and abject
poverty also experienced by urban minorities are endemic in the rural realities experienced on American Indian reservations, in the Latino *colonias*
in the lower Rio Grande Valley, and in African American communities in
the rural south (Snipp 1996). These social problems only become more

prominent in the context of rural dual isolation: geographical isolation and marginalization resulting from prejudice and denied participation.

Another indicator of the economic state and well-being of a society's health is the extent of coverage under medical insurance. DHHS reports that although Medicaid[1] covered 13.3 million poor people, an additional 30.7 percent of the poor had no health coverage in 2001. *Health Insurance Coverage: 2001* reported an increase of 1.4 million people without health insurance coverage in 2001, reflecting an increase of .4 percent from 2000. Mexican Americans have uninsured rates averaging 40 percent (U.S. Census Bureau 2002a).

It is not too strong to suggest that in contemporary American life the absence of health insurance can prove fatal. An Institute of Medicine report "Care without Coverage: Too Little, Too Late" found a 25 percent higher mortality rate for the uninsured (Institute of Medicine 2002). The report estimates that approximately eighteen thousand deaths a year can be attributed directly to absence of health insurance.

For the nation's minority populations, this additional burden is evident. The 2001 report of the Center for Studying Health System Change indicated that blacks and Hispanics have less overall access to medical care in comparison with white Americans, as well as lower rates of insurance coverage. In 2000 the percentage of blacks and Hispanics without health insurance was 19 percent and 32 percent, respectively, while the rate for whites was 11 percent. Further, simply being employed is no assurance of adequate coverage, as 48 percent of employed but poor persons were without health insurance (Hargaves 2002). When these statistics are transposed onto rural America, a bleak picture emerges. A portrait of triple jeopardy for many of the nation's minorities is a rural reality. As this picture comes into focus, it portrays a population that is geographically isolated and overrepresented by persons living in poverty, a significant percentage of whom are without health insurance and far fewer formal health care options because of limited resources.

Rural Minority Health Status

The literature dealing with rural minority health needs is too limited to offer a complete disease-by-disease inventory. However, the lack of health care resources and diminished health care access in rural areas is sufficiently established as a general profile that there have been efforts to deal with the disparities affecting minorities regardless of residence. In 1998 President Clinton initiated the "Race and Health Initiative" campaign. The goal of this campaign was to eliminate the racial and ethnic disparities in six health gap areas: infant mortality, cancer, cardiovascular disease, diabetes, AIDS, and immunization rates (Scanlan 2000). "Healthy People 2010," another national campaign, is designed to achieve two overarching goals: (1) increase quality and years of healthy life; and (2) eliminate health disparities (US DHHS 2000).

African Americans continue to have the worst health profile as a group in the American population . Today African American men have some of the highest mortality rates for cancer, as well as the highest incidence. However, other minority groups have similar profiles. The Native American population is devastated by diabetes (Ross 2001). Some of the highest rates of cervical cancer are found among Hispanic and Vietnamese women (Ross 2000). Although white women are more likely to develop breast cancer, black women are more likely to die from the disease (Ross 2000). The concerns of the Clinton administration begin to describe the mosaic of America's health care inequalities. Unfortunately the Clinton policy initiative has not received the same emphasis with the change of federal administrations following the presidential election in 2000.

Among the health care disadvantages for minorities in rural America are the absence of care providers (physicians, nurses, dentists, etc.); a higher incidence of chronic diseases; higher rates of infant and maternal mortality; a higher incidence of age-related loss of health status; shortages of mental health workers; and rural cultural barriers. A number of these parameters are accepted as general indicators of the state of health and well-being of a society as a whole, and these health measures have been persistently less favorable for blacks and American Indians than for other groups (National Center for Health Statistics 2001). A similar picture is presented by other indicators. According to the Centers for Disease Control and Prevention (CDC), the infant mortality rate for whites in 2000 was 5.7 percent, while that of African Americans was 14 percent. Infant mortality rates are also higher for American Indians and Hawaii Natives than for other groups (CDC 2002).

While life expectancy and overall health have improved for most Americans, health status for many is related to their race, gender, and economic status. The Centers for Disease Control and Prevention report that African American men have a 26 percent greater chance of having fatal heart disease than white men. Forty percent of this fatal heart disease will occur before age sixty-five. While in the population as a whole the life expectancy for men is 76.9 years, for African American men it is more than eight years less — 68.3 years. Eighty-one percent of AIDS cases reported between July 1999 and June 2000 were seen among black and Hispanic women (U.S. DHHS 2001). With health status indicators such as these, the picture is clear: minority populations in the United States are losing more children in infancy, facing more chronic life-threatening illnesses as adults, and experiencing shorter life expectancies well below national averages. And these problems are particularly acute among those minority populations that have the highest proportions of rural residents.

In addition to the disparities already mentioned there is a particular health care disadvantage experienced by minority populations that has its roots in America's history of oppression and discrimination, namely, differences in treatment by the health care delivery system. Studies cited in Guidance for the National Healthcare Disparities Report (Swift 2002) examined a number of health conditions for racial and ethnic differences. These studies reported disparities in the availability of health care resources for racial and ethnic minorities as followed:

1. Black patients with myocardial infarction were less likely (9 percent versus 17 percent) than whites to receive thrombolysis (Ayanian et al., as cited in Swift 2002);

2. White women are more likely (15 percent) than black women (9 percent) to receive mammograms (Burns et al., as cited in ibid.). This may be an important reason why African American women have the highest rate of mortality from breast cancer (26.7 per 100,000) compared to white women (18.9) (Office on Women's Health, as cited in ibid.);

3. Seventy-eight percent of whites with colorectal cancer compared to 68 percent of African Americans underwent surgical resection (Cooper et al., as cited in ibid.);

4. Pap smears are provided less often to Hispanic women than to white women (Harlan, Bernstein, and Kessler, as cited in ibid.).

The report goes on to cite additional studies with similar outcomes indicating a demoralizing reality of not only unequal access to health care facilities but also fewer treatment and procedural options offered to minorities even when equal facilities are available. An additional study completed by Mukamel, Murthy, and Weimer (2000) found that, "on average, nonwhites enrolled in fee-for-service plans were treated by surgeons with higher RAMRs [risk-adjusted mortality rate] than were whites enrolled in fee-for-

service plans" (1776). In other words, even when receiving appropriate treatment, minority group members may be at greater risk. The study also provides information which highlights additional disparities that racial
minorities encounter in accessing equitable high-quality health care. The
solution to such discrepancies in both disease rates and treatment practices
is not to reduce the levels of care provided to whites but to provide equitable
levels of treatment for minorities.

Native Americans

Native Americans, like other racial and ethnic minority populations in
the United States, face health care barriers of poverty, isolation, and access,
as well as additional barriers of language and cultural differences in the
expression of illness and help-seeking behavior. Recent census data, as reported by Mather in *Patterns of Poverty in America* (2003), indicate that
poverty rates at the county level were highest in certain rural areas, particularly Central Appalachia, the Northern Plains, the Lower Mississippi Valley,
and the Rio Grande Valley in southern Texas and New Mexico. Four out of
five counties with the highest poverty rate are located in South Dakota and
have significant numbers of Native Americans. Native Americans are twice
as likely as whites to be unemployed or underemployed (Population Reference Bureau 2000). In 1996 the U.S. Census data reported that 30.9 percent
of Native Americans lived below the poverty line. Many of the health status
issues for Native Americans are related to their poverty status (Schneider
and Martinez 1997) — this despite the fact that Native Americans who are
members of federally recognized tribes are eligible to receive services from
the Indian Health Service (IHS).

While the health status of Native Americans has begun to improve somewhat, they still have the second highest infant mortality rate (CDC 2002)
and, together with Alaska Natives, are five times more likely (38.4 percent)
to die of alcohol-related causes than are whites, (6.8 percent) (Indian Health
Service,1997). The rates of death and injury due to accident and violence,
including suicide and homicide, is also higher for Native Americans than
for the U.S. population as a whole (Schneider and Martinez 1997, 2).

Diabetes is one of the most serious health care challenges facing Native
Americans. The CDC reports that diabetes is the fourth leading cause of
death among American Indians. Diabetes has historically affected Native
Americans disproportionately. According to 1996 data from the IHS, the
prevalence of diabetes for American Indians and Alaskan Natives is three

times that of non-Hispanic whites, and, in all likelihood, this is an under-estimation since the data only measure those persons who use IHS medical facilities (CDC 1998). Native Americans are nearly three times more likely to die of diabetes than the general population. "The diabetes mellitus mortality rate for the IHS service area population was 31.7 (per population over the 1991–1993 period) in comparison with the rate of 11.9 among the entire U.S. population in 1992" (Schneider and Martinez 1997). Native Americans also experience a higher incidence of end-stage renal disease (ESRD) than both whites and African Americans. ESRD is a known complication of diabetes (U.S. DHHS 2001b)

The IHS within the Department of Health and Human Services was established in 1955. This relatively late date may surprise those who are not familiar with the sorry history of American Indian treatment by the U.S. government. The mission of the IHS is to provide a comprehensive health service delivery system for American Indians and Alaska Natives. Indian Health Service clinics are predominantly located on reservations, and thereby access only 20 percent of all American Indians. Even when one takes into account those living near the reservation, the access rate only rises to around 40 percent. The Surgeon General's report also indicates that one-third of American Indians and Alaska Natives do not receive regular preventive care or have a usual source of health care through a regular or primary care physician (Brown et al., as cited in U.S. DHHS 2001b). Taking all this into account, there appears to be ample grounds for concluding that high poverty and disease rates among the American Indian and Alaska Native population are closely associated with rates of undertreatment and lack of access, and the latter factor is complicated by rural isolation and distrust of a government that has historically failed to fulfill its promises.

Hispanic

The Hispanic population in the United States more than doubled between 1980 and 2000. Approximately one in eight people in the United States today is of Hispanic origin. Between now and 2050 the Hispanic population will grow at a higher rate than any other group in the United States (Day 1996). The recent immigrant status of much of the Hispanic population predicts linguistic difference for this group. Language problems often prove to be an important inhibitor of adequate treatment for this population.

Hispanics reside all over the United States but tend to be geographically concentrated most heavily in the West (44.7 percent) and in urban areas everywhere (46.4 percent). Only about 8 percent of Hispanics live in non-metropolitan areas (U.S. Census 2001a). Like the immigration of Southern Italians a century ago, the Hispanic immigration to the United States has often been a case of rural people in their countries of origin moving to take up urban residence in the United States. The small number of Hispanics found in rural areas of the United States together with their high rate of poverty and linguistic differences define their language and cultural isolation. Hispanics are a very heterogeneous group. The Hispanic population is primarily comprised of Mexicans (66.1 percent), Central and South American persons (14.5 percent), Puerto Ricans (9 percent), and Cubans (4 percent) . Mexicans are more likely to be in rural and nonmetropolitan areas than the Cubans or Puerto Ricans, who are heavily concentrated in urban New York and South Florida (Therrien and Ramirez 2000).

Education poses a serious problem for the Hispanic population in general. More than half the Hispanic population who are twenty-five years old and older has not graduated from high school, and another 25 percent have less than a ninth-grade education. With their high rate of poverty (22.8 percent) (Therrien and Ramirez 2000), owing, in part, to low educational attainment as well as associated linguistic and social difficulties, Hispanic people also face many health care challenges.

A large percentage of Hispanics are without health insurance coverage; 35 percent lacked such coverage in 1998 (National Council of La Raza 2001). The leading causes of unintentional injury deaths for Hispanics in 1999 were heart disease, cancer, stroke, and diabetes. Approximately 10 percent of Puerto Ricans and Mexicans have diabetes, which is twice the rate of non-Hispanic whites. All other Hispanics with the exception of Cubans also have an increased prevalence of diabetes greater than whites (Office of Minority Health 2002) and are twice as likely to die as a result of diabetes as are non-Hispanic whites (Kington, Tisnado, and Carlisle 2001; U.S. DHHS 2001b). Hispanics represented 20 percent of the new cases of tuberculosis in 1996 and have higher rates of hypertension and obesity than whites (U.S. DHHS 2001b). A study by Weinick and Krauss (2000) revealed that blacks and Hispanics are at greater risk than the general population for poor health care outcomes because of a lack of access. The same study showed that black and Hispanic children incurred persistent health care access disadvantages even when health insurance and socioeconomic status were held constant .

An additional disparity shared with other ethnic minority groups is the issue of access to quality health care. Lack of health care insurance benefits and a usual source of care, as well as linguistic and cultural differences, present disadvantaged minorities with barriers and often relegate them to sick and emergency care rather than health promotion and preventive care. Weinick and Krauss's findings suggest that, for Hispanic children, language ability and culture are the defining differences in health care access.

African Americans

The literature addressing issues of health disparities between African Americans and whites is copious. The issue with this minority group is not in the lack of study but in the persistent lack of parity. African Americans, like Native American, have higher rates of morbidity and mortality from a large variety of chronic illness than do non-Hispanic whites.

The connection between negative health outcomes and economic disadvantage is never seen as clearly as it is for this population. Twenty-six percent of African Americans live in poverty. Of all American families living in poverty, 23 percent or almost one-quarter are African American (McKinnon and Humes 2000). African Americans are more likely to live in severe poverty at a rate three times that of whites. Thus all the findings of the connection between low income and inadequate health care apply directly to this population.

According to the Rural Policy Research Institute as cited in U.S. DHHS (2001b), approximately 53 percent of all African Americans live in the South, and 15 percent of all African Americans live in rural communities. The African American family also has a different portrait than other American families. Of the 9 million African American families in the United States, 62 percent are living in single-parent families compared to 31 percent of other U.S. families. African American children are most likely to live in a female-headed family. For children who lived with one parent, African Americans were more likely to have lived with their mothers than were U.S. children overall (92 percent versus 69 percent) (U.S. Census Bureau, as cited in U.S. DHHS 2001b).

Ng-Mak and Dohrenwend (1999) conducted a longitudinal study to investigate the association between race and specific causes of mortality among adults twenty-five years old and older. The alarming results indicate that "black persons younger than 65 years were at higher risk than others *for all-*

causes (emphasis added) and cardiovascular mortality; the strongest effects were observed among persons aged 25 through 44 years" (1748). African Americans experience a disproportionate share of health problems as may be seen in the following:

- The diabetes rate is more than three times that of whites;
- The heart disease rate is more than 40 percent higher than that of whites;
- The prostate cancer rate is more than double that of whites;
- HIV/AIDS rates are more than seven times that of whites;
- The infant mortality rate is twice that of whites. (National Center for Health Statistics 1996)

A disparity in access to appropriate, high-quality service, deliverable through a "usual source" of care is indicated as a prime contributor to the disproportionately high level of morbidity for the African American population. In 1996, 76 percent of whites received most of their health care from an "office-based usual point of care." Such care is associated with health promotion and prevention. In contrast, African Americans are more likely to receive health care from emergency and outpatient hospital departments (U.S. DHHS 2001). Such care is not designed to include health promotion and disease prevention.

With the significant number of African American women who are heads of families, a review of the health and well-being of this population may serve as an indicator of the future health of the African American population. This picture provides no silver lining. African American women are more than twice as likely to die from heart diseases before the age of sixty-five and have twice the risk factor for hypertension, kidney disorders, diabetes mellitus, and septicemia. Moreover, this condition is not easily attributed to lack of awareness of health problems. African American women are also more likely to report "being in 'fair' or 'poor' health" (Rowland Hogue 2002, 222). The problem also appears not to lie in ignorance about health risks but rather in knowing what can be done about the risks.

Policy Issues

Many studies have been conducted regarding minority health issues. There is tremendous consistency in the finding of these reports: Racial and ethnic minorities in the United States continue to experience lack of parity in health status and access to health care. Access may be a particular issue for rural populations.

There have been efforts at the federal level to deal with the problem of minority health issues. The Office of Minority Health (OMH) was created by the U.S. Department of Health and Human Services (U.S. DHHS) in 1985 in response to the *Report of the Secretary's Task Force on Black and Minority Health*. For nearly two decades the mission of OMH has been to improve the health of racial and ethnic populations through the develop-ment of effective health policies and programs that eliminate disparities in health. OMH also monitors efforts to achieve the goals of *Healthy People 2010* (OMH, n.d.). In part, this mission involves special attention to the impact of general health policy on minority populations.

Healthy People 2010 provides a set of health objectives for the nation to achieve over the first decade of the new century. *Healthy People 2010* is designed to achieve two overarching goals, one of which is to eliminate health disparities among different segments of the population. In light of the goals of the OMH, a report by the Institute of Medicine (IOM) released in March 2002 indicated that minorities in America are still receiving poorer health care than whites, even when income, insurance, and medical con-ditions are similar. The report goes on to explain that minority death rates are higher for a number of chronic conditions (IOM 2002). Although rural minority groups were not explicitly singled out in the report, it is safe to assume that all these conclusions apply fully to them, given the relationship others have found between rural residence and access to health care, poverty, and so on. These findings are particularly discouraging given the time that has passed since OMH was created.

Cultural Competence

A great deal needs to be achieved before parity in health care can be realized for racially and ethnically diverse groups. One of the initiatives that may have a powerful role to play in reducing the disparities in minority health is cultural competence. Certainly the competence, including cultural competence, of those delivering health care has a role to play in achieving parity. Having health care providers who are culturally and linguistically diverse will help achieve parity. The U.S. Department of Health and Human Services defines cultural and linguistic competence as follows:

Cultural and linguistic competence is a set of congruent behaviors, attitudes, and policies that come together in a system, agency, or among professionals that enables effective work in cross-cultural situations. (2001, 1)

Consistent with this notion, U.S. DHHS also directs that health care must include:

- Care that is respectful of the patient's health-related beliefs and values;
- The recruitment, retention, and training of staff that reflect the demographics of the communities served and that are respectful of the beliefs, attitudes and behaviors of the individuals, families, and communities they serve (U.S. DHHS 2001);
- Knowledge of the community and a willingness to incorporate the voice of the community in designing and delivering health care services.

The need to have clear and effective communication between patients and their health care providers is of great importance. The Commonwealth Fund 2001 Health Care Quality Survey indicates that African American, Asian American, and Hispanic citizens all report difficulty communicating with their physicians. This was found to be most true for Hispanics and Asian Americans.

Language barriers can account for some of this communication difficulty; however, African Americans with English as their first language also indicated communication difficulties. In such cases the problems are clearly more psychosocial than linguistic. They reported that physicians did not listen fully, that they did not understand what their physicians said, and that they left their visits with unasked questions. Patient-physician communication, in all likelihood, is also related to cultural dissonance that is reflected in the inadequate number of physicians from the diverse racial and ethnic groups represented by patients. The Commonwealth Fund Survey also suggests that the problem is likely owing in part to a lack of familiarity among majority group physicians with the cultural background of their minority patients. Where rural minority citizens do succeed in accessing health care, communication problems because of these factors, and also because of the potential influences of more overt forms of discrimination on the part of providers, are sure to reduce the overall quality of care that can be expected. Problems of cultural competence in themselves represent formidable obstacles to be overcome in efforts to achieve adequate access to health care for minority populations.

Conclusions and Recommendations

At a time when America is becoming more diverse, significant portions of its population continue to experience lags in accessing high-quality culturally competent health care. Compared to their urban counterparts, rural communities face additional challenges indicative of physical isolation. Like their urban counterparts, rural minorities are significantly overrepresented in lower-income brackets and lower academic achievements.

The health care delivery system in the United States is plagued with rising cost, increasing numbers of underinsured and uninsured, and a practitioner pool that is unreflective of the diverse faces of the American populous. This bleak picture can be seen within the large densely populated urban mosaics. It is also evident within the more subtly emerging heterogeneous rural landscape. The failure of the health care system to address the unique health care needs of minority populations is as simple as monoculture-English-only-speaking white physicians and as complex as the antebellum history of oppression and discrimination that is still evident in today's lower quality of care provided to ethnic minorities.

Assuming equal access, if socioeconomic inequality were eliminated, "minority patients have a lower likelihood of receiving appropriate management of and treatments for their condition" (Kington, Tisnado, and Carlisle 2001, 60). However other factors also contribute to pervasive health care disparities, including cultural and linguistic barriers. For Native American persons, cultural and linguistic barriers are complicated by the history of distrust of mainstream America. When Native Americans do seek health care, the legendary poverty and social ills of the reservations and surrounding Indian communities result in fewer health care facilities, and in facilities with fewer resources and personnel that are less likely to be representative of the patients they treat. Some studies indicate that these personnel are less medically competent. A study by Brennan et al, as cited in Swift (2002) indicates that "these same hospitals [those that serve primarily minority patients] have significantly higher rates of adverse events due to medical negligence or errors compared to those hospitals not treating predominantly minority patients" (84). Linguistic challenges are evident in other ethnic minority groups such as Hispanics and Asian Americans. Simple interpretation services are not sufficient to enable heath care providers to understand how culture impacts help-seeking behavior, health behaviors, patients' perceptions of health, illness, treatment, and health care personnel. All these factors influence health status.

Disparity in health status, access to health care, and unequal quality of health care is still common for all minority group members and is exacerbated for those living in rural areas. Minorities lack access to regular health care providers and have few if any opportunities to secure services from providers that share their race or ethnic background or that have cultural similarities. Moreover, the evidence of race-based health care is growing with evidence of social inequalities reflected in both overt and subtle discrimination and bias. Studies show disparities in health care even when socioeconomic status and education are controlled for. The theory that improved patient knowledge, universal health care coverage, and elimination of the socioeconomic gap between minority and white Americans is the way to eliminate health care disparity is inadequate

Health care practitioners need to be aware of existing health care disparities and receive cross-cultural education. Health care practitioners and policy makers must advocate and provide care that is culturally sensitive. They must improve physician-patient communication. They need to develop treatment approaches that are culturally competent and deliver services that are responsive to racial and ethnic minority groups and their concerns. Practitioners must become comfortable with exploring possible cultural explanations of illness and at the same time not dismiss valid clinical information. Practitioners need to be sensitive to issues of distrust through their knowledge of past breaches of ethics and resulting harm to minority populations.

There are those who believe that the only way to convincingly decrease health care disparities is through the recruitment of underrepresented minority physicians. This presents a particular dilemma at a time when many minority communities are suffering from physician shortages and rural America is in the designation of Health Professional Shortage Areas (Health Resources Services Administration. as cited in Kington, Tisnado, and Carlisle 2001).

Health care consumers need information regarding health care resources as well as the financial resources to pay for health care. Health care providers need knowledge and skills related to working with patients who have had a different American experience from theirs, an experience of discrimination, abuse, and oppression as well as stereotyping. Patients with this experience may be dealing with issues of trust, cultural barriers related to the use of traditional remedies, and culturally specific beliefs and behaviors that make communication around health issues difficult.

Note

1. Medicaid is a combined program of the federal government and state governments that provides health care for those who are medically indigent.

References

Camasso, M. J., and D. E. Moore. 1985. Rurality and the residualist social welfare response. *Rural Sociology* 50 (3): 397–408.

Center for Disease Control and Prevention. 1998. "Prevalence of diagnosed diabetes among American Indians/Alaskan Natives: United States 1996." *Morbidity and Mortality Weekly Report* 47 (42): 901–904.

————. 2001. *Deaths: Preliminary data for 2000.* NVSR Vol. 49, No. 12, PHS 2001–1120.

————. 2002. *Infant mortality statistics from the 2000 period linked birth/infant death data set.* NVSR Vol. 50, No. 12, PHS 2002–1120.

Dalaker, J. 2001. *Poverty in the United States: 2000.* U.S. Census Bureau, Current Population Reports, Series P60–214. Washington, D.C.: U.S. Government Printing Office.

Day, J. C. 1996. *Population projections of the United States by age, sex, race, and Hispanic origin: 1995 to 2050.* U.S. Bureau of the Census, Current Population Report, P25–1130. Washington, D.C.: U.S. Government Printing Office.

Gornick, Marian E. 2000. Disparities in Medicare services: Potential causes, plausible explanations, and recommendations. *Health Care Financing Review* 21 (4): 23–44.

Henry J. Kaiser Family Foundation. 1999. *Perceptions of how race and ethnic background affect medical care: Highlights from focus groups.* Available online at http://www.kff.org/content/1999/1524. Retrieved August 12 2002.

Hargraves, J. L. 2002. *The insurance gap and minority health care 1997–2001.* Center for Studying Health System Change. Available online at http://www.hschange.com/CONTENT/443/. Retrieved October 12 2002.

Health Resources and Services Administration. 2001. *Cultural competence works: Using cultural competence to improve the quality of health care for diverse populations and add value to managed care arrangements.* U.S. Department of Health and Human Services. Available online at www.hrsa.gov/financeMC/ftp/cultural-competence.pdf. Retrieved October 29 2002.

Humes, D., and J. McKinnon. 2000. *The Asian and Pacific Islander population in the United States: March 1999.* U.S. Census Bureau, Current Population Reports, Series P20–529. Washington, D.C.: U.S. Government Printing Office.

Iceland, John, Daniel H. Weinberg, and Erika Steinmetz. 2002. U.S. Census Bureau,

Series CENSR-3, *Racial and ethnic residential segregation in the United States: 1980–2000*. Washington, D.C.: U.S. Government Printing Office.

Indian Health Service. 1997. *Trends in Indian health*. Rockville, Md.: Published by the author.

Institute of Medicine. 2002. *Care without coverage: Too little, too late*. Report from the Board on Health Care Services Committee on the Consequences of Uninsurance. Washington. D.C.: National Academy Press.

Kington, Raynard, Diana Tisnado, and David M. Carlisle. 2001. "Increasing racial and ethnic diversity among physicians: an intervention to address health disparities?" Summary of the Symposium on Diversity in Health Professions in Honor of Herbert W. Nickens, M.D.

Mather, Mark. 2003. *Patterns of poverty in America*. Population Reference Bureau. Available online at http://www.prb.org/template.cfm?template = Interest-Display.cfmandInterestCategoryID = 238. Retrieved January 21 2003.

McKinnon, J., and D. Humes. 2000. *The black population in the United States: March 1999*. U.S. Census Bureau, Current Population Reports, Series P20–530. Washington. D.C.: U.S. Government Printing Office.

Mukamel, D. B., A. S. Murthy, and D. L. Weimer. 2000. Racial differences in access to high-quality cardiac surgeons. *American Journal of Public Health* 90 (11): 1774–1778.

National Center for Health Statistics. 1996. *Leading causes of death by age, sex, race, and Hispanic origin: United States 1992*. Vital and Health Statistics; PHS Report No. 96–1857. Washington, D.C.: U.S. Government Printing Office.

———. 2001. *Health, United States 2001, with Urban and Rural Health Chartbook*. Hyattsville, Md.

National Council of La Raza. 2001. *Twenty most frequently asked questions about the Latino community: Updated March 2001*. Available online at http://www.nclr.org/about/nclrfaq.html. Retrieved October 26 2002.

Ng-Mak, D. S., and B. P. Dohrenwend. 1999. A further analysis of race differences in the national longitudinal mortality study. *American Journal of Public Health* 89 (11): 1748–1752.

Office of Minority Health. N.d. *Overview*. Available online at http://www.hrsa.gov/OMH/overview.htm. Retrieved October 26 2002.

———. 2001. Assessment of state minority health infrastructure and capacity to address issues of health disparity. Available online at http://www.omhrc.gov/omh/sidebar/cossmo/sec_1c.htm. Retrieved October 29 2002.

Population Reference Bureau. 2000. *2000 United States population data sheet* [Wall chart]. Washington, D.C.: Published by author.

Ross, H. 2000. Lifting the unequal burden of cancer on minorities and the underserved. *Closing the Gap* (August): 1–2.

———. 2001. Office of minority health publishes final standards for cultural and linguistic competence. *Closing the Gap* (February/March): 1–2.

Rowland Hogue, C. J. 2002. Toward a systematic approach to understanding — and ultimately eliminating — African American women's health disparities. *Women's Health Issues* 12 (5): 222–237.

Rural Policy Research Institute. 1999. *Rural by the numbers: Information about rural America: Demographics.* Available online at http://www.rupri.org/policyres/ rnumbers/demopop/demo.html. Retrieved September 10 2002.

Scanlan, James P. 2000. Race and mortality. *Society* 37 (2): 29–35.

Schneider, A., J. and Martinez. 1997. *Native Americans and Medicaid: Coverage and financing issues.* Kaiser Commission on Medicaid and the Uninsured. Available online at http://www.kff.org/content/archive/2101/polbren.html. Retrieved October 12 2002.

Shambaugh-Miller, M. D., J. A. Stoner, L. G. Pol, and K. J. Mueller. 2002. Health services at risk in "vulnerable" rural places. RUPRI Rural Policy Brief 7 (5): PB 2002–5. Omaha: RUPRI Center for Rural Health Policy Analysis.

Slifkin, R. T., L. J. Goldsmith, and T. C. Ricketts. 2000. *Race and place: Urban-rural differences in health for racial and ethnic minorities.* University of North Carolina, North Carolina Rural Health Research Program. Available online at www.unc.edu/research_programs/Rural_Program/rhp.html. Retrieved September 20 2002.

Snipp, M. C. 1996. Understanding race and ethnicity in rural America. *Rural Sociology* 61 (1): 125–142.

Summers, G. F. 1991. Minorities in rural society. *Rural Sociology* 56 (2): 177–188.

Swift, E. K., ed. 2002. *Guidance for the National Healthcare Disparities Report.* Washington, D.C.: National Academies Press.

Therrien, M., and R. R. Ramirez. 2000. *The Hispanic population in the United States: March 2000.* U.S. Census Bureau, Current Population Reports, Series P20–535. Washington. D.C.: U.S. Government Printing Office.

U.S. Census Bureau. 2001a. *The Hispanic population.* Census 2000 Brief. Available online at http://www.census.gov/population/www/cen2000/briefs.html. Retrieved June 30 2002.

———. 2001b. *Profiles of general demographic characteristics: 2000 Census of population and housing, United States.* Available at http://www2.census.gov/census_2000/datasets/demographic_profile/0_National_Summary/2khus.pdf. Retrieved June 30 2002.

———. 2002a. *Health insurance coverage: 2001.* Available online at http:// www.census.gov/hhes/www/hlthin01.html. Retrieved June 30 2002.

———. 2002b. *The American Indian and Alaska Native Population: 2000.* Census 2000 Brief No. C2KBR/01–15. Washington, D.C.: Published by the author.

U.S. Department of Health and Human Services. 1998. *The initiative to eliminate racial and ethnic disparities in health.* Available online at http://raceandhealth.hhs.gov. Retrieved September 15 2002.

———. 2000. *Healthy people 2010.* Rockville, Md.: Published by the author.

————. 2001a. *HHS Fact Sheet: Achieving new milestones in minority health*. Washington, D.C.: Published by the author.

————. 2001b. *Mental health: Culture, race, and ethnicity — A supplement to mental health: A report of the Surgeon General*. Rockville, Md.: Published by the author.

————. 2002. *One department serving rural America*. HHS Rural Task Force Report to the Secretary. July.

Weinick, R. M, and N. A. Krauss. 2000. Racial/ethnic differences in children's access to care. *American Journal of Public Health* 90 (11): 1771–1775.

12 Gay Men and Lesbians in Rural Areas

Acknowledging, Valuing, and Empowering This Stigmatized Invisible People

Chatman Neely

There is a particular need to educate social work providers who live in rural areas, where services may be more limited, about a population that is often invisible and subject to inappropriate, coercive, and even oppressive social sanctions (Atkinson and Hackett 1995; D'Augelli 1995; Mc-Carthy 2000; Smith and Mancoske 1998). The homosexual population in the United States is one of the more diverse minority groups in the country. Gays and lesbians are found in all social, economic, racial/ethnic, professional/work, and religious denominations (DuBois 1999). They may also be the most invisible minority group and one of the least understood (McDonald and Steinhorn 1990; Green and Herek 1994; Appleby and Anastas 1998; Wormer, Wells, and Boes 2000; Tully 2000; Ritter and Terndrup 2002). As the number of gay men and lesbian women coming out of the closet increases, so, too, does the need to understand their lives (Atkinson and Hackett 1995; D'Augelli 1998; McCarthy 2000; Smith and Mancoske 1998).

This chapter provides information about the experience of being gay or lesbian in a rural setting. It also addresses the commitment of the social work profession to advocate for those who are oppressed or marginalized or both (Zastrow 1998; Kirst-Ashman and Hull; 1997; Ginsberg 1998). With gays and lesbians, oppression and marginalization are largely due to the lack of institutionalized policies and laws that would provide universal recognition and protection. Oppressive and discriminating institutions, policies, and laws may, in fact, be more pervasive in rural settings than in more diverse urban settings (McFarland 1989; Fellows 1996: Lord and Reid 1995).

For social workers, dealing with gay and lesbian persons can evoke a variety of feelings, attitudes, and responses for both the seasoned and novice worker. Some research suggests that the intensity of these feelings, attitudes, and responses may be more pronounced in rural environments than in other settings (Appleby and Anastas 1998; Sears 1991).

Cohler and Galatzer-Levy (2000) and Ritter and Terndrup (2002) noted that institutional intolerance and personal hostility toward gay men and lesbians remain a fact of life in the United States. Gays and lesbians represent a challenge to the traditional beliefs and attitudes of many social workers (Herek 1995; O'Hare, Williams, and Ezovisk 1996; Weiner and Siegel 1990; and Appleby and Anastas). Some perceive homosexuality as an act against God, while others consider it a violation of the laws of nature. A helper with such attitudes may offer gay and lesbian consumers inferior service or no service at all. In response, gay and lesbian consumers may be less likely to seek help, and, when they do, they may be apprehensive about the effect of their sexual orientation on service delivery. Social workers need to understand that gay or lesbian clients may avoid treatment for fear of being perceived as deviant or mentally ill because of their sexual orientation instead of having helpers understand the issues of living in a homophobic culture.

While much research has been published on gay and lesbian identity development, little research has been conducted that addresses the life experience of being rural and gay or lesbian. The gay and lesbian community is very diverse in ethnicity, gender, race, and social class; however, most of what we know is based on the study of urban, white, and well-educated people (Appleby and Anastas 1998; Cohler and Galatzer-Levy 2000; Ritter and Terndrup 2002; Smith and Mancoske 1997; Fellows 1996). This research may have limited applicability to gays or lesbians of color, children and adolescents, older adults, and rural populations.

Discussion of the rural gay or lesbian experience is at best anecdotal. Research reveals that numerous social, political, financial, and religious factors affect tolerance for gays and lesbians in rural communities, where traditional morals, values, and behaviors still prevail (McDonald and Steinhorn 1993). Given the traditional expectations of rural areas such as the importance of family name and honor, race, gender, class boundaries, and fundamentalist religions, some suggest that being gay or lesbian in rural areas may be more challenging and difficult than in less traditional settings (D'Augelli 1995; McCarthy 2000). According to McDonald and Steinhorn (1993), life in some parts of rural America is "like living in a goldfish bowl where almost everyone knows everyone else's daily activities, associations, and comings and goings" (129). Consequently gays and lesbians may feel constant pressure to be discreet, to remain invisible, and to socialize with extreme selectivity (McCarthy 2000).

This may be changing, however. A recent issue of the national gay and lesbian magazine *The Advocate* (2000) published a special report on the growing number of sexual minorities in small towns and rural areas within the United States. Bull (2000) noted that the decision of many to remain in rural areas "is a reversal of the great gay migration of the latter half of the 20th century when many gay men moved to the cities where they believed they could live openly and free of discrimination" (66). In fact, with the onset of the information age (the Internet, political organizations, support groups, etc.) gay and lesbian inclusive social groups are now increasingly found in less-populated areas (Ritter and Terndrup 2002).

Gay and Lesbian Identity Formation

Much of the theory about personality structure assumes that behavioral characteristics are developed relatively early in life and that events in later childhood, adolescence, and adulthood represent an unfolding of these characteristics over time (Kegan 1998). Such approaches tend to be static. They don't allow for ongoing development, as Erickson's (1980) theory of personality development throughout adulthood does (D'Augelli and Patterson 1995). Human behavior surrounding sexuality, intimacy, affection, and identity is complex, and this complexity has to be acknowledged when dealing with sexual orientation (Appleby and Anastas 1998, 47). Sexual orientation is a derivative of developmental, interpersonal, experiential, and cultural influences that are associated with deep and complex intra psychic, personal, relational, and social meanings (Stein 1997). Sexual orientation is currently understood as a multidimensional constellation of characteristics that challenges precise definition but often is misunderstood as a singular concept, such as sexual behavior, sexual desire, or sexual identity (Michaels 1996).

Perhaps the best-known descriptions of gay and lesbian identity formation are found in the work of Cass (1979, 1990), Troiden (1989), Coleman (1982), and Grace (1992), all of which identify characteristic stages of identity formation and further propose that identity foreclosure may occur at any stage effectively stalling development at that level. All these models indicate that gay and lesbian identities form against a backdrop of stigma. The process maintains a back and forth movement as gay men or lesbians manage this "stigma" while they accept and apply their homosexual orientation to themselves.

The following brief summaries of these four contemporary models of gay identity development is followed by a discussion of the limitations of these developmental models. The four models represent current mainstream thinking about gay and lesbian identity formation. Although they list different numbers of stages to explain identity formation, they describe strikingly comparable patterns of growth and change as major hallmarks of such identity development. It is important to note that there is no model based on empirical evidence that examines how a rural gay or lesbian identity is formed. The following summaries are based on Ritter and Terndrup's (2002) discussions of identity formation.

The Cass Model

During several years of clinical work with gay and lesbian clients, Australian psychologist Vivienne Cass (1979, 1983–84) generated a theoretical model of identity formation which she applied to both men and women of homosexual orientation. Cass (1979) assumed that "identity is acquired through a development process" (219) and that the "stability and change in human behavior are dependent on the congruency or incongruence that exists within an individual's interpersonal environment" (220).

The Troiden Model

Sociologist Richard Troiden elaborated on his own previous work (1979) in which he synthesized the works of Cass (1979), Plummer (1975), and Ponse (1978) in order to formulate a four-stage model of gay and lesbian identity development. Troiden's (1989) model views identity formation as "taking place against a backdrop of stigma" (47) and developing over an extended period, incorporating a number of crucial transitions, and involving eventual self-labeling as gay or lesbian. Because Troiden's stages are nonlinear, they build on one another, sometimes recur, and often overlap. He identified these stages as Sensitization, Identity Confusion, Identity Assumption, and Commitment.

The Coleman Model

Psychologist Eli Coleman (1982) proposed a five-stage model of identity development. His model assumes that people enter into identity formation at different stages and that not everyone passes through every phase. Further, Coleman believes that some individuals are challenged by developmental tasks of more than one stage at a time and that identity synthesis depends on mastery of tasks at all previous levels. However, he posits that some people: "become locked into one stage or another and never experience identity integration" (32). His stages consist of Pre–Coming Out; Coming Out; Exploration; First Relationships: and Integration.

The Grace Model

John Grace (1992), a social worker, proposed another five-stage model of gay and lesbian identity formation, one that reflects a distinctly social work perspective on the interplay of person and environment. According to Grace, the concept of homophobia (or heterosexism) must be understood before the developmental dilemmas faced by gay men can be explained. He posits that heterosexism creates a climate that leads to homophobic beliefs, attitudes, and reactions. To facilitate such an understanding, Grace identified " extrinsic impediments to self-identification among four specific categories of homophobia: personal/active, personal/passive, institutional/active and institutional/passive" (34). He describes the final stage of identity development as "an open-ended, ongoing, and lifelong process" (46).

Several conclusions might be drawn from these studies:

1. An awareness of same-gender sexual desire initiates a developmental phase or transition where the individual reports feeling different. Many initially report feeling "confused" or "uncertain or questioning" during this period.
2. Individuals typically feel that they need to reconcile their potential gay or lesbian identity because it is negatively portrayed in their culture.
3. Gay men and lesbians look for ways to deal with the stigma associated with homosexuality.
4. The individual explores a gay or lesbian subculture and looks for other gay and lesbian people to "socialize" with.
5. Over time gay men and lesbians experience an increased desire to disclose their identity to a growing number of friends, family, and coworkers.

A rural setting may pose increased difficulties for the gay and lesbian person with regard to the steps listed above, because most gays or lesbians are likely to be isolated and do not have easy access to gay or lesbian peers, role models, or communities.

Although generally a stage-sequential linear progression is assumed in gay and lesbian identity development, the research indicates that the process might be better conceptualized as a repeating spiral pattern (Troiden 1988; Shelby 2000). It is important to remember that each model posits that development as a gay or lesbian is a process of interaction, not a set of stagnant categories. Reference to stages is useful in that it allows us to recognize significant shifts occurring in individual cognition and interactional relationships.

It is important, however, to be cautious about the generalizability of research findings or identity formation models developed on limited samples. For findings or models to be generalizable to the population as a whole, samples need to represent the characteristics found in the larger population. This is often not the case. Samples may not include both genders nor all ages, ethnicities, educational levels, religious backgrounds, geographic locations, or people of varying socioeconomic status. The definition of sexual orientation used in the research may further limit its applicability to a larger population.

The process of drawing research samples has resulted in individuals in rural settings often being underrepresented in research that has been conducted (Brady and Busse 1994). This means that much of the discussion of rural gays and lesbians is anecdotal. Several oral histories and researched novels (Bly 1982; Fellows 1996; Katz 1976; Reid 1973) have reported on the experiences of gay men living in rural areas. However, most of these studies were conduced on gay men who had moved to urban areas and reported on their previous experiences in rural areas.

Most of the research that has been done reports that numerous social, political, financial, and religious constraints exist in rural communities where traditional morals, values, and behaviors prevail (H. B. McDonald and Steinhorn 1993). It is important to recognize this when addressing unique aspects of rural gay and lesbian identity formation.

Public Perception of Gays and Lesbians in Rural Areas

What are the unique day-to-day realties of rural settings that may enhance or limit optimal living situations for gay or lesbian persons? Based on a review of existing research it is reasonable to assume that being different is not always welcomed in a rural setting (Drake 2001; Inscoe 2001; Ginsberg

1998). Sameness in many rural communities is a prescribed way of life, and being different often leads to social, familial, and personal isolation. Gay and lesbian persons may be more tentative in establishing social and personal associations in rural settings because of uncertainty as to how their "difference" may be perceived by others. This may also partially determine to what degree they are "out of the closet." Therefore it is important for social workers to be aware of verbal and nonverbal patterns of communication when dealing with issues of sexual orientation. It is essential for social workers to recognize and appreciate that while more gay men and lesbian women are visible today, in rural settings they are very aware that the world as they know and experience it is predominantly heterosexual.

Identity development is interpersonal and for many rural gay men and lesbian women, their sexual orientation is primarily an intellectual one because of limited opportunities to meet others like themselves. Gays or lesbians who have no access to other gay or lesbian persons must accept having little or no contact with others like them. Social workers need to understand how challenging it may be for a gay or lesbian person to know that what they want, need, sense, desire, and long for is different from what is socially, culturally, and family prescribed. For the concerned social worker it can be unsettling to recognize that gay and lesbian identity develops within the context of heterosexism, which socially constructs homosexuality as deviant or sick and can create varied levels of anxiety. The socially conservative and traditional rural climate and lack of role models and affirming culture results in many gays and lesbians reporting that they feel disconnected from the majority of their society.

While each client encounter is unique, nearly all rural gays and lesbians who have been treated by the author have reported a strong sense of discomfort regarding the discrimination they may experience because of their perceived or acknowledged sexual orientation. Some of the events they recall in their lives have had a major influence on how they see themselves. They report that living in a rural area is a difficult life for them.

Practice Issues Specific to Rural Gay and Lesbians

It is not uncommon for a rural social worker to say; "I don't know any gay men or lesbian women and don't believe there are any in my community." Such a statement reflects societal, cultural, and institutional bias, and demonstrates the need for ongoing education and training programs for rural social workers. It is essential for social workers to recognize that gay men and lesbians live as an oppressed group in a heterosexual society. Given that heterosexism is more apparent in a rural setting it may be that gays and lesbians in rural areas experience an even higher level of oppression. Social work has always seen part of its mission as serving the oppressed and minority populations with a goal of social change as an integral part of any intervention.

In order to apply affirmative knowledge and values to specific gays and lesbians, competent providers need to understand the impact of sexual orientation on presenting problems without feeling discomfort when discussing sex and sexuality. Discrimination that gays and lesbians may face in day-to-day living, education and employment needs to be addressed in all human service settings and advocacy endeavors. Social workers must be prepared to access current research and literature, continuing education, training workshops, and Internet resources (Tully 2000). Competent practice with rural gays and lesbians necessitates that social workers demonstrate knowledge and awareness of issues in a rural setting that affect identity development and the coming-out process. This issue is crucial for rural social workers because most have had minimal training and experience in working with rural gay and lesbian populations (Mallow 1998; Ryan and Futterman 1998).

Many authors writing on the subject of rural social work agree that a generalist approach is the essence of rural social work practice (Ginsberg 1993). Generalist social work practice techniques are important strategies but are not always affirming to gay and lesbian clients. Those techniques may not result in the specific knowledge and skills needed for effective social work with gay and lesbian clients in a rural setting. The generalist focus on understanding and incorporating macro, mezzo, and micro levels of practice is imperative for social workers when working with this population. Issues of sexuality, sexual orientation, traditional values, religious beliefs, and political climate need to be addressed and may not be sufficiently emphasized in generalist preparation. According to Mallon (1998, 42):

> Professional social workers must engage in a process of self-examination and change that in turn will contribute to the creation of more trustworthy professional relationships with clients and trustworthy programs and organizations for gay and lesbian clients.

A generalist approach coupled with a stance embracing affirmation of gay and lesbian people are needed to work effectively with this population. The author has identified several themes commonly reported by gay men and lesbians in rural areas seeking social services. These themes include social isolation, confusion of one's identity as gay or lesbian, fear of coming out, anxiety about feeling different, ambivalence toward sexuality, fear for self and family, fear of family abandonment, anxiety over religious intolerance, and uncertainty regarding staying in the community.

Personal and Professional Bias Toward Gay Men and Lesbians

Studies in social work, psychology, and other social sciences consistently show that bias against gay men and lesbians is high among practicing and teaching professionals (Garnets et al. 1991; Humphreys 1983). This homophobic bias likely leads to less content on gay men and lesbians being presented in seminars, in-service workshops, and courses than would be the case if the bias were not present (Appleby and Anastas 1998; Green and Herek 1995; Ritter and Terndrup 2002).

One of the most difficult tasks of social workers is to honor the dignity and worth of all clients. It is essential that rural workers be prepared to address personal biases that have formed because of their own ethnic, cultural, and regional background. Many times rural social workers must gain trust and earn respect from community members. Therefore social workers need to be highly visible and easily approachable (Ginsberg 1998; Ryan and Futterman 1998). Earning the rural community's trust may sometimes be at odds with adequately supporting gay and lesbian clients. Visibility and approachability are particularly necessary for effective work with gay and lesbian clients. In theory, social workers are prepared to address community bias, but in rural areas gay and lesbian populations are not commonly designated as a priority in terms of diversity training, ethical practice protocol, and service delivery. Acceptance occurs when social workers accept people wherever and whomever they are (Reamer 1995).

Competent social work practice with rural gays and lesbians requires that the social worker demonstrate a commitment to honor the dignity and worth of clients with diverse sexual orientations. It is important to promote safe and inclusive environments for both gay and lesbian workers and clients. It is equally vital that social workers find ways to promote social justice and human rights inclusive of gays and lesbians. Awareness of the political and practice stances of the National Association of Social Workers (NASW) and the Council on Social Work Education (CSWE) on gay and lesbian issues is a part of promoting social justice. Equally important is advocating for rural gays and lesbians.

A spectrum of feelings ranging from homophobic disapproval and rejection to an empowering attitude of affirmation may be found among social workers working with clients whom they know or assume are gay or lesbians. All social workers must confront homophobia at any level as an occupational hazard. Homophobia has profound implications for the delivery of social services. According to DuBois and Miley (1999, 201):

> In social work, ignorance and prejudice lead to the inaccurate identification of problems (erroneously assuming that homosexuality is the problem), inappropriate treatment goals (falsely targeting a cure for "sexual deviance"), and improper delivery of services (lacking sensitivity to the pervasiveness of homophobia in the delivery of services).

The creation of an atmosphere and attitude that allows gay and lesbian persons to be open, self-accepting, and self-affirming is essential (Cabji and Stein 1995). Therefore, if social workers want to be helpful to gay men and lesbian clients, it is important that they understand their own feelings about homosexuality. Many helpers have difficulty mastering this task. It can be especially difficult when the person they are to accept is from a different race, gender, religion, culture, or sexual orientation. At times the difference may be a violation of one of the helpers' closely held beliefs. Consequently their awareness can be clouded as they use these beliefs as their reason for not accepting people for who they are.

It is inevitable that providers' feelings about homosexuality will strongly influence their interactions with gay and lesbian clients (Domenici and Lesser 1995). Though many people may describe themselves as tolerant of gays and lesbians, tolerance alone is not sufficient. Affirmation of gay or lesbian identity allows for the free expression of concerns and joys related to being a a gay man or a lesbian, and it is the most appropriate client-oriented stance for working with gays and lesbians. To genuinely affirm gay and lesbian identity, social workers must be comfortable with their own sexual orientation so that they are able to celebrate and encourage their clients' exploration of gay and lesbian identity issues.

Managing "Difference"

Given the complicated stressors associated with gay or lesbian identity formation, it is not surprising that the most common experience of being a young gay or lesbian individual is "a profound sense of difference" (Cabaj and Stein 1995, 273). Because one's sense of sexual identity is formed when one is young, this experience is significant. While many gays and lesbians confront nonacceptance from the general population regardless of locality, they are perhaps nowhere more subject to hostility or more reminded of their differences than in rural communities (Harry 1990; McDonald and Steinhorn 1993). In rural areas, more than any other geographic setting, conformity is strongly urged, if not demanded. Deviation from the "traditional way of living" is often strongly discouraged (Drake 2001; Shapiro 1986).

Gay men and lesbians commonly disclose that a great deal of psychological and physical energy is needed to manage their feeling of being "different." This seems partially based on how they think others may feel or respond to them were their sexual orientation openly conveyed. The effort to manage this difference produces anxiety, fear, and ambivalence regarding various aspects of their lives. Hiding or disguising aspects of their self can lead to lowered self-esteem. Often school and other social settings become places of discomfort for fear, either real or imagined, of being verbally or physically harassed for being "different."

Social workers need to be aware of how gay men and lesbians manage these feelings and thoughts, and how they experience the sense of being different. The concept of "difference" is a main focus when working with rural gays and lesbians. For example, issues that relate to working, keeping busy, and taking care of oneself may become a focus that lends meaning to their lives and helps some to forget that they are different. Some gays and lesbians report a dread of the future, a fear of being alone, a sense of not being seen for who they are. Many dislike the feeling of being different and identify being invisible as a means of hiding their difference as one of the most pressing concerns in their daily lives. Some report not wanting to think about being different. Some even disavow their own recognition of being gay or lesbian simply because they cannot tolerate feeling different. It is also common for gays and lesbians to report that no one knows how they feel other than other gays and lesbians living in a rural area.

Isolation

Isolation is a key issue for rural gay men and lesbians. Using support or therapy groups can be an ideal intervention to address issues of isolation and help normalize the experience of a gay or lesbian person (Charde and Viets 1987; Mancoske and Lindhorst 1994). Such groups allow discovery that others do understand how they feel, that they themselves understand how others feel, and that others may exist as a reference group for them. Many gays and lesbians have turned to the Internet for many of the same reasons as a source of contact with other gays and lesbians, and as a place to obtain information. The Internet may provide a venue for rural gay men or lesbians to feel less isolated by providing links to others who understand and see them for who they are. It is important for Internet resources to be affirming of positive identity development as well as understanding of the complex bio-psycho-social needs of rural gay and lesbian people.

Work

Discrimination and on-the-job harassment facing gays and lesbians in the workplace need to be discussed in all human service settings as a regular aspect of advocacy. Many individuals consistently relate that being gay and lesbian is definitely a strike against them in the workplace. Work is often identified as a place where gays and lesbians are acutely aware that they are different. They want to do their best in their job in order to maintain a sense of security, sensing, perhaps, that if they work really hard they may not be discriminated against because of their sexual orientation. A central theme is the feeling that they need to interact in work settings in a self-protective way.

Family and Relationship Issues

The social worker engaged with this population needs to understand and be prepared to address family and relationship issues. It is important that workers realize that the stigma that exists in a rural setting is a barrier for gay men and lesbians who might otherwise seek help.

For some rural gay men, in particular, feeling "different" is most noticeable when they describe their relationships with their fathers. It is frequently reported that relationships with their mothers were more comfortable and did not seem to magnify their feelings of difference as much as relationships with their fathers. Stories of how their fathers would tell "fag" jokes are reported as being very disturbing and reinforcing the need to remain secretive about their sexual orientation. Gays in rural areas who seek psychotherapy also report that they are more fearful of their fathers than their mothers, although it is often unclear as to where this fear originates. The concepts of masculinity and femininity are frequently discussed in relation to how they felt they were viewed by their fathers and mothers. The important point is that it is not always clear whether they actually felt that they were different or if others were relating to them differently because of their sexual orientation. The process is reported as both an internal and external awareness. This is an area in need of further investigation.

Gay men and lesbians may also report that living an "out" and safe life in a rural area and in an open and affirming relationship is not possible. This awareness can impede their ability to start or maintain an intimate relationship. Dating and getting to know someone can be challenging as it involves having to deal with different levels of "coming out." Many relate that having a relationship would draw unwanted attention to them. Again, "managing difference" is a central theme in how a gay man or lesbian may approach each day. "Coming out" or "staying in the closet" is dictated by how others view and respond to them as being different. Although this may be true for all gays and lesbians, the consequences of coming out in rural areas may be more severe.

Religion

Church affiliations are very important in many rural communities. How a particular church or denomination addresses homosexuality can dictate how that community deals with gay men and lesbians. It is rare for fundamentalist and conservative religious denominations to discuss a homosexual orientation in an affirming context. According to Blumefield and Raymond (1988) and Goss (1993), organized religion has contributed considerably to the tormenting of gays and lesbians through an unending history of adverse bias. Such biases can lead to social isolation, exclusion, and discrimination (Haldeman 1994). It is important for rural practitioners working with gays and lesbians to identify both the strengths and conflicts involved in their relationship to religion and spirituality (Turluck 2000). Rural residents also tend to depend on, and in some cases be controlled by, a local church. As a result, a community member who is ostracized for being gay or lesbian may also have difficulty finding employment or a place to worship (Vaid 1996).

It is important for service providers to consider their own religious/spiritual values as well as those of the communities in which they practice. This

is especially important when dealing with the issue of homosexual orientation. Oppressive religious attitudes can have a tremendous impact on rural
gay men and lesbians. Spirituality should always be addressed when working
with this population. According to Cabaj and Stein (1995, 892):

> Understanding the importance of spirituality in a person's life and
> investigating the underlying meanings of religious attachments help
> to create a context in which the individual may fully integrate spiri-
> tuality into the gestalt of identity.

Practicing social service providers may find themselves in complex dilemmas
regarding how to challenge the existing religious values in rural settings.
The religious climate in a rural setting can impact the decision of a gay man
or lesbian to seek social services. Few small communities in the United States
have any provisions to protect gays and lesbians with regard to housing,
employment, parental rights, and partnered/domestic relations (Smith and
Mancoske 1997). A community that is "known" to be religiously conservative
presents a unique challenge to practitioners working with gay men and
lesbians.

Issues for Rural Gay and Lesbian Youth

Even though there is more visibility for gays and lesbians in general, there
is still a high level of invisibility in rural areas. This means that a place of
birth can be crucial to the development of a gay or lesbian identity. According to Siegel and Lowe (1995, 101):

> In more rural areas, however, even the concept of homosexuality as a
> statistical human reality may not be in a child's frame of reference.
> Alone without information or even a frame of reference for his think-
> ing, a youngster can create a lot of fiction about how he is , and so
> can everybody else. He then may base his life on the story he tells
> himself with the help of the frightened and ignorant population sur-
> rounding him.

Understanding issues specific to adolescents who identify as gays or lesbians
and are questioning their sexual orientation is useful in all settings where
services are provided for children and adolescents. There is an increasing
amount of research regarding the developmental perspectives of gay and

lesbian identity. However, the research is limited with regard to childhood and adolescence, especially in rural areas. When working with children and adolescents, very few social workers make sexuality issues a regular part of their assessment interview. Even fewer address sexual orientation concerns (Ryan and Futterman 1998). Until the 1990s few research studies existed showing that gay and lesbian youth were going through anything more than a disorder or a "passing phase" (Martin and Hetrick 1998). It can also be very difficult to find positive gay and lesbian role models in the rural setting. Some theorists (Coleman 1982; Grace 1992; Cass 1990) discuss the importance of gays and lesbians having access to role models who live their lives "out and open" in order to be able to identify with their own gay or lesbian feelings.

These factors present unique ethical, practice, and advocacy dilemmas for all who work with this population in rural areas. Recent research has indicated that gay/lesbian teenagers are at higher risk of suicide because of issues related to their sexual orientation and coming-out process (Hunter and Schaecher 1995). Some researchers posit that between 7 percent and 30 percent of all teen suicide attempts may be related to struggles with sexual orientation (Ryan and Futterman 1998). Research and data support the premise that being gay or lesbian can be associated with an increased risk of attempted suicide. Thus understanding suicide and preventing suicide are important challenges for all social workers working with gay and lesbian youth. There is also reason to suspect that this may be an even greater concern for gay and lesbian youth in rural areas because of the isolation and discrimination they may experience.

The very limited number of gay and lesbian affirming programs in rural settings means that individuals and families dealing with issues regarding gay and lesbian youth have even fewer opportunities for contact with positive role models. It is not uncommon for gay and lesbian youth and adults to report in counseling that they do not know anyone like themselves. Research reports that the most effective way to lower homophobic feelings, beliefs, and values is for a person to know and have contact with a gay male or a lesbian (Blumfield 1992; Fone 2000).

Civil Rights, "Passing," Confidentiality, and Ethical Treatment

Many gays and lesbians experience harsh reprisals in jobs, family, religious/spiritual, military and educational systems when they come out (Tully

1995; Miley et al. 2004). It is important that all human service providers understand that simply by being who they are, regardless of gender, age, social class, or religion, gays and lesbians are denied the rights that heterosexuals have in marriage, child custody and adoption options, insurance and inheritance benefits, as well as employment and educational opportunities. The Massachusetts Supreme Court recognized this in 2003 when it held that the state of Massachusetts must allow gays and lesbians to marry so they could experience equal treatment under the Massachusetts constitution.

Numerous factors affect the psychological and social health of gays and lesbians. However, the impact of institutional attitudes manifested through the courts, legislatures, and the military, as well as political and religious organizations, may have the most lasting and devastating consequences. Problems caused by discrimination, being victimized by hate crime attacks, differing needs related to developmental issues, and living in an oppressive environment can all provoke mental health crises. It is important to remember that rural life can increase many of these difficulties for gays and lesbians owing to the social, political, financial, and religious constraints existing in these communities. Thus it is essential when working with gays and lesbians to understand the lack of civil rights in their lives.

Many social workers erroneously believe that gays and lesbians are treated as fairly as heterosexuals. This can be seen as a cultural and institutional bias asserting that gay men and lesbians want "special rights." Only a handful of states and several urban areas have passed laws protecting gays and lesbians from discrimination on the basis of sexual orientation. And the passage of these laws has provoked a spate of counterattacks that characterize antidiscrimination efforts as attempts to gain special rights. Moreover, the situation is not getting better, as many states and localities seek to find ways to prevent such "special" treatment. In 1996 the Supreme Court overturned a Colorado law prohibiting antidiscrimination laws for gay men and lesbians. In June 2003 the United State Supreme Court in *Lawrence et al. v. Texas* overturned a Texas law used to convict two gay men of sodomy. The implications of this decision, which was unexpected, for other restrictive state and local laws is yet to be determined.

Despite these efforts to protect civil rights, gays and lesbians are subjected to frequent discriminatory practices in areas including housing, employment, and child custody (Leonard 1989). Such experiences can produce feelings of shame, anxiety, and depression in people who do not have strong support systems able to recast discrimination as homophobia rather than as the result of a deficit in the gay person involved. Therefore it is important for social workers to understand where a particular rural community is with regard to what is — or is not — provided for this population (McDonald 1990; Otis and Skinner 1996).

Homophobic prejudices that lead to discriminatory behavior can also lead to abusive and violent behavior. A grim underside to the process of coming out is the possibility of being targeted for verbal and physical harassment (Otis and Skinner 1996) or even violence. Several efforts are under way to document levels of harassment, and the National Gay and Lesbian Task Force has recorded numerous hate crime murders of homosexuals because of their sexual orientation (Vaid 1995). Even heterosexual people can be caught up in the violence if they appear to be gay, as can be seen in the report of murders of people falsely perceived as gay or lesbian. The impact of hate crimes lies in their ability to terrorize entire communities beyond the individuals involved (Dees and Friffer 1991). Threats and fear of violence can produce difficulties in coping that affect many areas of life.

There are numerous instances in which gays and lesbians have lost custody of their children because of their homosexuality and regardless of their ability to parent. When divorce, separation, or death occurs, the family members who are gay or lesbian may experience anxiety when confronted with situations where they are not allowed to participate with other family members in grieving and are made to feel invisible or otherwise punished because of their sexual orientation. This can be more of a problem in a rural area because of the more conservative legal climate and limited availability of civil rights lawyers willing to challenge the legal system. Many gay and lesbian parents will give up custody of their children without resistance for fear of being discriminated against because of their "differentness." Every year people are denied equal access to their property, inheritance, and medical benefits because they are homosexual.

A conservative rural community can place social workers in multiple ethical dilemmas, especially if they work for a particular state or private agency that actively discriminates against gays and lesbians, and is governed by policies that conflict with NASW practice and ethical guidelines for practice with gay and lesbian persons. This is more pronounced in the rural context for several reasons. In particular, there may be three major conflicts for both providers and clients:

1. Social work ethical standards may contradict state and private institutional policies regarding issues of sexual orientation.
2. Social services will inherently be limited in providing fully affirmative services to gay and lesbian clients.

3. Gay and lesbian employees may find themselves in a conflicted environment because of the need to "hide" their sexual orientation and pass as a heterosexual so as to find and maintain a job. Doing so becomes even more important because of limited employment opportunities in the rural setting.

Social workers must play an important role in educating themselves and their peers, colleagues, schools, and communities about gay and lesbian discriminatory laws and regulations. It is essential that social workers are aware that prejudice and discrimination against gays and lesbians is still rampant in society and that it may be even more pronounced in the rural environment.

Conclusion

All the dilemmas and challenges discussed in this chapter are exacerbated by aspects of rural settings. Ongoing attention needs to be paid to the training of social workers to prepare them to deal with the contradictions between social work values and ethics and the norms and mores that may exist in the rural setting. This is challenging for human service educators, administrators, and programs directors. The charge is to examine the multiple roles social workers must assume in the rural setting and to be fully aware of the potential for conflict or obstacles that may confront both the social worker and gay and lesbian clients.

Generalist social work practice could promote competent practice with gays and lesbians by requiring that social workers demonstrate the ability to use specific gay male and lesbian affirmative knowledge and value competencies. This will occur by conveying inclusivity, acceptance, and affirmation in order to effectively help gay and lesbian or questioning clients explore issues of diverse sexual identities.

The rural context challenges contemporary theories that discuss how gays and lesbians may experience multiple social conditions that can interfere with how they adapt to their identity. There is a consistent under-representation of gay men and lesbians in research regarding identity formation. This research bias must be taken into consideration when the social worker is practicing in a rural context.

It is essential that social workers and other human service providers understand the particular dynamics of each individual community and region where they practice. In order to understand the area in relation to gays and lesbians, it is important to be aware of the local social, institutional, and religious biases and views regarding human sexuality. This challenge, if met, will enhance service delivery for all potential clientele regardless of their sexual orientation. Competent social work practice with gay men and lesbian women requires that the social worker demonstrate a commitment to promoting a safe and affirming environment. It is critical that all human service providers are knowledgeable of agency and community bias and discriminatory practice with regard to gays and lesbians. These hindrances exist both on client and provider levels, as well as within the community. Social workers need to maintain reasonable expectations and to be aware of how delicate and problematic situations regarding sexual orientation can become in a rural setting. Increased professional attention must be directed toward helping gays and lesbians living in rural areas deal with the quandary of being homosexual. The need is both significant and compelling.

References

Appleby, G., and J. Anastas. 1999. *Not just a passing phase: Social work with gay, lesbian, and bisexual people.* New York: Columbia University Press.

Atkinson, D. R., and G. Hackett. 1995. *Counseling diverse populations.* Dubuque, Iowa: Brown.

Atwood, G., and R. Stolorow. 1984. *Structures of subjectivity.* Hillsdale, N.J.: Analytic Press

———. 1993. *Faces in a cloud.* Northvale, N.J.: Aronson.Batteau, A. 1983. *Appalachia and America.* Lexington: University Press of Kentucky.

Brown, L. 1989. Lesbians, gay men, and their families: Common clinical issues. *Journal of Gay and Lesbian Psychotherapy* 1:65–77.

Blumenfield, W. 1992. *Homophobia: How we all pay the price.* Boston, Mass.: Beacon.

Berzon, B. 1996. *Setting them straight: You can do something about bigotry and homophobia in your life.* New York: Penguin.

Bohan, S. Janis. 1996. *Psychology and sexual orientation.* New York: Routledge.

Bull, C. 2000, June 20. Pride Across America. *Advocate* 814:64–67.

Byne, W. 1997. Why we cannot conclude that sexual orientation is primarily a biological phenomenon. *Journal of Homosexuality* 34 (1): 73–80.

Cabaj, R., and T. Stein. 1996. *Textbook of homosexuality and mental health.* Washington , D.C.: American Psychiatric Press.

Cain, R. 1991. Stigma management and gay identity development. *Social Work* 35:67–73.

Campbell, J. 1983. The southern highlands and the southern highlander defined.

In B. Ergood and B. Kuhre, eds., *Appalachia: Social context past and present.* Dubuque, Iowa: Kendall/Hunt.

Cass, V. 1979. Homosexual identity formation: A theoretical model. *Journal of Homosexuality* 4:219–235.

Cohler, B. B., and R. M. Galatzer-Levy. 2000. *The course of gay and lesbian lives.* Chicago: University of Chicago Press.

Council on Social Work Education. 1995. *Graduate advancement for doctoral education.* Alexandria, Va.: Council on Social Work Education.

Commission on Accreditation. 1995. *Handbook of accreditation standards and procedures.* Alexandria, Va.: Council on Social Work Education.

Cramer, E. P. 1995. *Effects of a short-term educational unit about lesbian identity development and self-disclosure in a social work methods course.* Alexandria, Va.: Council on Social Work Education.

DeCrescenzo, T. 1994. *Helping gay and lesbian youth.* Binghamton, N.Y.: Harrington Park.

D'Augelli A., and C. Patterson. 1995. *Lesbian, gay, and bisexual identities over the lifespan.* New York: Oxford University Press.

Diagnostic and statistical manual of mental disorders. 1994. 4th. ed. Washington, D.C.: American Psychological Association.

DuBois, B. L. and K. K. Miley. 1999. *Social work: An empowering profession.* 3d ed. Boston: Allyn and Bacon.

Dupont, J., ed. 1988. *The clinical diaries of Sandor Ferenczi.* Cambridge, Mass.: Harvard University Press.

Edwards, J., and J. Bess. 1998. Developing effectiveness in the therapeutic use of self. *Clinical Social Work Journal* 26 (1): 89–105.

Erikson, E. H. 1980. *Identity, youth, and crisis.* New York: Norton.

Fahy, U. 1995. *How to make the world a better place for gays and lesbians.* New York: Warner Books.

Fellows, W. 1996. *Farm boys: Lives of gay men from the rural Midwest.* Madison: University of Wisconsin Press.

Grace, J. 1992. Affirming gay and lesbian adulthood. In N. J. Woodmen, ed., *Lesbian and gay lifestyles: A guide for counseling and education,* pp. 33-47. New York: Irvington.

Greenlee, R., and J. Lantz. 1993. Family coping strategies and the rural Appalachian working poor. *Contemporary Family Therapy* 15:121–137.

Ginsberg, L. 1998. *Social work in rural communities.* Alexandria, Va.: Council on Social Work Education.

Grmick, J. 1984. Developing a lesbian identity. In T. Darty and S. Potter, eds., *Women-identified women,* pp. 31–44. Palo Alto, Calif.: Mayfield.

Harper, K. 1986. Appalachian families: Aspects of working with developmentally disabled members. In A. Riemenschneider, ed., *Parent-professional interaction.* Columbus: Ohio State University College of Social Work.

Harper, K., and R. Greenlee. 1991. Workfare program in rural America: Joblessness in Ohio's Appalachian counties. *Journal of Sociology and Social Welfare* 18:71–85.

———. 1992. Promise and poverty in Appalachia's heartland. *Human Services in the Rural Environment* 13:42–47.

Hidalgo, H., T. L. Peterson, and N. J. Woodman. 1985. *Lesbian and gay issues: A resource manual for social workers.* Silver Spring, Md.: National Association of Social Workers.

Isay, R. 1989. *Being homosexual: Gay men and their development.* New York: Farrar Straus Giroux.

Jackson, H. 1997. *Using self-psychology in psychotherapy.* Northvale, N.J.: Aronson.

Johnson, M., C. Brems, and P. Alford-Keating. 1997. Personality correlates of homophobia. *Journal of Homosexuality* 34 (1): 57–69.

Jones, L. 1983. Appalachian values. In B. Ergood and B Kuhre, eds., *Appalachia: Social context past and present,* 2nd ed. Dubuque, Iowa: Kendalland Hunt.

Kaufman, G. 1996. *Coming out of shame.* New York: Doubleday.

Keefe, S., U. Reck, and G. Reck. 1991. Family and education in Southern Appalachia. In B. Ergood and B Kuhre, eds., *Appalachia: Social context past and present,* 2nd ed. Dubuque, Iowa: Kendall/Hunt.

Kegan, R. 1998. *The evolving self: Problem and process in human development.* Cambridge, Mass.: Harvard University Press.

Kirst-Ashman, K. K., and G. H. Hull. 1997. *Understanding generalist practice.* 3rd. ed. Chicago: Nelson-Hall.

Lantz, J. 1992. Meaning, nerves, and the urban-Appalachian family. *Journal of Religion and Health* 31:129–139.

Mallow, P. 1998. *Foundations of social work practice with lesbian and gay persons.* New York: Harrington.

McCarthy, L. 2000. Poppies in a wheat field: Exploring the lives of rural lesbians. *Journal of Homosexuality* 39 (1): 75–94.

McDonald, H., and A. Steinhorn. 1990. *Homosexuality: A practical guide to counseling lesbians, gay men, and their families.* New York: Continuum.

Miley, K. K., M. O'Melia, and B. L. DuBois. 2004. *Generalist social work practice: An empowering approach.* 2nd ed. Boston: Allyn and Bacon.

National Association of Social Workers. 1996. *Code of ethics.* Washington, D.C.: NASW.

———. 1996. *Committee on lesbian, gay, and bisexual concerns: Proposed policy statement.* Presented at the Delegate Assembly, Washington, D.C.

National Gay and Lesbian Task Force. 1992. *Hate crimes: Confronting violence against lesbians and gay men.* Newbury Park, Calif.: Sage.

Neisen, J. 1993. Healing from cultural victimization: Recovery from shame due to heterosexism. *Journal of Gay and Lesbian Psychotherapy* 2 (1): 49–63.

Obermiller, P., and M. Maloney. 1991. Moving on: Recent patterns of Appalachian migration. In J. Lloyd and A. Campbell, eds., *The impact of institution in Appalachia*, 2nd ed. Boone, N.C.: Appalachian Consortium.

Oles, T. P., B. Black, and L. Moore. 1995. Acknowledging and confronting homophobia among social work students. Paper presented at the Annual Program Meeting of the Council on Social Work Education, San Diego, Calif.

O'Neill. C. 1992. *Coming out within*. San Francisco: Harper Collins.

Orange, D., G. Atwood, and R. Stolorow. 1997. *Working intersubjectively: Contextualism in psychoanalytic practice*. Hillsdale, N.J.: Analytic Press.

Osborn, T. 1996. *Coming home to America : A road map to gay and lesbian empowerment*. New York: St Martin's.

Otis, M. D., and W. F. Skinner. 1996. The prevalence of victimization and its effect on mental well-being among lesbian and gay people. *Journal of Homosexuality* 30 (3): 93–121.

Palombo, J. 1987. Spontaneous self-disclosures in psychotherapy. *Clinical Social Work Journal* 15 (2): 107–120.

Plummer, K. 1975. *Sexual stigma: An interactionist account*. London: Routledge and Kegan Paul.

Ponse, B. 1978. *Identities in the lesbian world: The social construction of self*. Westport, Conn.: Greenwood Press.

Preston, L. 1998. Expressive relating: The intentional use of the analysts subjectivity. Paper presented at the Twelfth Annual Conference for the Institute for Human Identity, New York.

Ritter, K. Y., and A. I. Terndrup. 2002. *Handbook of affirmative psychotherapy with lesbians and gay men*. New York: Gilford.

Rosenblum, K., and T. Travis. 1999. *The meaning of difference*. New York: McGraw-Hill.

Ryan, C., and D. Futterman. 1998. Helping our hidden youth. *American Journal of Nursing* 98 (12): 37–42.

Rylant, C. 1982. *When I was young in the mountains*. New York: Dutton.

Shane, M., E. Shane, and M. Gales. 1997. *Intimate attachments: Towards a new self-psychology*. New York: Guilford.

Shelby, R., D. 2000. The self and orientation: The case of Mr. G In A. Goldberg, ed., *Conversations in self psychology: Progress in self psychology*. Volume 13. pp. 181-202. Hillsdale, NJ: The Analytic Press.

Shapiro, H. 1986. *Appalachia on my mind*. Chapel Hill: University of North Carolina Press.

Siegel, A. 1996. *Heinz Kohut and the psychology of the self*. New York: Routledge.

Siegel, S., and E. Lowe Jr. 1995. *Uncharted lives: Understanding the life passages of gay men*. New York: Penguin Books.

Skidmore, A., O. Thackeday, and W. Farley. 1997. *Introduction to social work*. 7th ed. Boston: Allyn and Bacon.

Smith, D., and R. Mancoske. 1998. *Rural gays and lesbians*. New York: Harrington Park.

Sophie, J. 1982. Internalized homophobia and lesbian identity. *Journal of Homosexuality* 14:53–65.

Stein, T. 1997. Deconstructing sexual orientation: Understanding the phenomena of sexual orientation. *Journal of Homosexuality* 34 (1): 81–86.

Sweet, M. 1996. Counseling satisfaction of gay, lesbian, and bisexual college students. *Journal of Gay and Lesbian Social Service* 4:35–49.

Troiden, R. R. 1988. Homosexual identity development. *Journal of Adolescent Health Care* 9 (2): 105–113.

Tully, C. 1995. Out of the closet and into the curriculum. Paper presented at the Council of Social Work Education, Annual Program Meeting, San Diego, Calif.

———. 2000. *Lesbians, gays, and the empowerment perspective*. New York: Columbia University Press.

Vaid, U. 1996. Hope versus hype. *Advocate* 723:80.

Wisniewski, J. J., and B. G. Toomey. 1987. Are social workers homophobic? *Social Work* 32 (5): 454–455.

Zastrow, C. 1996. *An introduction to social work*. 6th ed. Pacific Grove, Calif.: Brooks/Cole.

13 The Role of Religiousness/Spirituality and Social Support on Subjective Well-Being Among People Living with HIV/AIDS in Rural Communities

Dong Pil Yoon

AIDS is now more frequently characterized as a disease of heterosexual transmission increasingly affecting minorities, women, and rural communities rather than one of homosexual transmission predominantly affecting white urban males (Thomas and Thomas 1999). Rural areas have found it necessary to adapt to the needs of the growing numbers of persons living with HIV/AIDS, as people migrate from cities to the country, with some returning to their hometowns (Cohn, Klein, and Mohr 1994). National epidemiological reports indicate that there are increasing numbers of people living with HIV/AIDS in rural areas (Gardner et al. 1989; Shernoff 1997), which have resulted in tremendous increased demands on rural social services and health care facilities. Heckman et al. (1996) reported that people with HIV/AIDS in rural areas experience great difficulty accessing social support, the social contacts associated with employment, and, in many cases, an ongoing intimate relationship including death of the partner.

Despite the increasing needs of people with HIV/AIDS in rural areas, little attention has been paid to studying the quality of life among these individuals in situations where medical resources and medical care are limited, and emergency financial assistance and community support deficient. In particular, information about the role of spirituality/religiousness and social support on the health and well-being of persons living with HIV/AIDS

I would like to express my thanks to Judith Davenport, Ph.D., and Stacy A. Swenson, MSW, for their continuous assistance and insightful comments on my research.

in rural areas is limited because the majority of previous studies have focused on individuals with HIV/AIDS living in metropolitan or urban areas.

Literature Review

Factors Affecting Life with HIV/AIDS

Those who have been diagnosed as having either HIV or AIDS are confronted with many physical, psychological, social, spiritual, and financial needs. Anxiety, depression, and loss of hope may complicate the course of any life-threatening disease, interfering with compliance, self-care activities, and motivation toward recovery (Koenig 2001). Cohen (1985) observed that life events, including separation, loss, and feelings of hopelessness that are associated with the experience of loneliness might affect the endocrine system through abnormal secretion levels from the pituitary and adrenal glands. The deterioration in health through this process is most probable in persons with already compromised immune functioning, especially persons with AIDS (Rokach 2000). Current research suggests that psychological variables, including loneliness, have been associated with changes in immune functioning and may weaken the body's capacity to fight disease (Kennedy, Kielcolt-Glaser, and Glaser 1988; Kemppainen 2001). Rokach and Brock (1998) found that some individuals are unable to face loneliness and experience an overwhelming need to deny it so as to avoid the concomitant pain; in tandem with denying a diagnosis of HIV/AIDS, patients will temporarily deny its accompanying loneliness.

Social stigma is a constant challenge for people living with HIV/AIDS, resulting in feelings of low self-esteem, isolation, and discrimination (Collins 1994; Barroso 1997). Discrimination can be particularly devastating to gay men already struggling with their sexual orientation (Relf 1997). Heckman and Miller (2000) found that people with HIV who experience HIV-related discriminatory acts report severer depression and greater dissatisfaction in their lives that those who do not experience such discrimination. These multiple and profound stressors deeply affect the infected individual's quality of life and existing coping resources (Christ, Wiener, and Moynihan 1986; Robinson, Mathews, and Witek-Janusek 1999). Previous studies have demonstrated that more stress and less social support may accelerate the progression of HIV disease (Leserman et al. 1999). Because people in rural areas tend to be morally conservative (Martinez-Brawley 1990), the stigma may prevent them from reaching out to their natural helping networks for assistance in coping with emotional and psychological problems. Social stigma, uncertainty, and a lack of religious resources are major barriers to the spiritual support of HIV-infected persons.

Roles of Spirituality/Religiousness in Rural Communities

Spirituality is a resource that chronically ill individuals, especially people living with HIV/AIDS, use to cope with the physical and psychosocial challenges of illness (Fryback and Reinart 1999; Sowell et al. 2000; McComick 2001). Spirituality serves as support for some people with HIV/AIDS who experience fear, prejudice, and other unique challenges such as the inability to give life meaning, hopelessness, isolation, and low self-esteem (Peri 1995; Relf 1997). Individuals with HIV can find meaning in their lives by getting in touch with an ultimate power, focusing on self-improvement, assisting other people with HIV, and establishing closer ties with family and friends (Barroso 1997). Religious cognitions and behaviors, especially those centering on prayer, meditation, and other devotional pursuits, seem to be especially valuable in dealing with serious health problems (both acute and chronic) and bereavement (Ellison and Levin 1998; Pargament et al. 1998; Koenig 2001). There is mounting evidence that religious cognitions and behaviors can offer effective resources for dealing with stressful events and conditions (Larimore 2001). Investigations confirm that religious faith is important to many patients and that it provides them with meaning, strength, and hope as they face significant changes in their lives brought about by illness. Spilka, Shaver, and Kirkpatrick (1985) defined three roles that religion serves in the coping process: (1) offers meaning to life; (2) provides individuals with a greater sense of control over their situations; and (3) builds self-esteem.

It is widely asserted that at least part of the observed relationship between religious involvement and health outcomes results from the role of religious communities in providing social ties and support (Joseph 1988; Sloan, Bagiella, and Powell 1999; Koenig 2000). As rural people tend to be more religiously oriented than other groups, they prefer discussing their problems with their clergy rather than mental health personnel or social workers (Meystedt 1984; Furman 1991). Religious involvement may promote physical and mental well-being by regulating health-related conduct in ways that decrease the risk of disease and by encouraging positive, low-stress lifestyle choices. Reese and Kaplan (2000) found that both spirituality and social support had inverse relationships with worry about health among people with HIV. Somlai and Heckman (2000) also found relationships between higher levels of spirituality and social support, active problem solving, and life satisfaction among people infected with HIV/AIDS.

Roles of Social Support in Rural Communities

Social support is an important resource used to give life meaning for persons who live with the daily challenges of HIV/AIDS (Landis 1996; Barroso 1997). Kendall (1994) and Barroso (1997) found that individuals with HIV believed that what contributed most to their physiological and psychological health were meaningful relationships. With regard to individuals infected with HIV and AIDS, studies indicate that the more social supports were perceived to exist, the less hopelessness and depression were reported (Barroso 1997; Serovich et al. 2001). Social supports can be identified as reciprocated support to network members, the amount of emotional and informational support received from family, the number of close relationships, and the number of friends in one's support network. The consequences of social support may be a greater sense of coherence, higher self-esteem, decreased anxiety, better adjustment to the diagnosis of HIV disease, hardiness, improved quality of life, and psychological well-being. Support of family and friends has been found to be helpful in people with AIDS in maintaining their hope. Social support can increase self-esteem and psychological health, promote immune function, and decrease stress and isolation in people with HIV disease (Barroso 1997; Heckman et al. 1998). Rural residents rely heavily on social networks to provide social support and other services that, in urban areas, are often provided by more formal agencies (Davenport and Davenport 1982).

An extensive review of the literature indicates a sound basis for the significance of social support from both family and friends, and identifies religiousness/spirituality as a major contributory factor to psychological well-being among individuals with HIV/AIDS. The researcher tested the following a hypothesis about the effect of religiousness/spirituality and social support on subjective well-being among people living with HIV/AIDS in rural areas: Those who have higher religiousness/spirituality and receive more social support will have greater subjective well-being, specifically a higher level of life satisfaction and a lower level of depression.

West Virginia, a state with a population of less than 1.8 million, belongs to the Appalachian region which is characterized by small towns and rural areas. Over a ten-year period from 1990 to 1999, West Virginia reported 1,386 cases of HIV and AIDS, with 500 individuals reported as having HIV and 886 reported as having AIDS. At the end of this ten-year span in 1999, 538 of the individuals reported with HIV and 577 of the individuals reported with AIDS were still alive (Center for Disease Control and Prevention 2001).

Methods

Sample and Data Collection

A sample of 52 individuals infected with HIV/AIDS from nine counties in West Virginia was recruited through an HIV/AIDS social service agency in Morgantown, West Virginia, in 2002. Included in the sample were individuals who did not have a diagnosis of dementia or thought disorder. A population of 125 people with HIV/AIDS were asked to participate in this study. Sixty-one agreed to participate, but nine who agreed did not participate for a variety of personal reasons including illness and schedule conflicts. Each participant was interviewed in his or her home, and interviews lasted from two to two and a half hours and were conducted by an interviewer who had previous work experience with individuals infected with HIV/AIDS in West Virginia. At the start, the interviewer explained the purpose and format of the interview, emphasizing the confidentiality of all information collected. All participants signed a detailed informed consent form, and all responses were completely voluntary and anonymous.

Variables and Instruments

Religiousness/Spirituality   To measure various domains of religiousness/spirituality, as a short form, the Brief Multidimensional Measures of Religiousness/Spirituality (Fetzer/National Institute on Aging 1999) was used. For this study, the researcher selected seven subscales including daily spiritual experiences, values/beliefs, forgiveness, private religious practice, religious/spiritual coping, religious support, and organizational religiousness.

Daily spiritual experience measures the individual's experience of a transcendent (God, the divine) in daily life and experience of interaction with

God. This subscale consisted of six items and a 5-point response format was used, which ranged from 1 (never) to 5 (every day). Cronbach's alpha was .91 in the current sample.

The subscale *values/beliefs* measures religious values and beliefs. Studies reveal that many patients shape their personal responses to illness on the basis of their religious and spiritual beliefs; such beliefs play a major role in their decisions regarding specific treatments (Larimore 2001). This subscale consisted of two items with a 4-point response format ranging from 1 (strongly disagree) to 4 (strongly agree). Cronbach's alpha was .66 in this sample.

Forgiveness measures the degree of forgiveness of self and others, and belief in the forgiveness of God. Most religious traditions attempt to foster beliefs and teach methods that can facilitate forgiveness (Pargament and Rye 1998). This subscale consisted of three items rated on a 4-point response format ranging from 1 (never) to 4 (always). Cronbach's alpha was .67 in this sample.

Private religious practice measures behaviors (i.e., prayer, meditations, listen/watch religious programs, read religious materials, and pray before meals). This subscale consisted of five items and used a 5-point response format, ranging from 1 (never) to 5 (every day). Cronbach's alpha was .71 in this sample.

Religious/spiritual coping measures additional religious/spiritual practices and beliefs specifically related to coping with life's problems (i.e., "I think about how my life is part of a larger spiritual force"; "I work together with God as partners"; "I look to God for strength, support, and guidance"). This subscale consisted of seven items rated on a 5-point response format ranging from 1 (not at all) to 5 (a great deal). Cronbach's alpha was .80 in this sample.

Religious support measures the degree to which local congregations provide help, support, and comfort. This subscale consisted of four items and used a 4-point response format that ranged from 1 (none) to 5 (very often). Cronbach's alpha was .72 in the current sample.

Organizational religiousness measures the involvement of the respondents with a formal public religious institution. This subscale consisted of four items rated on a 4-point response format ranging from 1 (never) to 4 (daily). Cronbach's alpha was .86 in this study.

Social Support   To measure perceived social support, the Social Support Measurement was used (Zimet et al. 1988). In general, social support is thought to affect mental and physical health through its influence on emotions, cognitions, and behaviors (Cohen 1988). This scale particularly measures overall social support from family, friends, and significant others. This scale consisted of twelve items and a 4-point response format was used that ranged from 1 (strongly disagree) to 4 (strongly agree). Cronbach's alpha was .89 in this sample.

Subjective Well-being   For this study subjective well-being was conceptualized as consisting of two dimensions: depression and life satisfaction. The Center for Epidemiological Studies–Depression (CES–D) (Radloff 1977) and the Satisfaction with Life Scale (SWLS) (Diener et al. 1985) were used to measure subjective well-being. Cronbach's alpha for these two scales were .85 and .84, respectively, in this sample. The CES–D has been used to assess depressive symptomatology in the general population. The SWLS measures the degree of positive psychological well-being. The CES–D consisted of eleven items rated on a 4-point response format ranging from 1 (rare or none of the time: less than a day) to 4 (most of the time: 5–7 days), and the SWLS consisted of five items rated on a 4-point response format ranging from 1 (strongly disagree) to 4 (strongly agree).

Data Analyses   Hierarchical multiple regression analyses were used to determine the influence of variables including demographics, religiousness/spirituality, social support, and subjective well-being on the dependent variables. In these analyses, the first step of variables entered included the demographic variables of age, sexual orientation (dichotomously coded as 1 = heterosexual and 0 = homosexual), education (dichotomously coded as 1 = > HS diploma and 0 = ≤ HS diploma), annual income (dichotomously coded as 1 = > $10,000 and 0 = ≤ $10,000), and living arrangement (dichotomously coded as 1 = living with someone and 0 = living alone). The second step included religiousness/spirituality variables including values and beliefs, religious and spiritual coping, religious support, forgiveness, private religious practice, and organizational religiousness. Social support was entered in the final step to determine its effect on the level of subjective well-being consisting of life satisfaction and depression.

Results

Characteristics of the Participants

As can be seen in table 13.1, thirty-six participants identified as male (69 percent), with two identifying as bisexual, twenty-six identifying as homo-

TABLE 13.1 Characteristics of the Participants (n = 52)

Variable	Frequency	Percentage
Sex		
Male	36	69.2
Female	16	30.8
Age		
23–29	12	23.1
30–39	28	53.8
40–49	12	23.1
M = 36.0; SD = 6.65; Range = 23–49		
Sexual orientation		
Heterosexual	24	46.2
Homosexual	26	50.0
Bisexual	2	3.8
Education		
Some high school	10	19.2
High school diploma	20	38.5
Some college	20	38.5
College graduate	2	3.8
Annual income		
Less than $5,001	14	26.9
$5,001 to $10,000	22	42.3
$10,001 to $15,000	10	19.2
More than $15,000	6	11.6
Religion		
Protestant	38	73.1
Catholic	8	15.4
Other	4	7.7
None	2	3.8
Health insurance		
Yes	36	69.2
No	16	30.8

(continued)

TABLE 13.1 Characteristics of the Participants (n = 52) (Continued)

Variable	Frequency	Percentage
Number of doctor visits per year		
Less than 6	10	19.2
6–10	14	26.9
More than 10	28	53.9
Average travel mileage to see a doctor		
Less than 11 miles	8	15.5
11–30	6	11.5
31–50	6	11.5
More than 50 miles	32	61.5

sexual, and eight identifying as heterosexual. Sixteen participants identified as female (31 percent), with all identifying as heterosexual. Participants ranged in age from twenty-three to forty-nine, with a mean age of thirty-six years. Twenty individuals reported being single (38 percent), twelve reported being divorced (23 percent), another twelve reported living with a partner (23 percent), six reported being married (12 percent), and two individuals reported a deceased partner (4 percent). About 88 percent of the participants were white, with a small percentage being African American (8 percent), and Hispanic (4 percent). In terms of annual income, thirty-six individuals reported less than $10,000 (69 percent), ten reported between $10,001 and $15,000 (19 percent), and six individuals reported more than $15,000 (12 percent), indicating that most participants are financially below or near the poverty line (Department of Health and Human Services 2003). Fifty individuals (96 percent) had affiliated with some type of religion: thirty-eight (76 percent) being Protestant, eight (16 percent) being Catholic, and four (8 percent) in the category of "other." Forty-six (89 percent) had attended religious services before being diagnosed with HIV/AIDS. About 69 percent had health insurance: 73 percent had Medicaid and 47 percent had Medicare. Twenty-eight individuals (54 percent) had seen doctors more than ten times per year, and thirty-two individuals (62 percent) had traveled more than fifty miles to see doctors. About 62 percent had side effects from the medications.

Seven variables involving daily spiritual experience, values/beliefs, forgiveness, private religious practice, religious/spiritual coping, religious support, and organizational religiousness were used to measure religiousness/spirituality (see table 13.2). Daily spiritual experience scores ranged from 6 (never) to 30 (every day) with a mean of 23.9 (SD = 5.8), indicating that respondents reported experiencing spirituality most days. Respondents agreed to having a strong belief in God (Mean = 6.6; SD = 1.4), ranging from 2 (strongly disagree) to 8 (strongly agree). Forgiveness scores ranged from 3 (never) to 12 (always) with a mean of 9.7 (SD = 1.6), indicating that respondents reported often experiencing forgiveness. Respondents reported practicing religious activities a couple of days a month (mean = 13.5; SD = 3.7), ranging from 5 (never) to 25 (daily). Religious and spiritual coping scores ranged from 7 (not at all) to 28 (a great deal) with a mean of 21.1 (SD = 3.6), indicating that respondents reported using considerable religious and spiritual coping skills. Respondents reported receiving minimal religious support from the congregation (mean = 9.4; SD = 2.6), ranging 4 (none) to 16 (very often).

By and large, respondents agreed to having received social support from family and friends (mean = 38.0; SD = 5.7), ranging from 12 (strongly disagree) to 48 (strongly agree). Two variables involving life satisfaction and depression were used to measure subjective well-being. Life satisfaction scores ranged from 5 (strongly disagree) to 20 (strongly agree) with a mean of 11.7 (SD = 2.6), and depression scores ranged from 11 (rarely) to 44 (most of the time) with a mean of 30.7 (SD = 5.9), indicating that respon-

TABLE 13.2 Means and Standard Deviations of Measured Variables (n = 52)

Variable	Mean	Standard Deviation	Range
Daily spiritual experience	23.9	5.8	6–30
Values and beliefs	6.6	1.4	2–8
Forgiveness	9.7	1.6	3–12
Private religious practice	13.5	3.7	5–25
Religious and spiritual coping	21.1	3.6	7–28
Religious support	9.4	2.6	4–16
Organizational religiousness	5.5	1.1	2–10
Social support	38.0	5.7	12–48
Life satisfaction	11.7	2.6	5–20
Depression	30.7	5.9	11–44

dents were in disagreement with regard to finding satisfaction in their lives and occasionally having depressive symptoms.

Multivariate Analyses

Life Satisfaction   Table 13.3 also indicates that the full model accounts for 32 percent of the variance in life satisfaction (F = 3.92, p < .01). At the first step, age and living arrangement are significantly associated with greater life satisfaction, explaining 26 percent of the variance. At the second step, religious support is significantly associated with greater life satisfaction, explaining an additional 11 percent (p < .05) of the variance in life satisfaction. As expected, at the final step, social support is a significant predictor of a participant's life satisfaction, explaining an additional 6 percent (p < .05) of the variance in life satisfaction. Thus respondents reporting higher levels of life satisfaction are more likely to (1) be younger (beta = -.33, p < .05); (2) live with someone (beta = .32, p < .05); (3) receive more religious support (beta = .40, p < .05); and (4) receive greater social support (beta = .30, p < .05).

Depression   As can be seen in table 13.3, the results of the regression of depression have been summarized. The full model accounted for 59 percent of the variance in depression (F = 6.82, p < .001). At the first step, no factor relating to the participant's demographic information is significantly associated with depression and only 11 percent of the variance is explained. As expected, at the second step, more religious/spiritual coping skills and strong religious values/beliefs are significantly associated with lesser depression and explain an additional 53 percent (p < .001). Social support is, however, not significantly associated with depression at the final step. Therefore respondents reporting lower levels of depression are more likely to (1) have strong religious values and beliefs (beta = -.32, p < .05); and (2) have more religious and spiritual coping skills (beta = -.47, p < .01).

Discussion

Most of the previous studies investigating the relationship between quality of life and religiousness/spirituality have been conducted in urban or metropolitan areas. Furthermore, a unidimensional construct has been used to

TABLE 13.3 Summary of Hierarchical Regression Analysis for Variables
Predicting Participant's Subjective Well-Being
(standardized beta coefficients) (n = 52)

Variables	Life Satisfaction	Depression
Demographic information	$R^2 = .26; F = 3.12^*$	$R^2 = .11; F = 1.14$
Age	−.33*	.05
Sexual orientation	−.29	−.31
Education	.07	−.27
Annual income	.22	−.05
Living arrangement	.32*	.04
Religiousness/spirituality	$\Delta R^2 = .11; F = 3.57^*$	$\Delta R^2 = .53; F = 8.18^{***}$
Values and beliefs		−.32*
Religious/spiritual coping		−.47**
Religious support	.40*	−.17
Forgiveness		−.10
Religious practice	−.08	−.01
Organizational religiousness		.20
Social support	$\Delta R^2 = .06; F = 4.65^*$	$\Delta R^2 = .04; F = 4.39^*$
	.30*	−.22

* p < .05

** p < .01

*** p < .001.

measure religiousness/spirituality. This study was unique in that it attempted to capture multidimensional characteristics of religiousness/spirituality and social support as significant roles to enhance subjective well-being among people with HIV/AIDS in rural communities.

Consistent with findings of previous studies (Leserman et al. 1999; Somlai et al. 2000; McCormick et al. 2001; Kemppainen 2001), the results of this study indicate that certain religious and spiritual factors have an effect on the overall well-being of an HIV-infected individual, suggesting that those who receive more religious support and use more spiritual coping behaviors are likely to have higher levels of life satisfaction and lower levels of depression. More specifically, life satisfaction was found to be related to being younger, living with someone, and receiving support from family and friends. Depression was inversely related to having strong religious values and beliefs, and spiritual coping skills. Spirituality/religiousness and social support may work together to enhance levels of subjective well-being.

The small nonprobability sample in this study limits the ability to generalize the results to the population as a whole. In addition, a potential selection bias may have been created by excluding individuals diagnosed with HIV/AIDS from other geographic locations around the state. Because of the rural nature of West Virginia, there is a disparity among support and medical services available throughout the state, and life circumstances in all geographic areas would vary. Longitudinal studies with larger random samples are needed to understand the functions of spirituality/religiousness on quality of life throughout the progression of the HIV/AIDS disease. It is also suggested that research be conducted with the faith-based community in terms of its attitudes and beliefs about persons with HIV/AIDS.

Despite the limitations, this current study is important because it addresses issues faced by individuals infected with HIV living in a poor, rural state. The results of this study contribute to a growing body of literature that indicates the significance of addressing spirituality/religiousness in helping chronically ill clients, especially people living with HIV/AIDS in rural areas. Given the evidence concerning the significant influence of religiousness/ spirituality on subjective well-being, practitioners should routinely include assessment of spirituality and religious practices when working with people living with HIV/AIDS. Interventions that focus on spiritual perspectives may improve quality of life for spiritually or religiously oriented people living with HIV/AIDS. Helping HIV/AIDS patients to use religious and spiritual coping skills can reduce their level of hurt, anger, and perceived offense, and improve their mood and emotional status.

Findings of this study suggest that social workers and other health care professionals develop programs or services aimed at promoting religious or spiritual growth that assist in enhancing the quality of life and in improving psychosocial well-being of rural individuals living with HIV/AIDS. Religious and spiritual communities can be the source of support for clients because they can provide a sense of belonging, safety, purpose, and opportunities for giving and receiving service (Richard and Bergin 1997). Faith communities need to work closely with mental health professionals in providing environments that support the spiritual growth of individuals diagnosed with HIV/ AIDS. Rural models of health/mental health care for people with HIV/AIDS should be provided based on rural community life and the need for strong linkages with existing services and programs.

References

Barroso, J. 1997. Social support and long-term survivors of AIDS. *Western Journal of Nursing Research* 19 (5): 554–582.

Centers for Disease Control and Prevention 2001. *HIV/AIDS Surveillance Report* 5 (3): 11.

Christ, G., L. Wiener, and R. Moynihan. 1986. Psychosocial issues in AIDS. *Psychiatric Annals* 16:173–179.

Cohen, I. S. 1985. Psychosomatic death: Voodoo death in modern perspective. *Integrative Psychiatry* 16:46–51.

Cohn, S. E., J. D. Klein, and J. E. Mohr. 1994. The geography of AIDS: Patterns of urban and rural migration. *Southern Medical Journal* 87:599–606.

Collins, R. L. 1994. Social support provision to HIV-infected gay men. *Journal of Applied Social Psychology* 24:1848–1869.

Davenport, J., and J. Davenport III. 1982. Utilizing the social network in rural communities. *Social Casework* 63:106–115.

Department of Health and Human Services. 2003. The 2003 HHS poverty guidelines. *Federal Register* 68 (26): 6456–6458.

Diener, E., R. A. Emmons, R. J. Larsen, and S. Griffin. 1985. The satisfaction with life scale: A measure of life satisfaction. *Journal of Personality Assessment* 49:71–75.

Ellison, C. G., and J. S. Levin. 1998. The religion health connection: Evidence, theory, and future directions. *Health, Education, and Behavior* 25 (6): 700–720.

Fetzer Institute/National Institute on Aging, 1999. *Multidimensional measurement of religiousness/spirituality for use in health research*: A report of the Fetzer Institute/National Institute on Aging Working Group. Kalamazoo, Mich.: John E. Fetzer Institute.

Fryback, P. B., and B. R. Reinert. 1999. Spirituality and people with potentially fatal diagnoses. *Nursing Forum* 34 (1): 13–22.

Furman, L. E. 1991. The impact of the rural crisis on two-generational farm families. *Family Practice Quarterly Journal* 17 (1): 26.

Gardner, L., J. Brundage, D. Burke, J. McNeil, R. Visintine, and R. Miller. 1989. Evidence for spread of the human immunodeficiency virus epidemic into low prevalence areas of the United States. *Journal of Acquired Immune Deficiency Syndrome* 2:521–532.

Heckman, T. G., and J. G. Miller. 2000. Psychosocial distress among gay and bisexual men living with HIV/AIDS in small U.S. towns and rural areas. *Health Education Monograph Series 2000* 18:39–44.

Heckman, T. G., A. M. Somlai, J. A. Kelley, L. Stevenson, and K. Galdabini. 1996.

Reducing barriers to care and improving quality of life for rural persons with HIV. *AIDS Patient Care and STDS* 11:37–43.

Heckman, T. G., A. M. Somlai, S. C. Kalichman, S. L. Franzoi, and J. A. Kelley. 1998. Psychosocial differences between urban and rural people living with HIV/AIDS. *Journal of Rural Health* 14:138–144.

Joseph, M. V. 1988. The religious and spiritual aspects of clinical practice: A neglected dimension of social work. *Social Thought* 13:12–23.

Kemppainen, J. K. 2001. Predictors of quality of life in AIDS patients. *Journal of the Association of Nurses in AIDS Care*, 12 (1): 61–70.

Kendall, J. 1994. Wellness spirituality in homosexual men with HIV infection. *Journal of the Association of Nurses in AIDS Care* 5:28–34.

Kennedy, S., J. K.Kielcolt-Glaser, and R. Glaser. 1988. Immunological consequences of acute and chronic stressors: Mediating role of interpersonal relationships. *British Journal of Medical Psychology*, 61:77–85.

Koenig, H. G. 2001. Spiritual assessment in medical practice. *American Family Physician* 63 (1): 30–33.

Koenig, H. G., M. E.McCullough, and D. B. Larson. 2000. *Handbook of religion and health: A century of research reviewed.* New York: Oxford University Press.

Landis, B. J. 1996. Uncertainty, spiritual well-being, and psychosocial adjustment to chronic illness. *Issues in Mental Health Nursing* 17:217–231.

Larimore, W. L. 2001. Providing basic spiritual care for patients: Should it be the exclusive domain of pastoral professionals? *American Family Physician* 63 (1): 36–40.

Leserman, J., et al. 1999. Progression to AIDS: The effects of stress, depressive symptoms, and social support. *Psychosomatic Medicine* 61 (3): 397–406.

Levin, J. S., and P. L. Schiller. 1987. Is there a religious factor in health? *Journal of Religion and Health* 26:9–36.

Martinez-Brawley, E. E. 1990. *Perspectives on the small community.* Silver Spring, Md.: National Association of Social Workers Press.

McCormick, D. P., B. Holder, M. A. Wetsel, and T. W. Cawthon. 2001. Spirituality and HIV disease: An integrated perspective. *Journal of the Association of Nurses in AIDS Care* 12 (3): 58–65.

Meystedt, D. M. 1984. Religion and rural population: Implications for social work. *Social Casework* 65:219–226.

Pargament, K. I., and M. S. Rye. 1998. Forgiveness as a method of religious coping. In E. L. Worthington Jr., ed., *Dimensions of forgiveness: Psychological research and theological perspectives,* pp. 59–78. Philadelphia: Templeton Foundation Press.

Pargament, K. I., B. W. Smith, H. G. Koenig, and L, Perez. 1998. Patterns of positive and negative religious coping with major life stressors. *Journal for the Scientific Study of Religion* 37 (4): 710–724.

Peri, T. C. 1995. Promoting spirituality in persons with acquired immunodeficiency syndrome: A nursing intervention. *Holistic Nursing Practice* 10 (1): 68–76.

Radloff, L. S. 1977. The CES–D scale: A self-report depression scale for research in the general population. *Applied Psychological Measurement* 1 (3): 385–401.

Reese, D. J., and M. S. Kaplan. 2000. Spirituality, social support, and worry about health: Relationships in a sample of HIV+ women. *Social Thought* 19 (4): 37–52.

Relf, M. V. 1997. Illuminating meaning and transforming issues of spirituality in HIV disease and AIDS: An application of Parse's theory of human becoming. *Holistic Nursing Practice* 12 (1): 1–8.

Richard, P. S., and A. E. Bergin. 1997. Religious and spiritual assessment. In P. S. Richard and A. E. Bergin, eds., *A spiritual strategy for counseling and psychotherapy*, pp. 171–199. Washington D.C.: American Psychological Association.

Robinson, F. P., H. H. Mathews, and L. Witek-Janusek. 1999. Stress and HIV disease progression: Psychoneuroimmunological framework. *Journal of the Association of Nurses in AIDS Care* 10:21–23.

Rokach, A. 2000. Terminal Illness and coping with loneliness. *Journal of Psychology* 134 (3): 283–296.

Rokach, A., and H. Brock. 1998. Coping with loneliness. *Journal of Psychology* 132:107–127.

Serovich, J. M., J. A. Kimberly, K. E. Mosack, and T. L. Lewis. 2001. The role of family and friend social support in reducing emotional distress among HIV-positive women. *AIDS Care* 13 (3): 335–341.

Shernoff, M. 1997. Gay men with AIDS in rural America. *Journal of Lesbian and Gay Social Services* 7 (1): 73–85.

Sloan, R. P., E. Bagiella, and T. Powell. 1999. Religion, spirituality, and medicine. *Lancet* 353:664–667.

Somlai, A.M., and T. G. Heckman. 2000. Correlates of spirituality and well-being in a community sample of people living with HIV disease. *Mental Health, Religion and Culture* 3 (1): 57–70.

Sowell, R., L. Moneyham, M. Hennessy, J. Guillory, A. Demi, and B. Seals. 2000. Spiritual activities as a resistance resource for women with human immunodeficiency virus. *Nursing Research* 49 (2): 73–82.

Spilka, B., P. Shaver, and L. Kirkpatrick. 1985. General attribution theory for the psychology of religion. *Journal for the Scientific Study of Religion* 24:1–20.

Thomas, J. C., and K. K. Thomas. 1999. Things ain't what they ought to be: Social forces underlying racial disparities in rates of sexually transmitted disease in a rural North Carolina county. *Social Science and Medicine* 49:1075–1084.

Zimet, G. D., N. W. Dahlem, S. G. Zimet, and G. K. Farley. 1988. The multidimensional scale of perceived social support. *Journal of Personality Assessment* 52:30–41.

14 Demographic Characteristics of the Rural Elderly

Craig Johnson

This chapter concerns itself with the rural elderly, a large and, in some cases, growing population in rural areas. While attempts are made to draw some conclusions about the status of the rural elderly and the communities they live in, the heterogeneity of rural environments tends to undermine all but general assertions. Absolute population size, density, and occupational structure, as well as other criteria, can all be used to define and measure rurality. The Bureau of the Census defines as *rural* a place of twenty-five hundred or more inhabitants or one outside an urbanized area (U.S. General Accounting Office 1993, 26). The term *nonmetropolitan* refers to counties outside Metropolitan Statistical Areas (MSAs). MSAs "must include at least: one city with 50,000 or more inhabitants, or a Census Bureau–defined urbanized area (of at least 50,000 inhabitants) and a total metropolitan population of at least 100,000" (U.S. Bureau of the Census 2001, 892). Communities located within MSAs are not rural, but communities in proximity to MSAs may or may not be considered so. Thus making accurate comparisons between urban and rural areas is often difficult. This paper usually employs the terms *urban* and *rural* excepting those cases where information sources refer to an area's metropolitan, nonmetropolitan, or other specific status.

Size and Distribution of the Rural Elderly Population

Twenty-three percent of adults sixty years of age or older reside in nonmetropolitan areas. The elderly constitute more than 18 percent of all nonmetropolitan residents. While not all or even most nonmetropolitan elders require the services and assistance of social workers at any given time, they do represent a significant potential client population.

The southeastern states and the Midwest have especially high concentrations of persons sixty years of age and older, as do some areas on the Pacific coast. Nonmetropolitan counties possessing substantial urban populations as well as those immediately adjacent to metropolitan counties have tended in recent years to experience the greatest growth in the over-sixty population (18 percent). By contrast, the growth rate of that population in counties not adjacent to metropolitan areas has been a much more modest 5 percent (Rogers 1999; Johnson and Beale 1998).

Several factors account for the growth and concentration of the elderly in these areas. The outmigration of young adults to metropolitan areas is a phenomenon that has been observed for decades and continues in the present (Johnson and Beale 1998). This has been especially true in southern sections of the corn belt (Missouri and Illinois, primarily), the Mississippi Delta, east Texas, the dairy areas of Wisconsin and Minnesota, the southern Great Plains, and southern Appalachia (Fuguitt and Beale 1993), areas largely dependent on extractive industries and agriculture. Then, too, the fertility rate for nonmetropolitan women has declined. Many nonmetropolitan areas have experienced an influx of retirees (Johnson and Beale 1998). In addition to changing the age structure of such areas, the inmigration of retirees accounts for much of the growth of nonmetropolitan counties generally (Rogers 1999; Johnson and Beale 1998).

Economic Status

Poverty rates for the nonmetropolitan elderly exceed those of their metropolitan counterparts (Clifford and Lilley 1993; Rogers 1999). As the rural population of an area increases, so does the elderly poverty rate. In completely rural areas nonadjacent to any urban population, the poverty rate approaches 24 percent, almost ten percentage points greater than the highest poverty rate for elders in metropolitan areas (Rogers 1999).

At least two-thirds of the nonmetropolitan elderly poor are women. Less than 20 percent of rural men aged sixty years or older live in poverty, but for women the figure approaches 25 percent (Rogers 1999). The more rural a location, the higher the poverty rate is for elderly women (Rogers 1998), although poor elderly nonmetropolitan women are more likely to reside in areas adjacent to urban communities (Rogers 1999).

The "oldest-old," persons eighty-five years of age and older, are disproportionately present in nonmetropolitan areas, are more likely to be poor
than younger cohorts, and generally require more services, assistance, and
health care. Thus nonmetropolitan areas may be called upon to meet the
manifold needs of a growing and economically disadvantaged population
(Rogers 1999).

Social Security benefits are also disproportionately low for nonmetropolitan elders. Lingg et al. (1993) found that the nonmetropolitan beneficiaries
received an average benefit of $539 per month; metropolitan beneficiaries
received $60 more. This difference was most pronounced in the southern
states (exclusive of Florida, South Carolina, Virginia, and Arkansas) and in
the midwestern agricultural states of Missouri, Minnesota, and South
Dakota.

The nonmetropolitan elderly have less formal education than their metropolitan counterparts. When the educational attainment of rural age cohorts is examined, the results are even more striking. Fully 60.7 percent of
the oldest-old did not complete high school. Educational attainment is
much higher in the younger age cohorts, but limited education continues
to place the nonmetropolitan elderly at an economic disadvantage (Rogers
1999).

The migration of older adults to nonmetropolitan communities can be
economically advantageous for all (Rowles and Watkins 1993; Longino and
Hass 1993). Rogers (1999) observes that many "counties benefit significantly
from retirees, as seen in their population growth, increased family incomes,
greater economic diversification, and reduced unemployment rates" (Rogers
1999, 6). Longino and Haas (1993), citing findings from the Western North
Carolina Retirement Migration Impact Study, conclude that, during the
course of their residency, "the average retirement migrant household's overall impact on the local economy was $71,600. Measured by employment,
each household's expenditures create 1.5 jobs at an average income of
$14,900" (23). They further conclude that the economic benefits of retiree
migration at least cover the costs associated with providing services to this
population.

Housing

Home ownership is high among the nonmetropolitan elderly, but their
housing is generally older and in poorer repair (Belden 1993; Krout 1994;
McGough 1993). Belden (1993) found that "9.7% of the housing units oc-

cupied by the [nonmetropolitan] elderly were . . . substandard. Of all the substandard housing, 30% in nonmetropolitan areas and 17% in metro areas are occupied by elderly households" (73). Nonmetropolitan elders are more likely to be homeowners. The median value of elder-occupied nonmetropolitan housing units is lower (Rogers 1999), and nonmetropolitan elders with home mortgages have less equity in their homes than those living in suburban or urban areas (Belden 1993). Thus the homes of nonmetropolitan elders are less valuable as convertible sources of late-life income (Belden 1993).

Health Status

Rural elders may be less healthy than elderly persons living in more metropolitan settings, although research findings are not consistent. Mortality rates are highest in central city metropolitan areas, but rural areas rank second (Wallace and Wallace 1998). Yet reporting the findings of Wright et al. (1985), Wallace and Wallace (1998) also observe that rural mortality rates in the state of Georgia "were significantly higher than the urban rates in all age groups except for the population age 65 and over" (73). This anomaly may be attributable to higher rural mortality rates for unintentional injuries (Wallace and Wallace 1998), many of which may occur in the course of one's working years.

Nonmetropolitan residents suffer from a greater number of acute medical conditions than their metropolitan counterparts (Wallace and Wallace 1998). Chronic conditions are more frequently reported by the nonmetropolitan nonfarm elderly than by other groups of elders. Certain chronic conditions — "arthritis, cataracts, hearing impairment, absence of extremities, deformities or orthopedic impairments, ulcers, diabetes, kidney trouble, bladder disorders, heart disease, hypertension and emphysema" — occur at higher rates in nonmetropolitan areas (Wallace and Wallace 1998, 75).

Given higher mortality rates and lower life expectancy, it is difficult to justify the public's belief in the health-conferring advantages of rural residence. The nonmetropolitan elderly are more likely to report their health as being fair or poor (30 percent) than are metropolitan elders (27 percent). The nonmetropolitan black elderly are more likely than whites to rate their health fair or poor, a pattern also present in metropolitan areas (Van Nostrand et al. 1993).

Metropolitan versus nonmetropolitan differences on health measures are not otherwise so clear-cut. Several studies have indicated that cancer rates are higher in urban as opposed to rural areas (Wallace and Wallace 1998). Days of restricted activity per year are approximately the same for both groups, as are the rate of obesity and the percentage of people with a family history of cancer. Nonmetropolitan elders are as likely to smoke and drink as metro elders are, and certain health -promotion activities such as blood pressure screening, Pap smears, and breast self-examinations are equally common in both areas. However, compared to the metropolitan elderly, nonmetropolitan elderly women are less likely to receive mammograms or clinical breast exams. This might put nonmetropolitan women at increased risk for breast cancer, although the previously mentioned studies comparing rural-urban cancer rates do not support such a conjecture. Nonmetropolitan males are much more likely to be heavy drinkers than are metropolitan males (Van Nostrand et al. 1993). Nevertheless nonmetropolitan alcoholism rates are comparable to those of metropolitan areas (U.S. Department of Health and Human Services 1994).

Another way to evaluate the health of nonmetropolitan elders is to consider the extent to which they are unable to perform basic activities of daily living (ADLs) and instrumental activities of daily living (IADLs). ADLs consist of walking, eating, toileting, dressing, bathing, and transferring, and the ability to get in and out of bed or into and out of a chair. IADLs include the ability to do housework, go shopping, cook meals, and manage money. Both nonmetropolitan and metropolitan elderly experience similar levels of ADL and IADL impairment (Braden and Van Nostrand 1993). Redford and Severns (1994, 222) note that, while several studies have found more functional limitations and inability to perform ADLs among rural elders, "when factors such as age, sex, income, living arrangement, and education are controlled, many of these differences disappear."

It is not clear that the mental health status of older nonmetropolitan Americans differs from than of their metropolitan peers. Rurality per se has not consistently emerged as a significant predictor of either high or low subjective well-being or specific adaptive or maladaptive behaviors among the elderly (Scheidt 1998; Ortega, Metroka, and Johnson 1993; Amato and Zuo 1992; Mansfield, Preston, and Crawford 1988). Nevertheless the relationship between minority status, health, and poverty, on the one hand, and mental illness, on the other, has been established by research (Fox et al. 2001). Given that nonmetropolitan elders experience higher levels of poverty and ADL impairment, comparatively high levels of mental illness might be hypothesized for this population. However, Revicki and Mitchell (1990) found that economic deprivation and disabling illness accounted for the largest proportion of variance in emotional and psychosomatic distress and life satisfaction in a sample of both nonmetropolitan and metropolitan elderly. A Minnesota study cited by Rathbone-McCuan (1993, 146) found that "about 20% of the rural elderly population present significant mental health problems," a figure commensurate with the estimates for the general population of elders nationally.

Perceived adequacy of social support has been found to be a predictor of mental health among the elderly. The outmigration of younger people from rural areas may reduce the number of informal social supports available to rural elders, thereby negatively affecting the mental health status of older rural adults. McCulloch (1995), in a study of older Appalachian adults, reconfirmed the relationship between social support and mental health but also found that family proximity was not a predictor of mental health outcomes.

It is possible that changes occurring in rural towns may tend to undermine the well-being of some older rural residents. Norris-Baker and Scheidt (1994) argue that the deterioration of the physical environment of small towns may lead to psychological stress among elderly longtime residents. Windley and Scheidt (1982) found a positive relationship between satisfaction with dwelling and community, on the one hand, and mental health, on the other. Given the comparatively poor condition of rural housing, and the decline of small towns, negative mental health consequences for the rural elderly might be postulated.

Services for the Rural Elderly

The preceding discussion has highlighted the differences existing between rural and urban elders. While differences do exist, they are not always especially striking. In many ways nonmetropolitan elders closely resemble their metropolitan counterparts, and research has failed to yield evidence that they are, on the whole, in some major way better or more ill-prepared to meet the challenges of old age.

But if rurality confers no particular strengths or weaknesses, nonmetropolitan areas are believed to be deficient in terms of the health, economic, and social services that help older adults to "age in place." Krout (1994) attributes these deficiencies to six problems: availability, accessibility, adequacy, affordability, appropriateness, and acceptability. Services are unavailable when they cannot be found in a community, as is the case, for example, for inpatient mental health care in the more rural of nonmetropolitan areas. Services may, as a practical matter, be inaccessible, a particular problem in rural areas where transportation alternatives to the privately owned and operated automobile are likely to be very limited.

Services may be inadequate to meet the needs of elderly clients. While chore services, personal care services, and home health services help to maintain the independence of frail older adults, the most dependent persons may also require considerable family or other informal assistance to remain in their own homes. In rural areas where younger people have outmigrated in search of better employment opportunities, informal support may be in short supply, and even the maximum allowable number of service hours may be inadequate to meet client needs.

Because nonmetropolitan elders are, as a population, poorer than their metro peers, the affordability of services is a critical issue. As an agency director in two substantially rural West Virginia counties, the author managed a program of Medicaid-funded personal care services for elderly clients. Clients with Medicaid cards could receive assistance at no cost; under the rules established by state Medicaid authorities, those ineligible for Medicaid were given the opportunity to receive services on a sliding fee scale. Although the sliding fee costs were generally very low, most potential clients declined to accept services, perceiving the additional expense to be prohibitive.

Problems with appropriateness of services often arise when service choices are limited, as is frequently the case in rural areas. Clients must either decline assistance or adapt to supports that may not be well tailored to their individual circumstances. Thus the absence of many types of assistance, including help with home repairs, personal care, home health, or transportation may cause predominantly high-functioning elderly persons to choose more restrictive residential options, such as personal care or nursing homes, when a few well-targeted service options might have facilitated their continued residence at home. Finally, to the extent that rural values emphasize personal independence and self-reliance, many social services and supports may be unacceptable to rural elders (Krout 1994).

Even if services and benefits are available, accessible, adequate, affordable, appropriate, and acceptable, they will be of little use to those who are unaware of them. In more rural areas, where distances, low population density, and a more limited communication infrastructure may be the norm, keeping potential clients apprised of service options has been a challenging task.

Bull, Howard, and Bane (1991) attribute the challenges of delivering services for the rural elderly to seven factors: (1) geographic isolation; (2) economic deprivation; (3) lack of a human service infrastructure; (4) inability to use economies of scale; (5) low availability of trained labor; (6)cultural antagonism; and (7) lack of consistent, potent advocacy coalitions. In their discussion of potential solutions to these problems, coordination of effort among disparate local, state, federal, nonprofit, and for-profit organizations is a prominent strategy.

The following sections examine the status of specific types of services for the rural elderly.

Transportation

The absence or inadequacy of transportation options in rural areas remains one of the most intransigent problems of health and social service delivery for the elderly. The Federal Transit Administration (1994, iii) reports: "Thirty-eight percent of the nation's rural residents live in areas without any public transit service and another 28 percent live in areas in which the level of transit service is negligible." Stunkel (1997) concludes that public transportation is fundamentally unavailable to two-thirds of the residents of small towns and rural areas. The demand for transporation, however, is high. Nationally the elderly constitute only 7 percent of public transportation riders, but where public transportation is available in rural communities, 18 percent of all riders are elderly.

The exodus of younger persons from rural communities in search of employment in metropolitan areas undermines reliance on family members for needed transportation. At the same time, the centralization of needed services and the relocation or closure of small-town businesses and agencies create increased demand for transportation (Schauer and Weaver 1994). However much individual rural elders may need transportation — more than half the elderly drivers surveyed by Kihl (1993) expressed concerns about their own driving — low rural population density, dispersed settlements, and poor roads impede efforts to establish comprehensive transportation options.

Schauer and Weaver (1994) identify three basic strategies commonly used to enhance rural transportation options for the elderly. In the first of these, networks of volunteers provide transportation. Sometimes the transportation is focused on a specific objective, as when churches provide rides to Sunday services for their elderly parishioners or senior center volunteers transport clients to physician appointments or shopping. But the network can also be more flexible, responding to the specific requests of elders on an as-needed basis. Although these networks are very useful, they may be difficult to sustain and could require "screening of volunteer drivers, vehicle inspections, and reimbursement for mileage for transporting individuals" (Schauer and Weaver 1994, 48) and insurance coverage (Kihl 1993). Second, agencies may transport clients to the services they provide using paid staff and agency vehicles. Senior centers, for example, frequently provide transportation to congregate meal sites. This may, however, drive the cost of providing service above acceptable limits. Third, there may be some agencies whose primary purpose is to provide transportation. Although such systems are not tied to specific programs and services, as a practical matter they can seldom be as flexible as clients might wish:

> The transit manager soon discovers that a demand-responsive taxi-type service, although perhaps preferred by riders, is not a satisfactory technique for serving a large number of riders. Hence trip priorities are generally developed and a regular schedule is encouraged in an attempt to get riders to fit the available system (Schauer and Weaver 1994, 49).

This assertion is echoed by Kihl (1993, 89) whose research on rural transit found that "despite the sizable proportion of elderly in the target area there would be an insufficient number of elderly alone to support a demand responsive system."

Financing for rural transportation is limited. Rural transportation systems are heavily dependent on federal funding but receive only about 10 percent of the federal transportation budget. In spite of the importance of federal funding for rural transportation, less than half the number of rural residents are served by federally funded transit (National Eldercare Institute on Transportation 1994). In addition to financial challenges, the development of rural transportation has been hampered by a shortage of proven planning tools and methods, service delivery standards, and adequately trained personnel (Schauer and Weaver 1994).

Medical Services

Health insurance through the Medicare system is available to almost all metropolitan and nonmetropolitan elders. However, the latter are less likely to have private insurance in addition to Medicare (Braden and Cooley 1993;

Mockenhaupt and Muchow 1994). This may be a consequence of underinsurance among nonmetropolitan elders during their working years. Although the uninsured rate is similar for metropolitan and nonmetropolitan areas, nonmetropolitan residents are much more likely to purchase their own health insurance or rely on health insurance provided by small-scale employers (Pol 2000). Such coverage is less likely to be maintained subsequent to retirement. Among the more functionally impaired nonmetropolitan elderly, Medicaid is responsible for covering a larger proportion of health care costs than among comparably impaired older adults in metropolitan areas (Braden and Cooley 1993).

Access to health care is more limited in rural areas. The ratio of health professionals to the elderly population is lower in nonmetropolitan areas (Krout 1986; Schick and Schick 1994), and primary care physicians are in shorter supply (Rogers 1999), although they make up the largest proportion of rural physicians (National Advisory Committee on Rural Health 2001). In nonmetropolitan counties, increased distance to primary care providers is associated with reduced utilization of health care (Nemet and Bailey 2000). Nonmetropolitan elders are less likely to visit the dentist than are their metropolitan counterparts, a fact that may be attributable to less access to dental care in more rural areas (Van Nostrand et al. 1993).

There are more than two times as many rural Health Professional Shortage Areas (HPSAs) as urban HPSAs. Medical specialists are less likely to be located in rural areas, and 57 percent of rural physicians are generalists (National Advisory Committee on Rural Health 2001). Access to medical professionals is more problematic for minority rural elderly. Lower physician densities are a particular problem for predominantly Hispanic-American rural communities in the west. Hospital services are also more distant for this group, as they are for African-Americans in the rural south (Pathman, Konrad, and Schwartz 2001).

Rural hospital closures have exacerbated health professional shortages in rural areas because "physicians, nurses, and other health professionals . . . depend on the hospital as a base of supportive technology and employment" (Redford 1998, 273). Until the 1980s, small rural hospitals were the usual locus for medical care in rural communities. However, rising health care costs attributable to expensive hospital-based care spurred the development of new payment regulations for federal health care programs. Changes to the Medicare system particularly affected rural hospitals, because Medicare expenses account for 47 percent of patient-care expenses in these facilities compared to only 36 percent for urban hospitals (National Advisory Committee on Rural Health 2001). Medicare's Prospective Payment System

(PPS) established reimbursement caps for hospital stays, thereby encouraging the early discharge of patients. Lower occupancy rates followed, producing substantial financial losses and consequent closures for many small rural hospitals (Redford 1998).

The rate of hospitalization for rural elders exceeds that for their urban counterparts but declines markedly among those who live a distance of half an hour or more from the hospital (National Advisory Committee on Rural Health 2001). Whereas rural elders "overwhelmingly select local care in preference to remote care" (National Advisory Committee on Rural Health 2001, v), younger or better-insured rural residents often willingly choose urban hospitals because they are perceived to be of higher quality. Consequently rural hospitals serve disproportionate numbers of poor and elderly persons (Redford 1998).

The Continuum of Care in Rural Areas

Title I of the Older American's Act establishes as an objective the provision of a continuum of care services for vulnerable elderly persons (Older Americans Act of 1965). This continuum of care constitutes "a system of social, personal, financial, and medical services that supports the well-being of any older adult, regardless of the person's level of functioning" (Wacker, Roberto, and Piper 1998, 9). Rural areas are believed to have fewer such services, both in terms of absolute number of programs and the range of support options available (Christianson and Moscovice 1993; Krout 1986, 1994, 1998). Krout (1994, 16) found that "services such as adult day care, respite care, guardianship, material aid, and housing were more likely to be reported as not available in rural than in more urban planning and service areas." Rural senior centers generally have lower budgets and offer fewer services than metropolitan centers (Krout, Williams, and Owen 1994). In general, dependent persons appear to have comparatively few alternatives to institutionalization in most rural communities, as reflected in high rates of nursing home usage, higher numbers of nursing home beds per capita, and lower levels of client impairment at the time of institutionalization (Krout 1998). Even if services are available, information about them may be less accessible to rural residents. McKinley and Netting (1994) note that the small populations of rural areas usually preclude private funding availability for information and referral services, leaving such services dependent on public funds in an era of constrained budgets.

Other findings present a more mixed picture. Braden and Van Nostrand

(1993) found that despite similar functional impairment, metropolitan elders received more home health care than did nonmetropolitan elders. On the other hand, Redford and Severns (1994) found that, although more home health agencies existed in rural than in urban areas, rural residents were less likely to utilize them. Nelson and Salmon (1993), reviewing studies (Salmon et al. 1991; Benjamin 1986; Hammond 1985; Swan and Benjamin 1990; Nyman et al. 1991) examining the effect of rurality on in-home service availability, found that rurality was a significant but not strong positive predictor of chore and homemaker service provision, a weak positive predictor of Medicare home health provision, a negative predictor of home health visits, and a weak positive predictor of the likelihood of admission to a skilled nursing facility. Likewise, they found a curvilinear relationship between rurality and the supply of institutional beds, one in which rural bed censuses tended to be either disproportionately high or low. Nelson and Salmon (1993, 194) did find that rurality is a positive predictor of congregate and in-home meal provision. However, they concluded: "When the different community-based services are aggregated into a composite community-based per capita spending figure, rurality is not a significant predictor of higher [public] spending — only poverty is."

Is there a rural disadvantage regarding the availability and array of services for the elderly? Evidence suggests that this is true in a general sense, although Krout (1998, 250) has observed that several studies have found "considerable variation in the availability of services in rural areas." Rurality may be associated with certain service development and delivery problems, but local capacity may overcome these. Thus Nelson and Salmon (1993) note that political connections, strong local leadership, networking, planning, attitudes, values, and public involvement may be better predictors of service delivery than rurality per se. This point underscores the importance of social work practice for planning, developing, and enhancing services for elders in rural areas.

Social Workers, Older Adults, and Rural Communities: Roles and Opportunities

Effective social work practice requires workers to assume a variety of professional roles. In rural communities, where health care and social service professionals are likely to be in short supply, the generalist social worker can fulfill an important function by bringing a broad repertoire of skills to bear on micro- and macro-level problems. Given the paucity of services available to elders in many rural communities, system linkage and system development roles (Hepworth and Larsen 1990) are important.

Two system linkage roles — brokering and case management/coordination (Hepworth and Larsen 1990) — are critical. Brokering involves connecting clients to the resources they require, and may also require direct assistance and case follow-up. McKinley and Netting (1994) note that information about available services may be limited in rural areas, and underscore the importance of these brokering functions for effective rural information and referral.

In rural areas, where resources may be located in geographically disparate communities or clustered in a few local areas, case management and coordination have the potential to improve overall client care. Ideally case management would coordinate the delivery of required community-based services to elderly persons, thereby reducing the number of frequently bewildering client-agency interactions and facilitating client-directed service decisions and scheduling. In practice, however, rural case management is often premised on a services-based model, in which each service employs its own case managers to oversee the delivery of its own services to its own clients. The result is multiple sets of client evaluations and service plans and very little communication among providers or thoughtful articulation of services (Urv-Wong and McDowell 1994). This is hardly surprising given that comprehensive multi-service case management is not generally a funded activity. The true potential of case management for rural clients is unlikely to be realized in the absence of more centralized case planning and coordination.

Developing and enhancing the service system is likely to be as important to rural elders as linking them to existing resources. Thoughtful planning is an important activity if the service delivery system is to respond to both the needs and predilections of the rural elderly, who may have reservations about utilizing social services. Genuine community involvement in planning is more likely to produce accurate assessments of local need than studies conducted solely by external agencies. Generalist social workers familiar with existing local service options and limitations, community dynamics, key informants, persons of influence, and assessment strategies can fulfill a critical role in organizing and coordinating the planning process.

Social workers can also be instrumental in developing new services identified as critical by community-based planning. Krout (1994, 15) observes that rural areas may experience a lack of "specialty staff (trained labor pool) that impedes the development of comprehensive and community-based services." Generalist social workers, many of whom may have training in the areas of grant writing, budgeting, policy development, supervision, and administration, may be able to address the multiple demands of initiating and maintaining rural services.

Both case and cause advocacy (Kirst-Ashman and Hull 2001) are important activities for rural social workers. Case advocacy may be required to obtain for clients those services that might otherwise be unavailable as a consequence of physical distances, limited service delivery infrastructure, poor service coordination, or inadequate funding. Cause advocacy may be more important, especially with regard to policy issues that affect rural communities. Proposed strategies for Medicare and Social Security reform are cases in point.

Medicare cost containment strategies may inequitably distribute health care services to the disadvantage of rural elders. Raising Medicare premiums to discourage health care overutilization has been proposed as a way to control rising Medicare expenditures. However, because rural elders experience more chronic health conditions and have lower incomes, this strategy may disproportionately burden rural beneficiaries (MacKinney 2001).

Reliance on managed care as a Medicare cost containment strategy may not augment health care services for rural beneficiaries. Historically, Medicare expenditures in rural areas per patient have lagged behind those in urban areas. While explicitly urban/rural reimbursement criteria are no longer in effect, methods employed to calculate payment rates for hospitals and providers in different regions may work to the disadvantage of rural health systems (National Advisory Committee on Rural Health 2001). One consequence of the historically low reimbursement rates has been the reluctance of insurers to participate in the Medicare + Choice plan, which allows elderly persons to choose a managed-care form of Medicare. These plans may offer more benefits than traditional fee-for-service Medicare. Higher base payments have recently been instituted in an effort to encourage insurers to expand Medicare + Choice into rural areas but has met with little success (Dubow 2001).

Social Security is a critical source of income for older rural Americans. Plans to preserve Social Security include both incremental reforms and major structural modifications. Raising the retirement age has been frequently proposed as a strategy to reduce program expenditures. Retirement age increases can be justified on ethical grounds because they are applied to all workers equally in the interest of the net welfare (U.S. General Accounting Office 1998). Currently mandated increases will be gradually implemented; no particular age cohort bears a disproportionate share of the reduction. But it can be argued that age increases will nonetheless be inequitable, as certain groups — including the rural elderly — may be more adversely affected than others.

Blue-collar workers are at greater risk than white-collar workers for certain health problems — musculoskeletal diseases, respiratory disease, diabetes, and emotional disorders — and these are associated with increased unemployment compared to that of their healthy counterparts and white-collar workers with similar health problems (*Social Security reform* 1998). Increasing the retirement age for these workers may result in additional years of low or inadequate income prior to full benefits eligibility. Blue-collar workers employed in agriculture, forestry, and fisheries, are at an added disadvantage, as these groups frequently lack private pension benefits (U.S. Bureau of the Census 1996). This suggests that raising the retirement age may have deleterious consequences for rural dwellers who are disproportionately employed in these occupations (Dorfman 1998).

Summary

Although the rural elderly resemble urban older adults in most respects, the circumstances of rural life pose unique challenges for rural elders and the health and social service systems that support their efforts to age independently. Generalist social workers can support these efforts by providing direct service in the areas of rural mental health, health care services, and long-term care. Equally important, social workers should direct their efforts to developing needed supportive services for elders and improving the coordination of rural aging-related services so that the rural elderly and their communities may derive the greatest benefits from limited resources.

Finally, national age-related public policies, such as Social Security, Medicare, and others not addressed in this chapter, are critical for the welfare of older rural residents. The future fiscal viability of these programs is uncertain at best, and a variety of proposals are under consideration by which costs may be controlled if not reduced. While changes in these programs probably cannot be avoided, social workers should keep themselves apprised of the consequences of specific reform initiatives and advocate for measures that will minimize their negative consequences for rural elders.

References

Amato, P. R., and J. Zuo. 1992. Rural poverty, urban poverty, and psychological well-being. *Sociological Quarterly* 33 (2): 229–240.

Belden, Joseph N. 1993. Housing for America's rural elderly. In C. Neil Bull, ed., *Aging in rural America*, pp. 71–83. Newbury Park, Calif.: Sage.

Braden, J., and S. G. Cooley. 1993. Health insurance, expenditures, and benefit use. In J. F. Van Nostrand, ed., *Common beliefs about the rural elderly: What do national data tell us?* DHHS Publication No. PHS 93–1412. Washington, D.C.: U.S. Government Printing Office.

Braden, J., and J. F. Van Nostrand. 1993. Long-term care. In J. F. Van Nostrand, ed., *Common beliefs about the rural elderly: What do national data tell us?* DHHS Publication No. PHS 93–1412. Washington, D.C.: U.S. Government Printing Office.

Bull, C. Neil, David Howard, and Share Decroix Bane. 1991. *Challenges and solutions to the provision of programs and services to rural elders.* Kansas City: National Resource Center for the Elderly, University of Missouri.

Christianson, J., and I. Moscovice. 1993. Health care reform and rural health networks. *Health Affairs* (fall): 58–80.

Clifford, William, and Stephen Lilley. 1993. Rural elderly: Their demographic characteristics. In C. Neil Bull, ed., *Aging in rural America*, pp. 3–16. Newbury Park, Calif.: Sage.

Deavers, K., and R. Hoppe. 1992. Overview of the rural poor in the 1980s. In Cynthia M. Duncan, ed., *Rural poverty in America*, pp. 3–20. Westport, Conn.: Auburn House.

Dorfman, Lorraine T. 1998. Economic status, work, and retirement among the rural elderly. In Rayond Coward and John Krout, eds., *Aging in rural settings: Life circumstances and distinctive features*, pp. 47–66. New York: Springer.

Dubow, Joyce. 2001. Medicare + Choice: Payment issues in rural and low payment areas. *American Association of Retired Persons Public Policy Institute Data Digest* 60. Available online at http://research.aarp.org/health/dd60_payment.pdf.

Federal Transit Administration. 1994. Status report on public transportation in rural America, 1994. Federal Transit Administration. Available online at http://www.fta.dot.gov/library/program/rurlstat/rurlstat.html.

Fox, J. C., M. Blank, V. G. Rovnyak, and R. Y. Barnett. 2001. Barriers to help seeking for mental disorders in a rural impoverished population. *Community Mental Health Journal* 37 (5): 421–436.

Fuguitt, Glenn, and Calvin Beale. 1993. The changing concentration of the older nonmetropolitan population, 1960–90. *Journal of Gerontology: Social Sciences* 48 (6): S278-S288.

Hepworth, Dean, and Jo Ann Larsen. 1990. *Direct social work practice: Theory and skills.* Belmont, Calif.: Wadsworth.

Johnson, Kenneth, and Calvin Beale. 1998. The continuing population rebound in nonmetro America. *Rural Development Perspectives* 13 (3). Available online at www.ers.usda.gov/publications/rdp/rdp1098/rdp1098a.pdf.

Kihl, Mary R. 1993. The need for transportation alternative for the rural elderly. In

C. Neil Bull, ed., *Aging in rural America*, pp. 84–98. Newbury Park, Calif.: Sage.

Kirst-Ashman, K. K., and G. H. Hull. 2001. *Generalist practice with organizations and communities*. Boston: Brooks-Cole.

Krout, John. 1986. *The aged in rural America*. New York: Greenwood.

———. 1994. An overview of older rural populations and community-based services. In John Krout, ed., *Providing community-based services to the rural elderly*, pp. 3–18. Thousand Oaks, Calif.: Sage.

———. 1998. Services and delivery in rural environments. In Raymond T. Coward and John A. Krout, eds., *Aging in rural settings: Life circumstances and distinctive features*, pp. 247–266. New York: Springer.

Krout, J., M. Milliams, and O. Owen. 1994. Senior centers in rural communities. In John Krout, ed., *Providing community-based services to the rural elderly*, pp. 90–110. Thousand Oaks, Calif.: Sage.

Lingg, B., J. Braden, A. A. Goldstein, and S. G. Cooley. 1993. Income, poverty, and education. In J. F. Van Nostrand, ed., *Common beliefs about the rural elderly: What do national data tell us?* DHHS Publication No. PHS 93–1412. Washington, D.C.: U.S. Government Printing Office.

Longino, Charles, and William Haas. 1993. Migration and the rural elderly. In C. Neil Bull, ed., *Aging in rural America*, pp. 17–29. Newbury Park, Calif.: Sage.

MacKinney, A. Clinton. 2001. Redesigning Medicare: Equity considerations for rural Medicare beneficiaries and health systems. In A. F. Coburn et al., eds., *Redesigning Medicare: Considerations for rural beneficiaries and health systems, RUPRI Rural Health Panel Special Monograph*, pp. 9–20. Columbia, Mo.: Rural Policy Research Institute.

Mansfield, P. K., D. B. Preston, and C. O. Crawford. 1988. Rural-urban differences in women's psychological well-being. *Health Care for Women International* 9 (4): 289–304.

McCulloch, J. 1995.The relationship of family proximity and social support to the mental health of older rural adults: The Appalachian context. *Journal of Aging Studies* 9 (1): 65–81.

McGough, Duane. 1993. Housing. In J. F. Van Nostrand, ed., *Common beliefs about the rural elderly: What do national data tell us?* DHHS Publication No. PHS 93–1412. Washington, D.C.: U.S. Government Printing Office.

McKinley, Anne, and F. Ellen Netting. 1994. Information and referral: Targeting the rural elderly. In John Krout, ed., *Providing community-based services to the rural elderly*, pp. 23–41. Thousand Oaks, Calif.: Sage.

Mockenhaupt, Robin, and Jennifer Muchow. 1994. Disease and disability prevention and health promotion for rural elders. In John Krout, ed., *Providing community-based services to the rural elderly*, pp. 183–201. Thousand Oaks, Calif.: Sage.

National Advisory Committee on Rural Health. 2001. *Medicare reform: A rural perspective*. Washington, D.C.: Published by the author.

National Eldercare Institute on Transportation. 1994. *Meeting the challenge: Mo-*

bility for elders. Washington, D.C.: National Eldercare Institute on Transportation.

Nelson, Gary, and Mary Anne Salmon. 1993. The rural factor in developing state and local systems of home and community care. In C. Neil Bull, ed., *Aging in rural America,* pp. 189–203. Newbury Park, Calif.: Sage.

Nemet, Gregory F., and Adrian J. Bailey. 2000. Distance and health care utilization among the rural elderly. *Social Science and Medicine* 50:1197–1208.

Norris-Baker, C., and R. Scheidt. 1994. From "our town" to "ghost town": The changing context of home for rural elders. *International Journal of Aging and Human Development* 38 (3): 181–202.

Older Americans Act. 1965. 42 U.S.C.A.,Chapter 35, Subchapter I, Section 3001. Available online at http://www4.law.cornell.edu/uscode/42/ch35schl.html.

Ortega, S., M. Metroka, and D. Johnson. 1993. In sickness and in health: Age, social support, and the psychological consequences of physical health among rural and urban residents. In C. Neil Bull, ed., *Aging in rural America,* pp. 101–116. Newbury Park, Calif.: Sage.

Pathman, D., T. Konrad, and R. Schwartz. 2001. *The proximity of rural African American and Hispanic/Latino communities to physicians and hospital services: Working paper no. 72.* Chapel Hill: University of North Carolina at Chapel Hill, Cecil G. Sheps Center for Health Service Research, North Carolina Rural Health Research and Policy Analysis Center.

Pol, Louis. 2000. Health insurance in rural America. *Rural Policy Brief* 5 (11). Omaha, Nebr.: Rural Policy Research Institute Center for Rural Health Policy Analysis.

Rathbone-McCuan, Eloise. 1993. Rural geriatric mental health care: A continuing service dilemma. In C. Neil Bull, ed., *Aging in rural America,* pp. 146–160. Newbury Park, Calif.: Sage.

Redford, Linda. 1998. Public policy and the rural elderly. In Raymond T. Coward and John A. Krout, eds., *Aging in rural settings: Life circumstances and distinctive features,* pp. 267–286. New York: Springer.

Redford, Linda, and Alison Severns. 1994. Home health services in rural America. In John Krout, ed., *Providing community-based services to the rural elderly,* pp. 221–242. Thousand Oaks, Calif.: Sage.

Revicki, D., and J. Mitchell. 1990. Strain, social support, and mental health in rural elderly individuals. *Journals of Gerontology: Social Sciences* 45:S267-S274.

Rogers, Carolyn. 1998. Poverty of older women across the rural-urban continuum. *Rural Development Perspectives* 13 (3). Available online at www.ers.usda.gov/ publications/rdp/rdp1098/rdp1098a.pdf.

———. 1999. *Changes in the older population and implications for rural areas.* Research Report Number 90. Washington, D.C.: Food and Rural Economics Division, Economic Research Service, United States Department of Agriculture.

Rowles, G., and J. Watkins. Elderly migration and development in small communities. *Growth and Change* 24 (4): 509–538.

Schauer, P. M., and P. Weaver. 1994. Rural elder transportation. In John Krout, ed., *Providing community-based services to the rural elderly*, pp. 42–64. Thousand Oaks, Calif.: Sage.

Scheidt, R. 1998. The mental health of the elderly in rural environments. In Raymond T. Coward and John A. Krout, eds., *Aging in rural settings: Life circumstances and distinctive features*, pp. 85–103. New York: Springer.

Schick, Frank L., and Renee Schick. 1994. *Statistical handbook on aging Americans.* Rev. ed. Phoenix, Ariz.: Oryx.

Social Security reform: Raising retirement ages improves program solvency but may cause hardship for some: Testimony before the Special Committee on Aging, United States Senate. 1998. Testimony of Barbara D. Bovbjerg. GAO Publication No. GAO/T-HEHS-98–207. Washington, D.C.: General Accounting Office.

Stunkel, Edith. 1997. Rural public transportation and the mobility of older persons: Paradigms for policy. *Journal of Aging and Social Policy* 9 (3): 67–86.

U.S. Bureau of the Census. 1996. *65 + + in the United States.* Current Population Reports, Special Studies, P23–190. Washington, D.C.: United States Government Printing Office.

———. 2001. *Statistical abstract of the United States:2001.* Washington, D.C.: U.S. Government Printing Office

U.S. Department of Health and Human Services. 1994. *Rural issues in alcohol and other drug abuse treatment.* DHHS Publication No. SMA 94–2063. Rockville, Md.: U.S. Department of Health and Human Services.

U.S. General Accounting Office. 1993. *Rural development: Profile of rural areas.* GAO Publication No. GAO/RCED-93–40FS. Washington, D.C.: General Accounting Office.

———. 1998. *Social Security: Different approaches for addressing program solvency.* GAO Publication No. GAO/T-HEHS-98–33. Washington, D.C.: General Accounting Office.

Urv-Wong, Ene, and Donna McDowell. 1994. Case management in a rural setting. In John Krout, ed., *Providing community-based services to the rural elderly*, pp. 65–89. Thousand Oaks, Calif.: Sage.

Van Nostrand, J. F., S. E. Furner, J. A. Brunelle, and R. A. Cohen. 1993. Health. In J. F. Van Nostrand, ed., *Common beliefs about the rural elderly: What do national data tell us?* DHHS Publication No. PHS 93–1412. Washington, D.C.: U.S. Government Printing Office.

Wacker, R., K. Roberto, and L. Piper. 1998. *Community resources for older adults: Programs and services in an era of change.* Thousand Oaks, Calif.: Pine Forge.

Wallace, Rachel. and Robert Wallace. 1998. Rural-urban contrasts in elder health status: Methodologic issues and findings. In Raymond T. Coward and John A. Krout, eds., *Aging in rural settings: Life circumstances and distinctive features*, pp. 67–83. New York: Springer.

Windley, P., and R. Scheidt. 1982. Ecological model of mental health among small-town rural elderly. *Journal of Gerontology* 37 (2): 235–242.

Part IV

Education for Practice

15 Social Work Education for Rural Practice

Nancy Lohmann

•

The preceding chapters in this book have dealt with those who live in rural areas and the nature of social work practice with these rural residents. They have done so in part by contrasting the experience of nonmetropolitan residents with those of persons living in more metropolitan areas.

This final chapter considers the nature of social work education for those who practice in nonmetropolitan areas. In doing so, it examines the recommendations for classroom education, field education, and continuing education. It reviews whether there is or should be anything different about educating for practice in rural areas and educating for practice in other areas.

History of Education for Rural Practice

Emilia Martinez-Brawley (1980) has traced the history of practice in rural areas, including efforts to educate social workers for rural practice. That history includes the 1909 *Report of the Commission on Rural Life* that called for "many young men and women, fresh from our schools and institutions of learning, and quick with ambition and trained intelligence" to focus on the problems of rural America (Martinez-Brawley 1980, 19). One of those providing recommendations early in the twentieth century for the education of rural practitioners was Jesse Frederick Steiner, whose paper on "Education for Social Work in Rural Communities: Rural Sociology — Indispensable or Merely Desirable?" (cited in ibid.) was presented at the 1927 National Conference of Social Work.

In the latter half of the twentieth century the Southern Regional Education Board, through its Rural Task Force of the Manpower Education and Training Project in 1972, identified some assumptions about rural practice and the characteristics of effective rural social workers (Levin 1974). Ginsberg (1976, 1–12; 1998 [1976], 3–22) has included this list in three of his edited books on rural social work practice suggesting their continuing relevance more than twenty-five years after they were first identified.

During the twentieth century, the suggestion of many writing about the preparation needed for rural social work practice was that a generalist model was the most appropriate approach. Davenport and Davenport (1995) indicate that the model was first advocated in the 1920s and 1930s. Such a model was adopted by 1984 as the basis for all beginning social work practice, indicating that the model is viewed as the sine qua non for all practice regardless of the setting. In 1974 the generalist model was adopted by the Council on Social Work Education (CSWE) as the basis for a Baccalaureate of Social Work (BSW), and in 1984 it was adopted as the basis for the foundation education of Master of Social Work (MSW) students. However, even with the adoption of a generalist approach for all beginning social work education, those interested in rural practice still struggle with the question of what rural practitioners may need to know. Every annual meeting of the Institute on Human Services in Rural Areas continues to include several papers on education for rural practice. This suggests that the perception of educators concerned with this field is that more than a generalist education is needed to prepare for work in the nonmetropolitan environment. What kind of education, including generalist education, is needed to prepare practitioners to be effective in rural environments?

What Is Generalist Practice?

The definition of *generalist practice* has changed over time. With those changes some of the concerns expressed by those writing about rural practice have been addressed. Mermelstein and Sundet (1976), for example, in a frequently cited chapter on education for rural practice, take issue with the definition of *generalist* that was current at the time. They were writing soon after the generalist model had been adopted for baccalaureate education (1974) and prior to its adoption as the foundation for masters education (1984). They indicated that the definitions tended to assume a therapeutic or remedial approach to practice and emphasized microsystems. They also pointed out that the rural social worker "assesses social phenomena in all of their systematic ramifications and identifies and intervenes at whatever level is efficient and effective to bring about desired social changes" (ibid., 16). Thus a therapeutic or remedial approach with microsystems was not sufficient in their view for nonmetropolitan practitioners. While Pamela Landon (1995), in the *Encyclopedia of Social Work*, indicates that complete agreement has not been achieved as to the definition of such practice, she adds that,

> there appears to be definitional agreement on the centrality of multi-method and multilevel approaches, based on an eclectic choice of theory base and the necessity for incorporating the dual vision of the profession based on private issues and social justice concerns. Differences lie in the emphases placed on the use of the planned change process, the ecosystem base, and the various central philosophical concepts such as empowerment; the centrality of context; and the definition of specific knowledge and skills needed. (1103)

Landon also discusses the advanced generalist model as an alternative MSW-level concentration and indicates that among the reasons for adopting such a model are the contextual issues confronted in rural practice.

Cody et al. (1998, 26) describe a generalist program as one that "entails clinical, management, and policy curriculum content. It teaches students to intervene at every level with an approach guided by planned change and an emphasis on the problem-solving process."

If, at this time, there is agreement that a generalist model is appropriate for rural practice, and if the definition of a generalist model appears to have broadened over time to incorporate the skills needed for rural practice, why do educators, concerned about preparing nonmetropolitan practitioners, continue to write about the education needed? The continued concern suggests that something in addition to that generalist foundation is needed. Educators have taken three main approaches to identifying what those additional knowledge, values, and skills may be. They have developed lists of the skills that may be needed, suggested theoretical orientations that appear especially appropriate for rural practice, and looked at research findings about the nature of rural practice. In effect, both deductive and inductive approaches have been taken to identify what may be needed to become an effective rural practitioner. Major findings with each of these approaches are discussed below.

Skills Needed

Ginsberg (1976) identified five elements that needed to be present in education for rural practice:

- Generalist preparation.
- Field instruction provided in a rural area or small town.
- Supportive curricular materials dealing with rural social problems, rural social policies, rural community behavior, and skill in rural and small-town intervention.
- Preparation for independent, minimally supervised practice. Ginsberg identifies this as perhaps the most important need.
- A high degree of sensitivity to and skill in relating to various socioeconomic classes and ethnic groups.

Nooe and Bolitho (1982), in their review of the literature on rural practice, concluded that the social work curriculum for rural practice, in addition to preparing students in the basic principles (14), needed to prepare students in the following areas:

- To understand rural change and its opportunities and challenges
- To recognize the need for specialized skills and ways to use them in rural practice
- To meet the task of gaining acceptance into the small town or rural area. (15–16)

Theoretical Orientations

Some of those writing about rural practice have suggested particular theoretical orientations that ought to be present in a generalist education intended to prepare practitioners for work in nonmetropolitan areas. Irey (1980) suggests that an ecological perspective be used to develop the foundation for rural practice. With such a base, she argues, problems will be reconceptualized as transactional problems, and the social worker will focus on improving the fit between the person and the environment (40).

Martinez-Brawley (1985) suggests a contextual approach in which context would be an added dimension to those of field of practice, social units of concern, and methods or social technologies. Jones (1998) suggests the use of a strengths perspective. Nooe and Bolitho (1982) call for a specialized degree for rural practice in addition to a generalist foundation. They argue that the absence of professional resources in rural areas may suggest that a clinical degree would be appropriate, given the level of treatment and consultation that may be required of the social worker.

Research on Rural Practice

Within the last few decades educators have also attempted to define the education needed by examining what practitioners in nonmetropolitan areas actually do.

Wodarski (1983), reporting on the results of a five-year National Institute of Mental Health project on preparation for practice in rural community mental health, indicates that the experiences of students participating in the project support a generalist model (1983, 183). He goes on to identify particular competencies needed by BSWs and MSWs for rural practice. BSW competencies include being aware of one's own biases, conducting oneself in a professional manner, being able to conduct assessments, having the ability to link clients with services, being capable of analyzing organizational workings, understanding cultural diversity, and having familiarity with psychotropic medications (Wodarski 1993, 183–184). MSW competencies build on BSW ones and include advanced practice technologies and enabling skills. Such technologies and skills incorporate competencies in the delivery of advanced clinical skills, administration and management, supervision, social policy planning, and intermediate research skills (Wodarski 1983, 184–187).

Doelker and Bedic (1983) surveyed twenty practitioners in southern Alabama and northwest Florida, and asked these practitioners seven open-ended questions about their practice. The researchers concluded that what was needed for practice was a generalist base that was broad in scope rather than role-specific. They also identified five process skills (acculturation, affiliation, ingress, accessing, and synergism) that would prepare the practitioner to assess the community and determine appropriate service roles (43).

Whitaker (1984) surveyed National Association of Social Workers (NASW) members practicing in rural and urban areas in Maine and used 87 dependent variables to identify the differences between rural and urban practice from the 243 usable questionnaires returned. The results showed that rural practitioners were more likely than urban ones to report:

- a broader range of administrative activities
- self-actualization as important to their practice
- the importance of freedom from prejudice
- the importance of a sense of humor
- identify inclement weather as a problem
- having encountered a lack of job security in the last year

Some surprising findings emerged on characteristics that did not differ in the way that conventional wisdom about rural practice might suggest. Rural workers were less likely than urban ones to

- indicate that knowledge of natural helping networks was important in their practice
- think that knowledge of local standards and mores was important to their practice
- report excessive travel time for client contact
- perform broker activities

One possible explanation that Whitaker offers for his findings is that "the survey results accurately describe a relative lack of substantial differences existing between rural and urban social work" (18). However, he does believe that the performance of the social worker is affected by forces in a rural area that his study may not have identified.

Jerrell and Knight (1985) surveyed 117 social workers in eleven service areas in twenty rural counties in western Pennsylvania. They reported the number of hours BSW and MSW social workers indicated spending on various activities. BSW workers spent the most time on intake (5.15 mean hours), emergency services (4.09), partial hospitalization (4.98), and community residential services (4.76). MSW workers spent the most time on inpatient services (13.70 mean hours) and administration (13.68). The researchers concluded that "the MSW's role more closely resembles a clinical practice model while the BSW is a true generalist" (335).

Waltman (1986), when reviewing the findings of Doelker and Bedic (1983) and Jerrell and Knight (1985) and reflecting on her own observations, indicates that rural baccalaureate-level workers are often involved in high-risk and complex clinical situations and administrative and supervisory responsibilities. Rural master's-level social workers, she has observed, are often in demand as consultants and field work supervisors.

Denton, York, and Moran (1988), like Whitaker, surveyed NASW members, surveying a systematic random sample of rural and urban social workers in North Carolina and receiving 177 useable responses. They focused on differing perceptions of the communities in which the social workers practiced and the emphasis they placed on various practice roles. The researchers found that social workers in rural areas tended to perceive their communities in more rural terms. The dimensions of the community examined included the formality of decision making, the pace of life, the stability of the lifestyle, the traditional nature of the values, the formality of support systems, the extent to which there was a focus on individuals or communities (internal-external focus), and the degree to which education was emphasized.

They found, however, that there was no significant correlation between the perception of the community and the role sets used in practice. Role sets were those of broker, mobilizer, advocate, clinician, and mediator. Denton, York, and Moran concluded that, "it appears that social workers who perceive that their communities possess rural characteristics do not practice in ways that are different from social workers who perceive that their communities possess urban attributes" (ibid., 20). They offer several possible explanations for this surprising finding. They suggest that the social workers may differ in the way they operate in the roles even though the roles may not differ. It is possible that the community dimensions they examined are not relevant to practice. Few of the MSWs surveyed had been educated in programs with a rural emphasis, and they suggest that it is possible that the nature of their education explains the absence of a difference.

Egan and Kadushin (1997) examined social workers' roles in rural hospitals in Iowa. Their findings supported a generalist education for rural practice at both the baccalaureate and master's level.

Gumpert, Saltman, and Sauer-Jones (2000) report on a snowball sample based on mailing lists for the 1993 and 1994 National Institutes on Social Work and Human Services in Rural Areas and the 1994 mailing list for the journal *Human Services in the Rural Environment*. Of the 6-page, 39-item questionnaires mailed, 155 responses from persons living in 19 states were received. This study did not attempt to contrast nonmetropolitan practice with that in more urbanized areas but instead described the nature of the practice of those in rural areas.

The researchers report that a majority of the respondents identified some aspects of practice that they considered uniquely rural, including informal networks of community knowledge, suspicion of outsiders, a slower pace of work with clients, lack of value on formal education, stigma associated with the receipt of mental health services, a tolerance of incest, and a value placed on independence (ibid., 30). Most respondents agreed that workers in rural areas needed special skills to practice effectively, but the survey did not ask respondents to identify the skills required. Gumpert, Saltman, and Sauer-Jones suggest that education programs focus on community systems assessment to prepare students for rural practice.

Hovestadt, Fennell, and Canfield (2002) surveyed 124 members of the National Association for Rural Mental Health using a modified Delphi process, and identified six skills needed to be an effective marital and family therapy provider in rural mental health settings. Of the seventy-four persons responding to the survey, twenty-three, or 31 percent, indicated that their primary professional training was in social work. The skills identified were (1) effective skills in marriage and family therapy; (2) rural community understanding, appreciation, and participation; (3) personal characteristics and flexibility; (4) generalist with a nonspecialization foundation; (5) education, training, and experience in marital and family therapy; and (6) utilizing formal and informal community resources (227–229).

Generalist and Beyond: The Advanced Practitioner

There appears to be a consensus supported by research findings that a generalist foundation is needed to practice in nonmetropolitan areas. Is anything else needed, in addition to the generalist base, to enable the MSW practitioner to work in a rural area?

As Landon (1995) indicates, some have argued that an advanced generalist education is necessary for the graduate-level practitioner. Landon surveyed twenty-two graduate programs that appeared to have an advanced generalist curriculum for the MSW degree. Of the twenty responses received, seventeen (85 percent) indicated that they were advanced generalist by title or content (1103). Eleven of the programs offering an advanced generalist degree are joint bachelor's-master's programs, which Landon believes may have provided a contextual influence on the choice of this focus. She indicates that reasons for selecting the advanced generalist approach include a program's focus on rural practice and developments in multicultural practice that raise questions about classical clinical practice.

Landon reports on three models of advanced generalist practice that appear to be used by different programs. Some use a multi-method conceptualization and address the traditional triad of methods. Others use an integrated model that focuses on "major interventive knowledge and strategies that can apply at all client system levels" (1103). Still others use a specific social problem, field of practice, or population group to demonstrate the application of the generalist model.

In her study Landon (1995) used the Council on Social Work Education (CSWE) *Summary Information on Master of Social Work Programs* to identify those programs that might have an advanced generalist focus. A more recent review of that information for 2001–2002 indicates that twenty-one accredited programs describe their degrees as providing advanced generalist content. Four programs in candidacy for accreditation also describe themselves as offering advanced generalist content. Programs offering such content range from the urban Columbia University School of Social Work to institutions in more rural settings.

Four accredited programs and two programs in candidacy describe themselves as having a rural focus. Not all those programs use an advanced generalist model, however. Three of the accredited and one of the programs in candidacy indicate that their rural focus is combined with an advanced generalist model. Several programs that are known to the author to have a rural and small-town focus do not self-identify as such in the summary information.

Martinez-Brawley (1985, 41), writing soon after CSWE adopted the generalist foundation and concentration approach for graduate programs, proposes the development of a rural concentration at the graduate level. She indicates that such a concentration would need to incorporate substantive content about rural issues in the policy, research, and human behavior in the social environment (HBSE) components, and pay attention to appropriate practice methods and field experience sequences.

Gibbs, Locke, and Lohmann (1990), writing about the generalist–advanced generalist continuum, indicate that it is supportive of practice in rural areas and small towns. They describe the curriculum then in effect at the West Virginia University (WVU) School of Social Work to illustrate the continuum. WVU has focused on rural and small-town practice since the late 1960s.

Field Practicum

The literature is limited on the field practicum approaches that are most supportive of rural practice. Ginsberg (1998 [1976], 20) indicates that field practica should be in smaller communities to prepare students for rural practice. He indicates that preceptors from fields other than social work may be needed for such placements because of the limited availability of social workers.

Mermelstein and Sundet (1976, 24–25), when writing about education for rural program development, identified six principles that field education should follow and that would alter the usual field instruction pattern:

1. The ideal pattern is a field instructor who is a member of the faculty and who assumes the role of middle manager within an agency or a consortium of agencies.
2. The field instructor and students are accountable for production.
3. Autonomy of practice must be integral to the placement.
4. Opportunities for collaboration with other professions must be provided.
5. There must be opportunities to observe and analyze agency and community decision-making processes.
6. The field instructor should demonstrate the role of professional learner.

Mermelstein and Sundet point out that the role of field supervision in this model would differ from the apprenticeship model "since both the instructor and student would be actively engaged in the same intervention, and the evaluation of performance and suggestion for improvement would be mutual responsibilities" (1976, 25). Mermelstein and Sundet focus on rural program development and they indicate that a student in a rural placement is more often called upon to do such program development.

Weber (1980, 210) suggests three basic models that can be used to design rural field placement. She suggests that students can be placed in a rural agency where the social work educator is located; they can be placed in another community agency with a task supervisor for all or part of their placement; or they can be assigned to work independently on a social problem in the community. She indicates that the first two models work best with a generic or micro level of intervention, while the third model is appropriate for a community organization placement.

Miller (1998, 59), in discussing the dilemma posed by dual relationships in rural areas, indicates that time needs to be spent in the field as well as in the classroom on the ethical issues posed by dual relationships. The nature of social relationships in rural areas makes it difficult to avoid dual relationships. The language added in 1994 to the National Association of Social Workers *Code of Ethics* on nonsexual dual relationships suggests the importance of assisting students in understanding how they may behave ethically when working in nonmetropolitan areas. Chapter 6 in the present volume addresses in detail the difficulties of dealing with dual relationships in rural areas.

Yevuta (1999) describes her experiences in developing a placement in a rural West Virginia county for an MSW student at West Virginia University. She indicates that the placement met a need that could not otherwise be met and, by doing so, demonstrated the value of social work services. The student used a generalist approach, and projects included direct practice and community organization. Only one or two MSWs lived in the county, and there were no MSWs working in the agency where the student would be placed. An arrangement was made for social work supervision to come from an MSW who taught part-time at a local community college. Meetings between the supervisor and the student occurred on Saturdays at the supervisor's home. Yevuta emphasizes the importance of advance planning for rural placements given that the educational support found in larger areas is often not available (321). She adds that the time and effort spent planning for the placement were well worth it, given the positive outcomes of the placement.

Planning for nonmetropolitan field practica may require greater flexibility than planning for field placements in other geographic areas. It can be challenging for the educational program to provide such placements while assuring that the expectations of the profession for a placement are met. The rewards for the student and the nonmetropolitan area in which the student is placed can be significant, however.

Continuing Education and Rural Social Work Practice

The need for continual development of one's knowledge and skills is a hallmark of all professional education. Social work licensure requirements have meant that continuing education is now a requirement for most social workers to remain eligible to practice. Continuing education can be especially important for the social worker practicing in rural areas where the number of other professional colleagues may be limited and isolation may characterize the practice experience. However, gaining access to continuing education may also be a challenge in rural areas.

Horejsi and Deaton (1977, 209) identify some of the barriers that are faced when attempting to provide continuing education to rural practitioners, four of which, listed below, they believe are unique to the rural situation:

- Courses and workshops must be scheduled at more locations because of the sparse population.

- Collaboration among continuing education providers is appropriate to avoid duplication or fragmentation of resources.
- Planning must recognize that the rural practitioner is a generalist who assumes a variety of roles.
- Rural continuing educators work with a wider variety of social service professions than the urban counterpart.

Horejsi and Deaton report on two home study courses that they have used with some success, one of which was supplemented by cassette tapes and long-distance conversations with the instructor. While they suggest that electronic technology is underutilized, they were writing before some of the contemporary technological approaches for distance education had been fully developed and available.

Bast (1977, 217) reported on the use of the agriculture extension model for continuing education in Wisconsin. At the time he described this process, Area Health and Social Service Education agents had been developed whose role was to link the needs of communities to the social development expertise of the university system.

Pippard and Bates (1983) contrast the urban continuing education program with that for rural areas. Among the differences they cite is that rural program objectives are often broader in scope because of the range of educational backgrounds of those being served by them (5). They indicate that private profit-making entrepreneurs are often not interested in providing continuing education in rural areas because it is "especially costly, complicated, [and] time- and energy-consuming" (5). The director of continuing education serving a rural area often has to do everything from developing the brochures to coordinating room and travel arrangements to providing refreshments and cleaning up when the activity is done. They, too, function as generalists, it would appear.

Pippard and Bates (1983) also indicate the importance of the natural helping system in developing programs for rural communities and the importance of word-of-mouth as a marketing technique for recruiting people to the programs.

Distance Learning Technology and Rural Education

One of the ways to meet the needs of those preparing to practice or already practicing in rural environments is through the use of distance learning technologies, which are increasingly available in rural areas (see chapter 3). Several social work programs now have a decade or more of experience in using such technology to offer graduate and undergraduate courses at distant locations.

Rooney and Bibus (1995) report on the delivery under Title IV-E of an advanced course on working with involuntary clients by the University of Minnesota School of Social Work. The course was delivered through satellite to forty-nine participants at five remote sites. Eighteen students also took the course at the studio classroom from which it was broadcast. Some participants took the course for graduate credit although most (82 percent) completed it for continuing professional education. Two-way communication via phone was possible with the students at remote sites.

Rooney and Bibus indicate that while it would have been possible to offer the course via interactive television at three state university locations, they chose satellite transmission because it was available at more locations in the state. While some form of distance technology is likely available in reasonable proximity to all but the most remote sites, the technology may not always be facilitative of interaction as was the case in this instance. In this course, arrangements were made for all participants to take part in a face-to-face session for the first and last sessions to reduce some of the limitations associated with the use of a technology that is not interactive.

Participants indicated that varied modes of presentation were helpful as was the program's use of facilitators to lead discussions at each site. The modes of presentation included the use of videotapes and transparencies. Most of the participants reported that the training was useful in improving their practice, although those at remote sites rated it as slightly less useful. Participants at remote sites attended the training sessions more frequently.

Coe and Elliott (1999) have reported on a graduate direct practice course taught through face-to-face and interactive television. The course was part of a program developed by the School of Social Work at the University of Texas, Arlington, to meet the need for master's-level social workers in rural Texas. Six of the fourteen class sessions were conducted face-to-face with instructors traveling to instructional sites, and the remaining eight sessions were taught by live interactive television. The experiences and performances of the distant students were compared to those of students enrolled in the same course on campus. Based on the grades earned, students at distant sites performed as well as those on campus. Among the suggestions for improvement in the course were the following:

- Increase training for instructors on ways to increase interactions.
- Increase the use of visual aids such as PowerPoint and overhead transparencies.
- Train students on accessing the library through the internet and the use of interlibrary loan.
- Increase faculty-student interaction through the use of a toll-free phone number for calls, e-mail and voice mail. (Ibid., 362–363)

Petracchi and Patchner (2000) have compared the experiences of students enrolled in three sections of a foundation research methods course: one section was in the classroom from which an interactive television broadcast originated, the second was at a remote site receiving the broadcast, and the third was in another classroom receiving face-to-face instruction with no interactive involvement. The course was offered by the University of Pittsburgh School of Social Work.

The researchers found no statistically significant differences between students in their rating of the instructor's interactive skills and also that an overwhelming majority of students indicated that they would again enroll in a course using the same format. Of those at the remote site, 96 percent, the highest proportion, indicated that they would again enroll in a course using that format. Four of the nineteen students at the remote site expressed concern about the adequacy of library and research facilities. Students at the remote site expressed interest in purchasing supplemental readings as a packet rather than having to go to the library to obtain them (ibid., 344).

Many of the reports of the impact of distance learning on rural students and practitioners deal with graduate education. Haga and Heitkamp (2000) report on the experiences of a midwestern university in delivering required undergraduate social work courses over interactive television to students in four rural communities between 1989 and 1993. They point out that the program was the first in the nation to offer the entire curriculum over interactive television. Their research on program impact was primarily descriptive in nature (323). However, they found few differences between the on-campus and off-campus cohorts in satisfaction levels and student outcomes. An alumni survey of the graduates seven years after graduation found that all the graduates were licensed and 92 percent were employed as professional social workers (318).

McFall and Freddolino (2000) compared the experiences of field instruction graduate students at distant sites to the experiences of students on campus. The on-campus students were at the East Lansing campus of the Michi-

gan State University School of Social Work. The distant students were in a
small city four hundred miles from East Lansing and in a rural area two
hundred miles distant.

Students at the distant sites were more positive in their assessment of
adequate agency resources than were the students on campus. The former
also had more positive assessments of the agency climate. Students at one
distant site and on-campus had a more positive assessment of the field office
resources than did students at the other distant site.

McFall and Freddolino conclude that "it is possible to implement a quality field instruction component in a distance education setting at least comparable to what is provided on campus, and in some cases, even better"
(ibid., 306). They indicate that, in part, this may be because of the energy
and creativity associated with distant education programs.

What Does It All Mean?

Given the findings about education for rural practice, some of which are
contradictory, what conclusions can we reach? How should we be educating
for rural practice?

It is appropriate to conclude that generalist preparation is the strongest
preparation for a social worker wishing to practice in a nonmetropolitan
area. Such preparation needs to prepare the social worker to address a variety
of issues using a range of intervention methods while dealing with varied
clients. Such preparation at the graduate level may come from programs
that self-identify as providing an advanced generalist education. It may also
be provided by programs that allow a limited degree of method or population
specialization while assuring that students have sufficient familiarity with
other methods and populations to work with them.

Some understanding of the rural environment and rural context is
needed. No one appears to assume that students coming from rural backgrounds already have such understanding. Content that will help provide
this understanding should be included in the curriculum. Among that content should be information about the relative absence of organized social
services in nonmetropolitan environments and ways to develop alternatives
to such services. Understanding the cultural practices and expectations of
one's clients is important in nonmetropolitan practice, as it is in all social
work practice.

Because the number of MSW practitioners in nonmetropolitan areas is
often limited, MSW students should be prepared to function with a high

degree of professional autonomy. They should also anticipate that they will be expected to have some advanced specialized knowledge. They may be among very few people in their geographic area with a graduate degree, and others will expect that some specialized knowledge or skill resulted from that degree. If the master's program has not prepared MSW-level practitioners with such knowledge, they may need to make use of continuing education programs to gain the needed information and skills.

Arrangements for field placements for students being prepared to work in rural areas need to be flexible. The greatest flexibility may be needed with MSW-level practica, given the limited number of persons in nonmetropolitan areas that may meet an educational program's expectations for field instruction. Programs with a history of preparing students for rural practice have demonstrated that it is possible to meet professional and accreditation standards while providing the flexibility that is needed. The experience of such flexibility is part of the student's preparation for his or her postgraduation practice in a rural area.

Technology holds promise for the delivery of basic and continuing education to nonmetropolitan areas. It also provides opportunities for consultation to the relatively isolated rural practitioner. As chapter 3 in this book illustrates, health services have often progressed further in the use of technology in consultation. When technology is used to provide a degree program, special attention needs to be paid to the provision of library and other instructional resources.

The adoption of a generalist foundation for all social work education means that all social workers, to a certain degree, are prepared with the essentials needed to practice in a nonmetropolitan area. However, the multifaceted demands of such practice and the practitioner's relative isolation means that not all will be successful in such an environment, let alone thrive. Thus the need will continue for education designed to prepare those who seek to practice in such an environment despite its challenges — or, perhaps, because of them.

References

Bast, D. 1977. Continuing education for rural social workers — Wisconsin style. In R. K. Green and S. A. Webster, *Social work in rural areas: Preparation and practice*, pp. 213–219. Knoxville: The University of Tennessee.
Cody, I., K. Collins, L. Mokarry, M. Morris, and K. Rosekrans. 1998. Social workers facing the 21st century: Are we ready? In S. J. Jones and J. L. Zlotnik, eds.,

Preparing professionals to meet community needs: Generalizing from the rural experience, pp. 26–33. Alexandria, Va.: Council on Social Work Education.

Coe, J.A.R., and D. Elliott. 1999. An evaluation of teaching direct practice courses in a distance education program for rural settings. *Journal of Social Work Education* 35 (3): 353–365.

Council on Social Work Education. 2002. *Summary information on master of social work programs: 2001–2002.* Alexandria, Va.: Council on Social Work Education.

Davenport, J. A., and J. Davenport III. 1995. Rural social work overview. In R. L. Edwards, ed., *The encyclopedia of social work*, 19th ed., pp. 2076–2085. Washington, D.C.: NASW Press.

Denton, R. T., R. O. York, and J. R. Moran. 1988. The social worker's view of the rural community: An empirical examination. *Human Services in the Rural Environment* 11 (3): 14–21.

Doelker, R. J., Jr., and B. C. Bedic. 1983. An approach to curriculum design for rural practice. *Journal of Education for Social Work* 19 (1): 39–46.

Egan, M., and G. Kadushin. 1997. Rural hospital social workers: Views of physicians and social workers. *Social Work in Health Care* 26 (1): 1–23.

Gibbs, P., B. L. Locke, and R. Lohmann. 1990. Paradigm for the generalist–advanced generalist continuum. *Journal of Social Work Education* 26 (3): 232–243.

Ginsberg, L. H. 1976. An overview of social work education for rural areas. In L. H. Ginsberg, ed., *Social Work in Rural Communities*, 1st. ed., pp. 1–12. New York: Council on Social Work Education.

——, ed. 1998 [1976]. Social Work in Rural Communities. 3rd. ed. Alexandria, Va.: Council on Social Work Education.

Gumpert, J., J. E. Saltman, and D. Sauer-Jones. 2000. Toward identifying the unique characteristics of social work practice in rural areas: From the voices of practitioners. *Journal of Baccalaureate Social Work* 6 (1): 19–35.

Haga, M., and T. Heitkamp. 2000. Bringing social work education to the prairie. *Journal of Social Work Education* 36 (2): 309–324.

Hovestadt, A. J., D. L. Fennell, and B. S. Canfield. 2002. Characteristics of effective providers of marital and family therapy in rural mental health settings. *Journal of Marital and Family Therapy* 28 (2): 225–231.

Horejsi, C. R., and R. L. Deaton. 1977. The Cracker-Barrel Classroom: Programming for continuing education in the rural context. In R. K. Green and S. A. Webster, eds., *Social work in rural areas: Preparation and practice*, pp. 197–212. Knoxville: University of Tennessee Press.

Irey, K. V. 1980. The social work generalist in a rural context: An ecological perspective. *Journal of Education for Social Work* 16 (3): 36–42.

Jerrell, J. M., and M. A. Knight. 1985. Social work practice in rural mental health systems. *Social Work* 30 (4): 331–337.

Jones, S. J. 1998. Professional development in the Human Services: Implications for the 21st century. In S. J. Jones and J. L. Zlotnik, eds., *Preparing professionals to meet community needs: Generalizing from the rural experience*, pp. 3–23. Alexandria, Va.: Council on Social Work Education.

Jones, S. J., and J. L. Zlotnik, eds. 1998. *Preparing professionals to meet community needs: Generalizing from the rural experience.* Alexandria, Va.: Council on Social Work Education.

Landon, P. S. 1995. Generalist and advanced generalist practice. In R. L. Edwards, ed., *The encyclopedia of social work*, 19th ed., pp. 1101 – 1108. Washington, D.C.: NASW Press.

Levin, L. I., ed. 1974. *Educating social workers for practice in rural settings: Perspectives and programs.* Atlanta, Ga.: Southern Regional Education Board.

Martinez-Brawley, E. E. 1980. *Pioneer efforts in rural social welfare: Firsthand views since 1908.* University Park: Pennsylvania State University Press.

———. 1985. Rural social work as a contextual specialty: Undergraduate focus or graduate concentration? *Journal of Social Work Education* 21 (3): 36–42.

McFall, J. P., and P. P. Freddolino. 2000. Quality and comparability in distance field education: Lessons learned from comparing three program sites. *Journal of Social Work Education* 36 (2): 293 – 307.

Mermelstein, J., and P. Sundet. 1976. Social work education for rural program development. In L. H. Ginsberg, ed., *Social work in rural communities*, pp. 15–27. New York: Council on Social Work Education.

Miller, Pamela J. 1998. Dual relationships in rural practice: A dilemma of ethics and culture. In L. H. Ginsberg, ed., *Social work in rural communities*, 3rd. ed., pp. 55–62. Alexandria, Va.: Council on Social Work Education.

Nooe, R. M., and F. H. Bolitho. 1982. An examination of rural social work literature. *Human Services in the Rural Environment* 7 (3): 10–17.

Petracchi, H. E., and M. A. Patchner. 2000. Social work students and their learning environment: A comparison on interactive television, face-to-face instruction, and the traditional classroom. *Journal of Education for Social Work* 36 (2): 335–346.

Pippard, J. L., and J. E. Bates. 1983. The care and feeding of continuing education programs in rural areas. *Journal of Continuing Social Work Education* 2 (3): 4–8.

Rooney, R. H., and A. A. Bibus III. 1995. Distance learning for child welfare work with involuntary clients: Process and evaluation. *Journal of Continuing Social Work Education* 6 (3): 23–28.

Waltman, G. H. 1986. Main street revisited: Social work practice in rural areas. *Social Casework* 67 (8): 466–472.

Weber, G. K. 1980. Preparing social workers for practice in rural social systems. In H. W. Johnson, ed., *Rural human services: A book of readings*, pp. 203–214. Itasca, Ill.: Peacock.

Whitaker, W. H. 1984. A survey of perceptions of social work practice in rural and urban areas. *Human Services in the Rural Environment* 9 (3): 12–19.

Wodarski, J. S. 1983. *Rural community mental health practice.* Baltimore, Md.: University Park Press.

Yevuta, M.A. 1999. Nitpicking in rural West Virginia: The small stuff does matter. In I. B. Carlton-Ney, R. L. Edwards, and P. N. Reid , eds., *Preserving and strengthening small towns and rural communities*, pp. 315–325. Washington, D.C.: NASW Press.

Epilogue

What Is Rural Practice?

Roger A. Lohmann and Nancy Lohmann

This book has explored the topic of rural social work practice as it exists in the United States at the present time. After reading all the preceding chapters, what conclusions might we reach about the nature of rural social work practice? Does it have any unique features? To answer these questions, we return to the subject of rural/urban differences first addressed in the opening chapter. Please note, however, that these are the personal conclusions of the editors and not the consensus of all the contributors to this volume. These are the conclusions we have drawn about the nature and unique quality of rural social work practice after our more than thirty years of practicing in the rural environment.

A standard feature of the rural social science literature is the seemingly endless quest to identify the signature differences between rural and urban areas. One might think that the term *rural* has no inherent meaning, that we can only understand the term in contrast to its urban counterpart. And yet this quest has been largely futile. One report after another, including several in this volume, indicates that no *major* differences have been identified. A tentative generalization we may draw from this vast thread in the social science literature is that, while real differences do exist, we must also recognize the many similarities shared by contemporary rural and urban life.

There are, for example, important differences in population density and other urban indicators between New York's Manhattan and Manhattan, Illinois. Both, however, tend to have access to more-or-less paved streets, grocery stores, newspapers, cable television, public schools, libraries, book and video stores, and restaurants. Surely any rural practitioner can point to communities where these features are absent in whole or in part, but most urban workers can also point to similarly deficient neighborhoods in such cities as Los Angeles, St. Louis, and Washington, D.C., without claiming that these are rural areas. Many features of contemporary American urban culture are found today in rural as well as in urban America. Thus, in an important sense, urban and rural in contemporary American life reflect merely differences in degree within what, in world historical terms, is the universal urban culture inhabited by all Americans. The much vaunted rural culture of Appalachia, for example, is no more. No longer would it be possible for a rural backwoods family of celebrated musicians like the Hammons to live within miles of a number of Civil War battle sites and plausibly claim not to have been aware that a war was going on until nearly a decade after it had ended (Williams, Jabbour, and Cuthbert 1999). That kind of rural isolation almost totally disappeared with the advent of modern communication and transportation. Television and radio, the Internet, and interstate highways have made this kind of cultural isolation almost impossible in contemporary culture.

Those seeking fundamental differentiation of urban and rural are, wittingly or not, diluting realism with the rural romanticism of the social philosopher Jean-Jacques Rousseau, the English poet William Wordsworth, and the writer John Ruskin. These and other critics of the Industrial Revolution not only saw the countryside as *different* from the city; they saw rural areas as the cure for the ills of industrialization. These and other Romantics saw in rural living not only an alternative to the emerging urban industrial order but also an antidote to the modern world. More recently a great many committed advocates of rurality in social work have joined the Romantics in this view. What is interesting about the present, however, are the many ways in which a suburban middle ground has emerged and sought to combine the best aspects of city and country life and, in the process, transformed both. City people wanted greater access to the natural world, while rural people sought more of the cultural and service amenities of the city. Not only did the suburbs provide such reconciliation, they also provided models for the subtle transformation of both city and rural community.

Within the rural social work literature the romantic distinction of urban and rural continues to hold sway despite evidence to the contrary. This futile quest for isolating rural/urban differences brought about a nearly thirty-year search for the essential differences between practice principles and methods employed in conventional urban practice and those most suitable for rural practice. As several of the chapters in this book note, such "difference" studies have been largely inconclusive. Rural social work is not a distinctly dif-

ferent mode of practice nor a unique method of social work, and there is
no strong case to be made for a separate rural practice theory base. Good
rural social work practice is, first and foremost, good social work practice.
Rural/urban differences, important as they are for social work practice, are
largely contextual in nature. These differences, however, are more akin to
the differences between social work in Boston, Atlanta, and Oakland than
to the categorical differences implied by the distinction. As we showed in
the case of aging services at the very first rural conference, and as others
have argued convincingly since, environmental and resource availability issues are of the utmost importance (Lohmann and Lohmann 1976; Resultan
2004).

Yet the quest for rural/urban difference in social work practice will likely
continue. The romantic spirit remains strong, and not everyone is convinced
that it is futile. Part of this impulse may be a result of the need for affirming
identity. There is an inherent insecurity to rural identity in a national culture
that is so overwhelmingly urban and increasingly suburban. This remains
true even as American urbanism in Manhattan and elsewhere seeks to capture the best features of rural life within the city and the suburbs, and rural
communities selectively adopt those features of city life that fit best with
rural sensibilities. Thus the reality of rural social work is explained in part
by the fact that rural people are as shocked and troubled by the brutal realities of poverty, alcoholism, domestic violence and abuse, and other social
problems as any urban reformer or suburbanite. Concern for identity is an
important aspect of rural social work. Social workers in rural areas need to
be reassured (and to reassure themselves) that their work is valued and important. Leon Ginsberg (2004, 10) reached a comparable conclusion, and
pointed out that "social work in smaller areas isn't so terribly different than
social work practice anywhere else, despite the strong interest of small town
practitioners in their identity."

Also driving the impulse to distinguish rural from urban is the simple
need for descriptive differentiations. Pairs of dichotomous variables are fundamental to the descriptive or demographic sections of research questionnaires and college textbooks. Certain stock descriptive dichotomies are almost inevitable in this sense: young/old; rich/poor; male/female; urban/rural.
Thus *rural* as a contrast term for *urban* will likely continue as long as the
need for such simple distinctions remains. In that context we would modestly
suggest that a three-part distinction is probably more accurate today: urban/
suburban/rural. Chuck Fluharty of the Rural Policy Research Institute has
made this same point in presentations available online at www.rupri.org.

The real significance of rural and nonmetropolitan life in the present only begins to emerge with the recognition that contemporary American rural areas need not be understood in simple contrast to the nation's urban centers. Indeed, poor rural communities, whether in New England, the rural South, the Midwest, the hollows of Appalachia, or the *colonias* of the Southwest borderlands, probably have a good deal more in common with distressed urban inner-city neighborhoods than any of them have in common with gentrified urban neighborhoods or gated, affluent suburbs within their own geographic regions. In many ways it would be a major improvement if national statistics moved one step beyond the simple dichotomy and reported rural, urban, and suburban figures.

All things considered, however, rural areas today are best viewed, sui generis, as phenomena in their own right, not as mere contrasts to urban or even suburban areas. Chuck Fluharty (2002) expresses an important truth with the phrase: "When you've seen one rural community. . . . You've seen one rural community!" It is less important how or whether rural areas are different from urban or suburban areas than that they simply exist in their own right. In the twenty-first century, as in the eighteenth and the tenth, rural communities are what they are; one should seek to understand them and deal with them on their own terms. The social work principle of individualization demands nothing less.

This is particularly the case in considerations of professional, agency, and service delivery issues in social work. It is certainly fair to say (as most rural social workers do, from time to time) that many urban and suburban social workers do not really understand the subtleties and nuances of rural practice, sometimes even after such matters are explained to them. This in itself is not evidence of great difference in forms of practice; rather, it is only evidence of a lack of experience in one group of practitioners.

A corollary of this statement, however, is that a great many rural social workers also do not understand or acknowledge the very real attractions of city or suburban life. In fact, at least some of the urban/rural comparisons in the rural social work literature are best understood as comparisons of the writer's working knowledge of rural life with fictional urban images and stereotypes grounded in Dickens, Dreiser, Lewis, and others, and the strain of anti-urban suspicion that runs deep in American culture and politics. Rural stereotypes notwithstanding, millions of people in urban areas know their neighbors, have close friends, live in extended families, and live coherent, meaningful lives that bear no resemblance to the images of social disorganization projected upon them from the rural heartlands.

Of course, it is also true that millions of rural folks already know this. Not only do many of them travel to the city and have close relatives living in urban areas, but perhaps, just as important, rural folk, too, have watched *I Love Lucy, The Cosby Show, Cheers, Friends, Frazier, Everybody Loves Raymond,* and decades of other urban-based sitcoms that show city life in positive, normal terms. Urban life in popular culture is pictured not only as livable but as downright pleasant; above all, it is portrayed as the cultural norm. Rural people simply prefer not to believe that this can be the case; and, in this sense, they construct for themselves one of the most important sets of subcultures in contemporary American life. Dealing with the rural subcultures of the deep South, the Midwest, Appalachia, New England, the West, California, and others, is one of the most interesting and challenging aspects of rural practice.

It is possible to recognize and understand that life in South Boston, Homestead near Pittsburgh, or the East Side of Manhattan is *different* from life in rural Appalachia without having to treat either in terms of the other. In fact, respecting such individualization is one of the foremost tenets of social work practice. Local places are different within their commonality, and social work practice requires recognizing and dealing with such differences.

Given all this, what conclusions do we reach about rural social work practice? Although we do think that certain aspects of such practice are unique, we believe that the differences that exist between social work practice in rural and urban areas are matters of degree rather than of fundamental distinction. For example, most rural areas are indeed characterized by limited resources but so, too, are areas that are not rural. Limited resources, in fact, presents a challenge to social workers to identify innovative solutions to problems. As we suggested in chapter 8 of this volume, an appropriate variation on the song "New York, New York" is that if you can practice effectively in rural America, it is likely that you can practice anywhere because you will have learned to be resourceful and creative.

Another difference represented by the rural/urban dichotomy is the personal nature of relationships. Of course, urban and suburban residents often also know their neighbors, and so this distinction is also one of degree. However, many urban residents may not have known their neighbors for generations nor see them as frequently as do their rural counterparts. This is another difference that offers a challenge to the rural social worker. A book about urban social work would probably not emphasize dual relationships to the extent that this book does, because such relationships are less common in urban areas and do not present the frequent ethical dilemmas that occur in rural settings.

The sense of a positive identity, both among rural residents and rural social work practitioners, may represent another difference. Rural residents tend to describe their environment in positive terms, despite whether those terms are justified or whether they are formed in opposition to urban culture. Rural practitioners also tend to be highly committed to the nature of their practice. As Ginsberg (2004) points out, they are a loyal group of social workers who have kept an annual Institute on Social Work in Rural Areas going even though there is no professional staff, headquarters, dues, news-letters, or any other kinds of support assumed to be required to maintain a specialized professional institute.

There will continue to be the need for social workers who focus on rural and small- community practice. It is our hope that the reflections on that practice found in this volume will help them in their practice.

References

Fluharty, C. W. 2002. Keynote Speech. Presented at the Twenty-seventh Annual National Rural Social Work Conference. Frostburg, Maryland, July 17.

Ginsberg, L. 2004. In rural communities, geography key to services, identity. *Social Work Education Reporter* 52, 2 (spring/summer): 9–10.

Lohmann, R. A., and N. Lohmann. 1976. Urban services for the rural aged: Are they exportable? In R. Green and S. Webster, eds. *Social Work in Rural Areas: Preparation and Practice*, pp. 284–297. Knoxville: University of Tennessee School of Social Work.

Resultan, V. 2004. Intolerance, transportation, housing costs target of rural social work services. *Social Work Education Reporter* 52, 2 (spring/summer): 8–9, 13.

Williams, D., A. Jabbour, and J. Cuthbert. 1999. Cover notes. *The Edden Hammons collection* (CD). Vol. 1. Morgantown: West Virginia University Press.

Contributors

Eleanor H. Blakely, Ph.D., ACSW, is an Associate Professor of Social Work at West Virginia University, where she teaches courses in social policy and administration. For the last five years she has been a member of the West Virginia University Interdisciplinary Research Task Force on Welfare Reform, which has conducted research on the impact of welfare reform on program participants in West Virginia. With Patty Gibbs she coedited *Gatekeeping in BSW Programs*, published by Columbia University Press in 2000.

Amy Brimer, MPA, is a Research Associate in the Center on Nonprofits and Philanthropy at the Urban Institute, a nonprofit social policy research organization in Washington, D.C. In addition to her research on nonprofit human service providers, her current research interests focus on volunteers and volunteer management practices. Amy was born and raised in a rural southern Oklahoma community and looks forward to her visits home.

Warren B. Galbreath, Ph.D., is an Assistant Professor of Social Work at the Eastern Campus of Ohio University where he teaches social welfare policy and practice courses. He has more than twenty-five years of experience working in child welfare and children's mental health programs in rural communities throughout West Virginia and Ohio. Warren has also conducted numerous workshops on dual relationships in rural communities. His MSW degree is from West Virginia University.

Mark A. Hager, Ph.D., is a Senior Research Associate in the Center on Nonprofits and Philanthropy at the Urban Institute in Washington, D.C. His work focuses on the characteristics and behavior of charities in the United States. He was born and raised in a small town in western Kansas, and the lessons he learned there continually influence his work and life.

Craig W. Johnson earned a BA from the University of Michigan and an MSW from West Virginia University. He worked with an Administration on Aging–funded project that provided training on aging and the needs of elderly persons for clergy and lay leaders throughout West Virginia. He also served as a family service agency director before joining West Virginia University's Center on Aging as a program specialist, teaching in the Gerontology Certificate program, writing grants, and providing continuing education programs. From 1997 to 2001 he was a visiting assistant professor at West Virginia University's School of Social Work. In 2001 he was an adjunct professor for Meredith College, North Carolina, and in 2002 he joined the clinical social work staff at the Geropsychiatry Institute of John Umstead Hospital in Butner, North Carolina.

Barry L. Locke, Ed.D., is an Associate Professor of Social Work at West Virginia University. He is former chair of the National Rural Social Work Caucus and served as program chair for the Third and Seventeenth Annual National Institutes on Social Work and Human Services in Rural Areas. His recent research work, as a member of the Interdisciplinary Welfare Reform Research Group at West Virginia University, has focused on rural poverty. He is also a coauthor, with Rebecca Garrison and Jim Winship, of *Generalist Social Work Practice: Context, Story, and Partnerships* published by Brooks/Cole in 1998.

Nancy Lohmann, Ph.D., is Senior Adviser to the Provost and a Professor of Social Work at West Virginia University, where she has been on the faculty since 1977 and has been a full- or part-time administrator since 1983. She is a former member of the Commission on Accreditation and Board of Directors of the Council on Social Work Education and former Dean of the WVU School of Social Work. With Roger A. Lohmann, she coauthored *Social Administration*, published by Columbia University Press in 2002.

Roger A. Lohmann, Ph.D., is a Professor of Social Work and Benedum Distinguished Scholar at West Virginia University, where he has been on the faculty since 1977. He is the author of *Breaking Even: Financial Management in Nonprofit Human Services* (1980); *The Commons: New Perspectives on Nonprofit Organizations, Voluntary Action and Philanthropy* (1992); and coauthor, with Nancy Lohmann, of *Social Administration* (2002). He is also the editor of the journal *Nonprofit Management and Leadership*.

Chatman Neely, ACSW, LCSW, is currently working toward a Ph. D. at the Institute for Clinical Social Work, Chicago, in clinical social work, specializing in psychodynamic psychotherapy and the strengths perspective. He earned a BSW from Concord College, West Virginia, an MSW from West Virginia University, and a Certificate for Individual Therapy from Smith College School of Social Work. He is an accomplished social worker, clinician, and instructor with more than fourteen years of experience. He has worked with children, adolescents, and adults in residential, substance abuse, community mental health, psychiatric hospital, and private practice settings. He is currently an adjunct faculty member at the West Virginia University Division of Social Work.

Neal Newfield, Ph.D., is an Associate Professor of Social Work at West Virginia University and teaches courses in direct practice and in marriage and family therapy. Dr. Newfield is a clinical member of the American Association for Marriage and Family Therapy. He is also a documentary photographer and has conducted a number of innovative programs in the use of documentary photography to document current social conditions, notably poverty, in West Virginia. He has also done work on the use of photographs in stimulating discussion of difficult subjects involving conflict.

Doris Nicholas, Ed.D., is an Assistant Professor at the West Virginia University Division of Social Work, where she teaches diversity and practice courses. Dr. Nicholas has extensive practice experience in health care having served for several years as the Director of Social Services for the WVU Hospitals. Her MSW is from West Virginia University.

Thomas H. Pollak, JD, is Assistant Director of the National Center for Charitable Statistics, a program of the Center on Nonprofits and Philanthropy at the Urban Institute. Current projects include the development of a Form 990 electronic filing and state registration system for state charity offices. He is the coauthor, with

Linda M. Lampkin, of *The New Nonprofit Almanac & Desk Reference*, published by Jossey-Bass in 2002.

Dennis L. Poole, Ph.D., is Dean of the School of Social Work at the University of South Carolina. He was formerly Professor of Social Work at the University of Texas at Austin, where he taught courses in nonprofit management, community organization, and evaluation. For many years Dr. Poole was the executive director of the Community Development Support Association in Oklahoma, and is coeditor of *Community Building: Renewal, Well-Being, and Shared Responsibility*, published by NASW Press. His MSW degree is from West Virginia University.

Elizabeth Randall, Ph.D, is an Associate Professor of Social Work at West Virginia University, with nineteen years of direct practice experience in behavioral health. Currently she serves as the NASW representative to the Behavioral Health Advisory Council for the West Virginia Bureau of Behavioral Health and Health Facilities.

Rev. Dennis Vance Jr., M.Div., is a minister and earned an MSW degree at West Virginia University. He specializes in clinical social work, and his previous education included courses in pastoral counseling. In both his secular and religious employment, Reverend Vance has worked with rural populations in a variety of settings related to rural mental health.

Norma Wasko, Ph.D., has worked throughout her career in both academic and practice settings. She has been a member of the faculty of West Virginia University's School of Applied Social Sciences and Adelphi University's School of Social Work. She has worked in health policy, planning, and program development for the State of Vermont Division of Health Care Administration and the Department of Public Health. Her recent publications include the article *Web-Based Technology Makes Clinical Data Systems Technically and Economically Practical: Are They Politically Feasible?* which appeared in the *Journal of Technology for Human Services* (spring 2001).

Jim Winship, D.P.A., is an Associate Professor of Social Work at the University of Wisconsin-Whitewater. Dr. Winship is coauthor, with Barry L. Locke and Rebecca Garrison, of *Generalist Social Work Practice: Context, Story, and Partnerships*, published by Brooks-Cole in 1998. Jim is the former chairperson of the Rural

Social Work Caucus and recently published a book chapter on homelessness in rural America. He also publishes materials about, and is active in, advocacy for homeless families and children.

Dong Pil Yoon, Ph.D., is Assistant Professor at the School of Social Work, University of Missouri at Columbia. He is a former faculty member with the Division of Social Work, West Virginia University. He has conducted a number of studies on religiousness/spirituality, social support, and subjective well-being among older adults in rural areas. The article "Religiousness/Spirituality and Subjective Well-being among Rural Elderly Whites, African-Americans, and Native Americans" will be published as part of the special Diversity and Aging issues of the *Journal of Human Behavior in the Social Environment*. His MSW degree is from West Virginia University.

Index